Wide-Open Town

Wide-Open Town
Kansas City in the Pendergast Era

Diane Mutti Burke,
Jason Roe,
and
John Herron,
Editors

 University Press of Kansas

Published by the University Press of Kansas (Lawrence, Kansas 66045), which was organized by
the Kansas Board of Regents and is operated and funded by Emporia State University, Fort Hays
State University, Kansas State University, Pittsburg State University, the University of Kansas, and
Wichita State University

Library of Congress Cataloging-in-Publication Data

Names: Burke, Diane Mutti, editor. | Roe, Jason, editor. | Herron, John, 1968– editor.
Title: Wide-open town : Kansas City in the Pendergast era / Diane Mutti Burke, Jason Roe, and
John Herron, editors.
Description: Lawrence, KS : University Press of Kansas, 2018. | Includes bibliographical references
and index.
Identifiers: LCCN 2018040153
  ISBN 9780700627059 (hardback)
  ISBN 9780700627066 (paperback)
  ISBN 9780700627073 (ebook)
Subjects: LCSH: Kansas City (Kan.)—History—20th century. | BISAC: HISTORY / United States
/ State & Local / Midwest (IA, IL, IN, KS, MI, MN, MO, ND, NE, OH, SD, WI). | SOCIAL
SCIENCE / Sociology / Urban. | HISTORY / United States / 20th Century.
Classification: LCC F689.K2 W53 2018 | DDC 978.1/39033—dc23.
LC record available at https://lccn.loc.gov/2018040153.

British Library Cataloguing-in-Publication Data is available.

Printed in the United States of America

10 9 8 7 6 5 4 3 2

The paper used in this publication is recycled and contains 30 percent postconsumer waste.
It is acid free and meets the minimum requirements of the American National Standard for
Permanence of Paper for Printed Library Materials Z39.48-1992.

Contents

Preface and Acknowledgments

The origins of this project—a partnership between the Center for Midwestern Studies at the University of Missouri–Kansas City (UMKC) and the Kansas City Public Library—trace to a previous collaborative effort that reexamined and commemorated the sesquicentennial of the Civil War era along the Missouri-Kansas border. Crossing the state line, the project disseminated new insights and sparked discussion among scholars, educators, museum professionals, archivists, and general enthusiasts. In the spring of 2011, a group of Civil War scholars convened at the Hall Center for the Humanities at the University of Kansas for a peer-review workshop during which they read and critiqued each other's original scholarship. The following fall, these historians shared their findings in a public symposium at the Kansas City Public Library. The product of this work was the award-winning anthology *Bleeding Kansas, Bleeding Missouri: The Long Civil War on the Border*, edited by Jonathan Earle and Diane Mutti Burke (University Press of Kansas, 2013). The project continued with an interactive website, Civil War on the Western Border: The Missouri-Kansas Conflict, 1854–1865 (www.civilwaronthewesternborder.org). This heavily visited website won multiple awards for digital and public history, including the prestigious Roy Rosenzweig Prize for Innovation in Digital History from the American Historical Association.

In consideration of the high level of public engagement with the Civil War project, the Center for Midwestern Studies and the Kansas City Public Library again partnered to explore a regional history project of national importance. We did not have to search long for a topic to succeed the Civil War. In the last decade, the revitalization of Kansas City's urban core has correlated with a resurgence of awareness and interest in the city's history and culture, especially the boom period between the two world wars when Kansas City developed a national reputation as a "wide-open town." In this era, the city's economy boomed and culture flourished, even as residents struggled with mob rule and ongoing strife along the lines of race, class, and gender. The current public conversation about this era often focuses more on the "colorful" aspects of this history rather than issues such as the dangerous consequences of corruption or racial discrimination. But if the present interest in this era lacks nuance, the focus on this city and this period provides a moment to better investigate the parallels between the present and the past.

This anthology, alongside its companion projects, seeks to fulfill several objectives. The first is to encourage conversations among scholars who research the history of this region. Our hope is not only to support the development of new research on the city but also to direct this work to a deeper understanding of how diverse historical populations navigate and influence the political, economic, and cultural life of urban America. A second, and in many ways more important, goal is to use this volume to create a public forum for an ongoing discussion of the historical and contemporary issues raised by Kansas City history. With resources that we hope will find a home in all educational levels, this project attempts to build on the widespread interest in this era and use historical scholarship to contribute to a more complete understanding of regional culture and politics.

With these goals in mind, we issued a call for new scholarship to challenge and deepen our understanding of this period. A range of scholars from several disciplines responded, and following the model of the Civil War project, we brought these researchers to UMKC for a peer-review workshop in the fall of 2015. In the spring of 2016, the group presented their work at a public symposium at the Kansas City Public Library. Nearly 1,000 patrons attended the two-day symposium that included a keynote address on the Great Depression by Stanford University's Pulitzer Prize–winning historian David M. Kennedy. We also incorporated a special workshop for K-12 educators from around the region. The revised public presentations form the core of this volume. Several scholars associated with this project also created versions of their work that appear on the Kansas City Public Library's website, The Pendergast Years: Kansas City in the Jazz Age and Great Depression (www.PendergastKC.org). This site takes advantage of multimedia features and a vast collection of primary documents to create a vibrant research tool for use by academics, educators, students, and the general public.

None of these pieces could have come together without the significant contributions of our organizational partners, funders, and of course, the scholars, librarians, and archivists who made this project a reality. We would like to extend special thanks to Executive Director R. Crosby Kemper III and Deputy Director of Public Affairs Carrie Coogan of the Kansas City Public Library for hosting the public symposium and providing ongoing support to the larger endeavor. The library's exceptional staff, including Steve Woolfolk, Andy Dandino, Leslie Case, and others from the public affairs department, as well as the staff of the Missouri Valley Special Collections, including its manager, Jeremy Drouin, and senior archivist Kate Hill, provided critical research support for the symposium and book. David LaCrone, digital branch manager, supported much of the labor for both the symposium and the website. Special thanks are owed to Eli Paul, retired manager of the Missouri Valley Special Collections, who was instrumental as a project advisor.

The symposium also received a boost from Tom's Town Distilling Co. The downtown distillery inspired by "Boss" Tom Pendergast hosted the participants and organizers of our symposium in a special venue complete with portraits of machine leaders (and mounted heads of goats and rabbits representing the various factions of local political parties) adorning the walls. In a final perfect touch, Tom's Town also provided drinks, including McElroy's Corruption Gin and Eli's StrongArm Vodka, to more than 400 guests at the symposium's keynote address.

We also appreciate the support of UMKC's vice chancellor for research and economic development Lawrence Dreyfus, who recognized the significance of this work and championed the project through a Funding for Excellence Grant. Chelsea Dahlstrom, grants and contracts administrator in UMKC's Office of Research Services, played a crucial role in the submission and administration of the various grants for this project and assisted with the keynote address dinner. Dean of the College of Arts and Sciences Wayne Vaught has long supported the initiatives of the Center for Midwestern Studies and generously underwrote the teacher workshop and the David Kennedy lecture through the Bernardin Haskell Lecture Fund. Carla Mebane and Cynthia Jones of the High School College Partnerships assisted us in the organization of the teacher workshop. Thanks also go to the UMKC History Department, and in particular Christopher Cantwell, for its support. We would like to express special gratitude to Amy Brost, formerly the director of programs and development for the Center for Midwestern Studies, who successfully orchestrated grants and fundraising avenues for the workshop and symposium in addition to arranging travel, dinners, receptions, and other logistics for all of the participants.

We are also grateful for the support of Bryan Le Beau, retired provost and vice president for academic affairs at the University of Saint Mary, who played a crucial advisory role for the scholarly content in the book and the Pendergast Years website. Jennifer L. Weber, associate professor of history at the University of Kansas, participated in both the workshop and symposium and offered key insights as the project took shape. Gary Kremer, the executive director of the State Historical Society of Missouri, also offered his support of this work. In addition to the staff of the Missouri Valley Special Collections, archivists who assisted with this project include Stuart Hinds from the LaBudde Special Collections at UMKC, Chuck Haddix from the Marr Sound Archives at UMKC, Lori Cox-Paul and Elizabeth Burnes from the National Archives at Kansas City, and Lucinda Adams and Whitney Heinzmann at the State Historical Society of Missouri, Kansas City Research Center.

A project of this scale is made possible only through the generous financial support from several sponsors. The Missouri Humanities Council provided significant program support for the Wide-Open Town symposium, as did the Freedom's Frontier National Heritage Area. The UMKC Office of Research Support, Bernardin Haskell Lecture Fund, and High School College Partnerships also provided resources to offset the symposium and public presentations. The Missouri Valley Reading Room at the Kansas City Public Library helped underwrite the scholars' travel to Kansas City, and the host institutions contributed both space and considerable staff hours to the workshop and symposium.

Planning an event of this size and scope (and bringing this project to its conclusion) has required countless hours of collaboration and work. We want to thank our families for their support and indulgence throughout the process.

Wide-Open Town

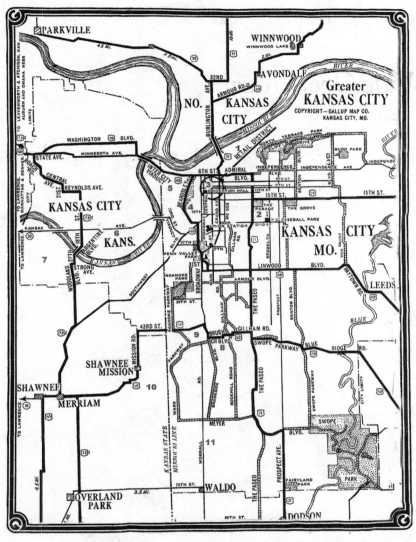

Greater Kansas City Map, Gallup Map Company, 1929. Courtesy of the Gallup Map and Art Company, Kansas City, Missouri

Greater Kansas City Neighborhoods and Districts

1. Little Italy
2. 18th and Vine
3. Garment District
4. Westside
5. West Bottoms
6. Armourdale
7. Argentine
8. University of Kansas City
9. Country Club Plaza
10. Mission Hills
11. Armour Hills

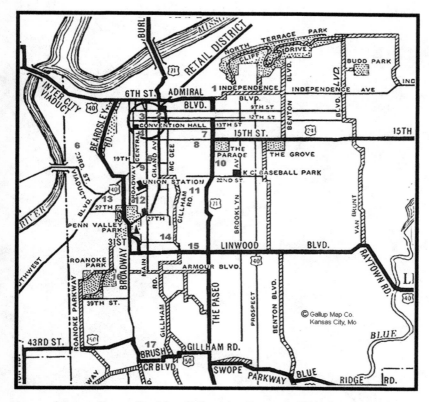

Insert of Greater Kansas City Map, Gallup Map Company, 1929. Courtesy of the Gallup Map and Art Company, Kansas City, Missouri

Pendergast-Era Kansas City

1. Dante's Inferno
2. Federal Reserve Bank and the Woman's City Club
3. Hotel Muehlebach
4. Orpheum Theater
5. Donnelly Garment Company
6. Livestock Exchange Building
7. Paseo Hall
8. Jeffersonian Democratic Club (Cas Welch's Office)
9. Jackson Democratic Club (Tom Pendergast's Office)
10. 18th and Vine District (Kansas City *Call* Office)
11. Hospital District (Hospitals #1 and #2)
12. Union Station & Liberty Memorial
13. Guadalupe Center
14. El Torreon Ballroom
15. The Athenaeum
16. Thomas Hart Benton Home
17. Arts District (Nelson-Atkins Museum of Art and Kansas City Art Institute)

Introduction

Diane Mutti Burke, Jason Roe, and John Herron

Near the corner of Twentieth and Main—on the same block as "Boss" Tom Pendergast's still-standing political machine headquarters—is the Rieger Hotel. The bustling hotel, which first opened in 1915, was built by Alexander Rieger, son of the
founder of a popular whiskey company located in the city's West Bottoms district.
The budget hotel catered to the many railroad workers and traveling salesmen who
passed through the city in the opening decades of the twentieth century. Today, the
Rieger is an upscale restaurant that serves a decidedly different clientele. On any
given weekend evening, the place teems with attractive young professionals who, in
recent years, have flooded back into downtown Kansas City.

Despite the building's refurbished appearance and hipster patrons, the place
remains awash in history. Mosaic tile work, plaster moldings, and a hand-carved bar
all remain from the original structure, but here history serves a different purpose.
Look, for example, to Manifesto, a straight-up-no-chaser speakeasy in the building's basement. To get a reservation, guests text a "secret" code to the manager. To
then get access to the space, these same guests must weave through the back of the
restaurant and buzz a speaker box beside an unmarked door. A bouncer meets your
party and leads you down a steep stairway and through a long narrow hallway into
a nicely appointed but dimly lit cellar with less than fifty seats. Once at your table,
a dapper waiter will offer an extensive list of handcrafted cocktails, many named for
figures from Kansas City's colorful criminal past. This is how to drink like a mob-
ster. Indeed, patrons visiting the men's restroom will find proof: an "Al Capone
Pissed Here" plaque hangs above the urinal.

That the famous Chicago mafioso may have drunk in this bar is part of the
appeal of the establishment and, perhaps now, even the culture of the city. The
popularity of the Rieger, and the many storefronts just like it that blanket downtown, suggests that many local residents really do want to party like it's 1929. The
embrace of the "wide-open" history of this community is far from universal, however. A quick survey of the traditional scholarly literature on urban development

1

reveals that many American cities, including Kansas City, are "at war with their own pasts." Cities, historian Thomas Frank argues, "have proceeded through the years in a frenzy of building, razing, and reconstruction, continually wrecking and then reconstituting themselves elsewhere, expanding over the surrounding countryside like an ever-spreading infection." Such sprawl, that includes a purposeful neglect of the city's downtown core, "involves more than mere physical growth," as the "character and design of the new metropolis" takes definition from "the razing of the old . . . [and the] indiscriminate destruction of obsolete buildings and neighborhoods." Frank is skeptical of any community that adopts such practice as a "blueprint for civic organization," but he is especially pointed in his criticism of Kansas City, his hometown. Kansas City, he notes, has long prioritized blandness and property values over history and the cultivation of a distinctive urban culture. "Detached from the particularities of time and place," contemporary Kansas City, he concludes, advanced urban renewal projects that deliberately obscured the city's "now-vanished cultural inheritance."[1]

Frank's critique is not without standing, and others have made similar points with even more force. Nearly thirty years ago, for example, Pulitzer Prize–winning historian—and Kansas City native—Richard Rhodes authored a cutting assessment of the city entitled "Cupcake Land," his term for the rolling "vanilla suburbs" of metropolitan Kansas City. The defining feature of the region was, he noted, a desire to disconnect from history: "Kansas City renounced its heritage when it pledged allegiance to Cupcake Land." In the middling decades of the twentieth century, city fathers led an effort to obscure the region's "bawdy history." The goal was to attract the kind of investment that could transform a midwestern cowtown into a "regular" American city, a telos best accomplished with a strategy of separation and historical denial.[2]

Frank, Rhodes, and others who comment on Kansas City's "everyplace" character make a significant, if still somewhat controversial, point. In their defense, their criticism was directed at the city's ever-expanding suburbs, and in the mid-twentieth century, there is little question that Kansas City accelerated its outward reach. When combined with a drop in corporate investment and white flight, the result was a central city marked as a place of indifference and neglect. In more recent times in Kansas City, however, residents have engineered a community revitalization that, perhaps ironically, takes its cues from the exact history now celebrated in places like the Rieger restaurant. Sprawl and conformity defined the city in the second half of the twentieth century, but in the years between the two world wars, the town was marked by a competitive brand of politics and a vibrant culture—an age that was anything but ordinary. To travel to any of the revitalized neighborhoods of the city today—the Crossroads Arts District, the West Bottoms, the Garment District, River Market, Eighteenth and Vine, Westport, and the Country Club Plaza—is to see ample evidence of a community that finds contemporary significance in the long tale of this distinctive history. Importantly, much of the recent focus on urban renewal has centered on the rejuvenation of the neighborhoods and public places that were first promoted by city boosters in the 1920s and 1930s. Developers now use carefully selected elements of history to reimagine many of the city's once over-looked landmarks and neighborhoods. To be sure, some of these efforts serve an entrepreneurial purpose, with boosting tourism and downtown business develop-ment a primary goal. It is not unexpected to see artisanal juiceries and craft distill-eries sharing refurbished neighborhood spaces with architectural firms and digital technology companies. Yet as a new generation of city residents search for meaning beyond suburban Cupcake Land, they have increasingly embraced the city's spirited past, focusing on the period they imagine to be their city's "golden age."

That a curated history could be used to sell the image of a revitalized city should not surprise us, but the results can lead to unexpected conclusions. For a city that rightly advertises itself as progressive, the continual backward glances to the Jazz Age contribute to an understanding of the present that is as messy as it is incom-plete. Finding proof of contemporary significance in the form of an animated past is not standard form for glossy Chamber of Commerce promotional brochures. Yet as this project illuminates, the border between nostalgia, history, and memory is often muddled, and in this gray space lies the importance of this period to under-standing Kansas City. Our goal in *Wide-Open Town* is to reexamine this critically important time in Kansas City history and to investigate how this city shaped na-tional narratives.

At the crossroads of American transportation networks and cultural norms, Kansas City in the 1920s and 1930s typified broad trends in American history. The decades bounded by the world wars were marked by intense political, social, and economic change as the United States reluctantly took its place on the world stage while simultaneously struggling with significant challenges at home. The upheaval of World War I, the massive migration of people of color into urban America, the entrance of women into both the labor force and electoral politics, resistance to Prohibition and changing social mores, and an economic collapse and near revo-lution in national politics, all redefined the national character. How these changes influenced Kansas City—and how the city responded—helps us understand how citizens of the age adapted to the rise of modern America.[3]

Kansas City's place in this larger national story has already received consider-able scholarly attention. We encourage readers interested in popular topics such as crime, the political machine, Harry S. Truman, race relations, and jazz to consult this growing and increasingly sophisticated body of regional history.[4] The chapters in *Wide-Open Town*, however, approach subjects that, although less known, reveal a complicated past. During this period, for example, Prohibition was barely (if ever) enforced; the mob was in ascendancy; and gambling, prostitution, and other hall-marks of urban vice were easily visible. All of that is true, yet this same "openness" allowed many of the city's residents to carve out autonomous spaces and challenge conventional social boundaries. Kansas City remained a community divided by the hard lines of race and class, but it was also a city of possibilities where the restrictions that governed life in a segregated state were often more fluid. With this premise as a foundation, *Wide-Open Town* explores how local residents navigated a city in transition. We believe this project will contribute to an ongoing conversation about the costs and consequences of Kansas City's maturation into a modern American city.

The volume is divided into three sections, each highlighting a key theme—politics, diversity, and culture—of the era. The first, "Politics and Progress in Kansas City's 'Golden Age,'" suggests that Kansas City of the early twentieth century stood on the leading edge of national political and economic change. Chapters from John W. McKerley and Jeffrey L. Pasley explore how the racial politics of the city transformed both the Democratic and Republican Parties. McKerley shows in Chapter 1 how the ability of African Americans to maintain the vote in Missouri provided them with opportunities for political influence that were not available to many other black citizens of this era. In Chapter 2, Pasley argues that the unique social and political structure of Kansas City's Democratic machine forged a demographic coalition—"blacks, immigrants, workers, and just enough partly reconstructed southern whites"—that would eventually dominate national Democratic Party politics in the age of Franklin D. Roosevelt. From these larger political shifts emerged an alliance of convenience between the corrupt Pendergast machine and the Kansas City business community as together they worked to promote their city as a major midwestern metropolis. Sara Stevens illustrates in Chapter 3 how the city's pioneering urban developer, J. C. Nichols, used aesthetic conventions and racially restrictive real estate covenants to create a model of American suburban development that was replicated throughout the nation. And in Chapter 4, Jaclyn Miller shows how city leaders used Kansas City's position as a national economic leader to demand the establishment of a branch of the Federal Reserve Bank. City boosters used similar logic to attract additional national attention, including hosting the 1928 Republican National Convention, a topic explored by Dustin Gann in Chapter 5. Civic leaders would leverage this moment of triumph to enact a long-term vision for city development, creating a template for federal investment in local affairs during the New Deal.

In the second section, "Breaking Barriers in a Segregated City," the chapters shift to the residents who altered social norms in the city. Kansas City's unique political environment created opportunities for historically disenfranchised residents to advocate for improved social welfare and civil rights. In Chapter 6, John Herron investigates Kansas City's first major industry, meatpacking, illustrating how workers, especially black laborers, attempted to organize for improved working conditions. Kyle Anthony follows with an examination of the city's other industrial power, garment making. Chapter 7 reveals that unlike the laborers in the packinghouses, garment workers were unable to organize at the Donnelly Garment Company, one of the foremost dressmaking companies in America. The organizers ran up against the maternalistic management style of the company's owner, Nell Donnelly Reed, one of the nation's most successful female business owners. In Chapter 8, K. David Hanzlick reveals how elite Kansas City women expanded their power and influence from traditional social and philanthropic clubs into the realm of party politics. Although they did not meet with significant electoral success, they forced political leaders to recognize women as an important constituency. Indeed, it would be women from Kansas City's Republican Party who played a key role in bringing down the Pendergast Democratic machine. Another prominent Kansas City woman, Lucile Bluford, managing editor of the city's main black newspaper, *The Call*, challenged racial segregation in Missouri when she attempted to enroll in the University of Missouri's prestigious journalism school. In Chapter 9, Henrietta Rix Wood explores how Bluford used rhetorical strategies in the pages of the paper to encourage readers to support her campaign for civil rights. In Chapter 10, Jason Roe shows how black community leaders pressed for the construction of a new public hospital to treat the city's residents of color. The result was a state-of-the-art hospital entirely staffed by African American doctors and nurses that reflected the newfound political influence of black Kansas City. Valerie M. Mendoza concludes this section by illustrating how the effort to build stronger ethnic communities was not limited to African Americans. She reveals in Chapter 11 how the Mexican community, the largest immigrant group in the city, reshaped a settlement house first established by white philanthropists into a community institution that reflected its own priorities.

In the final section, "Culture at an American Crossroads," the authors explore how Kansas City, one of the nation's primary transportation hubs, emerged as a significant site of cultural production. The city would use its central geography not only to blend diverse regional influences but also to export a distinctive brand of artistic expression. Kansas City is well known for the development of jazz, a trend best illustrated by the nightlife of the Pendergast years, but Marc Rice reminds us in Chapter 12 that the early luminaries of the music scene were sustained by elite black Kansas Citians who employed them at various charity and social events. Kansas City's famous black jazz musicians such as Bennie Moten, Count Basie, and Charlie Parker are rightly remembered as the founders of the Kansas City jazz style. Chuck Haddix argues in Chapter 13 that to national radio audiences in the 1920s, however, an earlier "Kansas City sound" was first introduced by a now-obscure local white dance band called the Coon-Sanders Nighthawk Orchestra. A few years after the Nighthawks left Kansas City in search of larger audiences, the internationally renowned artist Thomas Hart Benton returned to the Midwest from the East Coast in an attempt to elevate Kansas City into a cultural mecca. In Chapter 14, Henry Adams explains that Benton used his position as a prominent artist of American regionalism and the son of an influential Missouri politician to forge relationships with the city's cultural leaders and social elite. For a brief period, the Benton house was home to an avant-garde community of artists and expats. In a colorful example of the city's open cultural mores, Stuart Hinds examines in Chapter 15 how female impersonators performed in Kansas City's vaudeville theater and club venues long after similar performers were forced off the stages of many other American cities. And in the final chapter in the volume, Keith Eggener traces the construction, decline, and resurgence of Kansas City's Liberty Memorial. The monument, built with local funds and erected in the 1920s, was intended to honor the sacrifice of millions in World War I. Just as important, the impressive site was also meant to announce the arrival of Kansas City as a national economic and cultural power. The memorial was long a point of civic pride, but in the mid-twentieth century, the complex fell into disrepair, matching a similar decline of the downtown core. In the early years of the new millennium, however, Kansas City's leaders once again raised funds for the memorial, this time to refurbish the site in hopes of inaugurating a new golden age for the city.

With its heartland location, mild manners, and expansive suburbs, Kansas City has been stigmatized as generic "flyover" country. A look beneath the surface, however, reveals a much more complex and captivating story about American economic development, race relations, and cultural transformation. In an inversion of the everyplace narrative, the chapters in this volume illustrate that Kansas City holds significance to our understanding of America's past.

Notes

1. See Thomas Frank, "A Machine for Forgetting: Kansas City and the Declining Significance of Place," *The Baffler* 7 (1995).

2. See Richard Rhodes, "Cupcake Land: Requiem for the Midwest in the Key of Vanilla," *Harper's Magazine* 275 (November 1987): 51–57.

3. For a sample of the voluminous scholarship on the history of the United States during this period, consider Kristi Andersen, *After Suffrage: Women in Partisan and Electoral Politics before the New Deal* (Chicago: University of Chicago Press, 1996); David Burner, *The Politics of Provincialism: The Democratic Party in Transition, 1918–1932* (New York: Knopf, 1967); George Chauncey, *Gay New York: Gender, Urban Culture and the Making of the Gay Male World, 1890–1940* (New York: Basic Books, 1994); Norman H. Clark, *Deliver Us from Evil: An Interpretation of American Prohibition* (New York: W. W. Norton, 1976); Lizabeth Cohen, *Making a New Deal: Industrial Workers in Chicago, 1919–1939* (New York: Cambridge University Press, 1990); Nancy F. Cott, *The Grounding of Modern Feminism* (New Haven, Conn.: Yale University Press, 1987); Lynn Dumenil, *The Modern Temper: American Culture and Society in the*

1920s (New York: Hill and Wang, 1995); James Fentress, *Eminent Gangsters: Immigrants and the Birth of Organized Crime in America* (Lanham, Md.: University Press of America, 2010); Estelle B. Freedman, "The New Woman: Changing Views of Women in the 1920s," *Journal of American History* 61 (September 1974): 372–393; John Kenneth Galbraith, *The Great Crash* (New York: Houghton Mifflin, 1954); David J. Goldberg, *Discontented America: The United States in the 1920s* (Baltimore: Johns Hopkins University Press, 1999); John Higham, *Strangers in the Land: Patterns of American Nativism, 1860–1925* (1955; New Brunswick, N.J.: Rutgers University Press, 1988); James R. Grossman, *Land of Hope: Chicago, Black Southerners, and the Great Migration* (Chicago: University of Chicago Press, 1991); Kristin Hoganson, *Consumers' Imperium: The Global Production of American Domesticity, 1865–1920* (Chapel Hill: University of North Carolina Press, 2007); Kenneth T. Jackson, *The Ku Klux Klan in the City, 1915–1930* (New York: Oxford University Press, 1967); Matthew Frye Jacobson, *Whiteness of a Different Color: European Immigrants and the Alchemy of Race* (Cambridge, Mass.: Harvard University Press, 1998); Ira Katznelson, *Fear Itself: The New Deal and the Origins of Our Time* (New York: Liveright Publishing, 2013); David M. Kennedy, *Freedom from Fear: The American People in Depression and War, 1929–1945* (New York: Oxford University Press, 1999); James T. Kloppenberg, *Uncertain Victory: Social Democracy and Progressivism in European and American Thought, 1870–1920* (New York: Oxford University Press, 1986); William Leach, *Land of Desire: Merchants, Power, and the Rise of a New American Culture* (New York: Pantheon, 1993); William E. Leuchtenburg, *The Perils of Prosperity, 1914–1932* (Chicago: University of Chicago Press, 1958); David Levering Lewis, *When Harlem Was in Vogue* (New York: Knopf, 1979); Catherine Gilbert Murdock, *Domesticating Drink: Women, Men, and Alcohol in America, 1870–1940* (Baltimore: Johns Hopkins University Press, 1998); Humbert S. Nelli, *The Business of Crime: Italians and Syndicate Crime in the United States* (Chicago: University of Chicago Press, 1976); Charles Postel, *The Populist Vision* (New York: Oxford University Press, 2007); James Warren Prothro, *The Dollar Decade: Business Ideas in the 1920s* (Baton Rouge: Louisiana State University Press, 1954); Daniel Rodgers, *Atlantic Crossings: Social Politics in a Progressive Age* (Cambridge, Mass.: Harvard University Press, 1998); Kenneth D. Rose, *American Women and the Repeal of Prohibition* (New York: New York University Press, 1996); Vicki Ruiz, "'Star Struck': Acculturation, Adolescence, and Mexican American Women, 1920–1950," in *Small Worlds: Children and Adolescents in America, 1850–1950*, ed. Elliott West and Paula Petrik (Lawrence: University Press of Kansas, 1992); David E. Ruth, *Inventing the Public Enemy: The Gangster in American Culture, 1918–1934* (Chicago: University of Chicago Press, 1996); George J. Sánchez, *Becoming Mexican American: Ethnicity, Culture, and Identity in Chicano Los Angeles, 1900–1945* (New York: Oxford, 1993); and Mark Robert Schneider, *"We Return Fighting": The Civil Rights Movement in the Jazz Age* (Boston: Northeastern University Press, 2002).

4. For selective scholarship on Kansas City during the 1920s and 1930s, see A. Theodore Brown, *The Politics of Reform: Kansas City's Municipal Government, 1925–1950* (Kansas City, Mo.: Community Studies, 1958); A. Theodore Brown and Lyle W. Dorsett, *K.C.: A History of Kansas City, Missouri* (Boulder, Colo.: Pruett Publishing, 1978); Ann Brownfield and David Jackson, *We Were Hanging by a Thread: Kansas City Garment District Pieces the Past Together* (Kansas City, Mo.: Orderly Pack Rat Publishing, 2014); Janet Bruce, *The Kansas City*

Monarchs: Champions of Black Baseball (Lawrence: University Press of Kansas, 1985); Charles Coulter, *"Take Up the Black Man's Burden": Kansas City's African American Communities, 1865–1939* (Columbia: University of Missouri Press, 2006); Lyle W. Dorsett, *The Pendergast Machine* (New York: Oxford University Press, 1968); Fred W. Edmiston, *The Coon-Sanders Nighthawks: "The Band That Made Radio Famous"* (Jefferson, N.C.: McFarland, 2003); Robert H. Ferrell, *Truman and Pendergast* (Columbia: University of Missouri Press, 1999); Jane Fifield Flynn, *Kansas City Women of Independent Minds* (Kansas City, Mo.: Fifield Publishing, 1992); Charles N. Glaab, *Kansas City and the Railroads: Community Policy in the Growth of a Regional Metropolis* (Lawrence: University Press of Kansas, 1993); Kevin Fox Gotham, *Race, Real Estate, and Uneven Development: The Kansas City Experience, 1900–2010* (Albany: State University of New York Press, 2014); Chuck Haddix and Frank Driggs, *Kansas City Jazz: From Ragtime to Bebop–A History* (New York: Oxford University Press, 2006); Rudolf Hartmann, edited with an introduction by Robert H. Ferrell, *The Kansas City Investigation: Pendergast's Downfall, 1938–1939* (Columbia: University of Missouri Press, 1999); Henry C. Haskell Jr. and Richard B. Fowler, *City of the Future: A Narrative History of Kansas City, 1850–1950* (Kansas City, Mo.: Frank Glenn Publishing, 1950); Frank Hayde, *The Mafia and the Machine: The Story of the Kansas City Mob* (Fort Lee, N.J.: Barricade Books, 2010); Lawrence H. Larsen and Nancy J. Hulston, *Pendergast!* (Columbia: University of Missouri Press, 1997); Maurice M. Milligan, *Missouri Waltz: The Inside Story of the Pendergast Machine by the Man Who Smashed It* (New York: Charles Scribner's Sons, 1948); Diane Mutti Burke and John Herron, eds., *Kansas City, America's Crossroads: Essays from the Missouri Historical Review, 1906–2006* (Columbia: State Historical Society of Missouri, 2007); William Ouseley, *Open City: True Story of the KC Crime Family, 1900–1950* (Overland Park, Kans.: Leathers Publishing, 2008); Nathan W. Pearson, *Goin' to Kansas City* (Champaign-Urbana: University of Illinois Press, 1994); William M. Reddig, *Tom's Town: Kansas City and the Pendergast Legend* (Philadelphia: J. B. Lippincott Company, 1947); Sherry Lamb Schirmer, *A City Divided: The Racial Landscape of Kansas City, 1900–1960* (Columbia: University of Missouri Press, 2002); James R. Shortridge, *Kansas City and How It Grew, 1822–2011* (Lawrence: University Press of Kansas, 2012); Robert Unger, *The Union Station Massacre: The Original Sin of J. Edgar Hoover's FBI* (Kansas City, Mo.: Andrews McNeel Publishing, 1997); and William S. Worley, *J. C. Nichols and the Shaping of Kansas City: Innovation in Planned Residential Communities* (Columbia: University of Missouri Press, 1990).

PART ONE

Politics and Progress in Kansas City's "Golden Age"

CHAPTER ONE

The Other Tom's Town

Thomas T. Crittenden Jr., Black Disfranchisement, and the Limits of Liberalism in Kansas City

John W. McKerley

In the spring of 1908, Democrat Thomas T. Crittenden Jr., the son of a former Missouri governor, handily defeated his Republican opponent to become mayor of Kansas City, Missouri. His election marked a partisan as well as personal victory. Crittenden became only the second Democrat to win the mayor's office since 1894, and Democrats also took back both houses of the city council, including seats in several reliably Republican wards on the expanding south side. Crittenden and his allies had achieved this remarkable success by explicitly playing on white Kansas Citians' racial fears, turning white anxiety about crime, racial integration, and black political empowerment into votes. Over the next several months, they attempted to expand their local victory into a model for the entire state, pressing Missouri Democrats to commit the party to a vision of white supremacy centered on black disfranchisement.[1]

Crittenden's surprising 1908 election victory both reflected and responded to a system of racial and electoral politics that stretched back almost half a century. In the wake of the Civil War, Missouri Democrats had reorganized their party around opposition to Radical Republican rule and the threat of black suffrage. In 1870, with ratification of the Fifteenth Amendment to the US Constitution providing for black men's voting rights, they lost the fight against black suffrage but won, at least temporarily, against Republicans, with Democrats taking back statewide political control for the first time since the war. They were successful because of the assistance of self-styled Liberal Republicans, who supported black suffrage but broke

11

Thomas T. Crittenden Jr., mayor of Kansas City from 1908 to 1910, date unknown. Courtesy of the Missouri Valley Special Collections, Kansas City Public Library.

with the Radicals over voting restrictions on white wartime "disloyalists."[2] Although postwar Democrats had initially organized against such political liberalism being extended to black people, over the next several decades, they largely accommodated themselves to black men as voters, even appealing for black votes at election time.

Democrats took such an unprecedented step because they needed all the votes they could get. Although it would take Republicans decades to rebuild the statewide strength that they had wielded during the 1860s, they quickly recovered in Kansas City and other urban areas, where waves of black migrants joined with white new-comers to produce an exceptionally competitive urban political landscape. While Republicans downplayed their relationship with black voters to court the state's racially conservative whites, Democrats approached the same goal from the opposite direction, reaching out to black voters while assuring white Missourians that they were still the party of white supremacy. Over time, these political shifts produced a new "liberal" order. Eschewing a clear economic ideology or partisan orientation, this new liberalism was a style of politics rooted in city life that mixed elements of pluralism and paternalism with the social, political, and economic preeminence of white male property holders, especially those with political connections.[3]

This new order allowed Democrats to compete with Republicans in urban Missouri, but it failed to restore uncontested Democratic dominance and produced its own critics from within the party. Such criticism was particularly fierce from the generation of aspiring young white men who, like Crittenden, came of age at the turn of the century. In these years—from roughly the 1880s through the 1910s—new white supremacist political movements swept the former slave states, and anti-immigrant groups argued that "racial" hierarchies could be found even among otherwise "white" Europeans.[4] For many of these young white men, their fathers' generation—and its "boss" politicians in particular—had threatened white supremacy and good government through corrupt deals with working-class and black men in return for political power.[5] For Crittenden and his allies, black political equality necessarily entailed black social equality (whatever the denials of the boss politicians), and they were determined to demonstrate that they could seize and wield political power in the name of honest elections and the security of white, middle-class homes and families.[6] Their failure would establish Kansas City's place within the racial geography of the urban Midwest as well as set the stage for the rise of another "Tom," Thomas J. Pendergast, whose system of twentieth-century urban liberalism drew heavily on the lessons of its predecessors.

Race and Partisanship in Late Nineteenth-Century Kansas City

In 1863, when Crittenden was born, Missouri's laws restricted voting rights to white men.[7] Although the wartime struggle over slavery had begun to present black Missourians with opportunities to claim new rights, such as the right to testify against their white owners in Union military courts, the overwhelming majority of white Missourians still opposed full legal and political equality for black people.[8] As the war ended, however, Missouri's newly ascendant Radical Republican majority began to press for greater black rights—both on the grounds of resolving emancipation and as a result of persistent lobbying on the part of black Missourians—with Democrats rallying in opposition. As early as October 1865, over a hundred delegates to a meeting in Kansas City resolved "that the Constitution and Government of the United States were ordained and established by white men for the benefit of themselves and their posterity." The delegates further resolved that they were "opposed to negro suffrage, negro equality, miscegenation and all the kindred negroism of the Radical [Republican] party."[9]

In the decades following the ratification of the Fifteenth Amendment and Democrats' "redemption" of the state from Republican rule, however, such unnuanced commitments to black disfranchisement increasingly appeared both politically unwise and unnecessary. Indeed, Kansas City, and Missouri generally, changed a great deal during those years. In 1869, the Hannibal Bridge opened the city and surrounding areas to industrial development and sped Kansas City's eclipse of competing towns along the state's western border.[10] Fueled by economic expansion and the corresponding demand for wage labor, Kansas City's population, which stood at just over 55,000 in 1880, almost tripled by the turn of the century, reaching over 163,000 by 1900.[11]

Most of these new Kansas Citians could claim whiteness, but a significant number of black people arrived as well. Whereas only 190 black men and women resided in Kansas City in 1860, over the next twenty years the arrival of black migrants from rural Missouri and across the South pushed the city's black population to 7,914, a figure representing over 14 percent of the city's total. Although this phenomenal growth slowed after 1880, the city's black population still rose to 13,700 by 1890.[12] Most of these black men and women worked as laborers or domestic servants, but the community also contained skilled and semiskilled craftsmen—including stonemasons, bricklayers, and blacksmiths—as well as lawyers, doctors, and other members of the black professional class.[13] Moreover, these migrants represented a significant part of a larger rural-to-urban migration transforming black life in the state. By 1900, Missouri had become the first state of the former slave South to have a majority (55 percent) of its black population living in cities and towns (with 70 percent of these urban black people residing in either St. Louis or Kansas City).[14]

In this context, Missouri politicians from across the political spectrum began to reconsider their approach to black voters, especially as new migrants made urban politics more competitive. Republicans attempted to hold on to black loyalty at election time while simultaneously reaching out to the white majority, often resisting black calls for political patronage in the process. Democrats attempted to take advantage of black frustration over Republican patronage but remained willing and able to use various forms of race baiting and disfranchisement to ensure political victories. One example of this process took place in 1888, when a black Kansas Citian, Paul Jones, attempted to win the Republican nomination for city attorney. Republicans denied him the spot, with both white and black party members arguing that running a black man for such a prominent position would repel white voters (even party members), doom the ticket as a whole, and leave black Kansas Citians at the mercy of the Democratic Party, with its majority of overtly hostile whites. For their part, Democrats were happy to publicize what they characterized as Republican hypocrisy and bad faith toward black voters, all the while reinforcing their own commitment to white supremacy through racist depictions of black people. Jones and his supporters negotiated this difficult and dangerous political terrain by reaching out not to Democrats but to a third party—the Union Labor ticket. Jones's base of support came from black members of the Knights of Labor, a pro-cooperative, anti-monopolist union organization founded around the concept of working-class solidarity and empowerment across lines of skill, gender, ethnicity, and race.[15] Jones lost but pulled enough black support to garner more votes than any other candidate on the (otherwise white) Union Labor ticket, revealing the degree to which black Missourians had become willing and able to vote strategically to advance their individual and collective interests.[16]

Over the next decade, such episodic third-party experiments failed to produce sustainable, independent political alternatives for black Kansas Citians, but they did become a bridge into the Democratic Party. Facing a political world character-ized by varying degrees of white racism, black people increasingly offered electoral support to Democrats, if for no other reason than splitting their vote offered more meaningful opportunities to exert leverage in close elections and lay claim to public employment for themselves and members of their communities. Likewise, Demo-crats sought black voters in the context of not only growing partisan competition but also intraparty factionalism. As early as 1900, supporters of one Democratic faction, the "Goats," led by James F. Pendergast, organized a Negro Central League as part of their effort to attract black voters to the campaign of their faction's may-oral candidate, James A. Reed (the other main faction, the "Rabbits," were led by Joseph Shannon). After black Missourians contributed to Reed's narrow victory, he attempted to consolidate some of the gains by opening jobs in the fire department and other patronage opportunities to black supporters. Indeed, in 1902, when Reed ran again for mayor, his black support was so conspicuous that one white Democrat noted, "The Democratic party [in Kansas City] no longer claims to be a strictly white man's party."[17]

Reinventing Black Disfranchisement in Progressive Era Kansas City

By the turn of the twentieth century, Kansas City's white political leaders in both major parties had developed liberal politics that largely accepted black men as vot-ers. Such acceptance, however, was both situational and contested. These same white politicians (and the dense, white-dominated networks that made Kansas City electoral politics function) were willing and able to use various forms of disfran-chisement whenever black political access threatened to lead to black power over whites or to challenge partisan or factional priorities or broader social segregation and economic subordination. Black Kansas Citians were the primary opponents of such liberalism, even as they sought to use its opportunities to advance their indi-vidual and collective interests in the city.[18] But it was also opposed by a substantial minority of whites who regarded liberalism as a tool used by some unscrupulous white men to profit from a counterfeit white supremacist order. This latter group was increasingly dominated by a younger generation who had come to see the postwar system as corrupt and out of touch. Although such white Missourians from across the state had made periodic calls to overturn postwar liberalism, they did not coalesce into anything approaching a unified political "movement" in Missouri until 1908, when Thomas T. Crittenden Jr. and his allies in Kansas City tried to forge one.

Crittenden might have seemed an unlikely person for such a role. He came from a distinguished Kentucky family known for its relative political moderation and support for the status quo and the rule of law. His great-uncle, John J. Crittenden, had authored the famous "Crittenden Compromise," a failed proposal to avert the Civil War.[19] His father, Thomas T. Crittenden Sr., had moved the family to western Missouri, where he served on the side of the Union. After wartime military service and stints as Missouri's attorney general and in the US Congress, Crittenden Sr. settled into a law practice with Francis Cockrell, a pro-Confederate Missourian who would begin a long career as a postwar Democrat in the US Senate. In 1881, Crittenden, also a Democrat, became Missouri's governor, making his reputation (famously or infamously) as the governor who brought down Confederate-guerrilla-turned-outlaw Jesse James.[20]

At the same time, however, the younger Crittenden evidenced an outspoken commitment to white supremacy and black disfranchisement that suggested both the ways that racism undergirded reunion after the Civil War and a certain tension between those older Democrats, like his father and Cockrell, who had rebuilt the party amid the contested terrain of postwar politics, and those young white men like himself, who had come of age at the turn of the century.[21] As a deputy clerk of appeals and clerk of Jackson County, Crittenden had made no secret of his efforts to exclude black men from jury service and even campaigned on the issue. "If I had the making of the law I would not have provided for Negroes serving on the juries until their education and intelligence warranted it," he replied when pressed on black jury service by a Republican opponent. "I think it unfortunate that negroes and white people should have to serve on the same jury. I feel that, socially, the races are not equal."[22]

And Crittenden was not alone. During the first years of the new century, white Kansas Citians grew increasingly concerned about and suspicious of black people's political influence and the social and economic opportunities such influence enabled. For example, opponents of black suffrage could point to a 1905 scandal at the city's workhouse in which a black male guard had allegedly beaten a white female inmate, prompting action by white women as well as men. When white representatives of Kansas City's Woman's Christian Temperance Union conducted their own subsequent study of workhouse conditions, they were appalled to find that white women sometimes bathed around black guards and that black and white women were sometimes held in integrated cells. Another investigation revealed that a black physician in the city's employ, Dr. Thomas C. Unthank, examined the workhouse's white female inmates, leading the city council to call for the institution of segregated facilities.[23]

Such scandals and investigations softened white political support for black patronage and liberalism more generally. In 1906, when William T. Kemper, a local businessman, ran for mayor, he rejected an alliance with black voters (having courted them only two years before during an earlier mayoral race). Instead, he announced that he would refuse to hire any black public employees if elected. Although the announcement failed to win Kemper the Democratic nomination for mayor—and Rabbit leader Joseph Shannon denounced Kemper's use of racial rhetoric in a Democratic nomination fight as "a miserable and a weak attempt to curry favor on a question that has no place in Democratic caucuses"—the party nonetheless used the workhouse scandal in its unsuccessful 1906 campaign against Republican mayoral candidate Henry M. Beardsley.[24]

By 1908, therefore, when Crittenden made his run for mayor, Kansas City's white Democrats were especially anxious for a return to both partisan power and uncontested white supremacy. Still, the 1908 mayoral campaign did not initially hinge on race. Instead, the campaign revolved around the two parties' approaches to the development of an "effective" public utilities commission. Both parties publicly supported the formation of some sort of commission, but they differed on its structure and powers. The Republicans and their allies advocated placing considerable appointment power in the hands of the mayor, whereas Democrats supported a commission that diffused regulatory responsibility among three Republicans, three Democrats, and one labor representative. Although the Republican incumbent, Beardsley, was himself a moderate reformer, Democrats attempted to discredit him as the tool of street railway companies and other municipal monopolies. In particular, they argued that he was under the direct control of William Rockhill Nelson, the influential owner and editor of the *Kansas City Star*.[25]

At first, Crittenden's campaign emphasized the themes of anti-factionalism, bipartisanship, elevation of a new generation of leaders, and the overthrow of the Republican "machine" (a term, like "boss," used by various parties and factions to disparage their opponents, but generally associated with urban political organizations that used patronage to organize voting blocks, especially working-class men).[26] Crittenden claimed to have withheld his acceptance until he was convinced that a "united party" would back him, and afterward declared that one of the core principles of his campaign would be the promotion of "absolute harmony in the ranks of the local Democracy." Finding a base of support among the Young Men's Democratic Club, Crittenden represented the aspirations of those young white men on the make, "the brainy, brawny young men" who were "determined to aid in the overthrow of the machine." Such people, he argued, included even the "best" and "taxpaying" portions of the Republican Party, who also had a stake in stopping "the extravagance and corruption that now exists at city hall."[27]

The Democratic-aligned *Kansas City Post* first introduced race into the campaign through its efforts to link the Beardsley administration to growing white concerns over crime. In late 1907 and early 1908, whites in greater Kansas City had been shocked by a series of sensationalized crimes allegedly committed by recent black migrants. In January 1908, a police captain told the *Post* that it was his belief that "the recent wave of crime is due almost entirely to blacks." After a black man allegedly struck a white storekeeper during a daylight robbery near a police station, the paper concluded, "Certainly no man is safe when a negro will dare to commit an assault like that." Although some of the black men arrested in connection with the incidents confessed to the crimes, others maintained their innocence, and at least one later recanted his confession on the grounds that he feared a "beating" at the hands of the police if he had refused.[28]

Indeed, it was the actions of white, not black, criminals, that first inspired the *Post*. On March 1, 1908, the paper, after discovering that Mayor Beardsley had participated in the release of two white pickpockets, accused the mayor of pardoning "thieves and thugs" to bolster the Republican voting tallies. The next day, it further alleged that the Beardsley administration had remitted the fines of two white Republican "gun toters" who had been charged with carrying concealed weapons. Race only became the center of the allegations after March 11, when the *Post* reported that "[within] the period of seven hours a [white] woman and a little girl were assaulted by negroes in Kansas City." Without making any direct connection between the Republicans and the alleged assault, the paper rushed to the rhetorical defense of white womanhood, "the very fountain head of our society." Although the *Post* claimed to "have no quarrel with the colored race," the paper charged that "there is present in its membership an element whose lust and bestiality are menaces to society" and that lynching, or "natural law," would be called for if it were not stopped.[29]

As early as the following morning, Democrats of various stripes had already retooled their attacks on the Beardsley administration to include claims that the same black men responsible for these assaults had been brought into Kansas City ("colonized") by the Republicans to support the party's ticket. While James A. Reed charged Beardsley with buying "nigger votes," the *Post* claimed that "evidence is being developed daily which proves that the Republican bosses of Kansas City not only intend to buy negro votes, but that they are even now colonizing negroes for registration purposes." Keeping with some of the campaign's earlier themes, they suggested that the money for such colonization schemes "[had] been wrung from public appointees and . . . collected from corporations supporting Henry M. Beardsley." Anticipating that some readers, even party members, might wonder at Democrats' sudden discovery of electoral fraud, the paper claimed that Democratic corruption never produced the "numerous outrages by blacks upon white women" on the part of "negroes who . . . are not known here." Instead, portraying itself and the party as the defenders of white womanhood, the *Post* announced that Democrats would only "[inject] the race issue into the present political struggle" if the "Republican bosses" and "respectable negroes" refused to join them in repudiating political alliances with black criminals. Such a refusal, it warned, would require "the white people of Kansas City . . . [to] indicate their resentment in a manner which will effectually eliminate the purchased negro from local politics."[30]

Once established, these basic elements—black criminality, Republican corruption, and white Democratic manhood—became the interlocking themes of the party's strategy during the campaign. On March 13, the *Post* alleged that a Republican judge had reduced a black man's fine for insulting an "eminently respectable white woman" from $500 to $25. A few days later, it reported that Republican officials had used "threats of arrest and prosecution" against the "poorer class of Democratic white voters," and that white women had identified a black man who had allegedly "followed and made indecent proposals to three young white girls."[31]

Crittenden seized the opportunity to declare that his election would signal a new birth of white supremacy in Kansas City. Rejecting previous white politicians' willingness to make limited compromises with black Missourians in return for political support, he announced that his administration would make a decisive break with any quid pro quo with the black community by purging black men from public employment. In particular, he announced that he would not permit any "negro foremen." "I do not believe in a negro being a 'boss' over a white man," Crittenden told an audience on March 25, "and I promise you here and now that when I get into office there is going to be a mighty lopping off of heads along this line."[32] Crittenden's close friend and political ally, William S. Cowherd, a former congressman and Kansas City mayor with aspirations for the governor's office, had earlier bolstered these claims by asserting that Crittenden was man enough for the job. Cowherd described Crittenden as "a good man, a man who has the backbone and courage to do right and a man who will do things," adding, "we want no mamby-pamby [sic], molly coddle in the mayor's office."[33]

White Republicans and their allies struggled in their efforts to deflect these charges because of their unwillingness to engage in tactics they found distasteful, but also because they shared some of the basic assumptions about the existence, if not the consequences, of black corruption and criminality. In the wake of the alleged outbreak of black crime, the *Star* acknowledged that "bad niggers" were responsible, but the paper argued that the extension of progressive reform into the black community was the only way to keep from unfairly punishing the "decent, respectable negro members of society." Instead of "[retarding] prejudices and inequities," the paper called for "[correctional] influences for the criminally inclined; decent environment for the neglected, starveling negro children; [and] intervention where parents are too poor or vicious to have the guidance of the young ones."[34]

This Republican strategy seriously underestimated white residents' feelings of insecurity and their willingness to project those fears onto the city's growing black population. As the Democratic campaign gained momentum, the *Post* began publishing letters claiming to be from white Republican workers and homeowners who had abandoned Beardsley in favor of Crittenden and his racial policies. On March 23, the paper printed a letter to Crittenden from a white Republican "clerk" who had shifted his support to the Democratic candidate. The problem, the anonymous white clerk explained, was not job competition per se, but the relationship between the prestige of patronage employment, higher wages, and "social equality." According to the clerk, he had paid "hard earned money for a nice home," only to have "a negro" buy an "adjoining" property. Now, the clerk feared for the safety of his "daughters who are just out of their teens," but he could not afford to sell his home. He laid the blame for the situation squarely at the feet of "[the] city hall machine, [which] by giving negroes public offices encourage them to believe in racial equality and then they buy homes near us." The "solution," he claimed, was a residential segregation ordinance, which he believed most likely under a Democratic administration. "No more Nelson-Beardsleyism for me," he declared; "[let] them keep their 'niggers.'"[35]

Black Missourians, once again isolated from and by erstwhile white allies in both major parties, struggled to construct defenses against renewed threats to their community. For some of the more prosperous and "respectable" men and women among them, the best defense was to publicly demonstrate their opposition to the alleged criminals in their midst. Other black Missourians abandoned caution and respectability in favor of a more aggressive and oppositional stance. On March 20, 1908, the *Post* published the alleged confession of E. W. Clemmons, a black man charged with illegal voter registration. Clemmons claimed to have been pressured into voting illegally by black Republicans who had insisted that it was the duty of "[every] colored man in Kansas City to register" in opposition to Crittenden and his promised purge of black Missourians from public employment. According to these black Republicans, black men who avoided this obligation "should be taken back down South where they haven't either the right to register or vote."[36]

Something of the lives and labors of these aggressive black opponents of white supremacy in Kansas City could be seen in the testimony of George Williams (also known as George Hale), who was arrested on suspicion of election fraud. In a statement to authorities, Williams testified that he was thirty-six years old and had been born in Leavenworth, Kansas, sometime around 1872. He had come to Kansas City "as a little boy" and, as a young man, had spent some time in jail for vagrancy. After travels that took him up and down the Mississippi River valley, he returned to Kansas City "some little time before the [1903] flood," and moved between jobs in various meatpacking plants. Sometime in 1904 or 1905, he "got a job as an extra man in the street department of the city under [Republican] Mayor Neff's administration," eventually working his way into a foreman's position (perhaps making him one of the "negro foremen" Crittenden targeted for removal from public work). In 1908, the *Post* described Williams as the "negro boss of the Tenth precinct of the First ward," adding that "[h]e is president of the First Ward Negro Republican club, and 'handles' the negroes of his neighborhood for the Republican machine." For his part, Williams simply testified that he worked the polls on registration day, "and did what good I could."[37]

Unfortunately for the city's black residents, there was little good that could be done. In April, Crittenden defeated Beardsley with a plurality of almost 1,350 votes, and the Democrats captured the city council. Even Crittenden's former competitors in the Democratic boss factions acknowledged his success in the election's wake. Remarking on the lack of postelection Republican celebrations, Goat leader James F. Pendergast quipped that "the good people of the city will be spared the sight of [black Republican leader] Nelson Crews and his marching club parading the main thoroughfares this afternoon."[38]

From Kansas City to Jefferson City: The Campaign for Black Disfranchisement in Missouri

Crittenden and his allies (Cowherd especially) soon began to contemplate the possibility that their local victory held "at least a state-wide significance." Not only would Democratic control of Kansas City politics increase the likelihood that the party would carry the city and county in the general election later that year, but they also believed their successful use of race to overcome factional divisions suggested a winning strategy for regaining Democratic dominance in the state as a whole.[39]

Their hopes for the future came from growing public support in the wake of their success in Kansas City. Crittenden noted that Democratic "friends" had advised against his repudiation of black voters because it was not the "popular thing." After the election, however, they came around to his position.[40] In the weeks that followed the election, the *Post* announced an ever-growing list of politicians (and prospective politicians) who now openly endorsed literacy tests and other legal restrictions on black voting rights. On May 5, the paper published an interview with former Democratic governor Lon V. Stephens detailing his shift from supporter of black political independence to proponent of broad-based suffrage restrictions across class and racial lines.[41]

As the movement gained momentum, other white Missourians clamored to join the growing list of white men proclaiming their fealty to the protection and promotion of white homes and honest elections. On May 12, Missouri state senator A. L. Cooper wrote in support of an educational test for voting.[42] He was followed by Thomas B. Buckner, a candidate for the Democratic nomination for Congress in the Fifth District, which included Kansas City. In a letter to the *Post*, Buckner

THE BALANCE OF POLITICAL POWER

Kansas City Post illustrator Earl Hurd captured white Missourians' anxiety over black voting rights in his cartoon, "The Balance of Political Power," depicting the state balanced between a white family, the "Citizens of Missouri," and a "Political Corruptionist," who holds out the ballot and a bribe to a caricatured black man representing "The Ignorant Black Vote." *Kansas City Post,* May 20, 1908.

boasted of his willingness to endorse legislation that eliminated the "illiterate and purchasable vote."[43] Not to be outdone, one of Buckner's competitors, Henry M. Withers, declared that he was "unqualifiedly in favor of such a restriction of the suffrage in Missouri as will eliminate the ignorant, purchasable and unworthy negro vote."[44] As had happened in the 1908 Kansas City municipal election, support for disfranchisement at times even crossed partisan lines. On May 19, the *Post* reported that a study of "twenty-two young men from various parts of the state, taking examinations for admission to [the] bar" in Jefferson City, had found that twenty supported some unspecified form of "restriction," one opposed it, and one registered as "non-committal." Of these twenty-two, thirteen identified as Democrats and nine as Republicans, with one of the Republicans opposed and one of the Democrats uncommitted.[45]

Bolstered by these expressions of political support, Cowherd and Crittenden led the effort to place a black disfranchisement plank in Missouri's Democratic platform. On May 14, Cowherd delivered a speech in St. Louis in which he declared that black disfranchisement would be a major part of the political program with which he hoped to capture the governor's office later that year. Calling on white Missourians and party members to "rally to the flag of Democracy," he argued that the success of racial segregation and disfranchisement across the South was pushing black criminals into Missouri. Once inside the state, he believed, they easily became the tools of corrupt white politicians and a threat to white women and good government. Sounding a warning to black Missourians and a challenge to his white political opponents, Cowherd declared, "This is a white man's country and the negro must be taught to cast both an intelligent and an honest ballot, or must surrender the suffrage he has so long sought."[46]

While Cowherd attempted to spread the gospel of black disfranchisement in St. Louis, Crittenden led the disfranchisers at the state convention in Jefferson City, where he introduced a resolution committing "the Missouri state legislature, and . . . the people of Missouri, to so restrict the right of suffrage in this state that the ballot will be denied to the ignorant, the vicious and the criminal of the negro race." Crittenden's Fifth District delegation adopted the resolution with only one dissenting vote, and it quickly garnered praise from delegates from across the state.[47] Over the course of the convention, the Post recorded expressions of support for general educational tests and the restriction of "negro suffrage" from numerous delegates and party notables, including State Superintendent of Public Schools Howard A. Gass; J. Frank Morris, the editor of the Jefferson City Tribune; H. S. Simmons, a candidate for lieutenant governor; and rank-and-file Democratic delegates from locations as diverse as Atchison, New Madrid, and Cole Counties.[48] But even with this broad base of support and "a sharp fight over the question" in "several districts," the proponents of suffrage restriction were unable to convince a majority of the Resolutions Committee to recommend the measure.

The source and strength of this unexpected opposition became apparent when Crittenden attempted to go around the committee's decision and present the resolution as a minority report to the assembled delegates. Although the vast majority of delegates appeared to have agreed that black voters could threaten white supremacy (at least under certain circumstances), Missouri's white Democrats ultimately approached the reality of suffrage restriction through the lens of their own experience of race, class, and partisan politics. At the lead of the anti-disfranchisement forces was Alexander Monroe Dockery, a former governor and longtime representative from northwestern Missouri's Third Congressional District. Although he admitted, in reference to the Fifteenth Amendment, "that the enfranchisement of 4,000,000 blacks by the stroke of a pen was the greatest crime of history," Dockery decried Crittenden's minority report as an "innovation" that was both unconstitutional and unnecessary.[49] By specifically targeting black men, he argued, the report was in flagrant violation of federal law and might yet provoke federal retribution against such nakedly race-based disfranchisement.[50] Furthermore, the report was rendered redundant by the disfranchisement measures that already existed under state law. "If some negroes are criminals," Dockery noted, "the law of Missouri now disfranchises them, as it does all criminals."[51]

Other Democrats expressed concern that many of the state's white voters might be removed from the rolls in an effort to disfranchise black men. As Thomas A. Dunn, an assistant reporter at the Missouri Supreme Court, told the *Post*, "I think the proposition is good enough, but I am afraid that it will lead to such a restriction that later a property qualification will be required for voters. It is difficult to restrict the right of suffrage without danger, because the precedent thus established might lead to greater restrictions."[52] Still others opposed Crittenden's proposed restrictions because they had found methods by which to attract, cajole, or fraudulently add black men's votes into the Democratic column. For example, J. V. Conran, a delegate from New Madrid County who had earlier supported Crittenden, now argued "that the blacks were voting the Democratic ticket in New Madrid . . . and he didn't want to disfranchise them."[53] According to the Republican-leaning *St. Louis Star and Chronicle*, "[the] St. Louis members of the committee on resolutions backed up Dockery in his contention," because "[the] Fourth and Twenty-second district negroes are needed by the Democrats."[54]

Last, delegates from outside Kansas City may have resisted a measure that seemed poised to catapult Democrats from a competing part of the state into power. Cowherd still had competitors for the party's gubernatorial nomination, and competing delegations, especially that from St. Louis, had little incentive to commit the party to a policy with which he was identified, especially when it might have restricted their own local political options. Although many, perhaps even a majority, of delegates favored some form of expanded suffrage restriction, the report failed because they could not agree on the precise method, extent, or target of disfranchisement. Moreover, no statewide party leader was willing or able to overcome these divisions and unite the party around a common program. As the *St. Louis Republic*, a viciously racist Democratic newspaper that had nonetheless mocked Crittenden's efforts, reported, "A vive voce vote was taken and the Crittenden [report] was rejected by an exceedingly large majority. The report of the [Resolutions] committee then was adopted without objection and the convention immediately adjourned."[55]

The disfranchisers continued their fight into the fall of 1908, but their efforts were quickly buried amid growing party factionalism. The issue of race, however, did not disappear from the campaign. At a meeting in Kansas City in early October, James A. Reed and other Democrats told their listeners that they faced a choice between big business and "negro panderers" on the one hand and a "white man's government" and the suppression of "private monopolies" on the other.[56] They focused particular attention on Cowherd's opponent in the gubernatorial race, Herbert Hadley, a Republican reformer who had served as attorney general in the administration of progressive Democratic governor Joseph Folk and who had made a name for himself in reform circles for his aggressive prosecution of the state's antitrust law.[57] In addition to linking the Republican to the old tropes of "boss rule" and "negro domination," the *Post* declared that Hadley, who had been born in Kansas where, the paper alleged, segregated education was the exception and not the rule, would promote "mixed schools" in Missouri.[58]

By November, the damage was already done. Democratic factionalism had undermined the white supremacy campaign (instead of the other way around), and black Missourians once again swallowed their growing frustration with the Republicans in the face of a clear and present threat to their lives and interests. In October, the *New York Times* reported that Republicans claimed to have registered "10,000 negroes who have never voted before in Missouri."[59] On election day in Kansas City, the *Post* noted that black voters came out for Hadley in large numbers, but the paper doubted that they could overcome what it predicted would be a "Democratic landslide."[60] Instead, it was Hadley who was swept into office, defeating Cowherd by a significant margin. Likewise, a Republican, William Howard Taft, once again took the state's electoral votes, and Republicans carried a majority of seats in the state house. Democrats held the senate and many county-level offices, but papers across the state interpreted the results as a stinging defeat for the party at the hands of corrupt politics, Democratic factionalism, and black voters.[61]

The Legacy of Missouri's White Supremacy Campaign of 1908

Far from quieting factionalism and providing a firm foundation for Democratic and white supremacy, the 1908 campaign had not only divided the party but also united its opponents. In its wake, Democratic leaders quickly retreated to a position from which they could at once remove the issue from factional squabbles and allow for maximum flexibility when dealing with black Missourians. They found this new position during the 1910 statewide elections, when Governor Hadley attempted to rally black Missourians at the polls by stressing the recent Democratic attempt at disfranchisement. Led by Kansas City Goat James Reed and Rabbit Joseph Shannon, Missouri Democrats adopted a plank in their party's platform denying that the party had ever attempted black disfranchisement.[62] In accordance with their 1910 plank, "[The Democratic Party] never has discriminated and will not discriminate against the colored race, either by criminal laws on the question or their right to franchise, and we deplore the action of the present chief executive of this State in seeking to make political capital by creating race antagonism."[63]

Such a dramatic refashioning of the party's history was an implied repudiation of Crittenden, who declined to seek reelection in 1910 and lived out the rest of his life in relative obscurity, dying in Kansas City in 1938.[64] Following the lead of Reed and Shannon, most historians of the rise of boss politics in Kansas City have ignored Crittenden or used him to add color to their depictions of James F. or (especially) Thomas J. Pendergast, who began his rise to power in Kansas City just as Crittenden was ending his term as mayor. For example, William Reddig, author of *Tom's Town*, noted that Mayor Crittenden had once let off the younger Pendergast with a "light reprimand" after he was charged with interfering with an arrest.[65] But Crittenden and his white supremacy campaign deserve more attention than they have heretofore received.

First, the campaign helps us to rethink the relationship between race, gender, and partisan politics. Since the 1990s, a new generation of political historians has revealed the ways in which many debates previously thought to have been between white men in legislatures and other halls of power instead involved diverse actors fighting over power in the home, workplace, and community.[66] While this new generation has done critical work in establishing relationships between public and private power, such work has come at a certain price in terms of our understanding of the role of party and partisanship. By considering the successful Kansas City mayoral race against the disfranchisers' failure in Jefferson City, we can see the ways in which partisanship combined with ideologies of race and gender to produce different outcomes in different contexts. In the municipal election, a broad coalition of white men and women came together to support a candidate (Crittenden) who they believed would protect a particular racial and gendered order. At the state level, however, competing politicians and interests groups, even though they shared support for much of that order in the abstract, rejected the proposition that radical steps needed to be taken to preserve it, especially if such steps might disadvantage them in competition with other politicians, cities, or sections.

Next, Crittenden's campaign helps us understand Missouri's complicated relationship to region. While historians of the Midwest have rightly pointed out that the region's whites embraced their own vision of white supremacy through the expulsion of Native Americans and the effort to restrict black migration and settlement, historians of the South have made equally important appeals to the importance of disfranchisement in setting the stage for the entrenchment of Jim Crow after the turn of the century.[67] In Missouri, we can see the ways in which white supremacy was a national ideology with regional inflections that hardened under the influence of state borders and state laws. With Missouri Democrats' rejection of a southern-style disfranchisement regime, Missouri politics (and the role of race in those politics) settled into a pattern more akin to those of its midwestern neighbors. That pattern was neither "better" nor "worse" than that in the Jim Crow South, but it *was* different, with the absence of literacy tests and poll taxes preserving spaces for black political action without necessarily changing the ways in which white racism limited the power of coalition building or access to resources.

Lastly, and perhaps most importantly from the perspective of this volume, Crittenden's campaign helps us to reconsider the history of the Pendergast machine and twentieth-century urban liberalism more generally. As Jeffrey L. Pasley describes in Chapter 2, even as Tom Pendergast overcame party factionalism in Kansas City and asserted his influence across the state, as Crittenden had tried and failed to do, he did so not through the mechanism of overt black political exclusion, but through a reconstituted urban liberalism within the Democratic Party. In many ways, Pendergast's approach harkened back to the model practiced by his brother and other Democrats before 1908, a fact drawn into sharp relief by Crittenden's challenge to both liberal orders. On the one hand, Pendergast's liberalism could offer significant gains to black people in return for political support. On the other hand, while finally rejecting the wholesale exclusionary Democratic tradition represented by Crittenden and his allies, Pendergast's brand of liberal politics remained a far cry from genuine, independent black political power and, for decades, left unresolved many aspects of white supremacy.[68]

Moreover, as black Kansas Citians moved into closer alliance with Pendergast's Democratic Party, Missouri Republicans took the opportunity to pursue a proto–"southern strategy" by shifting ever farther to the right to pick up disaffected white voters. Over time, this shift cost black Missourians much of their ability to exploit partisan and factional differences between whites, but they remained open to political experimentation in an effort to find mechanisms that afforded both amelioration from the consequences of white supremacy and an autonomous path forward. For example, as historian Roger Horowitz has documented, in the 1930s and 1940s, black packinghouse workers on both sides of the state line worked with members of the Socialist Party to develop an interracial industrial union movement that echoed the efforts of Kansas City's black Knights of Labor in the 1880s. Although, as Horowitz notes, "the early radicalism of the local unions faded after 1940 as Socialists . . . became liberal Democrats," these unions remained alternative centers of power for interracial organizing outside machine politics.[69] While the history of black politics in Kansas City is that of the long movement of black people from alliance with the Republican to the Democratic Party, it is also a reminder that that history is strewn with contingencies and paths not taken.

In the forty years between 1908 and 1948, the distance between the Kansas City of Crittenden and that of Pendergast became the distance between the "southern," Dixiecrat conservatism of Strom Thurmond and the "northern," urban, Democratic liberalism of Harry Truman. But their common roots—in a national Democratic Party struggling to square the values of white supremacy with the political and legal legacy of Reconstruction—also established what would become the commonalities between black freedom struggles in the North and the South. Indeed, in the political context of the 2010s, with liberal democracy seemingly threatened by a new generation of right-wing authoritarianism, it might be easy to dismiss the flaws and blind spots of twentieth-century liberalism. The long history of Kansas City, however, suggests the need to look beyond the limits of liberalism to find a politics capable of at once addressing white supremacy and broader concentrations of wealth and power. Or, as a young black woman told a reporter during the uprising against yet another liberal regime in Kansas City in 1968, "If they'd been through the hell we've been through, they wouldn't be sitting up on no pedestals."[70]

Notes

1. Regarding the election and its consequences, see John W. McKerley, "Citizens and Strangers: The Politics of Race in Missouri from Slavery to the Era of Jim Crow" (PhD diss., University of Iowa, 2008), chap. 7.

2. John W. McKerley, "'We Promise to Use the Ballot as We Did the Bayonet': Black Suffrage Activism and the Limits of Loyalty in Reconstruction Missouri," in *Bleeding Kansas, Bleeding Missouri: The Long Civil War on the Border*, ed. Jonathan Earle and Diane Mutti Burke (Lawrence: University Press of Kansas, 2013), 205-224.

3. Shelton Stromquist, *Re-inventing "The People": The Progressive Movement, the Class Problem, and the Origins of Modern Liberalism* (Champaign-Urbana: University of Illinois Press, 2006), especially 191-192.

4. Ibid., 131-164.

5. Regarding the role of race, gender, and generation in postwar southern politics, see Glenda Gilmore, *Gender and Jim Crow: Women and the Politics of White Supremacy in North Carolina, 1896-1920* (Chapel Hill: University of North Carolina Press, 1996), especially 61-90.

6. Regarding the relationship between social and political equality in turn-of-the-century liberalism, see Jane Dailey, "The Limits of Liberalism in the New South: The Politics of Race, Sex, and Patronage in Virginia, 1879-1883," in *Jumpin' Jim Crow: Southern Politics from Civil War to Civil Rights*, ed. Dailey, Glenda Elizabeth Gilmore, and Bryant Simon (Princeton, N.J.: Princeton University Press, 2000), 88-114.

7. Crittenden's birthdate from his obituary, "Crittenden Rites to Be Tomorrow at Family Home," *Kansas City Journal-Post*, August 1, 1938; regarding Missouri's Civil War-era black suffrage laws, see McKerley, "Citizens and Strangers," chap. 3.

8. Regarding the wartime right to testify, see Sharon Romeo, "'The First Morning of Their Freedom': African American Women, Black Testimony, and Military Justice in Civil War Missouri," *Missouri Historical Review* 110, no. 3 (April 2016): 196-216.

9. *St. Louis Dispatch*, October 24, 1865.

10. William M. Reddig, *Tom's Town: Kansas City and the Pendergast Legend* (1947; reprinted Columbia: University of Missouri Press, 1986), 21–22.

11. Charles E. Coulter, *"Take Up the Black Man's Burden": Kansas City's African American Communities, 1865–1939* (Columbia: University of Missouri Press, 2006), Table 1.1, "Kansas City, Missouri's Black Population, 1860–2000," 26.

12. Ibid.

13. Ibid., 24–52.

14. US Census Bureau, *1880 Census*, vol. 1: *Statistics of the Population of the United States* (1883), 421; US Census Bureau, *Twelfth Census of the United States–1900*, vol. 1: *Population* (1901), 663–664.

15. Regarding the Knights in Kansas City (especially in Kansas), see Leon Fink, *Working-men's Democracy: The Knights of Labor and American Politics* (Champaign-Urbana: University of Illinois Press, 1985), 112–149.

16. Regarding Paul Jones and black Missourians' efforts at political independence during the late nineteenth century, see McKerley, "Citizens and Strangers," chap. 6.

17. Ibid. Quote from Larry H. Grothaus, "The Negro in Missouri Politics, 1890–1941" (PhD diss., University of Missouri, 1971), 28. Regarding the Goats and Rabbits, see Lawrence H. Larsen and Nancy J. Hulston, *Pendergast!* (Columbia: University of Missouri Press, 1997), 31–34.

18. Arguably the most prominent white Kansas Citian to challenge the limits of the city's racial order during this period was labor attorney Frank Walsh, who was allied with the Rabbit faction. Although Walsh was clearly influenced by the white supremacy that infused the Democratic Party and the Irish American culture in which he was raised, he also revealed the ways in which countervailing experiences and ideas, especially radical working-class politics, could sometimes challenge the assumptions of white supremacy and pave the way for interracial alliances based on more than paternalism and opportunism. Regarding Walsh and race, see Joseph A. McCartin, *Labor's Great War: The Struggle for Industrial Democracy and the Origins of Modern American Labor Relations, 1912–1921* (Chapel Hill: University of North Carolina Press, 1997), 22, 115. On the limits of Walsh's interracialism, see Sherry Lamb Schirmer, *A City Divided: The Racial Landscape of Kansas City, 1900–1960* (Columbia: University of Missouri Press, 2002), 68.

19. "Crittenden, Thomas Theodore (1832–1909)," *Biographical Directory of the United States Congress, 1775–Present*, http://bioguide.congress.gov/biosearch/biosearch.asp, accessed May 22, 2016.

20. William A. Settle Jr., "The James Boys and Missouri Politics," *Missouri Historical Review* 36, no. 4 (July 1942): 412–429.

21. David W. Blight, *Race and Reunion: The Civil War in American Memory* (Cambridge, Mass.: Harvard University Press, 2001).

22. Crittenden, as quoted in Grothaus, "The Negro in Missouri Politics," 21–22.

23. Regarding the workhouse scandal, see Schirmer, *A City Divided*, 66–68.

24. Shannon, as quoted in Grothaus, "The Negro in Missouri Politics," 44. Schirmer, *A City Divided*, 65.

25. Regarding the 1908 Kansas City mayoral election, see McKerley, "Citizens and Strangers," chap. 7.

26. Regarding the rhetoric of machine politics, see James J. Connolly, *An Elusive Unity: Urban Democracy and Machine Politics in Industrializing America* (Ithaca, N.Y.: Cornell University Press, 2010).

27. *Kansas City Post*, February 24, 27, 29, 1908.

28. Ibid., January 16 and 30, 1908.

29. Ibid., March 1, 2, and 11, 1908.

30. Ibid., March 12, 1908.

31. Ibid., March 13 and 16, 1908.

32. Ibid., March 21 and 25, 1908.

33. Ibid., March 13, 1908.

34. *Kansas City Star*, January 22, 1908.

35. *Kansas City Post*, March 23, 1908.

36. Ibid., March 20, 1908.

37. Ibid., March 27, 1908.

38. Ibid., April 8, 1908.

39. Ibid.

40. Ibid.

41. Ibid., May 5, 1908.

42. Ibid., May 12, 1908.

43. Ibid., May 13, 1908.

44. Ibid., May 14, 1908.

45. Ibid., May 19, 1908.

46. Ibid., May 15, 1908.

47. Ibid., May 20, 1908.

48. Ibid., May 19, 1908.

49. Ibid., May 21, 1908. Dockery's reference to the Fifteenth Amendment and the roughly 4 million black people emancipated during and after the Civil War ignores that the amendment enfranchised only black men.

50. *St. Louis Republic*, May 21, 1908.

51. Ibid.

52. *Kansas City Post*, May 19, 1908.

53. Ibid., May 19 and 21, 1908.

54. *St. Louis Star and Chronicle*, May 21, 1908.

55. *St. Louis Republic*, May 21, 1908.

56. *Kansas City Post*, October 6, 1908.

57. Steven L. Piott, *Holy Joe: Joseph W. Folk and the Missouri Idea* (Columbia: University of Missouri Press, 1997), 118–120, 146.

58. *Kansas City Post*, November 2, 1908; Randall B. Woods, "Integration, Exclusion, or Segregation? The 'Color Line' in Kansas, 1878–1900," *Western Historical Quarterly* 14, no. 2 (April 1983): 183.

59. "West Now Looks Strong for Taft," *New York Times*, October 27, 1908.

60. *Kansas City Post*, November 3, 1908.

61. For example, see *Chariton Courier* (Keytesville, Mo.), December 4, 1908.

62. Grothaus, "The Negro in Missouri Politics," 62–63.

63. *Kansas City Post*, May 20, 1908; Cornelius Roach, ed., *Official Manual of the State of Missouri, 1911–12* (Jefferson City, Mo.: Hugh Stephens, 1912), 367.

64. *Kansas City Times*, August 1, 1938.

65. Reddig, *Tom's Town: Kansas City and the Pendergast Legend* (Columbia: University of Missouri Press, 1986), 83–84. For a similar anecdote regarding James Pendergast, see Lyle W. Dorsett, *The Pendergast Machine* (New York: Oxford University Press, 1968), 47. Historians also mention Crittenden in regard to his role in the formation of the Kansas City Board of Public Welfare. For example, see A. Theodore Brown and Lyle W. Dorsett, *K.C.: A History of Kansas City, Missouri* (Boulder, Colo.: Pruett Publishing, 1978), 155–156.

66. For examples of historians' connections between public and private power, see the essay in *Jumpin' Jim Crow* cited elsewhere in this chapter, as well as Laura F. Edwards, "The Politics of Marriage and Households in North Carolina during Reconstruction," and Kari Frederickson, "'As a Man, I Am Interested in States' Rights': Gender, Race, and the Family in the Dixiecrat Party, 1948–1950," in Dailey, Gilmore, and Simon, *Jumpin' Jim Crow*.

67. Regarding the Midwest, see Leslie A. Schwalm, *Emancipation's Diaspora: Race and Reconstruction in the Upper Midwest* (Chapel Hill: University of North Carolina Press, 2009); and Matthew E. Stanley, *The Loyal West: Civil War and Reunion in Middle America* (Urbana: University of Illinois Press, 2017). Regarding disfranchisement in the South, see J. Morgan Kousser, *The Shaping of Southern Politics: Suffrage Restriction and the Establishment of the One-Party South, 1880–1910* (New Haven, Conn.: Yale University Press, 1975).

68. Regarding the limits and opportunities of integration in Kansas City, Missouri, during the early twentieth century, see Schirmer, *A City Divided*.

69. Roger Horowitz, quoted in *"Negro and White, Unite and Fight!" A Social History of Industrial Unionism in Meatpacking, 1930–90* (Urbana: University of Illinois Press, 1997), 102. See also John Herron's chapter in this volume.

70. Douglas E. Kneelands, "Beyond the Violence: Despair and Spring Madness," *New York Times* (April 12, 1968). The quotation, in its original context, presumably referred to Kansas City's black youth, who were expected (by whites, especially) to suffer nonviolently ("sit on pedestals") despite police violence, poverty, and the tragedy of the assassination of Martin Luther King Jr.

CHAPTER TWO

Big Deal in Little Tammany

Kansas City, the Pendergast Machine, and the Liberal Transformation of the Democratic Party

Jeffrey L. Pasley

One of the defining political trends of the mid-twentieth century was the switch of African American voters from the Republican to the Democratic Party, accompanied by a major shift in the party's policy platform toward social liberalism and civil rights. Nationally, this change is usually dated to the latter half of the New Deal, roughly around the election of 1936, but in Kansas City, it happened much earlier and in surprising circumstances that influenced national affairs. In fact, a strong argument can be made that an important dimension of the liberal transformation of the Democratic Party began not with idealistic New Dealers but with the calculating streetwise politicians of the Pendergast machine.[1]

The Kansas City Democrats of the interwar period were one of the most notorious local party organizations in American history. Tapping into the profits from Kansas City's status as a leading railroad stopover and exchange point for livestock and grain, the original operation was founded by James F. Pendergast, a saloon owner who parlayed his popularity into a long career as a powerful alderman. It was a textbook city machine: Irish politicians exchanged access to public jobs, credit, and an ad hoc social safety net for the support of voters in teeming industrial neighborhoods. A favorite political method was the mob primary, where nominations were made according to who could get the largest, surliest crowd to attend the party meeting. In Alderman Jim's First Ward, the city's poorest immigrants, along with black refugees from the Missouri countryside, lived in shanties in a crowded floodplain next to the packinghouses, stockyards, and rail yards. They shared the neighborhood with one of the country's most active and seedy red-light districts, catering to trail's end cowpokes and travelers passing through the adjacent railway station. From this domain along the Missouri River, which also included the Italian and black North End, the Pendergast machine, nicknamed the Goats, battled furiously for control of the Jackson County Democrats with their chief rival faction, the Rabbits, based in the newer and more upscale neighborhoods east of Prospect Avenue and led by a more sedate Irish politician, the self-styled Jeffersonian scholar Joseph Shannon.[2]

Thomas J. Pendergast spent his young manhood working in middle management for his older brother, keeping books and busting heads, before moving into such key posts as superintendent of streets and city marshal. The younger Pendergast became known for tolerance and relative humanitarianism as well as toughness and business acumen. Gradually, he took over the machine and built his brother's organization into something much more grandiose. By the late 1920s, "Boss" Tom had created a de facto regional government run openly from his office in the Jackson Democratic Club at 1908 Main Street. With his giant bald head and cigar, he became the very image of the political boss, remaking the city and earning a fortune in government contracts through his famous Ready Mixed Concrete business. Meanwhile, working with Italian organized crime and a thoroughly corrupt police force, his machine facilitated the spread of the old West Bottoms nightlife across the city. In the teeth of Prohibition and the Depression, liquor, drugs, prostitution, and every form of gambling flourished, until Kansas City became a renowned adult entertainment destination. The Pendergast machine, wrote noted national columnist Westbrook Pegler, "gives good, rotten government, and runs a good, rotten city whose conventional Americans of the home-loving, baby-having, 100-per-cent type, live on terms of mutual toleration with wide open vice." *Life* published glossy photos of middle-class ladies and gentlemen whiling away their afternoon in a betting parlor called Fortune at Thirty-Ninth Street and Main. Pegler dubbed the city the "Paris of the Plains," but Vegas before Vegas comes closer to the truth.[3]

Most surprising of all was that although "Boss" Tom had little personal interest in social justice or neighborhood building, he sponsored the growth and cultural efflorescence of Kansas City's black community. By providing a haven for the establishments that required round-the-clock live music and concentrating the city's vice district and cultural center on the black east side near downtown, the Pendergast machine helped attract black musicians to Kansas City from around the country. This was the environment in which Kansas City's influential jazz style developed, and it also fostered the growth of a complex alliance between the local Democratic Party and the black community that gave the Pendergasts their greatest significance in American political history.[4]

The Pendergast machine's real importance, however, is how it created and empowered the modern Democratic Party in Missouri and, to some degree, nationally.

This party would be liberal-leaning, tolerant, heavily urban, and ethnically diverse, the new political home for African Americans and immigrant groups. Long before the New Deal, Kansas City's Irish Catholic ward-heelers put together the basic elements of a coalition that, when replicated nationally, handed the presidency to Franklin Delano Roosevelt. It saw blacks, immigrants, workers, and just enough partly reconstructed southern whites join forces behind a vision of a government that helped ordinary people live their lives rather than judging how they lived. Ruthlessly practical and nonideological, it was socialism "Kaycee"-style, offering relative justice, cheap drinks, and public works for all, regardless of class, creed, or color.

Of course, there was nothing remotely radical or socialistic about this approach, perfectly suiting it for the Cold War era to come. Kansas City Democratic politics reflected the mildly statist liberalism and concern for balancing its many interest groups that would define the Democratic Party in the late twentieth century. Breathing the spirit of Harry Truman more than FDR, this same slightly left-of-center coalition would support successful national Democrats from John F. Kennedy through Bill Clinton. It was strenuously middle American in its outward values and rhetoric of equal opportunity and equal rights, but tolerant of diverse ethnicities and lifestyles and open to the claims of previously unrepresented groups. The party drew enough votes from black and immigrant urbanites, labor union members, and public employees to lessen the Democratic Party's historical dependence on southern white supremacists, but never completely lost its ties to rural white voters, especially in mining and manufacturing areas of the Upper South. Party leaders were committed to policies that used government to stimulate economic development and protect citizens from the worst prejudices of society and the worst vicissitudes of capitalism, without repudiating traditional American shibboleths about the virtues of small, efficient governments. It was a form of limited, conflicted social democracy that suited a mixed-up, bellwether sort of place like Kansas City: a northern-style industrial city with a southern-style population dominated by white and black Protestants.[5]

The Old Democrats and the Missouri Bellwether

The shift to any significant degree of substantive social liberalism was a huge change from the Democratic Party of the early twentieth century. The Old Democracy (as they liked to style themselves) was then the party of provincialism par excellence, dominated by rural, culturally conservative whites in the former slave states and the Great Plains, existing in an uneasy alliance with the immigrant machines that dominated large urban areas. The one common link between rural Democrats and their urban allies was racism, an antipathy that went back to the mid-nineteenth-century days when Irish Catholics competed with African Americans for unskilled labor at the bottom of the economy.[6]

Kansas City's major role in changing the Democratic Party arose from Missouri's outsized influence in national Democratic affairs during the early twentieth century. In the 1920s, it was the seventh-largest state in population and electoral votes, bigger than California or Michigan. It was a true bellwether that combined elements of the industrial Northeast, the cattle-ranching West, and the rural South, with industrial cities to counterbalance its rural interior. More than just a "swing" state, Missouri's electoral results were absurdly predictive of the final national outcome. In the twentieth century, every successful presidential candidate carried Missouri, and no Democrat before Barack Obama *ever* won the presidency without the state's support. Missouri's national significance showed in the fact that it hosted eight national political conventions between 1876 and 1928 and was the only state given two Federal Reserve banks.[7] Many nostalgic stories of the Missouri bellwether have been told, but usually without mention of the crucial element of race. The shift of African American voters away from the party of Lincoln and to the party of Jefferson was a momentous change in modern American politics. Why did it happen here?

On the one hand, Missouri, though a former slave state, was a haven of relative "racial liberalism." It never fully adopted the Jim Crow system of segregation after the end of Reconstruction, and, in particular, never barred blacks from voting through devious means such as the poll tax, grandfather clause, or white primary. At the same time, Missouri's cities proved unusually attractive places for black migrants from the deeper South and rural areas to resettle. The state's black population was heavily urbanized ahead of the World War I–era Great Migration that brought African Americans in large numbers to other northern cities.[8]

On the other hand, racial liberalism was practiced with great inconsistency in Missouri. The western Missouri border region, stretching into Oklahoma and Arkansas, eagerly participated in the new racism that spread through the Midwest in the 1910s and 1920s. Rebooted as a public fraternity in conjunction with D. W. Griffith's blockbuster film *The Birth of a Nation*, the Ku Klux Klan became a powerful social and political force in places like rural Missouri. Fearful moviegoers who had never seen the original Reconstruction-era terrorists thrilled to Griffith's images of heroic hooded cavalry riding to the rescue of endangered whites.[9] The new Klan craze fed off an existing racial panic that had emptied many rural counties of their black populations, sometimes in the face of violent pogroms. In the most infamous Missouri case, armed white mobs killed three men and banished the entire black population of Pierce City and four other southwestern Missouri towns in response to a 1901 murder. Even after the pogroms subsided, violent defenders of white supremacy were a persistent threat. At least one public lynching was carried out each year in the state from 1919 to 1925, including the 1923 murder of custodian James Scott in Columbia.[10]

Nor were things necessarily much better in the cities where blacks moved to escape the terrors and poverty of rural life. Open racism in Missouri politics and journalism was always an option, despite the fact that blacks voted. The standard-bearer for Kansas City's Democrats in those days was the splenetic senator James A. Reed, who made himself a presidential contender by turning against Woodrow Wilson, his party's president, and mounting a starkly racist crusade against the League of Nations. Reed's main argument was that by joining the League, the United States would have to submit to the decisions of nonwhite countries: "The majority of the nations composing the league do not belong to the white race of men. On the contrary, they are a conglomerate of the black, yellow, brown, and red races," Reed thundered on the floor of Congress, declaring that he would never agree to give "the dregs of civilization . . . one single atom of power" over "the American citizen."[11]

More importantly for African Americans, their ability to live freely and un-molested in Missouri's major cities was under constant challenge. After formal segregation ordinances were struck down by the courts, whites turned to market manipulations, legal chicanery, and violence in their efforts to confine blacks to certain neighborhoods. Just as serious was the sinister combination of neglect and violent overzealousness that blacks had long suffered at the hands of Kansas City law enforcement.[12]

"The Negro Democracy" and the Balance of Power

Despite, or perhaps because of this unique racial environment, a sophisticated African American political leadership developed in Kansas City. Black leaders in politics and business sought to extract the best treatment they could from the white majority and exert the maximum influence possible over the white power structure. Sometimes this was not very much, but in Kansas City it was absolutely crucial to a transformation that had national implications. Newspaper publishers Nelson Crews of the *Kansas City Sun* and staunch Republican Chester A. Franklin of the *Sun*'s successor paper, *The Call*, were two of the most important voices for the black community. Less well-known but especially significant for our purposes was a black leader who emerged among Kansas City's Democrats, Dr. William J. Thompkins. Thompkins had grown up a Democrat, working at the Madison Hotel next to the State Capitol in Jefferson City and marching at the head of local Demo-cratic parades. In 1906, after preliminary medical training at the University of Col-orado–Boulder and completing his MD at Howard University in Washington, DC, Thompkins moved back to Missouri to set up a medical practice in Kansas City. In 1914, he was appointed the first black superintendent of Kansas City's black public hospital, known as General Hospital No. 2 and examined in-depth in Chapter 10. For the next three decades, Thompkins made himself a pillar of the Democratic side of Kansas City politics, vigorously embracing the often-difficult task of selling Democratic candidates and platforms to black voters.[13]

Thompkins was thoroughly convinced that "the party of Jefferson and Jackson offered the best ethics for the welfare of the Negro race." This surprising statement of fealty to two slaveholding Democrats addressed their perceived egalitarianism and hostility to the power of wealth. Thompkins and his fellow black Democrats were seeking to set an independent political course and were angry at the Republicans' paternalist expectation that former slaves and their descendants would remain forever loyal in gratitude for Lincoln's act of charity in freeing them. According to a 1935 statement penned by African American Democrat James W. Hutt of St. Louis, the black Democrats hoped that a "tidal wave" of their votes would wash "away the blot of servile obligation, not owed, but always to be paid, to Plutocracy."[14]

One advantage the "Negro Democracy" had in Kansas City was that they often held the balance of power in both general elections and intraparty Democratic struggles. In addition to the Goats and Rabbits, the Democratic organization contained numerous other neighborhood fiefdoms capable of shifting their allegiances under the right circumstances. Before 1925, Tom Pendergast and his Goats controlled only the northern and western river wards. Joe Shannon's Rabbit base was in the northeast, especially in the Ninth Ward, where Kansas City abutted rural Jackson County. Other neighborhoods had their own bosses who lined up with the Goats or Rabbits as it suited them. Thompkins generally affiliated with the Rabbits but tried to maintain the black Democrats as an independent force that white factions had to court, with results that soon paid off.[15]

Black votes were desperately needed in the early 1920s, as the Democrats sank to one of their low ebbs of the twentieth century. With the party largely shut out of power in Washington, DC, and most states, the rural "dry" faction that supported Prohibition was ascendant. It was heavily infiltrated by the new Ku Klux Klan, which added nativism, anti-Catholicism, and anti-Semitism to its roster of hate. Feeling a new sense of potential solidarity with African Americans that counteracted a long history of racial antagonism, and facing a series of uphill battles, the Irish Catholic–dominated "wets" of the urban wing sank their teeth into the Klan issue. The 1924 Missouri state Democratic convention "was transformed into a howling mob," wrote the *Star*, when Kansas City and St. Louis Democrats, led by Tom Pendergast and Joe Shannon, tried to insert a platform plank condemning the Klan, only to be defeated by Klan sympathizers from the interior of the state.[16]

The same cast played the same roles in the national election later that year. At the national convention in New York, with the Klan marching in the city and present in the hall, attorney John W. Davis of West Virginia was nominated after 103 grinding ballots, in a victory for the forces of relative tolerance within the Democratic Party. Having successfully argued civil rights cases before the Supreme Court, Davis boasted a reasonably enlightened record on race. Kansas City's Thompkins was asked to organize a Negro Bureau to campaign for Davis, and Pendergast and Shannon were able to smuggle an anti-Klan statement back into the state platform during the fall campaign by praising Davis. Their candidate was crushed by Calvin

Coolidge in the general election, and many Goats and Rabbits lost local contests too, but Kansas City had played a crucial role in curbing the Invisible Empire's political ambitions in Missouri.[17]

The whole experience paved the way for salutary changes by indicating the potential utility of an increased reliance on the black vote, even though African Americans were still largely voting Republican. The need for redirection was reflected in the career of young Goat official Harry S. Truman. Truman's membership in the Klan was widely speculated, and he undoubtedly had associates who were members, but he later prided himself on rejecting the Klan's overtures. Even so, with his family's Confederate roots and Independence's hick reputation, word on the street in Kansas City held the rumors of Truman's racism to be true. In 1924, the local chapter of the National Association for the Advancement of Colored People (NAACP) announced its opposition to his reelection. Dr. Thompkins focused his attention elsewhere, and Truman soon found himself out of office, hustling to sell American Automobile Association memberships rather than making public policy. Thus the "Man from Independence" learned the hard way to be careful about his African American support.[18]

Elsewhere, other members of the Pendergast machine were learning similar lessons, with the Goats, Rabbits, and Republicans all scrambling for black votes. With black Republicans growing increasingly restive, the local GOP finally nominated its very first African American candidate for alderman, Reverend J. W. Hurse of St. Stephen Baptist Church on Independence Avenue. Both parties took out ads in The Call, the Democrats touting their opposition to the Klan and "Police Brutality," specifically the more-than-rumored use of torture against black suspects: "The Democratic Party Is Against Burning Negroes for False Confessions," one ad proclaimed. Meanwhile Republicans attacked the Democrats for making "our city government the feeding ground of the 'boys,'" including the graft-laden decision to locate a new garbage dump, or "swill depot," in a black neighborhood. Hurse lost, but otherwise the Republicans swept the spring municipal elections; Joe Shannon's Rabbits were suspected of playing both sides. In the middle of all this, the unpredictable Shannon told reporters about his sudden interest in the Progressive presidential candidacy of Fighting Bob La Follette and quietly prepared to "knife" his rival Pendergast in the fall county and state elections, selectively abandoning Goat candidates on the Democratic ticket, often for Republicans! Harry Truman and his fellow Goat on the county court, Henry F. McElroy, were among the many candidates the Rabbit knives struck down.[19]

Big Man in Little Tammany: Casimir J. Welch

This 1924 electoral disaster turned out to be a major turning point in the history of the Pendergast machine and its approach to the black community. To understand

Casimir J. Welch distributing aid to an unknown woman in a publicity photo in front of his Jeffersonian Democratic Club. Courtesy of the Kansas City Museum and Bernard Ragan.

this important shift we have to introduce a new character. In between the western Goat and eastern Rabbit bases, geographically and politically, was "Little Tammany," the bailiwick of Judge Casimir J. Welch. It was named after the New York City Democratic organization that Welch aspired to emulate. Operated out of a garage at Fifteenth Street and Troost Avenue, Welch's Jeffersonian Democratic Club covered a large swath of the Sixth and Eighth Wards just southeast of downtown Kansas City. One of the most crowded and ethnically and economically diverse sectors of the city, its population was sneered at by the *Star* as composed "chiefly of rooming house dwellers, manual workers and trade artisans, petty tradesmen and the city's indigent." The area also contained the heart of the black business and entertainment district and many African American residences of all classes.[20]

Though a lifelong Rabbit, Judge Welch was horrified by his mentor's perfidy in 1924. He ordered his followers to vote the straight Democratic ticket no matter what Joe Shannon said, bringing Thompkins and his friends into the camp of the Goats. They held onto nearly 1,000 black votes (and the aldermanic seat) against black Republican J. W. Hurse. With Republicans riding high in the outlying precincts, Little Tammany's defection eviscerated the east side Rabbits, and Joe Shannon's days as a serious rival to Tom Pendergast, able to command a "50-50" share of patronage, were over. In his stead, Casimir Welch suddenly rose to be the number two man in a rejuvenated Pendergast machine that increasingly relied on his longtime strategy of forging good relations with the black community.[21]

"Cas" Welch embodied many of the thorny contradictions of Kansas City's changing urban politics. A native of the scruffy neighborhood he ruled, Welch had been a Rabbit since Joe Shannon picked him out as prime political muscle at age eighteen. Having already distinguished himself as the toughest newsboy in town, young Welch became an "aggressive and influential member" of the Plumber's Union. Later, outfitted with a politician's suit and tie, Welch turned into the most feared political brawler in a town full of them, legendary with his fists and handy with a gun, too. But allegedly the gigantic enforcer had a softer side as well. Placed by the machine in a job at the city jail, Welch developed a reputation for being sympathetic to people in trouble, establishing a lifelong pattern of friendly offices toward ex-convicts and their relatives of all races. This allowed him to command a ready army of political bodies for "mob primaries" and also make connections to mobs of an entirely different sort. For all his frightening and repellent qualities, Welch seems to have been free of overt racial prejudice. Hours of wiretap recordings from the Jeffersonian Democratic Club's telephone have survived, and while Welch and his cronies discuss all sorts of misdeeds, their general tone of friendly helpfulness to callers from all walks of life is striking. No ethnic slurs or tensions of any kind are voiced.[22]

In 1910, Welch was elected to his long-term job as justice of the peace and effective boss of the neighborhood he grew up in, putting him in a position to apply the principles of machine politics more directly and bluntly than most. In addition to carrying on the usual charity work, he ran his court as a "justice mill," where workaday people could deal with their legal problems without need of expensive lawyers and time-consuming procedure. "I'll be their lawyer. . . . Justice quick and cheap is my motto," Welch announced. Such politicized local courts were a once-common institution that even the Kansas City machine's own propagandists admitted were a thing of the past in most other localities. As one of the last of his kind, Welch used his court to build a loyal following among the common people of Little Tammany, including its African Americans. "Regardless of nationality, race, or color, the people of his district swear by him," the *Kansas City American* claimed.[23]

Judge Welch's approach was especially well suited to serving a community where so many people had sporadic incomes earned both inside and outside the strict boundaries of the law and under the disapproving (if often averted) gaze of the white Protestant middle classes. At any rate, working with Thompkins and friends, Welch developed a significant bloc of black Democratic voters that became one of the bulwarks of Little Tammany. Believing himself a "Friend of the Lowly," Welch claimed to have "pioneered in the conversion of colored people to the Democratic faith." Though he ended up living in a Ward Parkway mansion just like Tom Pendergast, Welch was convinced enough by "the Democracy's" self-image as the party of the lower orders to find it "ridiculous" that blacks ever supported the Republicans. Imagine, he told a reporter, "the very poorest people in the nation voting to perpetuate in power the wealthy people who keep them poor!"[24]

Of course, there was another, probably more widely accepted view of Welch that cast a jaundiced eye on the judge's intentions toward the people of Little Tammany. Reformers, enemies, and frightened allies (including Harry Truman), called Welch a "primitive" and a "thug" who controlled his district through corruption and violence and profited indecently from his position. Like Pendergast, Welch owned a construction company, a messenger service, and other concerns that did business with the city and county. No doubt his sympathy was mixed with a high degree of self-interest, in the form of selective lenience and aid toward those working in the many machine-tolerated criminal and semi-criminal enterprises that flourished in his territory. Welch was one of the major access points for organized crime into the machine and the black community. In time, such a long list of his close associates had been assassinated or caught making assassination attempts themselves that he decided to stop hearing criminal cases in court.[25]

To black leaders with whom he was not closely allied, Welch veered uncomfortably close to regarding Little Tammany as his personal vote plantation, full of selflessly loyal and grateful black retainers. "Sympathetic, Charitable, Benevolent, Guardian of the 'Forgotten Man,'" the Jeffersonian Democratic Club's campaign ads sang of Welch, "a man whom the Negroes love and adore." Bitter detractor Chester Arthur Franklin, Republican publisher of *The Call*, offered a different narrative. Welch's solicitude for the African American citizens of Little Tammany did not extend to supporting black candidates for office or placing blacks in plum city jobs. Welch boasted of being the political "spokesman" for Kansas City blacks, *The Call* fumed, but his part in actually helping the black community was more "like Jeff Davis' part in freeing the slave."[26]

Naturally, Cas Welch saw his own activities in a considerably more charitable light, arguing that he had made the bold departure of trying to serve the interests of his black constituents. "In the past the Republicans showed some consideration for the Negroes on election day—usually $2, $3, or $5, and at times as much as $10," Welch recalled. "We Democrats hit upon the idea of doing something for the Negroes every day of the year." Paternalistic as it was, the Welch formula amounted to a more liberal and tolerant set of social policies. The focus was on getting indigent and struggling blacks food, fuel, and basic employment, but otherwise letting them live their lives without supervisory interference, except at election time. One of Welch's Christmas advertisements in the black press made both ends of the trans-action clear: "No man in the organization is too small to receive a hearing." ("The Organization" was the Pendergast machine's preferred term for itself.) In return for electoral support, the Democratic city government would help provide black neigh-borhoods with access to better public health, educational, and recreation services and would afford them less brutal and unfair treatment from the police and the courts. Welch helped ensure that a black-staffed city hospital was built and prom-ised new bathhouses for blacks at city parks and a state teacher's college in Kansas City. Some of these goals were accomplished more effectively and honestly than others, but the new attitude was nonetheless a welcome change. The black voters of Little Tammany responded to it with a higher degree of gratitude and loyalty than was perhaps deserved.[27]

African American Votes, the Kansas City Machine, and the "New Abolition"

"Machine Smashed! Home Owners Win! Hogpens Are Not Wanted," trumpeted the *Star* the morning after the 1924 elections, and indeed, with Republicans con-trolling the state, county, and city, the forces of Republican retrenchment and re-form seemed to be in the driver's seat. Immediately after, in 1925, they were finally able to get their long-planned new city charter approved, with a small unicameral city council, a weak mayor, and most power vested in a professional city manager appointed by the council. But with Welch now in his camp, and the city's wards geographically consolidated (including most of Little Tammany packed into the new Second), Pendergast found it child's play to get his men elected to a majority on the new council and control it immediately. One of the defeated Goats from the county court, Henry F. McElroy, was installed as city manager, in which capacity his "country bookkeeping" would allow the machine to rake off millions from city operations while executing a massive modernization program and still, according to McElroy, remain in the pink of fiscal health. The other defeated Goat judge, Harry Truman, was restored to his seat in 1926 and led much of the building program. Even though the finances behind it all turned out to be a fiction, the illusion of prosperity kept the Pendergast machine and Kansas City afloat for much of the Depression.[28]

Building up a permanent majority took more time, but a major part of the project was increasing the Democrats' share of the black vote. Control of the city government and its revenue streams left the machine so flush with cash that it immediately invested in political tools it hoped would increase its influence in the state and nation, while expanding and consolidating power at home. The media were a major target. The city's most widely read black and white newspapers, *The*

Call and the *Star*, were both Republican-oriented and inveterate enemies of the machine. "Boss" Tom was from the old school of American politics that said a political movement was nothing if it did not have a newspaper to represent your community and tell your story to your supporters. He paid for a new journal, the aptly named *Missouri Democrat*, with daily and weekly editions edited by his right-hand man, county chairman Jim Aylward.[29]

Approaching the presidential election of 1928, the machine forces invested in another newspaper project, this one aimed at furthering the "great switch" of Kansas City's black voters. This was the *Kansas City American*, a black Democratic newspaper that would compete directly with *The Call*. Published by Dr. William Thompkins, in association with machine-connected gambler and nightclub owner Felix Payne, the *American* was clearly well funded. Nearly full-page ads touted and illustrated the brand-new Goss Comet press that had been installed, "the last word in printing equipment . . . used by no other Negro newspaper west of the Mississippi River."[30] The *American*'s take on most substantive issues was not that different from Chester Franklin's *Call*, but in politics it embraced Thompkins's vehement conviction that blacks could only find true political independence and equality outside the Republican Party. As Democrats, the *American* argued, African Americans could join the broad category of "the people," whose rights would be equally protected. This claim went far beyond the available facts or reasonable predictions, but at least northern urban Democrats saw blacks as an interest group to be courted, at a time when prominent members of the Missouri Republican Party were courting the second Ku Klux Klan. "LIBERTY vs. INTOLERANCE: Which Shall It Be? Don't Be a Political Slave! Vote the Democratic Ticket Straight!!!" shouted one of the *American*'s campaign display ads.[31]

That slogan reads quite oddly today, and it was somewhat belied by the limited, double-edged benefits Kansas City blacks would receive from the Pendergast machine and the New Deal. Despite the high mutual regard between himself and the Roosevelt administration, Dr. William Thompkins would have to content himself with a patronage appointment to the traditionally black office of recorder of deeds in the District of Columbia, not the respected executive post he would have preferred. Thompkins and his allies made an especially strong push for an appointment as governor of the US Virgin Islands. That would have made Thompkins the first black governor of that black-majority territory, a development that would have conflicted with Roosevelt's deference toward southern segregationist allies in Congress and would not happen until two years after Thompkins's death, when Harry Truman was president.[32]

Pendergastian tolerance helped make Kansas City a cultural mecca for blacks that afforded more opportunities to pursue creative careers, live freely, and work lucratively than would have been available otherwise, but those opportunities came at the cost of turning the heart of the main African American business and residential district into a twenty-four-hour vice and entertainment center, with heavy Mafia influence. Yet the effort made from 1925 forward to make a place for African Americans in the Kansas City Democratic Party was very serious, and was partly reflected in the *Kansas City American* itself, believed in Missouri to be the only explicitly Democratic black newspaper in the country.[33]

The occasion for the *American's* appearance was the tremendous opportunity that arose for Missouri Democrats to make inroads with black voters as the Republican Party prepared to hold its 1928 national convention in Kansas City. With huge majorities of Klan-curious middle-class Protestant whites behind them, the Republicans showed decreasing interest in maintaining the allegiance of black voters throughout the 1920s. Presidents Warren G. Harding and Coolidge appointed fewer blacks to office than even southern-born Democrat Woodrow Wilson, and segregation was imposed in federal departments where it had not existed before. Then Herbert Hoover, the favorite for the 1928 nomination, decided on the GOP's first "southern strategy," looking to acquire more white and dry votes in the South. At the Kansas City convention, the local housing arrangements committee voted to bar black delegates from the convention hotels, and several southern states sent competing integrated and "lily-white" delegations. Hoover sided with the lily-whites, and thus some of the most prominent black Republicans in the country were not seated. *The Call* thundered that "Negroes Will Resent This Insult," as this purge of black Republicans was carried out in front of one of the country's most dynamic black communities.[34]

The *American* jumped vociferously into the Democratic campaign, putting out a daily edition during the party's convention in Houston and then actively supporting the party's Irish Catholic nominee, Al Smith of New York, in the fall. Making an analogy between anti-Catholic bigotry and racial bias, and seizing on Republican race-baiting of Smith for the relatively integrated conditions in his home state, the *American* depicted Smith as the "embodiment of true Americanism" and a patriotism that was "Non-Racial, Non-Sectarian." Thompkins became one of the most prominent organizers of a black "Smith for President" league. Unfortunately, while most of the African American political elite and press endorsed Smith, they stuck with the Republican Party in other contexts, and the doomed Smith campaign failed to capitalize.[35]

One underlying problem was the same one that Franklin Delano Roosevelt would encounter four years later: Smith's unwillingness to offend the South by openly welcoming black votes. NAACP official Walter White thought Smith might have tipped the race in some of the northern and border states if he had been willing to make "a detailed and unequivocal statement that, if elected, he would be president of all the people, and would not be ruled by the anti-Negro South." Smith never dared to make such a statement but after the election wished he had, confessing that he had been strategically wrong not to make "an all-out bid for the Negro vote."[36]

In Kansas City, however, the plunge had already been taken, and it paid off locally despite the national Republican landslide in 1928. Thompkins boasted that he had pushed the Democratic percentage of the black vote in Kansas City up to 47 percent, nearly twice what it had been in 1924. In 1930, with the Depression on and the new black hospital open, the Kansas City Democrats made electoral breakthroughs with the black community and the wider public that would build up in subsequent elections. Thompkins traveled the country for FDR in 1932 as he had for Davis and Smith earlier. He claimed that the shift in the black vote was key to Roosevelt's wins throughout the Midwest, telling an audience in Omaha after the 1932 election that the Democratic victory amounted to a "new abolition." According to modern scholars, however, this change was just getting started in most localities, with Hoover still pulling 70 percent or more of the black vote in Chicago, Cincinnati, Cleveland, and Philadelphia, and the most pronounced swing visible only in 1936. In contrast, the *American* bragged about a 70 percent black vote for the Democrats in 1930, and Welch claimed to have 80 percent of his black precincts voting Democratic by 1934. Unfortunately, one of the methods Welch and the Kansas City machine used to accomplish this precocious feat was manufacturing votes, not just in the usual sense of boosting turnout with money and liquor, but also by inflating precinct totals with ghost votes.[37]

Whatever its means of winning, the Pendergast machine did try to deliver for the constituencies that supported it within the limits of its control and self-interestedness. The Democrats' most popular move in Little Tammany and the North End, where much of the black population lived and most of the Italian, Irish, Jewish, and African American gangsters operated, was gaining "home rule" for the police. Even after the Pendergast takeover, the Kansas City force was still controlled by Republican officials out of Jefferson City, as it had been for years. One of the most emotional issues in the black community was violent, arbitrary, and excessive policing that seemed to disproportionately target African Americans and their neighborhoods. Tom Pendergast and Cas Welch were prepared to do something about this for reasons not unrelated to their growing alliance with organized crime. The Democrats hit the issue especially hard in the 1930 city elections, when they took back the mayor's office. The *American*'s pre-election headlines included such on-message items as "Cripple Brutally Assaulted by K.C. Police" and "Police Torture Chamber Revealed to Citizens." In the near term, home rule allowed the Democrats to end the rampage of Republican-appointed police chief John L. Miles. Miles's manic enforcement of country Protestant values in black and Catholic neighborhoods resulted in more than 100 raids on the East Side Musicians' Club, along with many other depredations. As even the Republican *Call* admitted, the machine's replacement, Police Director Eugene C. Reppert, at least temporarily put an end to the "reign of police brutality."[38]

Unfortunately, the Pendergast Democrats also allowed their criminal allies to take control of the police: Italian mob boss (and North End Democratic leader)

Johnny Lazia was known to be "one of three who had a voice in naming men to the Police Department, and the turnover was large and rapid." For a time, the gangsters and the Organization alike were able to operate with a disastrous impunity that soon spun out of control, leading to Lazia's murder and Pendergast's downfall within just a few years.[39]

The tangled web of disappointments and possibilities that characterized the Kansas City machine's relationship with the African American community can be seen in the political career of one of Welch's boys, Gil P. Bourk. Theoretically an insurance salesman, Bourk spent much of his time holding down the fort at the Jeffersonian Democratic Club, working the phones, distributing jobs, and collecting club "dues." Bourk was such a thorough creature of the machine that the lead item on his official state legislative bio was "Has always been an active and loyal Democrat." In the 1930 sweep, with African Americans voting heavily Democratic in the city, Bourk unseated black Republican state legislator L. Amasa Knox, a distinguished attorney, by a suspiciously large margin, to howls of protest from *The Call*. One of the campaign themes used in Bourk's race was denying that a Republican had freed the slaves. Instead of Abraham Lincoln, machine propaganda named Missouri Democrat John Brooks Henderson, author of the Thirteenth Amendment.[40]

Yet despite the injustice and underhandedness that got him there, once ensconced at Jefferson City, this white party hack became a dogged spokesman for the black community. Just a few days into the legislative session, one of the most gruesome events in Missouri's violent racial history occurred. An unmasked white mob removed Raymond Gunn, accused murderer of a white schoolteacher, from the Maryville jail and marched him three miles to the country schoolhouse where the crime had been committed. Gunn was then chained to the roof, and burned alive, with no interference from the law. Nationwide outrage greeted this barbaric action, especially from the black press. Bourk promptly launched a crusade against lynching. He first introduced a resolution condemning the atrocity and demanding an investigation; the resolution was tabled but then hastily approved a few days later by the embarrassed rural majority of the Missouri House of Representatives. Later in the session, Bourk introduced a strict anti-lynching bill that defined a mob as any group of three or more people assembled to do violence to a prisoner, empowered the governor to fire any law officer who allowed prisoners to be taken, and provided the penalty of death or life imprisonment for any person convicted of lynching. Anti-lynching legislation was a longtime and long-frustrated goal of the NAACP and other black activist groups. The Senate whittled Bourk's bill down, and Republican governor Henry S. Caulfield still vetoed even the weakened legislation. Republicans grumbled that the bill was just a "political measure to increase the Democratic Negro vote," but the Pendergast machine saw no problem with benefiting politically from social justice. What was a stunt to one party was seen by another as "the opportunity of their lives" to secure black votes. The African American St.

Louis Argus accurately predicted "that the Negroes of the state will see the Democratic party in a different light to what they have in the past."[41]

Harry Truman's Escape from Goathood

While we often think of the modern Democratic Party as the creation of Franklin Delano Roosevelt, the real origins of the "New Deal coalition" as it survived past the 1930s can be found in the Kansas City politics of Harry S. Truman. The parts of the New Deal agenda that were consolidated and expanded were those preferred by Democrats from southern border states generally and Truman personally, while the aspects they rejected were abandoned or faded in importance. Hence, the New Deal's experiments in cartelization and direct relief were retrenched and abandoned rather quickly, under the glares of Jeffersonian penny-pinchers who included Truman, Joe Shannon, and their myriad southern segregationist friends in Congress.[42] At the same time, New Deal programs like Social Security that aimed to prevent people from falling out of the lower middle classes got much warmer support and were even expanded. Truman first introduced the idea of a national health insurance program in September 1945, days after the Japanese surrender. After the more limited but still sweeping Medicare program was finally enacted in 1965, President Lyndon Johnson came to Independence for the bill signing and a few months later delivered the first two Medicare cards to Truman and wife Bess: "We wanted the entire world to know we haven't forgotten who is the real daddy of Medicare."[43]

The Kansas City experience made Truman perfectly comfortable with the idea of African Americans, immigrants, and workers as interest groups whose aspirations and sensibilities had to be respected if their votes were to be retained. So, he supported civil rights and labor legislation that southern committee barons feared, beginning with integration of the military, a triumph of astutely calculated high-mindedness over the baser instincts he was raised with. It was Truman, much more than FDR, who was able to break away from the southern domination of his party and cement urban African Americans as its new bedrock of support nationally. National black leaders had the ear of left-liberal New Dealers such as Eleanor Roosevelt and Harold Ickes, but FDR never left the southern wing of the party behind. Many New Deal programs benefited blacks because they helped the poor, but only the tiniest modicum of integration was allowed, and southern Democrats were able—with the administration's tacit support—to block anti-lynching legislation, relief for agricultural laborers, and other policies that would have specifically protected African Americans.[44]

Despite a penchant for crude racist humor in private and personal attitudes only a little more enlightened than those of his Confederate grandparents, Truman was a thoroughgoing professional politician who could compartmentalize his social attitudes from his official duties. He seems to have put greater store than did "Boss" Tom himself in the supposed Pendergast motto that had appeared in the

Senator Harry S. Truman with Thomas J. Pendergast at the Democratic
National Convention in Philadelphia, Pennsylvania, June 24, 1936. Courtesy of
the Harry S. Truman Presidential Library and Museum.

machine's glossy "youth" magazine *Democracy*—"The Man Whose Word Is Good." Having made public commitments to fair treatment for all in employment and public services, Truman regained some favor with black leaders and voters in Kansas City during his second stint on the Jackson county court. Serving as presiding judge (and thus chief executive) from 1926 to 1934, Truman had made sure African Americans had equitable access to county jobs and contracts—according to one study, one-third of Jackson County's employees were black by 1928—and protected the county's black social service institutions, warding off some of Casimir Welch's efforts to corrupt them. Truman found his integrity and relative liberalism extremely beneficial in the unlikely runs for the Senate that would eventually put him in a position to be president.[45]

Harry Truman won his first Senate race in 1934 as Pendergast's man, with the machine's power, corruption, and violence at its apex. Unlike Pendergast, he also had the support of Chester A. Franklin and *The Call*, who strayed from Republican incumbent Roscoe Patterson on the straightforward basis that "Judge Truman" had a far better record on issues of concern to the African American community. Having both sides of Kansas City's black press in his corner was a huge change from Truman's days as a suspected Klansman.[46]

In 1940, with Tom Pendergast in jail, Cas Welch dead, the gambling dens and brothels no longer tolerated, and the jazz scene faded away, Senator Truman stood fair to be Pendergast's goat, literally and figuratively. He faced opposition in the Democratic primary from the two men who had done the most to bring Pendergast down, Governor Lloyd Stark and Kansas City prosecutor Maurice Milligan. The *Kansas City Star* responded to Truman's reelection announcement with an editorial denouncing "his record of complete subservience to Pendergast," and Stark opened his campaign bragging that he was "firmly opposed to everything the Kansas City plunderbund has fostered." Determined to win while remaining loyal to his old chieftain, Truman took the advice and possibly the speechwriting help of Dr. William Thompkins and made a strikingly bold play for the black vote that he realized held the key to surviving the primary. (Chester Franklin gave similar advice.) His opponents had left a wide opening. Few of Tom Pendergast's reforming pursuers had ever been especially friendly to the state's African American communities. Governor Stark in particular had repeatedly used his official powers to thwart the aspirations of black Missourians, for instance sending the Missouri State Highway Patrol to put down a 1938 black farmworkers' protest in the Bootheel. Most gallingly for African Americans active in Missouri politics, of whom there were more than ever before in 1940, Stark approved bald-faced efforts to avoid the integration of the University of Missouri Law School (in defiance of a Supreme Court order) by creating a second, plainly inferior Jim Crow institution, and then fired Lincoln University's entire board of curators when they complained.[47]

Truman chose the small rural metropolis of Sedalia, home of the Missouri State

Fair, to officially open his reelection campaign on July 15, 1940. In a speech that his campaign touted as a historic event, Truman staked his claim to the strongest New Deal record of the three major candidates by making a speech that was, for a politician of pro-Confederate ancestry, a radical endorsement of truly equal opportunity and citizenship for African Americans, tied directly to their history of oppression and re-oppression in his home region. "When we speak of man and his labor, at least in this country and, more particularly, in this locality, we must consider the problem of our Negro population and bend our every effort that, at least under law, they may claim their heritage of our Bill of Rights to 'life, liberty, and the pursuit of happiness.'" In a passage that was inserted into the *Congressional Record* under the heading "Tribute to the Negro," Truman channeled the liberal version of Jeffersonianism that was popular with New Deal Democrats, but took it much further than most, to include African Americans unequivocally in the Declaration of Independence's promises. The freshman senator celebrated that

> a new wave of feeling, saturated with the spirit of the Declaration of
> Independence, which looks upon the poor with sympathetic eyes, is passing
> over our country. A heightened conception of the worth and dignity of human
> life is taking irresistible hold upon all sections of society. Man is no longer a
> breathing robot, but a living spirit endowed with the highest and holiest of
> powers, capable of touching the heavens in inspiration and desire.

Truman stuck to the traditions of white Missouri politics with a quiet caveat abjuring any interest in social integration of the races, but he even more sternly rejected social injustice. Obliquely referencing then-current events in Europe, the Sedalia speech noted that American democracy would never be truly sincere or stable as long as ruling groups were allowed to tyrannize over those who were less powerful or numerous than they were:

> I believe in the brotherhood of man; not merely the brotherhood of white
> men, but the brotherhood of all men before law. . . . In giving to the Negroes
> the rights that are theirs, we are only acting in accord with our ideals of a true
> democracy. If any class or race can be permanently set apart from, or pushed
> down below, the rest in political and civil rights, so may any other class or race
> . . . and we may say farewell to the principles on which we count our safety.[48]

By announcing himself as Missouri's great champion of civil rights, Truman could both step ahead of the New Deal into the future of the Democratic Party and also avoid the short-term reverses it was suffering in 1940. Roosevelt won reelection, but his liberal Republican opponent, Wendell Willkie, cut down FDR's margins considerably, partly by appealing to black elites more than any Republican candidate had for a generation. The local situation in Missouri was far worse. Increasingly dissatisfied with the crumbs of patronage, policy, and funding that the New Deal regime had allowed them, black and working-class white voters sent Democratic gubernatorial candidate Larry McDaniel and many of his ticket-mates down to narrow defeats in 1940. With his much more overt racial liberalism, Harry Truman earned a different result, not only beating Stark and Milligan in the primary, but running more than 20,000 votes ahead of McDaniel in the general and winning reelection.[49]

The nature of the Democratic Party's relationship with African Americans, especially the authenticity of its claims to serve the interests of black voters, remains a debatable question. Yet here is an undeniable observation: The messy mix that defines that relationship—of self-interest, corruption, and self-deception, along with genuine sympathy and a sincere rejection of hate—had one of its major formative moments in Kansas City.

Notes

This chapter would have been impossible without the enthusiastic research assistance of recent University of Missouri graduate (and new Kansas Citian) Isaac Pasley.

1. On the remarkably slow pace of the transition in the country at large, see Nancy J. Weiss, *Farewell to the Party of Lincoln: Black Politics in the Age of FDR* (Princeton, N.J.: Princeton University Press, 1989). Two overlooked works that do get the timing right are Franklin D. Mitchell, *Embattled Democracy: Missouri Democratic Politics, 1919–1932* (Columbia: University of Missouri Press, 1968); and Larry Henry Grothaus, "The Negro in Missouri Politics, 1890–1941" (PhD diss., University of Missouri–Columbia, 1970). For an example of the conventional wisdom that 1936 was the turning point, see Joseph Alsop and Robert Kintner, "Farley and the Future," *Life*, September 19, 1938, 24–27, 56–59.

2. On the Pendergast machine and its various activities and lieutenants, see Lyle W. Dorsett, *The Pendergast Machine* (Lincoln: University of Nebraska Press, 1968); William M. Reddig, *Tom's Town: Kansas City and the Pendergast Legend* (Columbia: University of Missouri Press, 1986); Maurice M. Milligan, *Missouri Waltz: The Inside Story of the Pendergast Machine by the Man Who Smashed It* (New York: Charles Scribner's Sons, 1948); Gene Schmidtlein, "Harry S. Truman and the Pendergast Machine," *Midcontinent American Studies Journal* 7, no. 2 (July 1966): 27–35; and Lawrence H. Larsen and Nancy J. Hulston, *Pendergast!* (Columbia: University of Missouri Press, 1997).

3. "America Gambling," *Life*, February 6, 1939, 46; "The Governor of Missouri Helps Indict the Boss of Kansas City and Becomes a Presidential Possibility," *Life*, April 24, 1939, 17; Pegler's syndicated column, "Fair Enough," as printed in *El Paso Herald-Post*, February 21, 1938, 4.

4. Frank Driggs and Chuck Haddix, *Kansas City Jazz: From Ragtime to Bebop—A History* (New York: Oxford University Press, 2005); Nathan W. Pearson, *Goin' to Kansas City* (Urbana: University of Illinois Press, 1994).

5. On the evolution of the Democratic Party, a topic on which a comprehensive work does not exist, see Peter B. Kovler, ed., *Democrats and the American Idea: A Bicentennial Appraisal* (Washington, DC: Center for National Policy, 1992); Jo Freeman, "The Political Culture of the Democratic and Republican Parties," *Political Science Quarterly* 101, no. 3 (1986): 327–356; Steve Fraser and Gary Gerstle, eds., *The Rise and Fall of the New Deal Order, 1930–1980* (Princeton, N.J.: Princeton University Press, 1989).

6. Noel Ignatiev, *How the Irish Became White* (New York: Routledge, 1995); Jean H. Baker, *Affairs of Party: The Political Culture of Northern Democrats in the Mid-Nineteenth Century* (Ithaca, N.Y.: Cornell University Press, 1983).

7. David Brian Robertson, "Bellwether Politics in Missouri," *The Forum* 2, no. 3 (October 2004), http://www.degruyter.com/view/j/for.2004.2.3_20120105083449/for.2004.2.3/for .2004.2.3.1052/for.2004.2.3.1052.xml, accessed September 19, 2015.

8. John W. McKerley, "Citizens and Strangers: The Politics of Race in Missouri from Slavery to the Era of Jim Crow" (PhD diss., University of Iowa, 2008). See also McKerley's Chapter 1 in this volume.

9. David M. Chalmers, *Hooded Americanism: The History of the Ku Klux Klan*, 3rd ed. (Durham, N.C.: Duke University Press, 1987); Charles C. Alexander, *The Ku Klux Klan in the Southwest* (Norman: University of Oklahoma Press, 1995), 1–4; Wyn Craig Wade, *The Fiery Cross: The Ku Klux Klan in America* (New York: Oxford University Press, 1997), 119–148.

10. Kimberly Harper, *White Man's Heaven: The Lynching and Expulsion of Blacks in the Southern Ozarks, 1894–1909* (Fayetteville: University of Arkansas Press, 2012); Patrick J. Huber, "The Lynching of James T. Scott: The Underside of a College Town," *Gateway Heritage* 12, no. 1 (1991): 18–37; Jason Navarro, "Under Penalty of Death: Pierce City's Night of Racial Terror," *Missouri Historical Review* 100, no. 2 (2006): 87–102; Elliott Jaspin, *Buried in Bitter Waters: The Hidden History of Racial Cleansing in America* (New York: Basic Books, 2007); James W. Loewen, *Sundown Towns: A Hidden Dimension of American Racism* (New York: Simon and Schuster, 2005).

11. Jan E. Hults, "The Senatorial Career of James Alexander Reed" (PhD diss., University of Kansas, 1987), 208; Lee Meriwether, *Jim Reed, "Senatorial Immortal": A Biography* (Webster Groves, Mo.: International Mark Twain Society, 1948), 66–92. Reed's lengthy speech against the League of Nations, a catalogue of racial stereotypes covering the whole of the globe, is quoted from the *Congressional Record*, 66th Congress, 1st Session, Senate, May 26, 1919, 235–246.

12. On the perils blacks faced in Kansas City, see Sherry Lamb Schirmer, *A City Divided: The Racial Landscape of Kansas City, 1900–1960* (Columbia: University of Missouri Press, 2002).

13. William Rufus Jackson, *Missouri Democracy: A History of the Party and Its Representative Members, Past and Present* (Chicago: S. J. Clarke, 1935), 3:846–847; Gary R. Kremer, "William J. Thompkins: African American Physician, Politician, and Publisher," *Missouri Historical Review* 101, no. 3 (April 2007): 168–182; Grothaus, "Negro in Missouri Politics," 78–79, and passim; Schirmer, *City Divided*, 65.

14. Kremer, "William J. Thompkins," 168–182; Jackson, *Missouri Democracy*, 3:846–847;

James W. Hutt, "The Negro in Missouri," in Jackson, *Missouri Democracy*, 1:431–434, quotation on 432.

15. On Kansas City political geography, see Dorsett, *Pendergast Machine*, 56, 61, 63, 76; Donald B. Oster, "Reformers, Factionalists, and Kansas City's 1925 City Manager Charter," *Missouri Historical Review* 72, no. 3 (April 1978): 296–327; and, especially, James R. Shortridge, *Kansas City and How It Grew, 1822–2011* (Lawrence: University Press of Kansas, 2012), chap. 4.

16. Quotation from Charles P. Blackmore, "Joseph B. Shannon, Political Boss and Twentieth Century 'Jeffersonian'" (PhD diss., Columbia University, 1953), 315. It should be noted here that Irish Catholic "wet" politicos attacking the new Klan was a relatively general phenomenon, not something that happened uniquely in Kansas City.

17. Mitchell, *Embattled Democracy*, 63–82; Chalmers, *Hooded Americanism*, 135–137, 198–215; Grothaus, "Negro in Missouri Politics," 110–111; Missouri Secretary of State, *Official Manual of the State of Missouri, 1925–1926*, http://cdm.sos.mo.gov/cdm/ref/collection/bluebook/id/13422, 528–529.

18. Grothaus, "Negro in Missouri Politics," 112–113; Alonzo L. Hamby, *Man of the People: A Life of Harry S. Truman* (New York: Oxford University Press, 1995), 125–131.

19. Grothaus, "Negro in Missouri Politics," 107; Charles E. Coulter, *Take Up the Black Man's Burden: Kansas City's African American Communities, 1865–1939* (Columbia: University of Missouri Press, 2006), 47; *Kansas City Call*, April 4, 1924; Reddig, *Tom's Town*, 114–115; *Kansas City Star*, October 5, 1924, 6, 8; October 8, 1914, 4, 15; October 1924, 20. Hurse was friendly enough with the Democratic machine to host Democratic speakers at his church. See *Kansas City American*, March 26, 1931, 2.

20. On Welch and Little Tammany, see Reddig, *Tom's Town*, 109–114; Dorsett, *Pendergast Machine*, 63; Schirmer, *City Divided*, 153; "Casimir Welch Always the Direct, Blunt Politician," obituary, *Kansas City Star*, April 17, 1938, 14; Percy B. Sovey, "Casimir J. Welch: Friend of the Lowly," *Democracy*, September 1935, 10–11.

21. Grothaus, "Negro in Missouri Politics," 107; Coulter, *Take Up the Black Man's Burden*, 47; Blackmore, "Joseph B. Shannon."

22. The wiretap recordings can be heard at the Marr Sound Archives, Miller Nichols Library, University of Missouri–Kansas City. No transcripts have ever been made, and one of the few discussions of the recordings and their contents is Joseph Popper, "'30s Bug Reveals Pendergast Plots," *Kansas City Star*, June 25, 1994, A1. My thanks to Chuck Haddix for allowing me to listen to some of the recordings remotely.

23. Reddig, *Tom's Town*, 111; Editorial, "Judge Welch," *Kansas City American*, December 4, 1930, 8.

24. Sovey, "Casimir J. Welch."

25. "Casimir Welch," obituary, *Kansas City Star*, April 17, 1938; "Northside Democratic Leader [Lazia] Appeals to Negroes to Follow Some Leader," *Kansas City American*, June 9, 1932; "Feed Thousands Every Day; John Lazia Heads Group in Movement," *Kansas City American*, January 12, 1933. Truman's fear and loathing for Cas Welch and most other Rabbits comes through in the so-called Pickwick Papers of 1934. Truman vents on the stationery

of the Pickwick Hotel in downtown Kansas City, where he stayed occasionally after late or distasteful nights on machine business. "Pickwick Papers," 1934, Longhand Note File, Harry S. Truman Library and Museum, Independence, Missouri.

26. Quotations from "The Jeffersonian Democratic Club Endorses These Candidates" (display advertisement), *Kansas City American*, July 28, 1932, 7; "Merry Christmas 1931," *Kansas City American*, July 24, 1931, 7; "Welch Does Not Make Good," Kansas City *Call*, October 3, 1930, 8; "The Way That Wins," Kansas City *Call*, November 7, 1930, 8.

27. *Democracy*, September 1935, 10–11; "Merry Christmas 1931."

28. *Kansas City Star*, November 5, 1924, p. 1; *Kansas City Times*, April 9, 1924, 1; Reddig, *Tom's Town*, 115–130; Dorsett, *The Pendergast Machine*, 86–91, 118–119, 134–135.

29. *Missouri Democrat*, October 16, 1925; Dorsett, *Pendergast Machine*, 83–84. On Kansas City's newspapers in the early twentieth century, see Harry Haskell, *Boss-Busters and Sin Hounds: Kansas City and Its Star* (Columbia: University of Missouri Press, 2007); Jan Lelain Lorenzen, "Kansas City, Missouri, Newspapers of 1932 and the Pendergast Political Machine" (MA thesis, University of Missouri–Kansas City, 2003). On the tradition Pendergast was following when he created the *Missouri Democrat*, see Jeffrey L. Pasley, *"The Tyranny of Printers": Newspaper Politics in the Early American Republic* (Charlottesville: University Press of Virginia, 2001).

30. Kremer, "William J. Thompkins," 173. Quotation from *Kansas City American*, September 13, 1928 (ad: "A Part of Our Equipment").

31. Editorial, "Negro Democrats," *Kansas City American*, August 16, 1928, "Liberty v. Intolerance," advertisement, October 27, 1928.

32. Kremer, "William J. Thompkins," 174–175.

33. Jackson, *Missouri Democracy*, 3:847; Schirmer, *City Divided*, 147–178.

34. For an expanded discussion of the 1928 Republican Convention, see Chapter 5 in this volume by Dustin Gann. Allan J. Lichtman, *Prejudice and the Old Politics: The Presidential Election of 1928* (Chapel Hill: University of North Carolina Press, 1979), 147–159; *Kansas City Star*, March 16, 1928, 1, and March 23, 1928, B-4.

35. *Kansas City American*, June 21 and September 6, 1928; Mitchell, *Embattled Democracy*, 122–123; Samuel O'Dell, "Blacks, the Democratic Party, and the Presidential Election of 1928: A Mild Rejoinder," *Phylon* 48, no. 1 (1987): 1–11; Grothaus, "Negro in Missouri Politics," 120–121; Kremer, "William J. Thompkins," 173.

36. Walter F. White, *A Man Called White: The Autobiography of Walter White* (1948; Athens: University of Georgia Press, 1995), 100–101.

37. Mitchell, *Embattled Democracy*, 122–123; Sovey, "Casimir J. Welch"; Omaha *Sunday World-Herald*, December 18, 1932, A-11; Weiss, *Farewell to the Party of Lincoln*, 29–32; "The Seventy Per-Cent Negro Democratic Vote," *Kansas City American*, April 3, 1930, 7; Larsen and Hulston, *Pendergast!*, 104–105; Popper, "'30s Bug Reveals Pendergast Plots."

38. Reddig, *Tom's Town*, 140–145; Schirmer, *A City Divided*, 160–162; Editorial, "Past Gains Show Future Possibilities," Kansas City *Call*, September 23, 1932, B6; "Police Brutality Ended by Reppert," *Missouri Democrat*, June 10, 1932, 5. The quoted headlines appear on the front page of the *Kansas City American*, March 20, 1930. For a trenchant discussion of

law enforcement's brutal, partial treatment of Kansas City's black community, see Schirmer, *A City Divided*, 122–146.

39. Reddig, *Tom's Town*, 252–253; Larsen and Hulston, *Pendergast!*, 105–120.

40. *Official Manual of the State of Missouri, 1933–34*, 63; Coulter, *Take Up the Black Man's Burden*, 158–160; Editorial, "Welch Does Not Make Good," Kansas City *Call*, October 3, 1930, 8; "The Way That Wins," Kansas City *Call*, November 7, 1930, 8; Jeffersonian Democratic Club endorsement ad, *Kansas City American*, July 27, 1932, 1. On Henderson, see Zachary Dowdle, "John Brooks Henderson," *Historic Missourians*, State Historical Society of Missouri, accessed May 31, 2018, https://shsmo.org/historicmissourians/name/h/henderson/.

41. Mitchell, *Embattled Democracy*, 136–137 (includes quotations from St. *Louis Argus*); St. *Louis Post-Dispatch*, January 13, 1931, 1, and January 30, 1931, 20, and April 9, 1931, 20.

42. Ira Katznelson, in *Fear Itself: The New Deal and the Origins of Our Time* (New York: Liveright, 2014), calls these limitations the New Deal's "southern cage," but I would argue that Truman managed to wriggle through the bars on race. Harvard Sitkoff's *A New Deal for Blacks* (New York: Oxford University Press, 2008) makes the best case it can for the Roosevelt administration.

43. Monte M. Poen, *Harry S. Truman versus the Medical Lobby: The Genesis of Medicare* (Columbia: University of Missouri Press, 1979), 1–2, 58–59; Lyndon B. Johnson, "Remarks in Independence, Mo., at a Ceremony in Connection with the Establishment of the Harry S. Truman Center for the Advancement of Peace," *American Presidency Project*, accessed June 7, 2017, http://www.presidency.ucsb.edu/ws/?pid=27593; Muriel Dobbin, "Red View U.S. Will Quit Delays Peace, Johnson Says," *Baltimore Sun*, January 21, 1966, A6, https://www.newspapers.com/newspage/376754531/.

44. For positive assessments of the Truman civil rights record, see David Goldfield, "Border Men: Truman, Eisenhower, Johnson, and Civil Rights," *Journal of Southern History* 80, no. 1 (February 2014): 7–38; Robert Shogan, *Harry Truman and the Struggle for Racial Justice* (Lawrence: University Press of Kansas, 2013); Michael R. Gardner, *Harry Truman and Civil Rights: Moral Courage and Political Risks* (Carbondale: Southern Illinois University Press, 2002); and Larry Grothaus, "Kansas City Blacks, Harry Truman, and the Pendergast Machine," *Missouri Historical Review* 69, no. 1 (October 1974): 65–82.

45. Hamby, *Man of the People*, 186–199; Reddig, *Tom's Town*, 252–264; Larsen and Hulston, *Pendergast!*, 107–117; *Kansas City Star*, August 12, 1933, 1. On Truman's record as presiding judge and its impact on black public opinion, see Thomas D. Wilson, "Chester A. Franklin and Harry S. Truman: An African-American Conservative and the 'Conversion' of the Future President," *Missouri Historical Review* 88 (October 1993), 57–59. Quotation from *Democracy*, July 1935, 4.

46. "Like an Answer to Prayer," Kansas City *Call*, May 11, 1934, 1; "Judge Truman Is the *Call*'s First Choice; Patterson's Failures Cause Him to Lose Support in Senatorial Race," Kansas City *Call*, October 12, 1934, 2; "Missouri Negro Voters Like Judge Truman Because of His Record," Kansas City *Call*, October 26, 1934, 5. For an informative but speculative

study of the Franklin-Truman relationship, see Wilson, "Chester A. Franklin and Harry S. Truman," 48–77.

47. Richard Lawrence Miller, *Truman: The Rise to Power* (New York: McGraw-Hill, 1986), 325–327; Editorial, "Truman Servant of Pendergast," *Kansas City Star*, June 17, 1940; Curtis A. Betts, "Gov. Stark Opens Campaign, Citing Record in Office," *St. Louis Post-Dispatch*, May 18, 1940, 1; Hamby, *Man of the People*, 238–239; and Robert H. Ferrell, *Truman and Pendergast* (Columbia: University of Missouri Press, 1999), 93–98, 116.

48. 86 Cong. Rec. 4546 (1940).

49. Grothaus, "Negro in Missouri Politics," 164–165.

CHAPTER THREE

J. C. Nichols and Neighborhood Infrastructure

The Foundations of American Suburbia

Sara Stevens

Jesse Clyde Nichols developed upper-middle-class subdivisions in early twentieth century Kansas City. Essentially, he built and sold suburban infrastructure: he did not construct houses, turnkey-style, but laid roads, buried water and sewer lines, and subdivided land into lots. He is most known for two things: the Country Club Plaza, an early shopping center, and for the much-copied deed restrictions—limitations added to a property's deed, including everything from setbacks to the race of the inhabitants—that determined the outlines of all future construction. As subterranean and contractual as much of his work was, though, it also had a decidedly aesthetic component. Unlike most developers at the time, Nichols hired landscape architects to lay out his subdivisions and to design public green spaces on medians, esplanades, and other remnant spots of vegetation. Hardly large enough to qualify as park spaces, these enhancements were in some sense eye candy, decorated with statuary and fountains, but Nichols saw them as much more: as aesthetic devices for ensuring stable property values, maintained through the legal device of the home-owners' association.

In this chapter I argue that Nichols believed the aesthetics of curving lanes, birdbaths, and shrubbery not only bolstered but also steadied property values, providing Kansas City with an expansive landscape that showcased his vision of private-market city planning. Nichols did not see his investments in plant material as a sales tool for moving empty lots as much as he saw them as an infrastructure that would bring long-term dividends. In this way, leftover spaces gained productive value, signaling as well as ensuring through their aesthetics the high value of

Kansas City real estate developer J. C. Nichols, 1935. Courtesy of the State Historical Society of Missouri, Kansas City Research Center.

surrounding properties. Like his shopping centers, homeowners' associations, and deed restrictions, these leafy suburban accoutrements were but another component of Nichols's system of legal and economic standardizations aimed at producing steady property values for his purchasers, insulating them from the dangers of investing in real estate, what he called "unstable merchandise."[1]

Nichols was a singular but key player in creating the cul-de-sac landscape of suburbia, whose designs and deed restrictions would later be promoted by the Federal Housing Administration as standards to follow. A leader in his field, Nichols regularly borrowed from the language and techniques of city planning and landscape architecture to achieve his projects, and he repeatedly and explicitly defined his work and that of other "real estate men" in relation to the discourse on city planning. Nichols wiped any off-putting politics from city planning discourse in his retelling of it, casting city planning as a business-friendly initiative that would work hand in hand with developers to grow American cities.[2] His deed restrictions established self-perpetuating, private controls to development that became the model for other developers, forming the legal groundwork for private land use control, aes-

Billboard referencing racial and class restrictions in the Country Club District, 1912.
Courtesy of the State Historical Society of Missouri, Kansas City Research Center.

thetic controls, and an intractable urban fabric. Nichols capitalized on techniques from landscape architecture, paired with his own legal innovations, to establish and maintain in perpetuity the romantic, leafy-green aesthetic commonly associated with suburbia. The un-urbanized southwestern outskirts of Kansas City in the early decades of the twentieth century was the canvas on which he experimented.

Nichols began subdividing in 1904, having no experience in the business and little capital to launch his plans. He borrowed the equipment to put in the first curbs in the Country Club District and salvaged wood from a barn to build sidewalks.[3] Those curbs and sidewalks were some of the first of the physical "improvements" to the Country Club District—the name given to the aggregation of smaller, contiguous subdivisions Nichols developed piecemeal southwest of Kansas City until his death in 1950. Early on in that span of decades, at the end of a streetcar line on undeveloped land, Nichols built a temporary sales building for the company, calling it their "little white colonial office." In regular newspaper ads and from the office, he offered copies of the plat to potential buyers, and he toured visitors around the neighborhood to show them construction progress and tout the area's benefits. The wood-framed sales building, which existed for only a few years, mixed the appearance of a residential building and the symmetrical pomp of a small civic structure complete with a flagpole. Already a sales tool itself, the small building's design suggested the genteel traditions of an elite suburb—Palladian windows at the ends of the two protruding wings of the building, a small pediment over the central door, roof cornices, many large windows, a curving stone wall at the street, and a pair of domestic fireplaces as bookends. The edifice greeted potential buyers and projected the aesthetic standard that the Nichols Company imposed on its subdivisions.

A local comparison is useful for understanding how Nichols came to define the role of the state in urban development, that is, how he understood the alignments or conflicts between real estate and an idea of civic improvement. The Rockhill District of southern Kansas City (roughly bounded by Warwick Boulevard, Harrison Street, Forty-Third Street, and Forty-Seventh Street, though some properties extended south of Brush Creek) was developed by *Kansas City Star* publisher William Rockhill Nelson. Nelson's developments, though at the high end of the market, represent the norms of real estate that Nichols would eventually rewrite. Before expanding into real estate development, Nelson had worked with local leaders on Kansas City's foray into the City Beautiful movement, a parks and boulevards system designed by landscape architect George Kessler in the 1890s, and had become interested in landscape architecture as a tool for real estate development.[4]

Unlike the innovative approach Nichols would take, Nelson attempted to make his Rockhill District exclusive through more conventional methods. He retained architectural control of the neighborhood solely through the original sales contract of each lot he sold, which unlike covenants, did not apply to resold lots. The cost of all common improvements like streetcar rights-of-way, low stone walls along arterials, and services like water, electricity, and sewers were funded only by the initial sale, without replenishment from homeowners' association fees.[5] He put his own profits toward neighborhood improvements like landscaping and road upgrades; there were no deed restrictions controlling construction on purchased lots or subsequent changes to the properties by their new owners. While Nelson's move to develop the southwestern side of Kansas City and connect to the Kansas City Country Club were models for what Nichols would do, Nelson's overall approach was, in terms of standard practices for suburban developers of the time, conventional.

Nelson's own role as a developer and his political power in the city as a newspaper publisher led to some criticism from those who saw a conflict of interest.[6] Nelson organized an effort to get approval for a new landscaped boulevard, part of Kessler's original plan, that would extend from downtown out to his Rockhill District. Though eventually successful, the effort harmed his reputation, with Nelson disparaged in the process as "fantastically selfish, and wrapped in a vision of hundred foot boulevards . . . built out of the public treasury."[7] Around 1904, Nelson built his own formidable house and more modest stone houses to rent to his employees and then sold off other lots for residential use. He also built curving streets lined with trees and stone walls within the development, connecting it to the existing Kansas City Country Club to the southwest.[8] These landscaped streets, larger lots, and proximity to the country club helped attract wealthy people to the area. J. C. Nichols hoped that this demographic shift would rub off on his first venture in the area, located between the country club and the Rockhill District.[9] But perhaps Nichols also learned a lesson from Nelson's political snafu—reliance on public funding for neighborhood improvements carried political risks to one's reputation and projects. Unlike Nelson, Nichols would come to see the public sector as having a weak role in developing cities; real momentum could only be generated by private individuals and private funding. The relation between private-sector businesses and public funding required careful navigation for entrepreneurs. The costs of civic improvements like tree-lined boulevards ought to be borne by residential develop- ers if those developers wanted to remain above the fray of local politics. Though Nichols saw the interconnectedness of city planning and land development, he also recognized the political risks of too much cooperation. Nichols's successes with the Country Club District, noted in local newspapers including Nelson's *Kansas City Star*, confirm that his decision to insulate himself from any political agendas too directly tied to his own financial interests was smart.

Creating Exclusivity: Landscape Architecture

One important difference between the work of an innovator like J. C. Nichols and that of a typical practitioner like William Rockhill Nelson is that Nichols employed landscape architects to design his subdivisions, and most developers, like Nelson, did not. Landscape architects were an added expense that was usually avoided, but Nichols mined the techniques of landscape design to make his subdivisions more exclusive and more profitable. Put simply, Nichols hired landscape architects to increase land values in his neighborhoods. Nelson, by contrast, often designed the layout of the streets himself, without hiring a landscape architect, and his street lay- outs do not show the expected signs of a landscape architect's hand—curved interior streets, small park areas, or a hierarchy of roads. Though he was familiar with some of the techniques of landscape architects from working with George Kessler on the parks and boulevards plan for Kansas City in the late 1890s, Nelson relied only on low stone walls, one curved boulevard, and tree-lined streets to convey continuity with Kansas City's City Beautiful plans.

The role of landscape architecture in Nichols's work reflects a long-standing and significant association between picturesque ideals and residential design. Nichols's reliance on the traditions of garden design did not change or heavily influence that field, but rather continued and amplified a thread started by other developers elsewhere in the United States. Picturesque traditions came to American shores by a slow route. American garden designers of the mid-nineteenth century bor- rowed from the traditions of seventeenth-century Dutch landscape painters, whose scenes of romantic, meandering gardens featured exotic plants or ruins and looked like set pieces for narrative action. American garden designers like Andrew Jackson Downing adopted this style as they simultaneously wove a moral imperative into the meaning of proper domestic spaces, envisioning the domestic sphere as a naturalistic space separated from the fast-changing, noisy industrial metropolis. Downing's 1842 book, *Cottage Residences*, was a pattern book for consumers that promoted curved lanes and meandering garden paths, even defining different roles in creating and maintaining the garden for men and women. His ideas were widely popular, influencing consumers and builders alike for generations to come. When Nichols began to develop neighborhoods, the mode of setting houses in picturesque settings that Downing promoted was still popular, and Nichols's subdivisions—green and sylvan, with curved roads—capitalized on it.

Histories of US suburbia have shown how the picturesque represented a timelessness and escape from the city and its industry. The landscape designs of suburbia held a cultural meaning intended to provide separation for the domestic sphere and stability against the fluctuations of modern capitalism. As David Schuyler has shown regarding picturesque suburban cemetery designs of the mid-nineteenth century, the creation of a timeless, domestic space of permanence and rest for the dead explicitly countered the hustle of the unpredictable market in the gridiron city.[10] Even in the Country Club District, the association between cemetery design and residential spaces was not so far-fetched. Indeed, one of Nichols's landscape architects, Sidney Hare, was a cemetery designer before opening his own landscape architecture firm.[11]

The new field of landscape architecture that Nichols accessed through Kessler and Hare and Hare (another of the earliest landscape architecture firms in the country) was growing in popularity but also suffered from its gendered associations. Due in part to Downing's stress on the different roles for men and women in caring for a garden, the beautifying aspects of a manicured landscape carried the association of being unmanly. In order for men to legitimize their work as landscape architects and professionalize their field, they had to distance themselves from feminine associations of gardening.[12] Like landscape architects, Nichols focused on the masculine and infrastructural work of laying roads and building sidewalks and gutters rather than the beautifying work of designing and planting flower gardens. Even so, this need to transform landscape architecture into a masculine pursuit downplayed, but did not overwhelm, the feminized picturesque aesthetic so commonly understood, then and now, as suburban. Nichols continued to build on these cultural meanings and to promote the production of such landscapes through his speeches, writing, and professional organizing, and in doing so helped to bring more landscape architects into the production of middle-class subdivisions as part of his legacy.

As early as 1907, Nichols worked with George Kessler to subdivide a large farm he was purchasing west of land that had already been subdivided. Nichols began his first projects in Kansas City with family friends from Olathe as investors, gradually increasing the project size with each new iteration and shifting to Kansas City banks as his financial partners. This slow and steady approach kept his relationship with bankers strong and focused his attention on the bottom line. At this time,

Nichols platted other smaller subdivisions whose layouts also suggest that Kessler might have been involved, perhaps offering suggestions and advice but not creating the drawings himself.[13] The plats show streets curved to accommodate nonrectilinear conditions and topography and still produce the maximum number of salable lots. The November 1907 plat of Rockhill Place, for example, had to contend with streets to the west of the site that did not align with the streets on the east, and did so by creating a curved interior street to discourage nonlocal traffic. Also to this end, the blocks were reoriented to run east-west, giving the bounding north-south streets more hierarchy for traffic coming south from downtown. This arrangement also improved southern exposure for the houses and broke the prevailing northerly winter winds.[14]

George Kessler worked in Kansas City early in his career, preparing the parks and boulevards plan for the city with Nelson's support, and working with Nichols on a few subdivisions. Kessler was trained in Europe in botany, landscape design, and civil engineering before returning to the United States to work as a landscape architect, and briefly as a gardener in New York's Central Park. Nelson engaged him to design the parks and boulevards system after seeing his work in Merriam, Kansas, where he had designed a park at the railroad station.[15] The Kansas City commission led to more prestigious work designing the fairgrounds for the Louisiana Purchase Exhibition in St. Louis in 1904, and further work elsewhere as his national profile increased. The parks and boulevards plan that Kessler created for Kansas City in 1893 called for land clearance of working-class residential neighborhoods in order to shore up values in existing and planned upper-class neighborhoods. Here the egalitarian goals of city planning and landscape architecture met the realities of capitalist urban development with striking discord. Kessler's City Beautiful–inspired report was, according to historian William Worley, "a call for public funds to bolster private real estate values" more than it was an attempt to improve conditions in the city for the betterment of all citizens.[16] The green space Kessler proposed alongside enhanced boulevards created buffer zones protecting expensive residential properties from encroachment by undesirable land uses that might appear along busy streets. Tellingly, the roads selected to become green-scaped boulevards almost always abutted highly valued property. In contrast, Kessler's task in working on subdivisions with Nichols (and also with Baltimore developer Edward Bouton on that city's Roland Park) was to create—not just reinforce—higher land values through landscape architecture. Economic exclusivity and enhancement of lot values was the goal and landscape architecture the tool.

To further this aim, construction details were calibrated to attract high-paying buyers. J. C. Nichols paved the roads in his subdivisions, matching his commitment to landscape architecture with a commitment to bump-free car rides. By 1908, he specified an eight-inch base of crushed stone covered with two-inch heavy macadam, crowned for drainage, and bordered by a two-foot-wide cement curb and four-foot-

Two children watch construction machinery smooth the substrate for roads in the Country Club District, with statuary fountain in the background, date unknown. Courtesy of the State Historical Society of Missouri, Kansas City Research Center.

wide granite ("granitoid") sidewalks. The curb design and size were important for keeping cars off lawns in these early days of the automobile.[17] In accommodating the automobile, only a year after the Model T was introduced, Nichols set his subdivisions apart (and presaged the symbiosis between cars and suburbia). The well-paved roads and sidewalks illustrated readiness for the family car in promotional material. Nichols's two sons even worked on road-building and maintenance crews in the summers, learning to lay heavy stones as base, breaking up that stone with a napping hammer, and "enduring the suffocating asphalt fumes as they spread the macadam top."[18] Nichols increased the depth of the road beds with a twelve-inch stone base below the macadam top in 1917, exceeding local and national standards for road construction.[19] Well-maintained, well-constructed streets were a selling point for the Nichols Company, a feature Nichols leveraged to convince buyers of his progressive vision. Explaining how the large-lot design improved automobility for residents, Nichols told the *Ladies Home Journal* in 1921, "In these days of the motor car you can whisk around these long blocks in a jiffy."[20]

To show buyers the desirability of the Country Club District, Nichols's firm needed to present an exclusively residential landscape that offered the right amenities and was more than simply a larger home on a sizable lot away from the smoke of industry. Nichols, like other developers, bet that buyers craved more than "not-city" and wanted instead a new kind of picturesque suburbanism that contrasted with the dirty, harsh conditions of early twentieth-century American industrial capitalism. The vision Nichols and other developers had of high-end suburban living at the intersection of class, culture, and price point would justify the great energies

Decorative statues and a low stone wall frame a small park with a playground for children at Arbor Villa Park at Edgevale Road and Main Street, County Club District, 1923. Courtesy of the State Historical Society of Missouri, Kansas City Research Center.

spent on, say, smoothing the asphalt or on the legalese of deed restrictions. Similarly, it called for the inclusion of an additional layer of aesthetic accoutrements. Nichols's landscape architects used statuary fountains to sell buyers this vision of suburban living. The neighborhood's traffic-directing street layouts created small, postage stamp–sized parks as islands surrounded by roads. These Nichols turned into selling points by filling them with fountains and sculptures. He collected the art on trips to Europe, adding to the general cachet of the endeavor, and held receptions to unveil new acquisitions. More than mere ornaments in the landscape, Nichols believed these objets d'art established an aesthetic tone that reflected the street design and helped build a long-term vision for the quality and financial stability of the area.

Like real estate development, landscape architecture was a nascent field. After Kessler had moved his practice from Kansas City to St. Louis, Nichols hired the local firm Hare and Hare to create the street layouts and plans for his subdivisions. The younger Hare of the father-son pair trained with Frederick Law Olmsted Jr. at Harvard University; the elder Hare began his career as a civil engineer in Kansas City, was the established authority on the local geography and landscape, and came

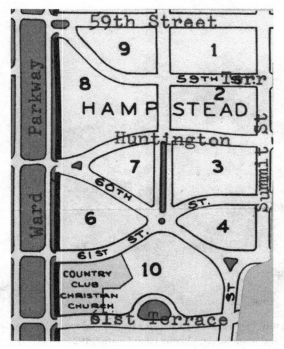

Plan of the Hampstead Gardens section of the Country Club District, showing curved streets and triangular parks at intersections, c. 1913. Courtesy of the State Historical Society of Missouri, Kansas City Research Center.

to landscape architecture through working with Kessler on the city's parks and boulevards plan.[21] Nichols benefited from the connection to Olmsted that brought him Hare's talents as a landscape architect, but more noteworthy is the small and close-knit world of landscape architecture in this time period. As Nichols would look to professionalize real estate development, these contacts in landscape architecture modeled for Nichols the beginnings of an allied field.

Nichols's landscape architects used site design and street layouts to sell buyers a vision of high-end suburban living. Though Hare and Hare's practice would never be as influential as Kessler's, the firm designed features in Nichols's subdivisions that reflect a new approach to real estate development. Their first project for Nichols was the small Hampstead Gardens subdivision. Blocks were generally oriented to run east-west, as in Nichols's previous projects, accentuating the hierarchy of arterial roads. The east-west orientation also allowed for ideal sun exposure on the majority of homes that would face north-south. More generally, if a gridded city plan would give equal importance to all roads, suburban superblocks create a hierarchy of roads—major arterials for faster traffic and smaller neighborhood streets for residential enclaves. In Hampstead Gardens, smaller neighborhood streets branch off Ward Parkway. By curving the roads gently, Nichols slowed traffic on them, and encouraged drivers to use the arterials instead of the indirect smaller streets. The plat introduced a few tiny triangular parks at three-way intersections to direct car traffic and soften the view. These small triangular parks became a recurring theme in the Country Club District, defining the area as automobile-friendly and showcasing Nichols's collection of public art. Curved streets, Nichols believed in an echo of the picturesque, offered an "ever-changing vista" that was "more pleasing to the eye," as his son later recalled his father saying on drives through the district.[22] Unspoken but easily inferred is his dislike of the monotonous, gridiron, pothole-ridden city, conjuring too much of the hard edges of capitalism. By contrast, his well-paved roads and sidewalks were all highlighted in advertisements for the district to illustrate readiness for the family car.[23]

Early in their collaboration with Nichols, Hare and Hare designed the high-end Mission Hills subdivision, a 240-acre development of large lots on the Kansas side of the state line.[24] Platted in 1912, Mission Hills was bisected by a creek that divided the residential area from the country club and golf course to the north. The traffic arteries that continued into the subdivision from the east curved to follow the topography and creek, creating the visual interest Nichols liked. One exception at the center of the subdivision was "Colonial Court," a block-long divided road with a formal planted median. Triangular parks at intersections were again laid out in accordance with the turning radius of an automobile. Lots were very large, some with as much as 175 feet of street frontage, and varied in size. They were intended to draw high-paying buyers. Nichols also planted thousands of trees in the subdivision between 1912 and 1919.[25] Since the subdivision was in Kansas (not Missouri) and in an unincorporated area, all services—sewers, water, and electricity—were provided by the Nichols Company.

Nichols's picturesque schemes became more confident as time passed. His seeming success in selling lots, the larger sites he acquired, and the ongoing lack of city oversight on unincorporated land allowed him to continue the experimentation. By the early 1920s, Nichols's street patterns regularly disregarded the preexisting grids within tracts of land—atypical for residential development at the time.[26] In the Armour Hills development, Hare and Hare designed a subdivision that continued the numbered streets running roughly east-west on the site, but modified them to curve gently and break the grid's regularity. Like a landform palimpsest, an aerial photograph of the development early in its construction shows a straight line of trees from the previous grid pattern that covered the site, in contrast with the new, curving street pattern that disregards the older plan. The plat plan responds to the relatively flat topography of the site and the lack of any outstanding landscape features by highlighting the slight changes in topography with the lines of the streets and transitioning from a regular, gridded street system on the western boundary to a more curvilinear scheme in the center, and then returning to a regularized street pattern at the eastern boundary. The site design distinguished the Country Club District from the straight lines and gridiron plan of Kansas City's downtown. But

A straight line of trees suggests older farmland property lines and contrasts with the new curving streets. Aerial photograph looking east from Wornall Road at Sixty-Seventh and Sixty-Eighth Streets, Armour Hills, Country Club District, 1925. Courtesy of the State Historical Society of Missouri, Kansas City Research Center.

landscape architecture was not enough in itself to maintain property values over time, and Nichols looked to legal mechanisms to stabilize value and to further increase exclusivity, both racial and economic.

Creating Exclusivity: Deed Restrictions and Homeowners' Associations

Deed restrictions are well known as the real estate industry's most explicitly racist tool. Racially restrictive clauses in deed restrictions produced an intentionally seg-regated landscape that white power elites wanted for their city in order to maintain racial, hegemonic control. This process was not accidental, and its repercussions for the United States continue today. A Supreme Court ruling (1948, *Shelley v. Kraemer*) might have ended enforcement, but as other scholars have shown, that decision did not end residential segregation—other mechanisms enabled a racialized landscape to continue.[27] Nichols, lauded as he is in Kansas City for his many good works, actively helped construct the racialized landscape of Kansas City by putting racially restrictive clauses into the deeds of all the properties he sold.[28]

Nichols used deed restrictions to do many things; he promoted the use of deed restrictions to control not just the race of the inhabitants but also land use, setbacks, minimum costs, construction standards, and materials. Nichols saw the deed restriction as another tool, in addition to zoning, that could control urban development. City builders and planners had struggled for generations over the best ways to control development, and in the early twentieth century two competing ideas rose to prominence: zoning and deed restrictions. Zoning offered a public process—a government policy that could control land use and direct new construction that could align with a broader city plan. The deed restriction offered another method—a private practice, essentially a contract between buyer and seller, that could control many things from land use to building setbacks. Enforcement relied on individuals or a development company bringing suit against others' infractions. Nichols gave a speech to a conference of city planners in 1916 describing how he saw the two tools, zoning and deed restrictions, as mutually supportive.[29] Real estate developers were keen to understand what the deed restriction, as a private mechanism for controlling development, could offer, and suburban developers like Nichols were at the forefront of exploring its possibilities. He saw that by controlling aesthetics, he could influence a neighborhood's financial stability and increase its market value, and so he designed deed restrictions that dictated paint colors, materials, and landscaping. Other developers tested similar ideas; Nichols mainly copied developers of high-end subdivisions before him, like Llewellyn Park, New Jersey, an elite planned residential community from the 1850s; Lake Forest, Illinois; Olmsted's Riverside, Illinois; and mentor Edward Bouton's Roland Park in Baltimore. The Olmsted Company's extensive catalog of restrictions was published in *Landscape Architecture* magazine in 1925 as a template for others to follow.[30] That the venerated Olmsted firm published its restrictions shows what currency this discussion held for other practitioners. Even though he was not ahead of the Olmsted firm, Nichols was in good company. No other developer looked to extend and finesse this device to more middle-class homes, and no other developer had found a way to extend the life of the restrictions with automatic renewals.[31] Nichols did, and he did so to secure his own corner of the market in Kansas City.

Other developers were using deed restrictions when Nichols began subdividing land in Kansas City, but only unevenly and without legal teeth.[32] Nichols filed deed restrictions with his plats (the publicly recorded maps of a subdivided land) before a single lot in the Country Club District had been sold. Legally, this expansion of the use of deed restrictions—combining blanket restrictions with the neighborhood (the plat) and individual restrictions with each lot—offered new and enduring possibilities. A deed is a private contract between buyer and seller; the restrictions or special covenants attached to that deed by the seller are said to "run with the land"—that is, these restrictions, once established by this private transaction, are attached to the land itself and remain, often as public record, for as long as the contract outlines.

Legal historians have traced the way these restrictions became codified in law, case by case, from the late nineteenth century into the early twentieth century before their legal grounding was established.[33] More recently, historians have mostly (and rightly) focused on the racially restrictive covenants attached to deeds, but deed restrictions more generally can and have performed in a variety of ways, establishing land use, setbacks, community provisions, and architectural design standards. Plats were typically used as selling tools by developers to show customers how lots were laid out in the area. As private contracts, deed restrictions were not typically filed with the plats to the city or county. But Nichols realized the advantages of filing some restrictions with the plat to show customers his commitment to high-class residential development. It proved consistency to the buyers. Nichols's earliest deed restrictions controlled land use by allowing only residential use, they controlled class by setting a minimum construction cost for the not-yet-built houses, and they controlled the urban fabric by mandating setbacks from the street and orientation of the building.

While the restrictions solved one set of problems, another remained. Developers had to pay for the maintenance of large tracts of land, not only during the development phase, but potentially for a much longer term, after most of the lots were sold and houses built and occupied. This uncertain and long-lagging cost was a major stumbling block for subdividers, and none before Nichols had discovered a satisfactory solution. While selling the first lots, the development company would maintain the area and provide city services in unincorporated areas, with the hopes that through annexation city governments would take over eventually. Deeds could then be amended. Purchasers had no guarantees, and the riders on sales contracts that other developers used had no longevity. But Nichols used the deed restriction to recuse his company from the maintenance costs (borne by residents instead) and extend provisions in perpetuity. Nichols also invented the homeowners' association as we know it. Upon purchase of a property, a buyer was automatically given membership in the association, which charged assessments based on lot size. The association's responsibilities included maintenance and upkeep of common areas and parks, as well as overseeing utilities and services like snow removal. In order for this to happen, the associations had to have the legal powers to provide or contract for city services. Otherwise, a well-maintained neighborhood could fall into disrepair if the development company went bankrupt, and property values would fall. With deed restrictions and homeowners' associations, Nichols innovated and employed increasingly sophisticated legal techniques for controlling development that other developers would copy and redeploy in similar and in vastly different environments.

Building up his holdings, Nichols had accumulated over 1,000 acres by 1908, and over the following decades those acres would be built out by home builders and owners. Nichols began advertising his larger plans in the *Kansas City Sun* by highlighting the large size of the development and the deed restrictions as protection against market instability. "Have You Seen the Country Club District? 1,000 Acres Restricted for Those Who Want Protection," the advertisement read. And in a subsequent company brochure: "In the Country Club District you are given the protection that goes with 'a thousand acres restricted.'"[34] The limitations on property use and buildings translated into good sales practices for the Nichols Company and success that was lauded nationally. Careful to avoid negativity, the language of Nichols's ads suggests the exclusivity accompanying a members-only club and responded to consumers' concerns that in a volatile real estate market rife with speculators, their investment in a property might disappear. The substance of the restrictions—setbacks, common space, racial exclusion, and land use limitations—implicitly played off those concerns and were the central focus of Nichols's sales pitch.[35]

Conclusion

Real estate, Nichols declared, was "unstable merchandise."[36] The goods he and his fellow real estate developers sold were subject to market volatility outside their control. He believed that the Country Club District was "a practical demonstration of the value of good planning, as is shown by its effect upon the banks and insurance companies, simply because they feel that by our planning we are securing values, stabilizing values."[37] Developers and bankers believed stricter restrictions were favored by property owners because they were designed to stabilize that "unstable merchandise."[38] Without zoning regulations or deed restrictions, and without the authority of a city planning department, a home buyer would have no assured expectations for the development of neighboring properties. Not only would the bank be more likely to renew a loan on a covenant-restricted property, so the thinking went, but noxious industrial or commercial tenants could not move next door. While these protections offered the developer the obvious incentive of greater profit and interest in the property, and have been criticized as private governments (for whites only), they afforded the buyer significant benefits as well. Residents of the Country Club District would promote the benefits of the homeowners' association, and in 1944, the executive secretary published an article in *House Beautiful* examining how the restrictions supported by the association kept the neighborhood in line.

The application of techniques from landscape architecture to Nichols's subdivisions offered greater marketing potential for the Nichols Company. Company advertisements highlighted these features to potential buyers, and later assessments of the district would praise Nichols's achievements with regard to landscape architecture as different from the "ordinary way to prepare this tract for building," which "would have been to lay it off with streets and alleys in rectilinear fashion, without regard to its topography, the adaptability of its building sites or its natural lines of communications. Hilltops would be graded down to fill up hollows. Streets would cut ugly gashes in hills and go across 'fills' in the valleys. Trees in the way . . . would be cut down."[39] Nichols's subdivisions have held their value, and scholars agree that comprehensive site planning and deed restrictions explain a significant part of their high value today.[40] Nichols's vision for landscape design set his subdivisions apart from the "ordinary way." It also laid the groundwork for the legal and managerial codes that would regulate future development and land use on the site. The curving streets that follow the topography, triangular mini-parks that ease traffic flow at intersections, and attention to landscaping created a visual tableau that attracted buyers and provided copy for newspaper ads. From Nichols's whitewashed, neocolonial sales outpost, potential buyers could survey the landscape and imagine stately homes and mature trees behind each sidewalk. And with the assurances of the deed restrictions and homeowners' associations, buyers were insulated from the risks of a volatile real estate market. Understanding J. C. Nichols's role in Kansas City in the early decades of the twentieth century sheds light on how the shape of Kansas City informed broader patterns of suburbanization in the United States. Nichols would go on to shape federal policy as the founding president of the National Association of Home Builders. Nichols's deed restrictions were the model that the Federal Housing Administration would recommend other developers to follow in *The Community Builder's Handbook* (1947).[41] Through this document, the subdivisions he built in Kansas City influenced subdivisions across the continent. But more than this, studying Nichols sheds light on how real estate developers saw the relationship between city and suburb, and between private market controls on development and the public powers of city planning. As historians have explored the aesthetic underpinnings of the nineteenth-century romantic suburb as a precursor to mass suburbia, they have said less about how it related to the cultural economy of suburban landscapes. Considering Nichols's explicit linking of aesthetics and market economics, the aesthetics of suburbia depended as much on cultural constructions of the picturesque as they did on managing the risks of the market.

Notes

1. J. C. Nichols, "Financial Effect of Good Planning in Land Subdivision," in *Proceedings of the Eighth National Conference on City Planning* (New York: National Conference on City Planning, 1916), 37.

2. This was a very different approach from that of city planner Harland Bartholomew, which focused on city planning as ideally separated from private business initiatives and more ensconced in the public sector. Joseph Heathcott, "'The Whole City Is Our Laboratory': Harland Bartholomew and the Production of Urban Knowledge," *Journal of Planning History* 4, no. 4 (November 2005), 322–355. For more on Nichols's relationship to the discourse of city planning, see Sara Stevens, *Developing Expertise: Architecture and Real Estate in Metropolitan America* (New Haven: Yale University Press, 2016), chap. 1.

3. He borrowed from Peter Larson, William Rockhill Nelson's foreman. J. C. Nichols, "Jesse Clyde Nichols (1880–1950) Memoir with Epilogue by Ethel V. Treshadding," 13, Collection KC0206, State Historical Society of Missouri, Kansas City Research Center, Kansas City, Missouri (hereafter SHSM-KC).

4. William H. Wilson, *The City Beautiful Movement in Kansas City* (Columbia: University of Missouri Press, 1964). The City Beautiful movement, relying on staid, symmetrical neoclassical designs for monumental civic centers, captured the attention of American city planners in the decades following the 1893 World's Columbian Exposition in Chicago.

5. William S. Worley, *J. C. Nichols and the Shaping of Kansas City: Innovation in Planned Residential Communities* (Columbia: University of Missouri Press, 1990), 96; Wilson, *The City Beautiful Movement in Kansas City.*

6. Worley, *J. C. Nichols and the Shaping of Kansas City*, 29–31, 52–53; Brad Pearson and Robert Pearson, *The J. C. Nichols Chronicle: The Authorized Story of the Man, His Company, and His Legacy, 1880–1994* (Lawrence: University Press of Kansas, 1994), 30–32.

7. Quoted in Gary Molyneaux, "Planned Land Use Change in an Urban Setting: The J. C. Nichols Company and the Country Club District of Kansas City" (PhD diss., University of Illinois at Urbana Champaign, 1979), 62; Wilson, *The City Beautiful Movement in Kansas City*, 20. See also the advertisement by the J. C. Nichols Company, "1,000 Acres [Advertisement]," *Kansas City Star*, June 12, 1908, 13.

8. That is, the existing country club with a golf course, before Nichols invented the Country Club District of single-family homes and Country Club shopping center by the same name. Worley, *J. C. Nichols and the Shaping of Kansas City*, 59–62.

9. Called Bismark Place, Nichols advertised it in Nelson's newspaper as being in the Rockhill District, a claim to which Nelson took offense. Ibid., 67–69.

10. David Schuyler, *The New Urban Landscape: The Redefinition of City Form in Nineteenth-Century America* (Baltimore: Johns Hopkins University Press, 1986), 37–56.

11. Hare and Hare archives, microfilm volume 1, 115–117, Collection KC0206, SHSM-KC.

12. Ann E. Komara, "The Glass Wall: Gendering the American Society of Landscape Architects," *Studies in the Decorative Arts* 8 (October 2000), 22–30. A master's thesis also addresses the question of gender in Nichols's work: Clinton D. Lawson, "Suburban Cowboy: J. C. Nichols, Masculinity, Landscape and Memory in the Shaping of an American Neighborhood" (MA thesis, University of Missouri–Kansas City, 2012).

13. Worley, *J. C. Nichols and the Shaping of Kansas City*, 70, 79–80, 94.

14. Ibid., 70. See "Restrictions Book," J. C. Nichols archive, Box 279, page 115, J. C. Nichols Company Records (K0106), SHSM-KC.

15. Kessler biography, from Kessler papers on microfilm, George Kessler Papers (K0355), SHSM-KC. Kessler worked for the St. Louis and San Francisco Railroad as head gardener, designing parks at railroad stations, after he worked for Central Park. He also designed a section of Hyde Park, a fashionable neighborhood in Kansas City that was financed by the same team that Edward Bouton was involved with. Worley, *J. C. Nichols and the Shaping of Kansas City*, 53.

16. Worley, *J. C. Nichols and the Shaping of Kansas City*, 56. Worley is responding to claims

in Wilson, *The City Beautiful Movement in Kansas City*. See also William H. Wilson, *The City Beautiful Movement* (Baltimore: Johns Hopkins University Press, 1989).

17. Pearson and Pearson, *The J. C. Nichols Chronicle*, 49. Platted in 1909, Sunset Hill also had Nichols's first cul-de-sac at 51st Street. This was not the first cul-de-sac in the country (Tuxedo Park in New Jersey had some of the first), but Nichols's use of this device is interesting given that New Urbanists, who bemoan the cul-de-sac, adore Nichols.

18. Ibid., 51, 280, note 215.

19. Ibid., 49.

20. A. B. McDonald, "A Home District Beautiful," *Ladies Home Journal*, February 1921.

21. Kessler departed to design the fairgrounds for the Louisiana Purchase Exhibition in St. Louis in 1904. Hare and Hare was one of the first landscape architecture firms in the country, alongside John Nolen, the Olmsteds, and Henry Vincent Hubbard. Olmsted recommended Hare and Hare to Nichols on a trip to the East Coast in 1913. Formal education in landscape architecture was still very new when Herbert Hare attended school (he did not graduate); the Harvard program in landscape architecture was the first in the country. The father, Sidney Hare, had worked as a civil engineer for Kansas City, beginning first as a "rodman," progressing to draftsman, levelman, and transitman; when Kessler was hired to do the parks and boulevards plan, he consulted with Hare to obtain local knowledge. The exposure to concepts of landscape design that Hare received through Kessler convinced him to change careers, working first in cemetery design and eventually opening his own landscape architecture firm, with his son later joining the practice. Hare opened his office in 1902; his son Herbert joined the practice in 1910. Microfilm volume 1, 115–118, Hare and Hare Company Records (K0206), SHSM-KC. Norman T. Newton, *Design on the Land: The Development of Landscape Architecture* (Cambridge, Mass.: Belknap Press of Harvard University Press, 1971), 416.

22. Pearson and Pearson, *The J. C. Nichols Chronicle*, 49.

23. Ibid., 49, 51, 280, note 15.

24. There are references that point to George Kessler and John Nolen as additional designers of Mission Hills, but the drawings in the archive are all by Hare and Hare. See the draft chapter of "The Historical Context of Mission Hills Development," in folder "F Residential–Mission Hills," Box 170, Collection KC0206, SHSM-KC. Construction began in 1912 and continued through 1919.

25. See draft chapter, "The Historical Context of Mission Hills Development," 8.

26. Community Builders' Council of the Urban Land Institute, *The Community Builders Handbook* (Washington, DC, 1947); Robert M. Fogelson, *Bourgeois Nightmares: Suburbia, 1870–1930* (New Haven: Yale University Press, 2005).

27. *Shelley et ux. v. Kraemer et ux; McGhee et ux. v. Sipes et al.*, 334 US 1 (1948).

28. Other scholars have addressed this. See Kevin Fox Gotham, *Race, Real Estate, and Uneven Development: The Kansas City Experience, 1900–2010* (Albany: State University of New York Press, 2002); Worley, *J. C. Nichols and the Shaping of Kansas City*, 144–155. For discussion of early twentieth-century developers, including Nichols, on the inclusion of Jews in race-based restrictions, see "Stenographic Report of [the] First Annual Conference of the Developers [of] High-Class Residential Property," Jemison Company Papers, Department of

Manuscripts and University Archives, Olin Library, Cornell University, Ithaca, N.Y., 1917, B52–B53; and Paige Glotzer, "Exclusion in Arcadia: How Suburban Developers Circulated Ideas about Discrimination, 1890–1950," *Journal of Urban History* 41, no. 3, 2015, 479–494. On the legacy of racism in real estate today, see Beryl Satter, *Family Properties: How the Struggle over Race and Real Estate Transformed Chicago and Urban America* (New York: Metropolitan Books, 2009); Ta-Nehisi Coates, "The Case for Reparations," *The Atlantic*, May 21, 2014, http://www.theatlantic.com/magazine/archive/2014/06/the-case-for-reparations/361631/ (accessed May 10, 2016).

29. Nichols, "Financial Effect of Good Planning in Land Subdivision," 108–109.

30. Henry Vincent Hubbard, "Land Subdivision Restrictions: Notes and Table," *Landscape Architecture* 16, no. 1 (October 1925): 53–54. Since the Olmsted firm was in business for over a century and kept good records, tracking their use of deed restrictions is much easier than tracking other developers' use of the tool. Earlier examples, like Llewellyn Park, Lake Forest, and Tuxedo Park, left few records for comparison. See also Worley, *J. C. Nichols and the Shaping of Kansas City*, 26; and Fogelson, *Bourgeois Nightmares*. Nichols had discussed deed restrictions with other developers who had worked with Olmsted at least as early as 1917, so he was likely familiar with them. Nichols had also been in conversation with Bouton since 1911. See "Stenographic Report"; Glotzer, "Exclusion in Arcadia."

31. Worley, *J. C. Nichols and the Shaping of Kansas City*, 124.

32. Worley, *J. C. Nichols and the Shaping of Kansas City*, chap. 5. For a more detailed history on the use of deed restrictions in the United States, see Fogelson, *Bourgeois Nightmares*.

33. William P. Stoebuck, "Running Covenants: An Analytical Primer," *Washington Law Review* 52, no. 4 (October 1977): 861–921.

34. Worley, *J. C. Nichols and the Shaping of Kansas City*, 124.

35. In a longer discussion about marketing fear in the suburbs, historian Robert M. Fogelson gives a vivid description of discussions between developers on how to instruct salesmen to use a language of "protections" rather than "restrictions" in discussing deed restrictions. See Fogelson, *Bourgeois Nightmares*, chap. 2.

36. J. C. Nichols, "Home Building and Subdividing Department," *National Real Estate Journal* (August 27, 1923): 27.

37. Nichols, "Financial Effect of Good Planning in Land Subdivision," 95.

38. Ibid., 137.

39. McDonald, "A Home District Beautiful." See also draft chapter of "The Historical Context of Mission Hills Development."

40. Worley, *J. C. Nichols and the Shaping of Kansas City*, 303; Mary Corbin Sies, "Paradise Retained: An Analysis of Persistence in Planned, Exclusive Suburbs, 1880–1980," *Planning Perspectives* 12, no. 2 (January 1, 1997): 165–191, see especially 177, 179–180.

41. Stevens, *Developing Expertise*, 60–63. Community Builders' Council of the Urban Land Institute, *The Community Builders Handbook* (Washington, DC: Urban Land Institute, 1947); Marc Allan Weiss, *The Rise of the Community Builders: The American Real Estate Industry and Urban Land Planning* (New York: Columbia University Press, 1987), 157.

CHAPTER FOUR

"A Magnificent Tower of Strength"

The Federal Reserve Bank of Kansas City

Jaclyn Miller

On November 16, 1921, the Federal Reserve Bank of Kansas City opened the doors of its new headquarters at 925 Grand Avenue. The 300-foot skyscraper became the city's tallest landmark. The building featured both classical and modern elements, including a colonnade of Doric columns at its base and a "field of windows" looking into sixteen floors of airy, open offices. Encased in stone, the building strove for "simplicity and dignity" as well as for "strength and solidity."[1] A pair of panels featuring the seal and eagle, "symbolizing the power of a Government institution," and "figures with upraised arms typifying the Spirit of Commerce and the Spirit of Industry," flanked the Grand Avenue doors and finished the imposing effect of the bank. The marriage of traditional stylistic elements with the modernity of skyscraper design and the pathbreaking scale of a government-sponsored central banking institution embodied the substantial power the bank would wield in Kansas City's financial future. The officers of the bank took understandable pride in the building. They intended passersby to understand that "here stands a building representing some thing greater and more important than an ordinary commercial institution."[2]

When the US Congress established the Federal Reserve System with the enactment of the Glass-Owen Act on December 23, 1913, it built on over a decade's momentum within banking and reform circles. The nation had not had a central banking system since President Andrew Jackson rejected the charter of the Second Bank of the United States and it disbanded in 1836; a mixed system of state and national banks with diverse regulations had since developed. The lack of a central banking system created a number of problems for the national financial structure, including the uneven flow of credit toward New York and away from the interior,

⊛ FEDERAL RESERVE BANK OF KANSAS CITY ⊛

Sketch of the new Federal Reserve Bank of Kansas City, 925 Grand
Avenue, December 31, 1920. Courtesy of FRASER, an online
records repository operated by the Federal Reserve Bank of St. Louis.

and the propensity for the whole economy to dissolve into crisis when the stock market stuttered. Lawmakers had witnessed this most recently in the Panic of 1907. The design of the Federal Reserve system, with twelve regional banks located in smaller cities such as Minneapolis and Kansas City, as well as in the large financial centers of New York and Chicago, dispersed the power of the nation's elite bankers. Many bankers and politicians in the nation's interior favored the new system, which promised to distribute credit among farmers, merchants, and industrialists throughout the country.[3] The Fifth District representative from Kansas believed that the regional banks would ensure "elasticity and stability" in the nation's currency, more equitable interest rates among all regions, and new opportunities for the "little fellow."[4] President Woodrow Wilson equally recognized the momentous step, commenting upon the opening of the Federal Reserve banks in November 1914 that the system would correct "fundamental wrongs," so that "all the differences will clear away."[5]

The Federal Reserve Bank of Kansas City was supposed to provide a more secure and equitable system of distributing credit for agricultural, industrial, and commercial development throughout its region. The institution's goal was to serve as the "banker's bank"—to purchase or "discount" the loans of member banks so they had the liquidity for further local investment. Encouraging member banks to provide adequate credit to the Great Plains—a region economic elites had dismissed as the "hinterlands"—would allow it to flourish under its own financial power. Residents of the region viewed Kansas City as their "gateway" market and financial center. This perception marked the city's increasing importance within the national economy and shaped the manner in which the Federal Reserve Bank viewed its own power. The Federal Reserve System, however, struggled to stabilize the regional agricultural economy during the post–World War I readjustment period and the Great Depression. Its policy of raising interest rates and depressing prices alienated residents of the broader region. As the economic consequences spread to other industries, unstable banks closed by the thousands in Kansas City's Federal Reserve District (District Ten) alone. For a financial institution now viewed as a crucial policy-making and economy-molding institution, this era of distress presents an interesting paradox. It took decades to shape the power the Fed now holds, despite early promoters' best efforts to identify the central bank as a "magnificent tower of strength."[6]

The Organization of the Federal Reserve Bank of Kansas City

The selection of Kansas City as a site for a regional Federal Reserve Bank in 1914 confirmed its economic strength as a western "gateway city," second only to Chicago and equal to St. Louis and Minneapolis.[7] Agriculture constituted a central pillar of Kansas City's financial success; the railroad hub shipped grains and livestock, and the city developed large meatpacking, flour, and other food-processing industries. Wholesale and retail commerce joined agriculture and industry as the foundations of Kansas City's economic power. The city's status as an emerging center for business interests and financial connections with several states to its west formed a key part of the argument for it to receive a Federal Reserve Bank. William Rockhill Nelson, publisher of the Kansas City Star, represented the spirit of city boosters in writing to the committee that would ultimately choose Kansas City for a Reserve center. He urged visiting committee members to view the "West Bottoms which receives a steady stream of cattle from the whole West up to the Rocky Mountains," the "immense industrial development that is going on in North Kansas City," and the "New Union Station," which symbolized the railroads' commitment to shipping the region's goods through Kansas City.[8] These institutions represented the city's growth as a commercial center and its promise to maintain a strong stake in the regional economy.

Many in the Great Plains relished the prospect of establishing a Federal Reserve Bank in their vicinity, but Kansas City was not assured of selection. Denver offered the chief alternative, and its proponents argued that the Colorado city might host a Federal Reserve Bank and preside over a Mountain West district consisting of Montana, Idaho, Colorado, Wyoming, Utah, Arizona, New Mexico, and the western part of Texas.[9] Under this plan, Kansas, Missouri, and the central Great Plains states would belong to one of the St. Louis, Chicago, or Minneapolis districts. Sentiments of bankers within the proposed Denver district, however, helped sway the organizational committee toward a Kansas City Reserve Bank. J. M. Williams of the Citizens State Bank of Lamar, Colorado, wrote to a colleague in Kansas City, "We, of Eastern Colorado and Northern New Mexico, look to Kansas City as our financial center, which supplies us with practically all the money used in our great sheep and cattle business, which is the greatest business we have in this territory." Williams noted that livestock naturally moved eastward on railways through the Arkansas River Valley, while funds for the business flowed westward from Kansas City. As an example, the banker cited his bank's recent financing of 170,000 sheep (nearly a third of the regional business). Out of a total of $680,000 in financing, more than $500,000 "was furnished by Kansas City banks either directly or through commission men."[10] A banker from Roswell, New Mexico, argued, "We feel in this part of the country that Kansas City could serve our needs better than any other city located any place in the country from the fact that we get our mail there about one day quicker than to any other point that we are able to use."[11] Mail service was important for the banking business, which needed rapid and safe delivery of currency, loan documents, and cleared checks.

Similar reasoning defined the official testimony for Kansas City's hearing before the Reserve Bank Organization Committee. Kansas City representatives included a map of mail routes and delivery times in their file, along with a map of banks in

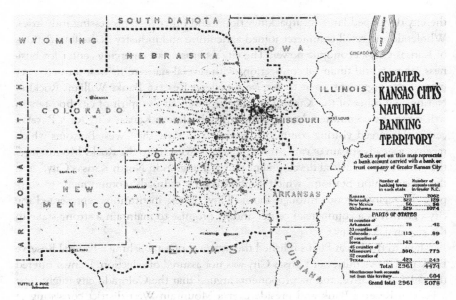

Kansas City's proponents offered several maps demonstrating the city's central economic position within the region, 1914. Courtesy of FRASER.

the region already holding correspondent relationships with Kansas City banks. In this system, state and national banks in the countryside made deposits with city banks; city bankers could use these funds as the basis for their own loans, but they remained readily recoverable—and thus liquid—in case the depositing bank needed to meet immediate community needs.[12] John R. Mulvane, a politically powerful banker from Topeka, Kansas, noted that his bank did 95 percent of its business with Kansas City banks. Kansas State Bank Commissioner Charles M. Sawyer added that 900 out of 930 state banks in Kansas kept accounts in Kansas City banks.[13] The Federal Reserve Bank would not serve as a commercial bank receiving deposits and making direct loans to consumers, but its function built upon the city's strength in correspondence banking. By purchasing bank loans, a process known as discounting, the central bank would also add to the liquidity of financial institutions throughout its district. Visual representations of Kansas City's economic reach, the testimony of area bankers, and discussions of Kansas City's sixteen major rail lines, thirty-two subordinate rail lines, and superb freight facilities ultimately helped to shape Kansas City's Federal Reserve District Ten.[14] As Verne Hostutler, the cashier for the Centerville State Bank in Kansas, concluded, Denver might seem "from a geographical standpoint, to be the logical location for a bank" west of St. Louis. But business concerns suggested otherwise: "The bank clearings show that Kansas City could serve many times the business interests."[15]

Maps of money, mail, and commodities flowing into Kansas City underscored its status as a gateway of commerce. Letters addressed to the organization committee from Kansas City and from bankers and business interests in parts of Missouri, Kansas, Nebraska, Colorado, New Mexico, and Oklahoma drew upon this rhetoric. E. G. Boughner, cashier at the First National Bank of Natoma, Kansas, commented, "Kansas City is to be the 'New York City,' the center of business of this great agricultural country in the center of the U.S."[16] J. C. Hopper, president of the Citizens National Bank of Ness City, Kansas, stated it even more conclusively. He wrote to William Gibbs McAdoo, secretary of the treasury and chairman of the Reserve Bank Organization Committee on January 14, 1914: "The railroads of this western country are focused at Kansas City, and it is the gateway of a great territory, young in development, but with possibilities beyond even the imagination of men."[17]

Kansas City itself would gain a great deal from the establishment of a Federal Reserve Bank, not least the pride of recognition as a financial and commercial center of the nation. Among those writing letters to the organization committee were Kansas City associations such as the Commercial Club, the Cooperative Club, the Millers' Club, the Motor Car Dealers Association, the Life Underwriters' Association of Kansas City, Missouri, the Livestock Exchange, the Rotary Club, the Southwestern Lumbermen's Association (which held its meeting in Kansas City in January of 1914), and the Western Retail Implement, Vehicle, and Hardware Association. R. J. Thresher, president of the Kansas City Board of Trade, made it clear that increased credit operations close at hand would grease the wheels of growing industries: "This is the largest primary winter wheat market in the United States. Last year we handled over seventy million bushels of grain. It is the second largest live stock and packing center. These interests together with various other industries which are rapidly growing demand the best possible banking facilities."[18]

The Commerce Trust Company, presided over by William T. Kemper as president and future Federal Reserve Bank governor Jo Zach Miller Jr. as vice president, issued a letter in support of the city's bid. Kemper was among the dignitaries present to speak for the city and region at the organization committee hearing on January 23, 1914.[19] It was clear that designating Kansas City as a Reserve Bank site would build upon the region's current financial affiliations, contribute to the economic development of the agricultural and natural resource sectors in the region, and shape the industrial and commercial development of the city itself. Kansas City's selection as one of twelve regional banks proved its coming-of-age as a true gateway for financial and commercial interests in the West.[20] While Denver, Omaha, and Oklahoma City would ultimately host branches of the Federal Reserve, Kansas City received the true prize as the district's headquarters. Residents of the city expressed pride at its new status. Senator James A. Reed noted before the Commercial Club that whereas few had known of the city before, now it "is recognized by the best authorities as a factor which must be considered in any scheme of business plan-

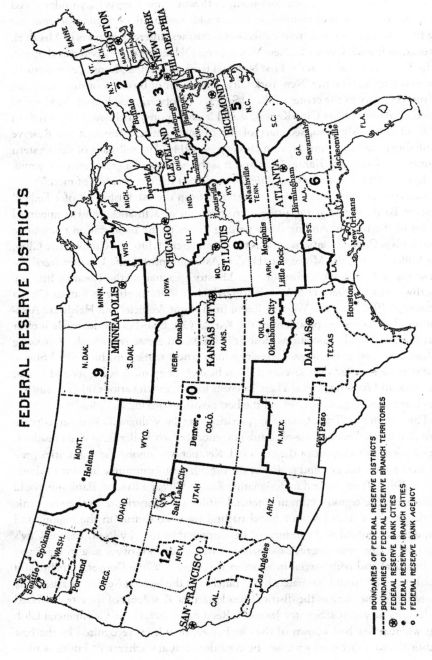

FEDERAL RESERVE DISTRICTS

BOUNDARIES OF FEDERAL RESERVE DISTRICTS
BOUNDARIES OF FEDERAL RESERVE BRANCH TERRITORIES
⊛ FEDERAL RESERVE BANK CITIES
• FEDERAL RESERVE BRANCH CITIES
○ FEDERAL RESERVE BANK AGENCY

The final delineation of the twelve Federal Reserve Districts, October 1922. Courtesy of FRASER.

ning."[21] The *Kansas Citian,* a journal published by the Commercial Club, demonstrated high hopes for future development as a result of the founding of the Federal Reserve Bank of Kansas City: "With the richest area capable of unlimited development, of any American city . . . this metropolis must become greater and more extensive. . . . The forecast of the committee that named it for a Reserve Bank will be justified by the outcome."[22]

City boosters envisioned promising civic developments resulting from the founding of the Federal Reserve Bank of Kansas City, but it also had important implications for the conduct of banking throughout the district. The framers of the Federal Reserve System intended it to fulfill several vital purposes of a government-regulated but privately held central bank. Its diffuse structure theoretically would ensure funds for all sections of the nation. As the guardian of the national gold supply, the system could move credit and currency quickly around the system to meet emergency needs. World War I demonstrated the importance of this function. In a period of incredible upheaval in international financial markets, the Federal Reserve allowed for the transferal of immediate credit among international banks and industries without necessitating the movement of actual gold. As Kansas City banker and American Bankers Association president P. W. Goebel commented in April 1917, the Federal Reserve enabled the conscription of American finances to the democratic cause and helped make the United States a financial leader for the world. As Goebel put it, "In the face of a declaration of war with a world power, not a trace of uneasiness has been apparent in financial circles. We can thank God that the federal reserve bank was established when it was."[23] For many observers, the Federal Reserve's response to World War I demonstrated its ability to navigate perilous economic conditions and prevent nationwide panic.

The Federal Reserve also facilitated financial services for member banks that paid in capital to the Federal Reserve Bank. It did not transact business directly with the public, but rather served as a "banker's bank."[24] It aided regional financial institutions in discounting their agricultural, commercial, and industrial loans, providing liquid currency in exchange for holding these assets. It also served as a clearinghouse for bank checks, provided wire services to expedite the transfer of funds among member banks, and offered educational and professionalization services to bankers across the nation. In its regulatory capacity, the Federal Reserve performed examinations of banks throughout the system and ensured that its members met reserve requirements based on their deposits.[25] Table 4.1 illustrates the clearinghouse function of the Federal Reserve Bank of Kansas City between 1919 and 1921. The central bank's handling of checks from city and country (rural) banks makes it clear that although country banks were more numerous and submitted millions more items for clearing than city banks, the latter institutions submitted items of substantially higher value. While submitting between 78 and 85 percent fewer items than country banks, city banks represented, on average, 36 percent greater value in their

Table 4.1. Clearinghouse items for city and country banks in District Ten, 1919–1921

	Year		
	1919	*1920*	*1921*
City Banks' Items	2,002,947	6,078,269	6,291,000
City Banks' Amount ($)	3,392,275,705	6,320,074,000	4,682,326,000
Country Banks' Items	9,173,290	40,238,898	43,365,000
Country Banks' Amount ($)	2,211,792,134	4,227,488,000	2,740,027,000
Total Items	11,176,237	46,317,167	49,656,000
Total Amount ($)	5,604,067,839	10,547,562,000	7,422,353,000

Data compiled from the *Annual Reports of the Federal Reserve Bank of Kansas City, 1919–1921*.

cleared checks. The Federal Reserve performed clearinghouse and wire services free of charge, as a perk for member banks. Discounting loans did earn the central bank interest, but as a not-for-profit institution it distributed the profits (after paying operating expenses and a federal franchise tax) to member banks based on their capital stock in the bank.

From the standpoint of banking operations and revenues, the Federal Reserve Bank of Kansas City performed well through 1921. Its directors managed to build the new headquarters, despite initial objections from a few prominent Kansas City businessmen. Robert A. Long, William T. Kemper, and J. C. Nichols opposed the construction of a skyscraper taller than the R. A. Long and Commerce Trust Company buildings. Nichols suggested that the bank "should purchase more frontage and build wider rather than higher than adjacent buildings," preventing the skyline from looking "uneven." It took several months for Kemper, a longtime friend and colleague of Federal Reserve Bank governor Jo Zach Miller Jr., to assure the Federal Reserve Bank's directors that the National Bank of Commerce would withdraw its objection. The building proceeded, but the three principal opponents declined to attend the bank's cornerstone-laying ceremony in April 1921.[26] Still, it was a victory for the central bank; the height of the new building symbolized its self-perception as a leader of the regional economy and suited an expansionary vision for it and its district. Unfortunately, the bank stood at the brink of two decades of uncertainty, years that would undermine confidence in its powers to mitigate economic contractions.

Unstable Economic Conditions of the Interwar Period

The first signs of crisis in the region became evident in the agricultural sector during the first few months after World War I. Stock speculation and the prices for consumer goods rose, while farmers in the nation's midsection faced low prices. Senator Arthur Capper of Kansas criticized banks for sending money to New York for investment in industrial stock, the prices of which were surging now that private business did not have to compete with wartime demands on materials. He urged the Federal Reserve to intervene on behalf of the livestock raisers of the West, trying to get the central bank board to "use their influence with western banks" and convince them to extend credit to cattlemen.[27]

In its first major peacetime policy, issued at the close of 1919, the Federal Reserve increased interest rates in an attempt to stem speculation and inflation.[28] Bankers in the Kansas City region, including Federal Reserve Bank director Willis J. Bailey, applauded the move. Bailey maintained, "Business men are borrowing too much money to float their schemes. The federal reserve bank should increase its interest rates in order to force down the spending proclivities of the public, fostered by business men all over the country."[29] Early the next year, in another move to reduce speculative lending of funds deposited to city banks, an amendment to the Federal Reserve Act allowed the Federal Reserve branches to adopt a progressive discount rate for member bank borrowers. If a bank wished the Federal Reserve Bank to discount loans in excess of its reserve limits, the borrowing bank would have to pay increased interest rates. The directors of the Kansas City Federal Reserve believed that "the new discount rule would have an immediate tendency to curb undue extension of credit." They considered this policy decision a momentous step in the development of the Federal Reserve Bank's influence over financial markets.[30] Although it should have addressed the issue of bank funds leaving District Ten to some degree, Great Plains residents remained deeply dissatisfied because banks passed the higher interest rates on to borrowers.

As farmers and ranchers pointed out, local banks continued channeling money toward New York investment banks. Senator Robert Owen of Oklahoma, one of the authors of the Federal Reserve Act of 1913, complained that the Federal Reserve was complicit in the loss of funds to speculation. He pointed out that its higher interest rate policy did nothing to impede the flow of money toward New York, and he considered the action an "abuse of the powers of the Reserve Banks." Owen called for a reduction in the normal discount rate as well as a stronger push to discourage banks "from abusing their trust by sustaining stock speculation."[31] The senator's criticisms struck at the heart of the Federal Reserve's policies. Owen pointed out that banks should know why they loaned money and that the Federal Reserve should "curtail or shut off absolutely loans for any but productive purposes, if this is desirable, without having to resort to high rates on loans for the most necessary purposes."[32] To Owen and other critics, the bank's failure to exercise restraint on its members' use of borrowed funds indicated its lack of power, or worse, its lack of will to come to the assistance of ordinary Americans.[33]

The Kansas City Federal Reserve governor, Jo Zach Miller Jr., recognized that food producers needed more assistance and made promises to the district's agricultural sector. He said in an interview with a *Topeka Daily Capital* reporter, "This bank is a public institution, and the public is entitled to our entire confidence. We are here to serve the people of the Kansas City federal reserve district whose paramount interest is in agriculture."[34] Miller insisted that the progressive interest rate on the funds exchanged by the Federal Reserve and member banks was not harmful to agricultural interests because it discouraged city banks from exceeding their lending capacity and expending all of their funds on unproductive ventures.

Such statements provided little comfort to the region's rural communities. Writers for the *Topeka Daily Capital* lamented the shrinking value of the dollar, continued high prices for consumer goods, the difficulties of transporting agricultural products owing to a lack of train cars to move crops and livestock after the war, and the lack of credit for farmers and ranchers trying to wait out the situation and invest in future seasons.[35] The senators of Kansas, Nebraska, and Wyoming accused the central bank of discriminating against their constituents, and they requested special government funds to support producers. Furthermore, the issue spread from the countryside to city industries dependent on agricultural production. The president of the Kansas City Livestock Exchange reported difficulties obtaining or renewing loans, high interest rates, and a reduction in livestock production among its members.[36]

It was becoming apparent that farmers could not rely on the Federal Reserve to relieve shortages in credit; instead, market forces ruled. Though commodity prices increased somewhat in the coming years, the agricultural sector remained unsteady throughout the 1920s, thus presaging the worldwide depression of the 1930s. Crises in agriculture were meaningful for Federal Reserve District Ten and for Kansas City itself, because so much of the regional economy relied upon the production of commercial crops and livestock, and the ability to process those commodities into marketable goods. When agricultural markets were weak, as they were through 1922, corresponding industries in the city, such as meatpacking and flour milling, declined. If commodity prices and agricultural production rose, as they did between 1923 and 1929, industry and commerce in the city recovered. Yet in 1930, the value of farm products in the district fell 31.7 percent, despite average production levels. The prices in food-processing industries then decreased, followed by lower values of wholesale and retail trade. These conditions prevailed until 1933, when benefit payments from New Deal programming began to intervene in supporting crop prices and providing a small measure of stability to the agricultural economy as a whole, including Kansas City's processing industries.[37]

The Federal Reserve's inability to stem the losses in agriculture and related industries suggested that the institution was not the economic stronghold it wished to appear. Persistent accusations that the Federal Reserve was injuring agriculture by driving bankers to call in loans and raise reserves boded ill for the institution's influence in the region. As a *Topeka Daily Capital* editorial in August 1921 pointed out, banks in District Ten that year had liquidated agricultural loans at twice the rate of

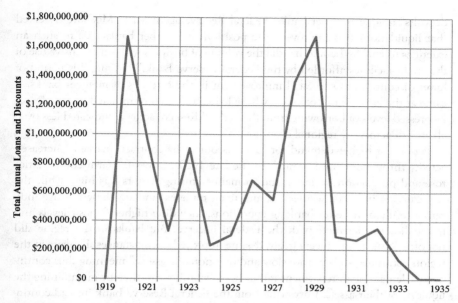

Figure 4.1. Loans and discounts issued by the Federal Reserve Bank of Kansas City, 1919–1935. Data compiled from the *Annual Reports of the Federal Reserve Bank of Kansas City, 1919–1935.*

commercial loans. The article concluded, "The hammering of agriculture should be stopped. The bank reserves are already too high. The bank statements show a high prosperity and a fine condition—for the banks. Not any prosperity but a demoralized condition for agriculture, which makes the existence of these banks possible. Call off the raid on the farm thru the country banks, Mr. Federal Reserve Banker."[38]

Economic conditions in the countryside improved slightly throughout the 1920s, but credit levels within District Ten remained subject to market forces and the whims of bankers, who preferred to earn higher profits from investments in stocks and securities. Federal Reserve policy did little to protect regional producers, despite the institution's stated commitment to agriculture and the related industries that had shaped Kansas City's development as a powerful trade center. The Federal Reserve had not yet set a precedent for preventing or correcting economic malfunctions through activist policies. The only tactic the institution was willing to try—raising the discount rate on the loans banks sold to the Fed—only served to attract banks toward stocks and securities as more profitable investment prospects.[39]

Figure 4.1 illustrates the instability of the regional economy during the interwar years. The steep decline between 1920 and 1922 indicated the agricultural crisis and a constriction of credit following the Fed's raising of interest rates. Another decline in 1924 reflected "heavy liquidations of indebtedness to banks and increased deposits" among member banks. Federal Reserve agent M. L. McClure observed that liquidations had improved "the position of member banks . . . to such an extent as to enable them to handle the volume of business without extensive use of the credit facilities afforded by the Federal Reserve Bank."[40] While this period of lower discount rates suggested improvement in the fortunes of member banks, it came at the expense of borrowers whose loans had been terminated or foreclosed. Depressed levels of borrowing from the Federal Reserve actually indicated less overall growth across the regional economy.

Periods of higher demand for loan discounts, by contrast, marked "increased activity throughout the District." In the late 1920s, prices for farm commodities rose and production on farms and in manufacturing centers was high, while the construction industry, wholesales, and retail trade expanded. These positive indicators resulted in better banking conditions, including higher deposit levels and larger discount balances with the Federal Reserve. But banks in the region did not offer loans to producers freely, despite improved circumstances. Bankers in the region continued to "improve slow and questionable assets," meaning they continued to demand loan repayment rather than extend terms, thereby maintaining the liquidity of their assets. Borrowing from the Federal Reserve Bank instead continued to support member banks' investments in stocks and securities, and deposits in city banks for investment in short-term "call" loans. These practices provided banks with relatively liquid assets but made it difficult for local borrowers to obtain credit. This situation recreated the credit shortages that producers had experienced from 1920 to 1922, and again the Federal Reserve did little to restrain member banks from these practices. The Fed noted that banks' Wall Street investments drove up the interest rates for local credit, and in 1929 suggested that the strong investment opportunities in the first three-quarters of the year (before the stock market crashed in October) meant that "banks were having difficulty in caring for all the credit needs of their communities."[41] Banks' ability to profit from the stock market brought the rate of Federal Reserve borrowing to a peak in 1928 and 1929; however, such feverish activity did not necessarily create good opportunities for producers needing credit.

The Federal Reserve Bank's research team and academic economists remained fearful that runaway stock prices constituted destructive speculation. Yet efforts to contract the expansion of credit and thus curtail this speculation in the late 1920s failed, as evidenced by the crash of October 1929. The Federal Reserve proved equally unable to stimulate credit in the coming years. Annual reports from 1930 to 1935 speak to the bottoming out of the lending business during the Great Depression, as represented by Figure 4.1. The Federal Reserve purchased fewer loans from member banks; such discount activity declined 83 percent from 1929 to 1930. In 1935, the Federal Reserve's lending volume reached only 0.2 percent of the total for 1929.[42] Solvent banks in the region had the funds to loan to local borrowers but were extremely cautious in doing so. As the Great Depression deepened, good borrowers became even harder to find, and banks' earning capacity was limited.[43] The Federal Reserve rejected some discount offers from member banks, judging them ineligible or lacking in collateral.[44] The institution failed to embrace its role as "lender of last resort," which would have meant refinancing loans backed by poor securities. Manipulation of the discount rate did little to effect a recovery when the Fed itself proved unwilling to follow through by purchasing bank loans.[45]

The Federal Reserve's inability to control the regional and national economy was magnified in the large number of failed banks throughout the region in these years. Many of these failures (which included voluntary bank liquidations and consolidations as well as suspensions) occurred in the countryside, resulting from local banks' inability to collect on farm mortgages and livestock loans during poor market years. Some of the banks that went out of business were Federal Reserve members, which suggested that the system could not prevent major losses as its founders had hoped. Still, a greater proportion of the failed banks were small, non-member state banks. The Federal Reserve Bank of Kansas City attributed such closures to these banks' lack of capital and reserves, or inability to afford good management. Failed banks often had been unable or unwilling to meet the standards of the central bank, such as its reserve and capitalization requirements and demands for federal auditing. State banks operated with much smaller capitalization than national banks (only $5,000 for a bank in a town of 3,000 people, compared to $25,000) and had greater freedoms in lending on farm real estate. State bankers were loath to cede their independence in joining the Federal Reserve, even though the government made multiple efforts to protect state banks' charter rights, lending abilities, examination practices, and ability to withdraw voluntarily from the system. Federal Reserve officers viewed the high bank failure rate as the result of banks' refusal to become Federal Reserve members.[46] In its 1927 annual report, the Reserve Bank called this trend "the process of elimination of weak or unprofitable banks." Around 900 fewer banks operated in the district at the end of 1927 compared to 1920, and the number of member banks in the region continued to fall, from 3,593 in 1928 to 2,430 in 1932.[47] Banks in Kansas City were not immune to these troubles; the city witnessed 33 bank failures between 1920 and 1928, though some reorganized or consolidated. The decade started with 55 banks operating in Kansas City, and only 40 existed by 1928.[48]

Kansas City and other urban areas in District Ten did begin to see signs of relief in 1934. Retail trade increased 16.4 percent, wholesalers did 14.8 percent more business, and construction increased 3.5 percent. Some urban production industries improved, including flour and cement processing, and regional production of zinc, lead, coal, and petroleum rose. A large part of the city's growth during these years fulfilled the aims of the Ten-Year Plan, a $50-million, bipartisan bond project approved by Kansas City voters in 1931 to finance infrastructural improvements and the construction of a new city hall, county courthouse, and municipal auditorium. Tom Pendergast's Ready Mixed Concrete Company, along with his coordination of pick-and-shovel work for thousands of unemployed laborers, provided much of the momentum for these projects even before the New Deal gave such work relief programs federal authority and funds. Two other major developments, the Nelson-Atkins Museum and the University of Kansas City, opened in 1933 as the culmination of decades of planning. Although the business community furnished leadership in the establishment of the Ten-Year Plan, these projects did not develop due to any strong financial incentive from the city banks. Wealthy donors, the political machine, and the voters offered the vision and the willpower to keep Kansas City moving forward even during the depths of the Great Depression.[49]

The level of activity in the city did not reach the farms of Federal Reserve District Ten. Farmers suffered through the worst drought in memory, and amid the Dust Bowl (beginning in 1931) produced the smallest harvests on record. Still, New Deal allotment contracts for reducing planted acreage or breeding in several key commodities provided much-needed subsidies to farm incomes, some $127,490,000 throughout District Ten in 1934. The federal government also purchased $170,297,000 worth of livestock, seed, and other farm commodities, and then channeled them into urban processing centers. Government accounts meant that flour production was "only 8 percent below the ten year average," and "operations at meat packing establishments were unusually heavy throughout the year."[50] Some of these trends continued through 1935. Retail and wholesale rates improved again that year, while residential construction rebounded with an incredible 83.5 percent increase in contract value.[51] New Deal programs, rather than renewed bank investment, deserve the credit for propping up the district's linked rural and urban economies. As illustrated in Figure 4.1, interbank lending within the Federal Reserve System remained close to zero throughout the early 1930s.

Despite a vision of its own strength projected through the construction of its twenty-one-story bank tower in downtown Kansas City, the Federal Reserve Bank did not play a particularly strong role in shaping the regional economy during the 1920s and 1930s. It promoted principles of conservative banking by encouraging banks to terminate questionable loans, but did little to encourage lending to viable producers who needed it. The bank also failed to push regional institutions away from investing in stocks and city call markets and toward in-district lending to farmers and industrialists. The Federal Reserve was not yet a major national economic policymaker, and the system would require congressional strengthening during the New Deal to achieve its undisputed status as the arbiter of the national financial system. The Banking Acts of 1933 and 1935 introduced the Federal Deposit Insurance Company and stipulated that banks with deposits of more than $1 million that wished to remain members of the FDIC had to join the Federal Reserve by July 1942. These laws finally gave many banks a powerful incentive to join the central banking system.[52] With greater control over more of the national banking structure, the Federal Reserve would become its chief regulating force and an important source of public confidence. Kansas City, too, would finally take its place as the heartland's financial center during the postwar years.

Conclusion

The Federal Reserve Bank of Kansas City at 925 Grand maintained its status as the tallest building in the city skyline until 1929, when the Bell Telephone Company built a several-story addition to its "Oak Tower." Its physical overpowering was perhaps symbolic of the general struggles the central bank faced in maintaining its authority within the district during the 1920s and in preventing financial disaster as the Great Depression set in. Newspaper reports surrounding the farm credit crisis of 1920–1922 showed how the institution struggled to support the agricultural base that had first earned Kansas City its gateway status. The Federal Reserve also failed to intervene when member banks' investment policies constricted opportunities for local credit during the late 1920s. In each of these cases, the central bank risked its reputation within the broader region and undermined efforts to bring order to the rural banking structure. Annual records of the Federal Reserve reflected an even worse decline in agriculture and the broader economy of District Ten from late 1929 to 1935, and again indicated that the bank made few, if any, major policy decisions to promote general recovery.

Considering the volatility in urban sales and manufacturing, and especially in the agricultural sector that undergirded Kansas City's status as a gateway city, scholars must question whether the interwar years were as "golden" as anecdotes might suggest. Though the Pendergast era in Kansas City was one of strong cultural advancements and some infrastructural improvement supported by philanthropic giving, a city bond, and New Deal funding, the economic development attributed to the machine era perhaps may have been overstated. The glitzy façade of the Jazz Age seems to have masked underlying cracks in the city's financial foundation. The Kansas City Federal Reserve, and the central banking system as a whole, struggled to react to unprecedented economic conditions. Disappointing as this was for a region with high expectations for its leading city, it was symptomatic of the age of nascent big government.

Notes

1. Federal Reserve Bank of Kansas City, "Operation of Federal Reserve Bank of Kansas City, 1920: Sixth Annual Report to the Federal Reserve Board," *Annual Report of the Federal Reserve Bank of Kansas City as of December 31, 1920,* 4, 34–35, https://fraser.stlouisfed.org/scribd/?item_id=18326&filepath=/files/docs/historical/ frbkc/1920_frb_kansascity.pdf.

2. "Operation of Federal Reserve Bank of Kansas City, 1920," 34–35; Ceremonies of the

Laying of the Corner Stone of the Federal Reserve Bank of Kansas City, Missouri, April 16, 1921, Missouri Valley Special Collections, Kansas City Public Library, Kansas City (hereafter MVSC), Missouri; and "Bank's Family Is Home," *Kansas City Star*, November 16, 1921, 2.

3. Chad R. Wilkerson, "Senator Robert Owen of Oklahoma and the Federal Reserve's Formative Years," *Federal Reserve Bank of Kansas City Economic Review* (Third Quarter 2013), 95–117.

4. "Why G. Helvering Favors Glass Bill," *Topeka Daily Capital* (hereafter *TDC*), November 26, 1913, 4.

5. "Wilson Sees Promise of Best Things Ahead," *TDC*, November 18, 1914, 1.

6. A characterization of the efforts of Federal Reserve governor Jo Zach Miller Jr.'s spearheading of the construction of a new bank building at Tenth and Grand, in "10-J: The History of the Kansas City Fed" (Kansas City Public Television, 2013), 44.40–44.55.

7. William Cronon theorizes that gateway cities controlled the agricultural goods, commodities, and financial relationships of their hinterlands, utilizing infrastructure such as railroads to move goods to and from the city. The development of Kansas City as a railroad hub contributed to its development as a trade and processing center, especially of animal products. See William Cronon, *Nature's Metropolis: Chicago and the Great West* (New York: W. W. Norton, 1991).

8. W[illiam] R[ockhill] Nelson, Publisher of the *Kansas City Star*, to Secretary [David F.] Houston and Secretary [William Gibbs] McAdoo, January 19, 1914, in United States, Reserve Bank Organization Committee, #51 Missouri (Kansas City), Box 2657, Folder 2, *Records of the Federal Reserve System, 1878–1996, Record Group 82*, United States National Archives and Records Administration, https://fraser.stlouisfed.org/archival/1344 (hereafter Record Group 82).

9. Map of Proposed Denver District, United States, Reserve Bank Organization Committee, #85 Maps—Denver, Colo., Box 2656, Folder 6, Record Group 82.

10. J. M. Williams to G. M. Smith, President of Commonwealth National Bank of Kansas City, Mo., January 15, 1914, in United States, Reserve Bank Organization Committee, #55 Miscellaneous States (Kansas City), Box 2657, Folder 3, Record Group 82.

11. Roy Ammerman, Cashier of the First State Bank & Trust Company of Roswell, New Mexico, to Jerome Thralls, Manager of the Kansas City Clearing House Association, January 2, 1914, in United States, Reserve Bank Organization Committee, #55 Miscellaneous States (Kansas City), Box 2657, Folder 3, Record Group 82.

12. Murray N. Rothbard, *A History of Money and Banking in the United States: The Colonial Era to World War II* (Auburn, Ala.: Ludwig von Mises Institute, 2002), 136–141, 144.

13. "Kansans Favor K.C. for Regional Bank," *TDC*, January 24, 1914, 3.

14. United States, Reserve Bank Organization Committee, #86 Maps—Kansas City, Box 2657, Folder 7, Record Group 82; and United States, Reserve Bank Organization Committee, Hearing at Kansas City, Friday, January 23, 1914, Box 2657, Folder 6, Record Group 82.

15. Verne Hostutler to Federal Bank Organization Committee, December 31, 1913, in United States, Reserve Bank Organization Committee, #50 Kansas (Kansas City), Box 2657, Folder 1, Record Group 82. The Hearing file (Box 2657, Folder 6, Record Group 82) con-

firms Hostutler's conclusions about Kansas City's clearings capacity, noting that its turnover of bank checks had increased 165 percent between 1903 and 1913.

16. E. G. Boughner (Cashier, First National Bank of Natoma, Kansas) to Reserve Bank Organization Committee, January 16, 1914, United States, Reserve Bank Organization Committee, #50 Kansas (Kansas City), Box 2657, Folder 1, Record Group 82.

17. J. C. Hopper (president, Citizens National Bank of Ness City, Kansas), to William Gibbs McAdoo, secretary of the treasury and chairman of the Reserve Bank Organization Committee, January 14, 1914, United States, Reserve Bank Organization Committee, #50 Kansas (Kansas City), Box 2657, Folder 1, Record Group 82.

18. R. J. Thresher, President of the Kansas City Board of Trade, to Organization Committee of Federal Reserve Banks, December 27, 1913, in United States, Reserve Bank Organization Committee, #51 Missouri (Kansas City), Box 2657, Folder 2, Record Group 82.

19. Richard C. Menefee (Commerce Trust Company) to W. G. McAdoo, December 30, 1913, in United States, Reserve Bank Organization Committee, #51 Missouri (Kansas City), Box 2657, Folder 2, Record Group 82; and Names of Persons to Appear before the Reserve Bank Organization Committee, Hearing at Kansas City, January 23, 1914, Box 2657, Folder 2, Record Group 82.

20. Federal Reserve Board, "Map of Federal Reserve Districts," *Federal Reserve Bulletin* (October 1922), 123, https://fraser.stlouisfed.org/scribd/?toc_id=384425&filepath=/docs/publications/FRB/1920s/frb_101922.pdf.

21. "Our Latest Achievement," *Kansas Citian* 3, no. 4 (April 1914), 78–79.

22. "Kansas City through Eastern Eyes: What This City Means to the Student of Civic Progress and Possibilities," *Kansas Citian* 3, no. 6 (June 1914), 132.

23. "Handle War Loans Free; Money Called to Colors," *TDC*, April 12, 1917, 12.

24. Jerome Thralls, "The New Bank's Value: Its Purposes, Procedure and Its Relations to the Public and the Banks," *Kansas Citian* 3, no. 4 (April 1914), 82–83.

25. A cashier of the Federal Reserve Bank of Kansas City offered a concise overview of the functions of the central bank to members of the Kansas Bankers Association in 1915. See Jerome Thralls, "Working Relations between the Federal Reserve Bank of Kansas City and the Banks within Its Jurisdiction," in *Proceedings of the Twenty-Eighth Annual Convention of the Kansas Bankers Association* (Topeka, Kans.: H. M. Ives & Sons, 1915), 165–171. These operations are described in much more detail in the Kansas City Federal Reserve Bank's annual reports, available in the Federal Reserve Archive online database (FRASER), at https://fraser.stlouisfed.org/title/474.

26. The ceremony's attendees included many politicians and bankers from throughout the different states of District Ten, but not these three major Kansas Citians. See "Objection to Height," Jess Worley, Unfinished Manuscript on the History of the Federal Reserve Bank of Kansas City, n.d., MVSC.

27. "Federal Reserve Board Urged to Assist Stockmen," *TDC*, July 29, 1919, 1; and "Kansas Growers Are Facing Ruin, Appeal for Help," *TDC*, July 2, 1919, 1.

28. "Hikes Interest Rates," *TDC*, December 12, 1919, 10.

29. "To Check Speculation," *TDC*, December 30, 1919, 1; "Trim Those Sails Now,"

TDC, January 30, 1920, 4. The governor of the Federal Reserve Bank of Kansas City echoed these sentiments in "An Address by J. Z. Miller, Jr., Governor of the Federal Reserve Bank of Kansas City," ca. 1920, Federal Reserve Bank of Kansas City Archives.

30. "Credits Curbed by New Reserve Bank Orders," *TDC*, April 19, 1920, 1.

31. "Federal Banks, Liberty Bonds, and Stock Gambling," *TDC*, February 23, 1920, 4. See also Wilkerson, "Senator Robert Owen of Oklahoma and the Federal Reserve's Formative Years."

32. "The Federal Reserve Loan Rate," *TDC*, May 22, 1920, 4.

33. The Federal Reserve Banks, it should be noted, were doing extremely well financially by 1920. Kansas City, which was in the bottom third of the regional branches in terms of capital investment, at $8,031,000, was in the top third in terms of net earnings as a percentage of capital, with profits for the previous year listed at $3,774,000, or 47 percent. Only New York, Atlanta, and San Francisco ranked higher by this measure. See J. R. Burrow, "Just Like a Mint," *TDC*, July 17, 1920, 17.

34. Frank G. Odell, "Federal Reserve Banks Will Help Agriculture," *TDC*, June 6, 1920, 11.

35. "Our Shrinking Dollar," *TDC*, April 25, 1920, 32; "Prices Are Still High," *TDC*, May 7, 1920, 11; "Finance New Crop," *TDC*, May 29, 1920, 18; "Will Speculators Euchre Farmers Out of Wheat?" *TDC*, July 17, 1920, 17; "Financing the Farmer," *TDC*, December 10, 1920, 4; and "Investigation of Agricultural Bank Loans," *TDC*, December 18, 1920, 4.

36. "Western Senators Offer Meat Shortage Proof," *TDC*, May 29, 1920, 1, 9; and "Grazing Lands Are Idle, No Cattle to Pasture," *TDC*, August 2, 1920, 3.

37. *Annual Reports of the Federal Reserve Bank of Kansas City, 1919–1935*, FRASER, https://fraser.stlouisfed.org/title/474.

38. "The Banking Raid on Agriculture," *TDC*, August 28, 1921, 4.

39. Perry Mehrling, *The New Lombard Street: How the Fed Became the Dealer of Last Resort* (Princeton: Princeton University Press, 2011), 41.

40. *Annual Report of the Federal Reserve Bank of Kansas City, 1924*, 7.

41. *Annual Reports of the Federal Reserve Bank of Kansas City, 1926–1929*.

42. Discounts in 1929 totaled $1,673,244,950; in 1930 they totaled $290,628,489; and in 1935 they totaled only $3,217,475. See *Annual Reports of the Federal Reserve Bank of Kansas City, 1929–1935*.

43. *Annual Reports of the Federal Reserve Bank of Kansas City, 1934*, 8–9; and 1935.

44. In 1931 the Fed declined 6.6 percent of notes worth $4,625,000, or 1.6 percent of the total value of discounts that year. In 1932, it declined 7.5 percent of discount offers. See *Annual Reports of the Federal Reserve Bank of Kansas City, 1931*, 12–12; and 1932, 7–8.

45. Perry G. Mehrling, *The Money Interest and the Public Interest: American Monetary Thought, 1920–1970* (Cambridge, Mass: Harvard University Press, 1997), 79.

46. "Reserve System Changes Rules to Aid State Banks," *TDC*, June 10, 1915, 1; "State Banks Are Called upon to Help Whip Kaiser," *TDC*, October 16, 1917, 1, 10; and Wayne D. Angell, "A Century of Commercial Banking in Kansas, 1856 to 1956, Volume II" (PhD diss., University of Kansas, 1957), 385–386. State bankers in Kansas expressed some of the prevailing doubts about joining the Federal Reserve, and even went so far as to attempt founding

a competing state reserve system. See "Reserve Banks Should Not Fight State Banks," *TDC*, October 4, 1919, 3; J. R. Burrows Jr. "Property Rights No Longer Held Sacred," *TDC*, June 26, 1921, 5; "State Banks Protest," *TDC*, January 24, 1920, 1; "State Bankers Aroused," *TDC*, October 21, 1920, 2; and "Don't Like Discount System," *TDC*, April 13, 1921, 10.

47. *Annual Reports of the Federal Reserve Bank of Kansas City, 1927–1932.*

48. Monroe F. Cockrell, "Banking in Kansas City, Missouri, 1920-1928," 1962, MVSC.

49. Lawrence H. Larsen, Nancy J. Hulston, and William E. Foley, *Pendergast!* (Columbia: University of Missouri Press, 2013), 88–95; and James R. Shortridge, *Kansas City and How It Grew, 1822–2011* (Lawrence: University Press of Kansas, 2012), 70–73.

50. *Annual Report of the Federal Reserve Bank of Kansas City, 1934,* 3, 8.

51. *Annual Reports of the Federal Reserve Bank of Kansas City, 1935.*

52. Angell, "A Century of Commercial Banking," 429–431.

CHAPTER FIVE

Our Time to Shine

The 1928 Republican National Convention and Kansas City's Rising Profile

Dustin Gann

During the first two decades of the twentieth century, Kansas City experienced a profound period of transformation. Its centralized location and bucolic natural beauty drew new residents and businesses that invigorated the city. The University of Kansas City and the Nelson-Atkins Museum, as well as the establishment of a World War I Memorial, enhanced local culture. Sustained progress, however, required ongoing urban planning and infrastructure expansion. City leaders worked continuously to build upon the aesthetic legacy of the late nineteenth-century City Beautiful movement and the recently completed Get-It-Done infrastructure campaign. Optimism surrounding recent growth was tempered by knowledge that regional rivals were experiencing similar development. Anxious city leaders continually sought new ways to expand the city's national profile.

According to a May 29, 1928, editorial in the *Kansas Citian*, a newsletter published by the Kansas City Chamber of Commerce, the Republican National Convention promised to "bring more influential people in industry, business, and financial circles than ever brought here by a convention." The editorial purposefully connected the convention with potential growth:

> when a city is engaged in an intensive drive or industry, it must of necessity,
> in order to succeed, cultivate acquaintance, friendship and goodwill in
> high places, so that when the location of a new factory, refinancing of an
> old one, extension of credit to the city, or any of its institutions, are under
> consideration in the directors' rooms of great financial institutions located in

the big money centers, Kansas City will be sure to have present one or more of those sold on Kansas City during the Republican National Convention.[1]

Local leaders envisioned the 1928 Republican National Convention raising the national and regional profile of Kansas City in two related ways. First, delegates and visitors attending the convention could see the city's growth firsthand. Second, and perhaps more important, the event and subsequent attention would bolster the city's standing, particularly in relation to regional rivals such as Cleveland and St. Louis. Both cities boasted similar amenities to Kansas City, and Cleveland had recently hosted the 1924 Republican National Convention.

Ultimately, the plan worked. Efforts to organize and host a national political event energized Chamber of Commerce leaders and united Kansas Citians behind efforts to improve their city. Goodwill generated by the convention galvanized support for a comprehensive, strategic, ten-year plan that spurred municipal improvements, modernized many facilities, and positioned Kansas City for twentieth-century success.

Envisioning Growth

The 1928 Republican National Convention followed two distinct periods of municipal growth in Kansas City. During the late nineteenth and early twentieth centuries, multiple efforts had been made to direct development toward aesthetically pleasing and commercially viable goals. Architect George Kessler, along with the Commercial Club, the forerunner of the Chamber of Commerce, laid the foundation for Kansas City's park system during the City Beautiful movement. Their efforts "remade an ugly boom town [Kansas City], giving it miles of graceful boulevards and parkways flanked by desirable residential sections, acres of ruggedly beautiful parkland dotted with recreational improvements."[2] Many of the attractions promoted to visitors during and after the Republican's 1928 gathering were created during the heyday of the City Beautiful movement.

As the momentum behind the City Beautiful movement ebbed, the Chamber of Commerce played an increasingly prominent role in municipal improvement projects. During the early 1920s, a Get-It-Done campaign updated Kansas City's infrastructure without the help of bond financing. The effort included rerouted streets, new bridges, and widened thoroughfares. When the campaign ran up against financing limits, however, and bond initiatives failed, progress stalled. By the mid- to late 1920s, calls had begun for a renewed and systematic approach to municipal improvement. In 1926 a chamber subcommittee argued, "Kansas City has arrived at a point where if it is to maintain its position and prestige with other cities that are in keen competition with it and fighting for commercial supremacy, it must do more than it has been doing." The committee added, "If Kansas City is to forge ahead and advance as it should, a definite and ambitious Program of Development must be undertaken at once."[3] At a time when Kansas City leaders noted expansion plans across the state—the St. Louis Chamber of Commerce had "4500 members at $50.00 dues, [and] is now planning to raise a large amount by 'subscription activities'"—Kansas City's Program Development Committee sought to unite the business community behind a plan that would keep pace with "the stiff competition among the fast-growing cities of the country." The committee recommended "advertis[ing] Kansas City in a nation-wide way, just as St. Louis and many other points are doing."[4]

A long-term vision, the *Kansas City Star* argued, "would undertake systemically to plan for major needs that are to be undertaken, say, in the next decade." After all, the paper reasoned, "Every business plans for the future. Why should not a city, which is the biggest business of all?"[5] In December 1927 the Chamber of Commerce appointed six men to "a special committee to take up with the city manager the matter of a 10-year improvement plan for Kansas City."[6]

Ongoing mobilization during late 1927 created a cadre of officials who were active Chamber of Commerce members and integral parts of Republican National Convention planning. In April 1928, Arthur Hardgrave, chamber president, appointed five men—Conrad Mann, Walter Negbaur, Frank Dean, Max Dyer, and Ed North—to the Municipal Bond Committee.[7] Mann later served as general chairman for the Republican National Convention Committee, while both Dean and Dyer were members of the Republican National Convention Executive Committee. Dean also served on the Transportation and Housing Committees.[8] Overlapping leadership epitomized the interconnected relationship between public government and the business community within Kansas City.

On March 6, 1928, in advance of municipal elections, the *Kansas Citian* argued that, when compared to similar cities, Kansas City could easily afford the proposed bonds. The article reasoned, "Of the 22 cities of over 300,000 population, only eight cities show a lower per capita net bonded debt than Kansas City." Of equal importance, "Kansas City also has a relatively low tax burden, as compared with that of other cities."[9] In early 1928 the Trafficways Commission released a detailed assessment of Kansas City's roads. The group, which had begun meeting in 1926, recommended the creation of "a definite plan that would adequately meet our growing traffic needs" and identified twenty-two deficient roadways. Suggested improvements included new bridges, additional traffic lanes, grade reductions, and the construction of bypass routes.[10] The *Kansas City Star* relayed the commission's findings to a wider audience through articles that detailed recommended changes to existing routes and proposed construction projects, complete with diagrams, supporting arguments, and funding estimates.[11]

The Call, Kansas City's leading African American newspaper, proved a steadfast supporter of growth initiatives and urged its readers to vote for improvement bonds. On February 17, an editorial argued, "A city needs dressing up just like a person.

There is a certain utility as well as beauty that costs money, but pays big dividends. . . . Progress requires effort and is worth it."[12] Moreover, "the bulk of all public expenditures goes for labor. Readers of *The Call*, being almost wholly of the laboring class, will feel the increased demand for labor at once, when thirty-one million dollars is spent to improve the city." This equaled, the paper argued, "two dollars a year at most for taxes, and as much per day in wages, [and] is the kind of investment that Kansas City voters can well afford to make."[13]

The May 1928 special election, held a month before Republicans gathered in Kansas City, placed multiple bonds before voters. The Citizens' Bond Committee, "representing nearly 100 civic, labor, and business groups," distributed a twenty-three-page booklet in favor of the proposed improvements.[14] Unfortunately, a majority of the initiatives failed. Chester A. Franklin, the publisher of *The Call*, lamented, "the people have said 'no' to the bond proposals. . . . By their vote Kansas City might as well go to sleep, letting the grass in breaks in the pavement be the only thing at work. The old Kansas City spirit is sadly in need of repair."[15] The *Kansas Citian* observed many projects received over 60 percent voter support, but only "the Municipal Wharf, Swope Park, the County Hospital, and the County Highway System overcame the constitutional requirement of a two-thirds majority."[16] Despite ballot initiative failures, city leaders remained undaunted in their efforts to unite residents behind municipal improvements and promote Kansas City's potential for growth to regional and national audiences.

Convention Background

Prior to 1928 the Republican Party had held conventions in cities bordering or west of the Mississippi River on only two occasions—meeting in Minneapolis in 1892 and St. Louis in 1896. Six of the first nine Republican conventions during the twentieth century were held in Chicago. Between 1864 and 1932 the Democrats gathered five times in Chicago and four times in St. Louis.[17] Political gatherings reinforced Chicago's role as the preeminent midwestern city and established St. Louis as a formidable regional challenger. Consequently, when Kansas City decided to stake a claim for the 1928 gathering, community leaders balanced ambition against likely disappointment.

In early 1927 Chamber of Commerce minutes expressed an interest in either national party convention. When the Democrats selected Houston, attention turned to the Republicans' summer gathering.[18] On April 4, the Convention Executive Committee alerted the Chamber of Commerce board of directors to the "strong possibility" of hosting the 1928 Republican National Convention. Despite this news, members remained skeptical. Executive session minutes indicate many believed "there was no chance of getting this convention, as apparently it is all fixed to go to Cleveland, but as a matter of policy and publicity such a move might be made."[19] If enough community support could be garnered, the Chamber of Commerce committed itself to bidding on the 1928 convention.[20] Turnout at initial informational meetings failed to meet expectations, however, and in a subsequent letter Lyle Stephenson called upon individuals' civic pride. He argued it "is of far more import to you as a citizen of this town than securing of any convention. Kansas City is extremely slack in man power and unless we get behind the town on this movement and every other movement . . . we can anticipate a retrograde city."[21] At subsequent meetings the city answered Stephenson's call. Chamber president Arthur Hardgrave notified select chamber members that "it was enthusiastically determined that Kansas City should put forth a most serious endeavor to obtain the National Republican Convention."[22]

To ensure bipartisan support, the Chamber of Commerce reached out to the local Republican and Democratic Parties. In late 1927, Robert H. Tschudy, chairman of the Republican County and Congressional Committee in Kansas City, wrote that the process of securing the convention "has become a civic matter." Tschudy extended "to those members of the Democratic party its appreciation for their cooperation in this movement which will be of such wonderful financial and advertising value to the city as a whole."[23] Republicans and Democrats in Kansas City, with publicity and prosperity for the city in mind, put aside political differences in order to secure the convention.

Broad support for the 1928 convention continued through the June meeting of the General Executive Committee of the Chamber of Commerce. Republican mayor Albert I. Beach as well as his predecessor, Democrat Frank Cromwell, served on the General Executive Committee along with Democratic politicians Harry Truman and current city manager Henry F. McElroy.[24] In addition, committed Democrat Jouett Shouse served on the General Executive Committee and headed the publicity committee. Shouse had been a Democratic state senator, a member of the US Congress, and a delegate to the Democratic National Convention. He later chaired the Democratic National Executive Committee from 1929 to 1932.[25] The bipartisan commitment of Kansas City's business and commercial class demonstrates that civic concerns and capitalist self-interest, rather than partisan ambition, motivated support for the 1928 gathering.

Raising Money and Interest

In late 1927 attention turned toward mobilizing the money and labor needed to bid on, secure, and execute a large-scale event. Lou Holland, then Chamber of Commerce president, proclaimed, "I am impressed with the fact that public sentiment is favorable. All this campaign needs, as usual, is man-power."[26] Holland recognized without concerned effort, "a fall-down on our part will be far more damaging than if we had never entered the campaign."[27]

Fundraising cards distributed in November 1927 asked individuals and businesses to indicate potential financial pledges. These cards made clear "if Kansas City, Mo. is not selected as the Convention City that no part of this subscription shall be paid."[28] Subsequent fundraising efforts connected Kansas Citians' civic duty to the potential economic benefit. A December 1927 fundraising letter declared, "It is generally agreed that this will be one of the outstanding events in Kansas City's history and that it will be of immeasurable benefit to the city." Moreover, the letter noted, "It has been estimated by Chicago business men that that city lost $4,000,000 by not obtaining the convention. This will serve as an indication of the actual dollars and cents return which Kansas City may expect."[29]

Existing funds formed the basis of Kansas City's initial convention bid, and the Chamber of Commerce secured a loan for an additional $125,000 in early 1928. The group simultaneously initiated a larger fundraising campaign to repay all previously committed monies.[30] During a January meeting, members discussed plans "to raise an additional $50,000 to finance it [the convention] and take care of it in a way that will be creditable to Kansas City and bring big returns."[31] The chamber created a "National Republican Convention Fund," funded by member-solicited subscriptions. The stated goal of the fund was $150,000.[32] In total, Chamber leaders "estimate[d] the cost at $175,000. We have raised and paid the National Committee $125,000. We pledged an additional $25,000 for convention expenses. We need an additional $25,000 to finance the work of the local committee."[33]

As preparations intensified, a sense of optimism and anxiety settled over Kansas City. On January 31, an unsigned letter from chamber leaders ventured, "All Kansas City is rapidly arising to our possibilities in properly entertaining and caring for the Republican National Convention. It is conceded to be the big, outstanding opportunity for Kansas City for many years in our history." Fundraising proved difficult, however, and the chamber warned that if significant funds were not raised and "unless our guests can be properly handled, years will be required to clear our reputation."[34]

In February 1928, the Chamber of Commerce established the GOP Committee of 100, chaired by local insurance agent Lyle Stephenson. Members, under the direction of Stephenson and seventeen "'captains,'" set out in two-man teams to raise funds "for the conduct of the convention and for all of the preparation that must be made for it." The *Kansas Citian* explained, "One team will cover all of the prospects in one building or in one section of the city and so on, regardless of lines of business or personal acquaintance, every worker having pledged his best effort to do his share . . . in the short space of time possible."[35]

When Kansas City was announced as the host for the 1928 Republican National Convention, it marked a culmination of an intense lobbying campaign on behalf of the local business community.[36] The *Kansas Citian* noted that Kansas City had beaten out "such cities as San Francisco, Detroit, Chicago, Cleveland, and Philadelphia."[37] A full-page story in the *New York Times Magazine* attributed the decision to party chairman William M. Butler of Massachusetts. The article observed, "if the convention were to be a mere ratification meeting, such as that at Cleveland four years ago . . . San Francisco or some city on either ocean would be suitable."[38] Political concerns, especially the ongoing agrarian depression, demanded a centralized party gathering in "Kansas City . . . on the very edge of the great open spaces where men are men and Republican farmers are discontents." The paper argued that a midwestern meeting indicated "the Republican Party was keenly interested in their welfare and was not under the domination of those effete Eastern industrialists and financiers whose hearts are supposed to be cold to the desire of the embattled farmers of the West."[39] Though Kansas City might not have been the Republicans' choice during boom times, the combination of direct solicitation, local organization, and historical circumstance provided the city a unique opportunity. City leaders were determined to use the national spotlight to promote Kansas City's transformation and potential for future growth.

Championing Kansas City

With political forces leading Republicans to Kansas City, Chamber of Commerce leaders set about preparing for the national spotlight. On only one previous occasion—the 1900 Democratic National Convention—had Kansas City hosted a national political gathering. To meet the challenge, the Chamber of Commerce created a vast organizational structure. A General Executive, Finance, and Arrangement Committee, chaired by Conrad Mann, oversaw all convention planning. By 1928 Mann had been a prominent member of Kansas City's business community for almost two decades. He worked tirelessly to promote community development through numerous civic organizations and "in 1913 he founded the Convention bureau."[40] Under Mann's direction thirteen standing committees—some spawned additional subcommittees—were also created. One committee handled entertainment, while another planned receptions, for example, and individual committees coordinated transportation, housing, automobiles and parking, information bureaus, and distinguished guests.[41]

The publicity committee, chaired by Jouett Shouse, oversaw preconvention promotion and distributed positive press releases to journalists across the country. Rather than focus on politics, these stories emphasized the history and development of Kansas City and served two purposes: first, they created a sense of anticipation among delegates and journalists covering the convention; and second, and perhaps most important, the stories used the convention to reach individuals who might never have thought about Kansas City as either a tourist destination or viable commercial hub.

At the request of the Republican National Committee, Shouse's committee compiled *The Book of the Republican National Convention.* Focused primarily on the summer gathering, it included "all possible pertinent information relative to the Convention itself and its personnel." There was also "an accurate, concise, and full history of the Republican Party." The *Kansas Citian* proclaimed on March 6, 1928, "Kansas City will not be behind Chicago, Cleveland, or any other cities that heretofore have entertained the national political conventions. One of the ways it will measure up with these is in the publication of what will be known as 'The Book of the Republican National Convention.'"[42]

A myriad of national and regional businesses, some of which had branches in Kansas City, purchased advertisements in the publication.[43] While some indicated support for Republican policies, all expressed general national pride and civic solidarity. Local businesses ranging from banks, law firms, hotels, and restaurants to the Stine and McClure Undertaking Company hoped to catch visitors' attention. The Loose-Wiles Biscuit Company, for example, invited "all visitors to Kansas City during the convention week" to tour the factory and "see for yourself, why it is to your advantage to ask for these delicious biscuits and candies by name."[44]

Interspersed between party history and advertisements were articles touting Kansas City's character. An article headlined "Heart of America," for example, described Kansas City as "nearer the geographic center of the country than any other large city." The "active trade territory . . . embraces thirteen states, all rich in varied lines of productivity." The flow and trade of goods—specifically mentioned were "livestock, grain, oil, lumber"—made Kansas City "the central storehouse and distributing point for a vast domain." Consequently, Kansas City "contains manufactories for conversion into consumable form the countless products which have been so extensively developed in the great southwest and which have made this territory a veritable empire." Another section, headlined "Kansas City's Domain," boasted top-five national rankings in numerous agricultural, commercial, and manufacturing categories.

The publication attributed Kansas City's character to "a small group of recognized leaders," including City Beautiful architect George Kessler, who uncovered "the aesthetic possibilities contained in the peculiar topography." Photographs highlighted landmarks, many established by the City Beautiful movement, such as Swope Park and the Thomas H. Swope Memorial, Loose Park, the palisades along Kersey Coates Drive in West Terrace Park, the Paseo, and Penn Valley Park. Emphasis on natural beauty continued in a section labeled "Residential Districts of Charm." Visitors were told Kansas City's "residential sections partake of the aspects of immense gardens and fit, without break or jar, into the delightful irregularities of its charmingly rugged topography." While the aesthetics of the Country Club District, which is described in Chapter 3 in this volume, received specific praise, the article boasted that "nearly 40% of Kansas City's people are home owners." Moreover, "Most of these homes, like buildings in the downtown section and in the public and semi-public areas, are variously designed to blend harmoniously into the artistic keynote which has governed improvements . . . since the original planners of this 'city beautiful' dreamed their dreams."[45]

The promotion of Kansas City's outdoor recreational facilities also demonstrated coordination between the *Book of the Republican National Convention* and other aspects of convention publicity. A half-page feature, headlined "Kansas City—Golfers' Paradise," boasted that "Greater Kansas City [has] a greater number of clubs fostering the exhilarating outdoor sport than in almost any other city of similar size." Golfers were told that Kansas City's courses offered varying terrain and "are easily accessible by street cars or buses."[46] A May 24, 1928, article in the *Kansas City Star* explained "a feature of the entertainment for visitors [allows] entrance at nine golf clubs and the Rockhill Tennis club."[47]

The *Book of the Republican National Convention* was not published until June 1928 and so did not influence the selection of Kansas City. It did, however, allow Kansas Citians to trumpet the virtues of their town to visiting politicians, operatives, and reporters. City leaders used convention publicity to highlight Kansas City's commercial advantages and residential appeal. Civic pride played a role in spurring businesses to place advertisements within the publication and in promoting the boastful pronouncements made by chamber leaders regarding Kansas City's greatness. Economic incentive also influenced these decisions. Businesses were integral supporters of efforts to secure the convention and subsequently hoped to reach customers and make connections during the event. Similarly, city leaders hoped a positive convention experience might lure new residents and investment to Kansas City.

Welcome to Kansas City

Committee members and volunteers worked diligently to create a festive atmosphere during the summer of 1928. Flags, bunting, and other adornments enlivened streets surrounding Convention Hall. Over 300,000 brightly colored stickers bearing convention dates and a GOP elephant were distributed to businesses for use on outgoing mail.[48] As delegates and attendees arrived, convention organizers provided a *Visitor's Guide to Kansas City* that served as an introduction for those traveling during the summer of 1928. With less focus on Republican Party and convention history, the *Visitor's Guide to Kansas City* highlighted the city's geographic advantages and municipal amenities. For example, the text boasted, "Few, if any cit[ies] of equal size and area have more rapid and interurban transportation facilities than found here." The Convention Committee also staged several social events that welcomed visitors, including a grand parade, golf tournament, and polo match.[49]

A veritable army of ambassadors, adorned with buttons—featuring "G.O.P." along the top, "I Live Here" along the bottom, and with "Ask Me" in the middle

Eleventh Street, looking west from the intersection with Grand Street and showing decorations for the downtown Republican National Convention, June 13, 1928. Courtesy of Missouri Valley Special Collections, Kansas City Public Library.

standing out in large type—greeted delegates and visitors upon their arrival.[50] Ambassadors were stationed in various convention hotels and "furnished information concerning the whereabouts of places of meetings and points of interest in the city." They were asked to "assist your [hotel] staff in the entertaining and reception of your guests."[51] W. Ricket Fillmore, chairman of the hosts and hostesses committee, reminded volunteers, "Our Committees will represent Kansas City. Therefore, it is imperative that every Captain and every Lieutenant before going on duty, get all the information possible and familiarize themselves with data that they will be expected to dispense."[52]

William Morton urged volunteers to create "an atmosphere of genuine hospitality which will be appreciated by our guests." He suggested "hosts and hostesses exercise a friendly and gracious manner and evidence a real desire to greet visitors and make them feel at home."[53] After all, he concluded,

There will be approximately twelve hundred men and women enlisted in this particular assignment. If every man and every woman reports faithfully at the time and place assigned, and if they enter wholeheartedly into the spirit of the service we are attempting to render, our work will be a glorious success. Our guests will leave Kansas City fully convinced that we are in deed and in spirit the "Heart of America" as well as by geographic location.[54]

Individuals unable to serve as a host or hostess could volunteer as an auto tour driver. Convention publicity described scenic routes along with approximate drive times and points of particular interest.[55] Consequently, vehicles were desperately needed. Organizers solicited volunteers through a postcard that indicated, "I will be glad to help 'Sell Kansas City' to visiting G.O.P. delegates and their families . . . and will donate my time and the use of my car."[56] The card asked which day and time (morning or afternoon) volunteers were available, as well as the make of their car and the number of passengers it could carry. A note at the bottom reminded residents, "This is a Kansas City proposition. Not necessary to be a Republican to serve on this committee. Your car will be needed."[57]

Simultaneous to the 1928 convention, the Hotel Greeters of America promoted Kansas City tourism through the *Hotel Greeter's Guide to Kansas City*. This document began with a historical overview introducing visitors to Kansas City's frontier past and progression "from a trading post in 1850 . . . [to] a lively and hustling metropolis, with a population, cultural development, and business enterprise that places it among the leading municipalities of the world."[58] The guide proclaimed, "[Kansas City] offers two things preeminently American: two things without price, the outstretched hand of hospitality, such as only the West knows, and the key to the greatest gift of all, boundless opportunity."[59] Geographic location made Kansas City simultaneously "the gateway to the west" and the "heart of America."[60] Kansas City boasted the best of all regions, the text declared, because it "hears the call of the North, and the voice of the South. Here the East ends and the West begins."[61]

Beyond introducing Kansas City's cultural heritage, the *Hotel Greeter's Guide* also called visitors' attention to the civic achievements and benefits enjoyed by Kansas City residents. Local businesses were highlighted, much as in the *Book of the Republican National Convention*, and local residents were lauded as possessing an enduring entrepreneurial spirit. Short descriptions of major attractions were followed by auto-tour options, ranging from a forty-five-minute trip to a three-hour tour, as well as a list of nine motor coach routes that highlighted Kansas City's neighborhoods and park system.[62] Multiple sites were highlighted within the pamphlet—sites that are explored in greater detail in other chapters in this volume, including the Liberty Memorial, the Federal Reserve building, Swope Park, and the Kansas City stockyards.

Finally, the publication represented an ideal venue for Kansas City businesses to reach out-of-town visitors and concierge services. Thirteen theaters were listed, along with both full and partial page advertisements for all manner of Kansas City businesses. Lodging and transportation options could be found by perusing the advertisements of thirty-two hotels, three bus lines, and four car services. In addition, the guide touted retail shopping and vital resources for someone moving to Kansas City, such as hardware stores, banks, and utility providers.[63]

While the *Book of the Republican National Convention* had been published specifically for delegates and convention attendees, both the *Visitor's Guide to Kansas City* and the *Hotel Greeter's Guide* targeted visitors more generally. The commercial content and coordination of the latter publications represents the broader campaign on behalf of city leaders and the business community to highlight the benefits of visiting and living in Kansas City. Collectively, all three texts demonstrate a commitment by convention organizers to entice delegates and attendees to leave the convention floor and experience Kansas City. The emphasis placed on the unique commercial advantages and cultural opportunities within Kansas City demonstrates how governmental officials and business leaders sought to use the 1928 Republican National Convention as a springboard for future municipal growth.

Race and the Convention

While Chamber of Commerce leaders hoped to bring positive publicity to Kansas City, controversy erupted regarding the role of African American delegates and attendees. Despite the racial integration of previous conventions—both Chicago and Cleveland had housed African American delegates among all attendees—Kansas City maintained a rigid color line.[64] As the 1928 convention neared, Charles F. Curry, secretary of the housing committee, informed state delegations, "If you have any Negro delegates and will give us their names, we will make an assignment for them. We have excellent accommodations for them."[65] The decision enflamed the editorial page of *The Call*, and in an attempt to placate African Americans, convention organizers added three African American members to the General Executive, Finance, and Arrangement Committee.[66] They also established a separate Negro Entertainment Committee of 103 members, including Chester Franklin and his wife, Ada Franklin.[67] A venue for the entertainment of African American delegates and attendees was located at Thirteenth and Paseo.

Multiple articles in *The Call* vehemently condemned convention organizers and lambasted enforced segregation. In February 1928, the paper reminded readers, "It is not too soon for Negroes to begin thinking of the coming election in terms of their own interests." Readers were urged to become activists because "the hubbub raised about convention delegates [in reference to electing African American delegates] and party candidates is all white so far. Pretty soon we will be told it is too late. Yet it will not be too late for our votes to count."[68] Conrad Mann, in particular, became a target of scorn. Mann justified convention segregation as consistent Kansas City policy. He explained, "Our Negro population would have cause to reprove us if we accorded any different treatment to visiting Negroes, merely because they happen to be in Kansas City."[69]

Delegate segregation reverberated beyond Kansas City. On a national level, it marked a strategic decision by Herbert Hoover's presidential campaign. Samuel O'Dell asserts that "Hoover's southern strategy unfolded at the convention. In credentials disputes between southern black and tan and lily-white delegations, Hoover sided with the lily whites." The strategy continued during the campaign as Republicans sacrificed equality to win over southern whites.[70] In order to appease southern voters, Republicans avoided appearing too radical on questions of racial equality and civil rights. Chester Franklin labeled the lack of attention paid to African American issues in the 1928 platform "a sorry crumb."[71] Negative publicity in outlets ranging from the *New York Times* to the *Chicago Defender* undercut efforts of convention organizers to showcase Kansas City's unity. Delegate segregation also created an opportunity for local Democrats. In Chapters 1 and 2, John W. McKerley and Jeffrey L. Pasley explore the voting patterns of Missouri's African American population and Democratic efforts during the late nineteenth and early twentieth centuries to sever the link between African American voters and the Republican Party. Their work further describes how the strategies honed in the first three decades of the twentieth century established long-lasting electoral parameters. The treatment of African American delegates at the Kansas City Republican National Convention became an important factor in this political shift.

The performance of African American dancers during the convention parade also led to full-throated condemnation in the pages of *The Call*. A June 15 editorial lamented how "Negroes could be found to play the fool in the republican parade." The unfortunate juxtaposition of Republican Party regalia and racial caricature led *The Call* to note that "the sons of freedmen who were the occasion of the republican party's birth . . . to be doing grotesque dances on a float . . . as their part in a parade in the party's honor, is to prove that we are now just where we were before the Civil War." The article concluded that as "much as we want to condemn the parade's managers, we found ourselves compelled to soften our reproaches because the actions of our own people gave encouragement to the plan." Thus, "as a group we need to learn that the thoughtless actions of the humblest among us can discount the greatest efforts of our best."[72]

The 1928 Republican National Convention laid bare internal tension among African Americans in Kansas City. Franklin's condemnation of delegate segregation and the public actions of convention organizers and African American dancers foreshadowed a long-term shift in his overall conservative approach to community leadership and activism. Nevertheless, he remained an advocate for Kansas City's future. In the weeks after the convention he urged readers to support upcoming initiatives to improve the airport, waterworks, and streets. Franklin argued:

> City improvements are not all pleasant parks and boulevards, not frills for
> moments of leisure. In the main they are the city's housekeeping, which invites

or repels prospective business enterprises, in search of better location. These give preference to cities which offer the best surroundings for labor, and the best facilities for commerce. Kansas City has natural advantages. But it must develop them, or be counted out as a good place to live and do business.[73]

Not all African Americans, however, supported Kansas City's leaders. One reader of *The Call* proclaimed, "It is time that we call a halt on our ballots, tell our leaders either to stiffen their backbones or step out." The author reasoned, "The national convention in coming to Kansas City let the local committee ignore the constitution in segregation and discriminating against the delegates of our race, and still expect you, our leaders, to get our votes for whoever they may name regardless of their past." The author condemned "leaders [who] knowing full well these facts accept a handful of decorations on East Twelfth street, Eighteenth street, as a salve then place a button in the lapel of their coat and come to plead with the race to have confidence in you and to vote for the man or men you stand for."[74]

Capitalizing on the Convention

The 1928 Republican National Convention united business leaders and average voters and showcased the city's growth and potential. On June 18, Conrad Mann expressed sincere appreciation for "all that you did toward the success that has won Kansas City not only favorable world-wide publicity, but a new standing nationally for our ability to handle an undertaking of that kind, for genuine hospitality."[75] Following the convention reporters from over fifty publications, ranging from major outlets like the *New York Times* and national wire services to the *Tacoma News Tribune* and *Salt Lake News*, issued a collective statement of praise.[76] The *New York Times Magazine* noted, "Missouri's 'Gateway to the West' has grown up since the Democrats went there in 1900."[77] The editorial page of the *Dallas Herald* observed, "The people of the east were disappointed when it was announced that Kansas City had been chosen for the convention. We didn't think Kansas City could take care of such a large gathering . . . I have found our fears groundless. I was never as well taken care of as now. The tremendous hospitality of the people of Kansas City is equaled only by the life and energy of the people."[78]

Following the Republican National Convention, the Chamber of Commerce sought to sustain the focus on Kansas City's natural beauty. After receiving "quite a few favorable comments on the [auto] tour used during the G.O.P. Convention," debate ensued over "marking a route permanently." J. M. Guild noted, "This proposition could command newspaper space in the National Advertising Campaign [which] was to be launched shortly by the Industrial Committee."[79] Subsequent discussion considered adding additional points of interest. For example, Hospital Hill was praised as "one of the most effective views within the city." Members were particularly keen on the inclusion of Swope Park. On the one hand, it was suggested that the time and distance required to tour Swope Park might distract from other Kansas City amenities. On the other hand, broad public admiration and the belief "that the entrance to the park was as beautiful as any in the country" led several committee members to argue, "protests would be citywide if Swope Park was omitted."[80] As a compromise, members endorsed "placing a marker at Linwood and Benton and another some place on Meyer Boulevard, making it clear that Swope Park lay south and east respectively, thereby giving tourists the opportunity of going there if they wished, but at the same time retaining the inside route much the same as used during the G.O.P. Convention."[81] The decision to designate a permanent scenic route reveals the link between the City Beautiful movement, which had established the park system, and efforts to cement Kansas City's reputation as a tourist attraction following the 1928 convention.

Ten-Year Plan

The creation of the Ten-Year Plan for Kansas City represented a continuation of the civic pride and organizational momentum created by the 1928 Republican National Convention. When Conrad Mann, following the summer gathering, became Chamber of Commerce president, he "brought 600 business men to their feet as they cheered his declaration that 'Kansas City is going to have a civic awakening.'"[82] The Ten-Year Plan reintroduced municipal projects that had failed to gain voter approval in 1928 and also identified new priorities. The Convention Committee, for example, noted during a meeting in July that despite the success of the 1928 Republican National Convention, Kansas City failed to land numerous other national conventions due to inadequate meeting space and facilities. Members were optimistic, however, that "if the Chamber of Commerce and the public in general decide to endorse a ten-year program . . . a new convention hall can be included in such a plan." Members noted that Cleveland, which had hosted the 1924 Republican convention, had recently finished a new municipal auditorium in 1922 and St. Louis was also planning a new facility.[83]

In order to ensure broad citywide support, thus avoiding the failed ballot results of the previous year, Mann spearheaded a Civic Improvement Committee. The *Kansas City Star* noted that the committee's structure mirrored what had been used in Chicago to create an "outstanding city . . . in the manner of city planning."[84] To avoid the segregation on planning committees for the Republican National Convention, African American members were included on the Civic Improvement Committee. For example, both Thomas Unthank and Fred Dabney, who had been late additions to the General Executive Committee for the Republican Convention, were appointed to the committee. Other African American members of the Civic Improvement Committee included Chester Franklin, Mrs. Myrtle F. Cook, Edwin

S. Lewis, Dr. William J. Thompkins, and T. B. Watkins. As Kansas City entered its next phase of growth, the city continued to measure itself against regional rivals and grapple with racial division.

In 1938, to commemorate the accomplishments of the previous decade, the Chamber of Commerce published *Where These Rocky Bluffs Meet: The Story of the Kansas City Ten-Year Plan.* The book stands as an important resource regarding the Ten-Year Plan and contains detailed descriptions of all proposed projects, maps, and diagrams, as well as the estimated and final costs associated with each project. From 1928 to 1938, Kansas City's Ten-Year Plan set the city abuzz with construction. The initiative included infrastructure projects, such as an updated sewer system and waterworks facility, as well as improvements to numerous roads and parks. The plan also envisioned numerous building projects, such as a new courthouse, police headquarters, and municipal auditorium.[85] During the Great Depression, the Ten-Year Plan ensured that Kansas City was able "to obtain its full quota of federal work-relief millions, and to use those funds not in haphazard jobs of expedience, but in an orderly program of needed public improvement."[86]

Conclusion

By most measures the Republican National Convention proved a resounding success. The summer of 1928 political gathering brought concentrated attention to Kansas City. Reporters and newspaper columnists filed numerous reports on political developments and their impressions of the Kansas City community. Visitors from across the nation, many seeing Kansas City for the first time, packed the city's hotels, toured the city's sites, and enjoyed the city's amenities. Carefully choreographed pamphlets and newspaper publicity touted the achievements of Kansas City's residents and businesses to both delegates and attendees. Organizers' careful planning and the collective enthusiasm of countless volunteers ensured delegates and attendees were treated to a firsthand view of Kansas City. They enjoyed the landscape created by the City Beautiful movement and the updated infrastructure built during the Get-It-Done campaign.

In the eyes of many, a great deal of work still needed to be done, however. The projects rejected by voters in the spring of 1928 remained unfinished. The decision to segregate delegates during the convention revealed ongoing racial tension within the city. Consequently, the 1928 Republican National Convention represents a pivotal turning point for Kansas City. The event bolstered civic pride and reinvigorated interest in developing a plan for Kansas City's future. The event also helped to unify Kansas City's business community and provided numerous city leaders, most notably Conrad Mann, with valuable organizing experience. Adoption of a comprehensive Ten-Year Plan following the event guaranteed the 1928 Republican National Convention an ongoing legacy within Kansas City. The event also revealed persistent divisions that threatened to disrupt municipal growth and undermine the carefully choreographed vision of Kansas City's transformation.

Notes

1. "The G.O.P. Convention," *Kansas Citian*, May 29, 1928, 414.

2. William H. Wilson, *The City Beautiful Movement in Kansas City* (Columbia: University of Missouri Press, 1964), xvii.

3. Minutes of Meeting of the Subcommittee on Budget for the Program of Expansion, April 26, 1926, Greater Kansas City Chamber of Commerce Minutes, 1856–1991, Native Sons Archives, (K0274), State Historical Society of Missouri, Kansas City Research Center, Kansas City, Missouri (hereafter Chamber Minutes).

4. Ibid.

5. "Why Not a 10-Year Program?" *Kansas City Star*, October 14, 1927.

6. J. M. Guild to Gentlemen, December 22, 1927. See also Board of Directors Minutes, Kansas City Chamber of Commerce, December 20, 1927, Chamber Papers. Names mentioned for the Ten-Year Improvement Plan include Arthur Hardgrave, J. F. Porter, R. M. Maxwell, Walter Matscheck, Ed S. North, and Thornton Cooke.

7. *Kansas City Times*, April 6, 1928.

8. *Kansas Citian*, May 15, 1928, 384–385.

9. "Can Kansas City Afford to Issue Bonds?" *Kansas Citian*, March 6, 1928, 195.

10. "Report of Trafficways Commission," January 5, 1928. Kansas City's Ten-Year Plan Records, 1870–1938, Native Sons Archives, (K0272), State Historical Society of Missouri, Kansas City Research Room, Kansas City, Missouri (hereafter Ten-Year Plan Records).

11. The *Kansas City Star* articles appeared from January 9, 1928, to January 20, 1928.

12. "Improvement Bonds," *The Call*, February 17, 1928, 10.

13. "Vote for the Bonds!" *The Call*, April 13, 1928, 4-B. See also page 1 for a detailed description of the issues on the ballot.

14. Citizens' Bond Committee, "Information on the Proposed Bond Issues," May 8, 1928, Ten-Year Plan Records.

15. "Kansas City Spirit Needs Repair," *The Call*, May 11, 1928, 4.

16. "Four Bond Proposals Carry," *Kansas Citian*, May 15, 1928, 381. Included is a table detailing the percentage of votes cast and requested bond amounts for all ballot measures.

17. Chicago hosted the Democrats in 1864, 1884, 1892, 1896, and 1932. Democrats gathered in St. Louis in 1876, 1888, 1904, and 1916.

18. Minutes, Convention Executive Committee, Kansas City Chamber of Commerce, February 11, 1927, and April 4, 1927, Chamber Minutes.

19. Minutes, Executive Committee, Kansas City Chamber of Commerce, April 27, 1927, Chamber Minutes.

20. Minutes, Board of Directors Meeting, Kansas City Chamber of Commerce, June 16, 1927, Chamber Minutes.

21. Lyle Stephenson to unnamed, November 4, 1927, Chamber Minutes.

22. Arthur Hardgrave et al. to Committee of 100 members, November 9, 1927, Chamber Minutes.

23. Robert H. Tschudy to unnamed, November 21, 1927, Chamber Minutes.

24. "Committee Organization," *Kansas Citian*, May 15, 1928. See also *Book of the Republican National Convention* (Kansas City Chamber of Commerce, 1928), which describes McElroy as "a leading Democrat who aided materially in bringing the Republican National Convention to Kansas City."

25. Shouse, Jouett, Biographical Directory of the United States Congress, http://bioguide.congress.gov/scripts/biodisplay.pl?index=S000384, accessed May 2016.

26. Lou Holland to unnamed, November 11, 1927, Chamber Minutes.

27. Ibid.

28. Subscription Contract, November 1927, Greater Kansas City Chamber of Commerce Records, 1856–1990, Native Sons Archives, (K0527), (hereafter Chamber Records).

29. E. E. Amick to unnamed, December 15, 1927, Chamber Records.

30. J. M. Guild to unnamed, January 31, 1928, Chamber Records.

31. Ibid.

32. Lou Holland to unnamed, November 11, 1927, Chamber Records.

33. Chamber of Commerce letter, January 31, 1928, Chamber Minutes.

34. Ibid.

35. "To Finance the Republican Convention," *Kansas Citian*, February 7, 1928, 121.

36. The contract was signed in Kansas City, Missouri, on January 7, 1928, Chamber Records.

37. "To Finance the Republican Convention," *Kansas Citian*, February 7, 1928, 121.

38. "The 'K.C.' That Is Host to Republicans," *New York Times Magazine*, May 27, 1928, 4.

39. Ibid.

40. *Where These Rocky Bluffs Meet: Including the Story of the Kansas City Ten-Year Plan* (Kansas City, Mo.: Kansas City Chamber of Commerce, 1938), 113; see also the biography of Mann in ibid., 110–118.

41. "Committee Organization," *Kansas Citian*, May 15, 1928.

42. "Book of Republican National Convention," *Kansas Citian*, March 6, 1928, 197.

43. Ibid.

44. *Book of the Republican National Convention.*

45. Ibid.

46. Ibid.

47. "G.O.P. Tinge Downtown," *Kansas City Star*, May 24, 1928, 1.

48. "Stick Up for Kansas City!" *Kansas Citian*, May 22, 1928, 403.

49. Undated Invitation, Chamber Records.

50. Conrad Mann to unnamed, June 12, 1928, Chamber Records.

51. Wm. E. Morton to unnamed, June 5, 1928, Chamber Records.

52. W. Ricket Fillmore to unnamed, June 5, 1928, Chamber Records.

53. "Duties and Instructions to Captains," Chamber Records.

54. Ibid.

55. *Information for Visitors to the Republican National Convention* (Kansas City, Mo.: Lecht-man Printing, 1928).

56. Conrad Mann to unnamed, May 29, 1928, Chamber Records.

57. "Dear Mr. Barton," postcard, undated, Chamber Records.

58. The publication noted that Kansas City was at "the center of an intensive border warfare" and "acts of depredation were committed on all sides." The guide abstained from taking sides by noting, "Kansas City was a meeting place for all factions, and many important decisions were made in or near the new city." *Hotel Greeter's Guide to Kansas City* (Kansas City, Mo.: Hotel Greeters of America, 1928), 4.

59. Ibid.

60. Ibid., 2.

61. Ibid, 4.

62. Ibid, 52–56.

63. Ibid, 60.

64. For a more thorough examination of the racial divisions within Kansas City, see Kevin Fox Gotham, *Race, Real Estate, and Uneven Development: The Kansas City Experience, 1900–2000* (Albany: State University of New York Press, 2002).

65. Charles F. Curry to State Delegations, undated. Chamber Records. See also "Hotels Are Closed to Delegates," *The Call*, March 16, 1928, 1.

66. "Committee Organization," *Kansas Citian*, May 15, 1928. The three men added were Dr. Thomas C. Unthank, Fred Dabney, and Gideon W. Brown. Mrs. Myrtle F. Cook was also added to the Housing Committee.

67. The Negro Entertainment Committee was chaired by Mrs. A. E. Jenkins, with Mrs. Myrtle F. Cook as the co-chair.

68. Editorial Board, *The Call*, February 17, 1928, 10.

69. "Surely Mr. Mann Is Joking," *The Call*, March 23, 1928, 4-B.

70. Samuel O'Dell, "Blacks, the Democratize Party, and the Presidential Election of 1928: A Mild Rejoinder," *Phylon* 48, no. 1 (first quarter, 1987): 1–11, 4.

71. "Less Practical Politics," *The Call*, June 22, 1928, 10.

72. "Playing the Fool," *The Call*, June 15, 1928, 10.

73. "Again the Bonds," *The Call*, June 22, 1928, 10.

74. "For the Right of Citizenship," *The Call*, June 22, 1928, 10.

75. Conrad Mann to unnamed, June 18, 1928, Chamber Records.

76. "Newspaper Men in Lavish Tribute," *Kansas Citian*, June 26, 1928, 498.

77. "The 'K.C.' That Is Host to Republicans," *New York Times Magazine*, May 27, 1928, 4.

78. *Dallas Herald*, quoted in "Visualize G.O.P. Convention Publicity," *Kansas Citian*, July 3, 1928, 514.

79. Chamber of Commerce Meeting, July 31, 1928, Chamber Minutes.

80. Ibid.

81. Ibid.

82. *Where These Rocky Bluffs Meet*, ix.

83. Convention Committee, July 16, 1928, Chamber Minutes.

84. "For the 10-Year Plan," *Kansas City Star*, January 1, 1929, 1.
85. *Where These Rocky Bluffs Meet*, 192.
86. Ibid.

Breaking Barriers in a Segregated City

CHAPTER SIX

Making Meat

Race, Labor, and the Kansas City Stockyards

John Herron

There are world records for nearly everything, including cattle processing. And in September 1918, Kansas City broke them all. As World War I entered its final, fateful months, the Kansas City stockyards handled more than 55,000 cattle in a single day, and for the month, 475,000. That fall, during a remarkable three-month span, more than 1.3 million cattle passed through the city's yards. The Kansas City cattle business was impressive, but add to these figures hundreds of thousands of sheep, hogs, and horses, and more than 3.3 million animals were yarded in the city.[1] First seven, then twelve, and then thirty-four railroads brought these animals into the city and out again to distant markets. The Kansas City Livestock Exchange Building—the economic nerve center of the stockyards—contained nearly 500 of-fices, and—with its own network of banks, buyers, dealers, and railroad agents—it was the largest building in the world dedicated to commercial stock transactions. Stockyard managers rattled off these statistics easily and frequently. Livestock was, after all, a numbers game—the higher the tally, the greater the profit. From its ability to efficiently weigh, kill, and process thousands of animals, the Kansas City stock-yards became the city's first million-dollar-a-year industry. Steady growth meant that livestock also became the first million-dollar-a-month and then million-dollar-a-day business.[2] Only Chicago could claim to put more meat on America's dinner tables. Civic boosters pointed to the city's paved streets, distinctive architecture, and public parks as evidence of their community's maturation and development, but as Kansas City entered its "Golden Age," it was livestock that made the city hum.[3]

Other figures, however, get less attention. On that record-breaking day in 1918, for instance, every cow in the Kansas City yard required at least ten gallons of fresh water. That same cow could consume thirty pounds of feed and produce three

A photograph of cattle pens at the Kansas City stockyards, looking northwest from atop the Kansas City Livestock Exchange Building, c. 1920s. Courtesy of the Kansas Historical Society.

pounds of urine and sixty pounds of manure each and every day. Do the math and it quickly becomes evident that a large infrastructure equivalent to a small city—hundreds of miles of discharge pipes and water mains, a massive system of levees and revetments, independent power and lighting plants—was required to keep the pens in operation. The environmental footprint of the stockyards was massive, with pollution of the nearby Missouri and Kansas Rivers and with an all-pervading stench in the city's bottoms part of the cost of business.

But a final set of numbers, this time measured in human capital, is required to complete this introduction to the Kansas City stockyards. At the end of World War I, the yards sprawled over 230 acres, where several major packinghouses and a handful of smaller related operations employed more than 20,000 workers—double the number from 1900 and more than 70 percent of the city's manufacturing labor force.[4] In the Kansas City yards, this contingent of industrial laborers systematically deconstructed animals for the American market and, in the process, transformed work routines and labor politics in the city.

The size and shape of this laboring community challenges the stereotype of Kansas City as a western "cowtown." Longhorn cattle, cowboys on horseback, and wide-open spaces are part of the iconography of the mythic American frontier, and for much of its early history Kansas City traded heavily on this imagery, sharing more with Dodge City and Abilene than Pittsburgh or Detroit. A more complete picture of the city, however, should include the long line of low-paid wage workers required to mechanically transform meat on the hoof.[5] Stockyards workers in Kansas City labored in an industry that was just as mechanized as steel and just as dangerous as coal. In this chapter I argue that more than any other enterprise, it was the stockyards and laboring thousands that propelled Kansas City into the modern age. Far from a quaint frontier effort, the stockyards represented a new industrial order that used modern corporate structures, efficient technologies, and an endless supply of workers to transform the nation's relationship with food. More significant from a labor perspective was the composition of the stockyards labor pool. Drawing white workers from midwestern hinterlands, immigrants from eastern and southern Europe, and African Americans from the agricultural South, the stockyards built a multiethnic labor force. In an era of divisive labor politics and race-based unionization efforts, the diverse working class in the Kansas City stockyards altered the history of labor activism in the Midwest. Stockyards labor in the city often found common cause, providing a rare glimpse of racial cooperation in an increasingly segregated working America.

Building the Yards

At the moment of this 1918 peak, the Kansas City stockyards were already more than fifty years old. After a decade of strife along the Missouri-Kansas border stretching from the political hostilities of "Bleeding Kansas" to the vicious guerrilla conflict and battlefield carnage of the Civil War, Kansas City shook off its nervous unease and, in 1865, welcomed the tracks of the Pacific Railroad Company into the city. Kansas City boosters embraced the railroad, thinking it would connect them to the wealth of Colorado gold fields and the silver mines of Nevada; instead, the rail line enabled the city to take advantage of a more local growth opportunity in meat.[6] In 1867 an Illinois merchant, Joseph McCoy, purchased 250 acres of open range near a newly constructed rail depot in Abilene, Kansas, and established a small stockyard. His plan was to give Texas cattle ranchers better access to American consumers. The war had prevented southern beef from reaching northern markets, but now, he hoped, the railroad offered a corrective. In midsummer of that year, cattle driven north on the Chisholm Trail began arriving at his midwestern outpost, and by early September, the first shipment of beef was on its way by rail to urban America.[7]

The first cattle out of McCoy's Abilene stockyards headed for Chicago, but Kansas City was not far behind. Chicago, the western hub of many eastern railroads and a booming metropolis, was a natural destination for midwestern livestock. The massive Union Stockyards, built in 1865, covered more than 300 acres of former swampland in the southern part of the city, and by 1870 Chicago was processing more than 2 million animals annually. Yet such size also became a liability as stock-yard overcrowding and increasing distance from western livestock fields eventually ended Chicago's meat monopoly.[8] Given an opportunity, Kansas City was eager to grab its share of the livestock market. In 1870, a group of local railroad executives, headed by James Joy and L. V. Morse, fenced off five acres in the city's West Bottoms neighborhood and built a series of small stock pens. Growth was immediate, and in 1871, thirteen additional acres on the banks of the Kansas River were added to handle the 100,000 animals then coming into the city.[9]

Kansas City was primarily a rest area where livestock could be fed and watered before continuing their journey eastward to markets, but in 1874 an infusion of eastern capital transformed the operation. Charles Adams Jr., the Harvard-educated grandson and great-grandson of American presidents, purchased additional land in the bottoms and immediately made plans to expand. He hired Charles Morse, a fellow Harvard man, to manage his Kansas City investments. Morse pursued the task with unusual vigor. As he admitted to a close friend in 1879, "the object of my life now is to help make Kansas City the Chicago of the Missouri Valley."[10] With nearly unlimited access to Boston financial networks, Adams and Morse began to think big. They joined with Philip Armour, a noted Chicago meatpacker, to build one of the most modern livestock-processing facilities in the country. Armour's factory employed 3,000 laborers working across an eight-building campus. In the first year of operation, Armour processed 45,000 animals, a tenfold increase in the city's production. With equal parts qualification and enthusiasm, a newspaper later described the plant's opening as "probably the greatest event in the history of Kansas City."[11] Gustavus Swift, another Chicago packer, arrived in 1887 and built a larger and more expensive thirteen-acre facility. Other major players like Cudahy Packing Company, the Fowler Packing Company, the Reid Brothers, Nelson Morris and Company, the Ruddy Brothers, and the New York–based Schwarzschild and Sulzberger soon joined the Kansas City market and elevated meatpacking into the city's main economic engine.[12] In 1893, one local newspaper crowed that the city would soon "strip from Chicago the proud plumage of first place in the live stock world." A second outlet was even more bullish. The city had received more than its share of "sneers and jibes" from eastern peers, the paper noted, but such "slander" was of little importance. "With the greatest cattle and livestock market in the world . . . the greatest packing industry in the world . . . there is nothing that stands in the way of [Kansas City] becoming the greatest city in the world."[13]

The local press was often filled with such breathless hyperbole, but in truth, the Kansas City stockyards were impressive and capable of processing nearly 5 million animals a year by 1900. In the first year of the new century, meatpacking represented an amazing 91 percent of the city's industrial output.[14] The Kansas City stockyards were able to expand so rapidly because of the wise application of tech-

Armour Packing Company, site of a 1938 sit-down strike. Courtesy of the Missouri Valley Special Collections, Kansas City Public Library.

nology. Chicago, St. Louis, Cincinnati, Louisville, and Milwaukee were also home to substantial meatpacking interests, but in comparison, Kansas City was relatively late to the game. Lack of transportation infrastructure hampered industrial growth in the city, although this liability became an advantage in the twentieth century as packers began closing out-of-date facilities in other locations, especially those without refrigeration, and constructing more modern plants in Kansas City. As a result, the city's meatpacking plants became some of the country's most advanced. A national industry trade paper confirmed this development with a survey of the city's Morris packing plant. "At every step of the operation in every department of the plant," the paper began, "large and small labor-saving devices have been developed." Visitors to the Kansas City factory, a seven-acre facility built at a cost of more than $2 million, saw technology everywhere with mechanized stokers, automatic scrapers, steam-powered saws, advanced pulley systems, electric motors, and modern transportation systems throughout the plant.[15] The Morris factory was not unusual; each of the other large packers built advanced facilities throughout the city's sprawling stockyard district.

Modern technology did not translate into a pleasant work experience, however. Indeed, it was often the opposite. Despite an abundance of advanced machinery, livestock processing in Kansas City remained a labor-intensive industry. Live animals that varied in size and shape made automation difficult and, when combined with a competitive market and low profit margins, pushed packers to organize work routines to control the high cost of labor. The result, as in other assembly-line environments, was that Kansas City's meat producers based their work demands on a "minute and unparalleled subdivision of labor." The above survey of the Morris factory, for example, found that more than 125 workers were required to process a single hog. "What is true of one task is true of all," the report noted, and each operation was expected to "proceed straightway without interruption."[16]

Thanks to labor journals and muckraking exposés, the workflow in the Kansas City packing industry is well known. The process began with livestock driven into the factory, where a knocker hit the animals with a heavy sledge, rendering them unconscious. Another worker attached the animal's hind legs to a mechanical hoist and then onto overhead rails. A sticker moved in and, in one quick motion, sliced the throat, causing the animal to bleed out. One packinghouse worker in Kansas City's Armour factory recalled that the sticker in his plant was a "huge German," who within the first minutes of every shift "was covered in blood." "He drank blood," the laborer remembered, "and said nothing to anybody."[17] A team of knifemen, with sharp tools in each hand, then removed the animal's valuable hide. A header followed and removed the skull, a gut-snatcher took the intestines, and a kidney puller removed the animal's other internal organs. Splitters, armed with heavy cleavers, sliced down the backbone, cutting the animals in two, and as the carcass moved across the killing floor, the animal was met by rumpers, backers, grinders, trimmers, cheekers, boners, pullers, and luggers, who processed the remaining meat. A small army of entry-level laborers helped the process along by moving carcasses, cutting off tails and horns, and cleaning up blood and other offal. Such practice was celebrated as efficient, but by reducing jobs to the lowest skill level, Kansas City packers were also able to replace experienced craftsmen with general laborers. This transition reduced wage levels in the packing industry, and with the repetition of basic operations, management could control the pace of production. No longer reliant on trade knowledge, factory foremen could, whenever possible, turn to what was called "continuous-flow methods" to speed up conveyor lines and increase work output.[18]

The average work routine in the meatpacking industry, then, was not just unskilled but dangerous. In one three-year period between 1907 and 1910, thirteen workers died in a single meat-processing plant, and more than a decade later, conditions had hardly improved.[19] One of the chief complaints was the pace of work, a common reason for injury. Laborers in the packing plants had but a few seconds to perform their routinized task and little time between animals. After a visit to one Kansas City plant, a national reporter noted that workers had a "full 2 seconds" to "debristle a hog carcass" and less than ten seconds "to de-head" a cow.[20] The speed and dexterity displayed by packinghouse laborers often impressed visitors, but as one labor activist remarked, such achievement "is simply inhumane hard work."[21] Cuts and scrapes were a daily occurrence, but so too were swollen joints and knuckles, as well as back and neck pain earned from long hours hunched over a carcass. Factory seniority often led to a life of arthritis and other muscular disabilities. Worse still was the frequency with which workers suffered disabling injuries from minor accidents, like trips and falls, to the more serious like burns and lost limbs.[22]

No less significant than the speed of work were the conditions inside the plant. Summer temperatures on the killing floors in Kansas City could easily exceed 100 degrees, and workers, stripped to the waist and covered in blood and viscera, struggled to keep pace with production. Conversely, workers in the trim and cutting departments labored in bone-chilling rooms only a few degrees above freezing. And virtually all of this labor occurred in a working environment that was, to be generous, unpleasant. In the early years of packing in Kansas City, a visitor to one plant reported amazement at the "perfect cleanliness of the whole establishment. . . . No offensive odor is perceptible."[23] A decade later, visitors would have a much different experience. The stench and smoke from the West Bottoms made an impression on nearly everyone who saw the stockyards. Guidebooks warned visitors of stained clothing, ruined hairdos, and a powerful stink that would not easily wash off. Such conditions were not just disagreeable but unhealthy. A 1911 federal survey of packinghouse safety in Kansas City concluded that the air in these factories "is often damp, close, and unwholesome." Such bland phrasing downplays the significant diseases—tuberculosis, asthma, pneumonia, and rheumatism—that left a permanent mark on packinghouse laborers in the city.[24]

The distressed nature of life inside the meatpacking plants continued to plague workers after they left the workplace. When Charles Adams joined with Philip Armour to build a modern packinghouse in Kansas City in the late nineteenth century, they also designed a new neighborhood for their workers. Christened "Armourdale," the community reflected the Boston background of its backers. Platted on 600 acres, Armourdale was built to resemble a small New England town. Home lots were wide and spacious, streets were straight and clean, and a nearly ten-acre public park was set aside in the village square. In 1885, less than 2,000 people lived in the small riverside community, but just three years later, the population had swelled to nearly 5,000, stretching social services.[25] In the first decades of the next century, the population continued to expand on a marked pace so that by 1920, Armourdale, following a pattern recognizable in more established eastern urban centers, was overcrowded, economically depressed, and lacking in proper sanitation. A federal official from the Immigration Commission toured the community's muddy streets and closely spaced residences, describing it as a "labyrinth of narrow, dirty passageways, flanked by the most non-descript sort of shacks."[26] It is no surprise, then, that 1920s worker surveys often placed meatpacking among the worst industries in which to find employment.[27]

Making a Working Class

As a result of the challenges inherent in stockyard labor, the factories relied heavily on a malleable working class. Census data reveal that recent arrivals from Ireland, France, and Germany worked alongside Dutch, Scandinavian, and Italian laborers. The British Empire was well represented with Australian, Canadian, Indian, Scottish, and Welsh workers filling many different roles throughout the industry. After plant managers sent recruiters to central and eastern Europe, a trickle of workers from Russia, Bulgaria, Poland, Czechoslovakia, Slovenia, and especially Croatia became a steady flow. While publicly proclaiming that "nationality makes very little difference" in their labor force, Kansas City meatpackers continued to maintain a labor hierarchy. Germans and Swedes were considered "superior," and of the more recent immigrants, "the Russians are regarded as much more efficient than the Poles, and the Greeks are considered more efficient than the Italians, but not as good as the Croatians, Slovaks, and Lithuanians." Most employers approved of the Japanese "on account of their quickness and quietness while at work," and everyone agreed that the Greeks and the ever-troublesome Italians were "unsatisfactory."[28]

But in many ways, the most significant cohort of meatpacking laborers was African Americans. Blacks began arriving in the city in large numbers in the 1870s and were immediately drawn into livestock processing, a stark contrast to the later entrance of black workers into other meatpacking centers. Later that decade, the Exoduster migration to the Midwest increased the region's black population, and by the early decades of the twentieth century, the packinghouses were the single largest employer of African American laborers in Kansas City. In 1900, 22 percent of meatpacking workers were black. This percentage declined slightly in 1909 to 16 percent, stabilized at 20 percent by 1920, and expanded to 25 percent of the workforce in the 1930s.[29]

One popular narrative for the abundance of black workers in meatpacking was kind treatment of African American laborers. There "[is no] large employer of Negroes in Kansas City which treats colored workmen with more consideration than does the Armour Packing Company," one contemporary labor survey noted. "Dressing-rooms and free baths are provided, coffee is served at luncheon . . . and the old employees who are unable to keep up . . . are given other work, which they are able to do, at the same salary."[30] The Kansas City Sun, an African American weekly, similarly reported that Armour "has always given the black man a square deal." "Many a Negro who has spent years in the service of this house," the paper concluded, "is now drawing a pension and living the remainder of his days out of want."[31] Stories circulated throughout the black community of packinghouse managers who allowed black workers to take less marketable cuts—livers, hearts, kidneys—home to their families and of plant owners who provided charity to black institutions like hospitals, veterans groups, schools, and religious organizations. At

Schwarzschild and Sulzberger, owners paid employees in bank receipts rather than by check, freeing black workers from the predatory West Bottoms saloonkeepers who charged to cash pay stubs.[32] The packinghouses also expanded recreational services for black employees by sponsoring sports teams and all-black social events. Such actions were widely advertised in the local black press. "Honesty and fidelity are the only tests applied to applicants for employment in the Armour Packing Co.," reported the *American Citizen*, a short-lived African American newspaper. The company employs "representatives of every civilized race" and "does not discriminate against any nationality or creed."[33]

Stories of management benevolence toward African Americans were, of course, overblown. In Kansas City, the black press was not always an independent voice for the community, and tales of financial aid to black city residents were more often part of a savvy marketing and recruitment campaign by corporate packers. There is a more obvious and direct reason why black workers were drawn to meatpacking. In the segregated labor market that was Kansas City, meatpacking provided black residents with one of the few available options for industrial employment.[34] A study produced by the Kansas City Urban League revealed that in 1929, only 30 percent of Kansas City businesses employed African Americans, and of that percentage, nearly half of the jobs were listed as porters. African Americans were frequently excluded from skilled trades, and their average weekly wage in the city was about half that of white workers. For meatpackers, then, black workers in Kansas City were cheap and exploitable. Reflecting the stereotypes of the day, plant managers remarked that African Americans were well suited to "the most disagreeable" elements of meatpacking labor. A spokesman for one large packing interest explained that company policy directed black workers to the most unpleasant jobs on the killing floor, where "the heat is intense and the smell uncongenial to men of more sensitive disposition."[35] In a congressional employment investigation, one manager reported that "Negro laborers seem to take quite naturally to packing-house work, especially in the occupations where the hours are irregular."[36] Perhaps just as important, packers also maintained that a sizable percentage of black workers on the killing floor would prevent worker solidarity. Owners counted on the barriers of language, custom, and especially race to keep labor interests separate. Many black workers held the opposite view, however, and confined to the lowest paid and least pleasant jobs in the factories, black meatpacking workers frequently joined with their white co-workers to improve working conditions in the city.[37]

Indeed, meatpacking became one of the main sites of labor agitation in the city. First in 1893 and then again in 1894 and 1895, workers in the factories pushed back against owners' attempts to reduce wages and speed up production. These collective actions were small in scale and did not lead to the unionization of meatpacking labor in Kansas City, but unions soon came to the yards. First under the Knights of Labor and then later the American Federation of Labor, attempts to band together

African American man cleaning livestock pens with a water hose at the Kansas City stockyards, date unknown. Courtesy of the Missouri Valley Special Collections, Kansas City Public Library.

were more successful as the nineteenth century came to a close. Even as organizing remained difficult in the city, by 1897, the nation's largest meatpacking union, Amalgamated Meat Cutters and Butcher Workmen of North America, was drawing Kansas City workers to its banner. After several years of consolidation, in 1904 Amalgamated called a nationwide strike of packinghouse laborers that impacted racial solidarity in the city. In response to wage cuts and the continued use of immigrant labor to replace union workers, more than 7,000 Amalgamated members, black and white, walked off the job in July.[38]

Meatpackers tried to keep their plants open by recruiting new workers from the city and the surrounding rural communities. They also began importing nonunion labor from other midwestern packing cities. In response, the union assigned members to watch the main railway stops, including Union Depot, in an effort to keep scabs from entering the city. The strikers did their best to disrupt operations and created special patrol units to keep strikebreakers away from the plants. Owners, in turn, began housing strikebreakers inside the factories and, in an example of the extreme divisiveness of the strike, stepped up their efforts to recruit African American scabs and then provided them with weapons.[39] As historian Sherry Schirmer dryly noted, "In a strike-torn city with a southern heritage, arming black workers was an unusual tactic." But as the strike wore on, packinghouse managers proved "willing to risk a race riot" in order to alienate striker and scab.[40]

Violence would come to the city that summer as a series of small confrontations between workers and strikebreakers marred the West Bottoms, but unlike what occurred in other packing cities, racial conflict did not escalate in Kansas City. Despite labor's pronouncement to "stay out until Christmas," the 1904 strike did not last and workers returned to the factories without the wage guarantees and union protection they desired.[41] The blow to the Amalgamated Meat Cutters union was total, and Michael Donnelly, an Omaha sheep butcher and union president, was more than willing to blame African Americans. Donnelly portrayed black workers as barriers to human progress, whose only interest was to drive white workers from the meatpacking industry.[42] The official Amalgamated newspaper published several stories, editorials, and political cartoons linking the failure of the strike to black workers. One result was that racial tension in the early twentieth century, especially in larger cities like Chicago, escalated dramatically. In Kansas City, however, the local press was largely silent on race matters, and labor leaders rarely introduced race into labor politics.[43]

Race was downplayed in the local media because African Americans were present on both sides of the picket line. Black strikers and black scabs were involved in confrontations with police, white laborers, and, importantly, each other. Indiscriminate and black-on-black violence hardly seems evidence of racial harmony, but a larger point remains. Throughout industrial America, black workers were frequently imported as strikebreakers, including, of course, into Kansas City. But just as they held a variety of positions in packinghouse factories, African Americans also had long participated in industry politics. Meatpackers assumed that their black employees were docile—uninterested in unions or even the idea of strikes—but the events in Kansas City offered a powerful corrective to that mistaken notion as African Americans demanded a stake in the economic expansion of the city.

In the first decades of the twentieth century, as labor activists increased their demands for representation, Kansas City's black residents were engaged in a parallel pursuit for improved standing. Rigid residential segregation, supported by racial covenants, forced African Americans into crowded black districts, just as equally significant cultural prescriptions created sharp lines of social separation. The city's black citizens encountered restrictions and limits in virtually all public accommodations. Perhaps ironically, the city's pervasive discrimination encouraged the cultivation of a politically conscious black community. It was not only the jazz clubs and baseball teams that defined African American society in this period but also vibrant black social clubs, black churches, black-owned businesses, black protective associations, and participation in party politics that solidified the community.[44] The strength of these institutions, combined with a deep history in the stockyards, meant that African American labor remained a key constituency for union leaders.

"Solidly entrenched in meatpacking occupations . . . [and] with sufficient numbers to decide the outcome of an organizing drive," African Americans in Kansas City, labor historian Roger Horowitz explained, "were courted by both the nascent unions and packinghouse management."[45] The defeat of the first major strike in the meatpacking industry calmed, but did not end, labor agitation in the city, and at nearly the same moment that the stockyards broke production records, African American workers would once again seek common cause.

On September 4, 1917, more than fifty canners, black and white and mostly women, left the line at the city's Cudahy plant. With factories in several midwestern cities and an international distribution network, Cudahy was one of the largest meatpackers in the country. Common labor demands—a wage increase and an eight-hour day—precipitated the walkout, and by the late afternoon, more than 300 workers had joined the campaign. These strikers paraded from plant to plant in the packinghouse district, calling for other laborers to support the walkout. The *Kansas City Journal* described the racial composition of the march, noting that "many in the procession were women, and nearly half the number were negroes." Frustrated that owners were making "millions in war profits" while wage cuts continued in Kansas City, one striker told reporters that all workers desired was "enough to live on." When labor requested a 5.5-cent-an-hour raise, plant management countered with 2.5 cents, and the strike expanded. Cudahy strikers were joined by workers from Wilson, Ruddy Brothers, and Swift. Two days after the walkout, more than 2,000 laborers, once again both black and white, lined the streets of Armourdale.[46] Less than a week after the initial protest, sympathetic strikes spread to city railroad workers, freight handlers, and soap producers. As the event grew in significance, local workers asked Amalgamated Meat Cutters to direct the strike. Confirming African American support for the action, while at the same time reminding Amalgamated officials of their race-baiting more than a decade earlier, one black laborer explained succinctly, "When you divide up the pie, do not forget your colored brother."[47] A federal arbitrator ended the short strike by forcing Cudahy to rehire the strikers and agree to a pay increase for all laborers. A strike under similar circumstances less than a year later, in 1918, led to even more gains for black stockyard workers in Kansas City. The strike moved quickly to federal arbitration, where national union leaders, represented by Kansas City attorney Frank P. Walsh, former head of the Commission on Industrial Relations and co-chairman of the National War Labor Board, convinced mediators to grant workers a number of concessions, including an eight-hour day, equitable rules for overtime, and equal pay for equal work.[48]

These were important victories for stockyard labor, and Kansas City's African American packing workers were in an unusually strong position. World War I restricted immigration, limiting an important source of labor, while at the same moment, European demand for American meat reached record levels. With few options, the city's packinghouse owners tried to keep labor peace with frequent concessions to workers. But if the war created a unique moment of political leverage, black workers must also be given credit for maximizing their opportunities. African American laborers created a working-class movement for shop control that was designed to alter the conventional narrative of racial politics in the city. And there is little question that a key element of this strategy was to engage African American workers with organized labor. As one black newspaper editor reminded its readers, "Don't be a scab . . . we advise you to belong to the working class." If the "unions offer to be fair with you, join hands with them in struggle, capital against labor."[49]

These successful protests bracket the opening of Kansas City's important period of growth, and it was a strike two decades later that would serve as a capstone to this era of change and tumult. The events of 1917 and 1918 occurred within the context of World War I. Soon after, however, the federal labor apparatus designed to support worker rights was dismantled. Immigration returned to prewar levels and new arrivals, often less interested in old traditions and workplace politics, proved difficult to organize in the Kansas City yards. Further, the political constriction of the First Red Scare (1917–1920) targeted unionists as unpatriotic, and the devastating race riots that rocked several midwestern packing cities, including St. Louis, Omaha, and Chicago, eroded worker solidarity. Strikes in 1921 and 1922 ended poorly for the union, and throughout the rest of the 1920s, increasing segregation in Kansas City and a corresponding dependence on packinghouse labor meant that African American workers frequently sided with management. Sensing a moment to consolidate worker loyalty, packers introduced pension plans, stock systems, and incentive wage programs that hampered efforts to unify labor against meatpacking interests. Of these recent developments, a pleased Chamber of Commerce announced in 1925, "Kansas City labor is settled and contented." There "have been only seven strikes since 1898 and none since 1921." Here, all "industries operate on an open shop basis."[50]

That the Chamber of Commerce would make such claims should not surprise anyone, but the city's celebrated stability was short-lived. The Depression hit the Kansas City industrial market especially hard as more than 300 companies went bankrupt between 1929 and 1933, and meatpacking employment declined by 25 percent. Packers responded with expected wage cuts, a shortened workweek, and a reduction in welfare capitalism.[51] Workers across the city's meatpacking plants, faced with a deteriorating situation, turned once again to collective action. In this effort to improve working conditions, stockyard labor would also attempt to change the traditional discussion about unions. As the uneven record of labor protest in the city suggests, the strength of the union movement in the packing houses waxed and waned. The first attempt at organization, advanced by the American Federation of Labor, followed the model of craft unionism. Such practices worked in retail butcher shops where proprietors could organize based on shared skills and shared problems. In the packinghouses, however, skilled unions struggled. Not only were the houses continually deskilling, but they also separated workers by craft. In many of the packinghouses in the city, for instance, local craft unions dominated the shop floor. Hog splitters joined their union; rumpers joined theirs. These laborers were allied with similar workers performing the same job in other cities but often had little contact with other workers in their home plant. These craft unions negotiated work schedules and pay scales with management independently, so when large strikes occurred, not every local went out, limiting the effectiveness of the action. But now, in the 1930s, the idea of industrial unionism—a single union that championed working-class issues—came to Kansas City meatpacking.

There is little debate that this renewed local effort to organize was supported by the massive package of federal legislation during the New Deal. The National Recovery Administration (NRA), established in 1933, brought worker and industry together in an attempt to craft fair standards for labor. Although the Supreme Court would soon nullify many of the provisions of the NRA, much of its support for the American worker, including the right to unionize and to collective action, reappeared in the 1935 National Labor Relations Act. The bill, also known as the Wagner Act, was opposed by many business leaders who viewed the proposal as an unnecessary intrusion into commerce, but for many laborers, the Wagner Act provided the foundation for worker solidarity. Such legislation would also reshuffle management practices, mobilize immigrant labor, and bridge America's racial divide.[52] Collective bargaining had already proved effective in the auto and steel industries, and in 1938 a multiethnic coalition of stockyard workers in Kansas City would once again push for solidarity.

In late August 1938, Kansas City's largest packing plant, Armour, raised the "kill," the quota for daily beef processing. The move was announced without worker consultation or the addition of more laborers. Six hide cellar workers—five African Americans and one Croatian—complained to stewards on the killing floor, and the following morning, the men left the line to attend a grievance hearing with company managers. Jobs in the hide cellar were among the most menial and least desirable in the packing factories. After skinners removed the cow's valuable hide, it traveled down a chute to the hide cellar below, where workers, mostly African American, processed the leather. They shook, stretched, brushed, and eventually salted the hides, allowing them to cure for several months.[53] The stench in this part of the house was particularly oppressive, and chronic health problems plagued hide cellar workers. From 8:00 a.m. to 2:30 p.m., the workers met with plant officials and later returned to their positions in the factory. The following day, Armour officials not only rejected worker appeals to reduce the kill but also docked the pay of the workers who attended the grievance meeting. The United Packing House Workers of America Local Number 15 asked for $22.09 as payment for the workers and their "6½ hours away from the line." Armour refused.

At 10 a.m. on Saturday, September 10, after the processing chain was fully loaded with cattle, nearly 2,000 Armour workers left the killing line and occupied the plant. Under a headline banner that announced Adolf Hitler's takeover of Czechoslovakia, the *Kansas City Star* broke the news of "An Armour Sit Down." Reflecting the new emphasis on a single labor movement, the paper quoted a strike organizer who declared, "A grievance of one worker is a grievance of the entire union." Over the next four days, nearly 1,000 workers, including 400 African American laborers, remained in control of the plant. Inside the factory, workers reported a lively, even festive, atmosphere. Workers talked of card games, frequent union meetings, and entertainment. "We had some very good musicians that could play guitar . . . sax, and trombone, trumpet; you name it, we had it in there," remembered labor organizer Charles Fischer, and "there were several guys who had very good voices . . . they were fabulous, fabulous."[54] Workers sang and played music during the day and in the evenings were entertained by a "Negro quartet" and a black worker gospel choir. Local newspapers ran front-page stories of the sit-down, complete with pictures of workers perched atop locked factory gates pulling up buckets of food and coffee delivered by their families. Armour asked the Kansas City Police Department to remove the strikers, and the police refused because community support rested with the workers. As the possibility of a nationwide sympathy strike became likely, city leaders, including the mayor, forced Armour into mediation. In the final compromise, the company and the union agreed to split the cost of the beef that workers left to rot on the line, but Armour agreed to accept the strikers back without punishment and award the hide cellar workers back pay.[55] The strike was costly to both management and the union. Armour lost nearly $100,000 in revenue, and the union share of the spoiled beef was almost $15,000, but it was the $22 that was the most significant. The union stood firm behind six low-skilled ethnic and African American workers and, with the back pay concession, solidified control of the floor.

The events of 1938 built on the efforts of union leaders to create racial cohesion in Kansas City's packinghouse neighborhoods. The industrial union movement occurred not only in the factory but also in the community. The union sponsored concerts and picnics intended for both black and white workers (and their families) with the goal of building a common tradition. As one scholar noted, in a divided city, these social events were the "largest unsegregated cultural gatherings" in the city. The most important legacy of the strike and the grassroots community involvement that supported it, remembered one labor leader, was "a friendship there that couldn't have been created in any other way. It forged a bond between all of the races . . . it did the job that we couldn't have done otherwise."[56] White and black laborers lived in distinct and segregated worlds, yet for this strike to be a success, they had to collectively "plan the occupation [and] eat, sleep, and pass the time waiting for a settlement in the same physical space."[57] It was a remarkable achievement, and the Armour strike established a precedent for racial and ethnic collaboration throughout Kansas City's meatpacking industry. Racial division continued to mark the city in the 1930s and beyond, including in some packinghouses, but an indus-trial workforce that had experienced the deep cleavages of race since the 1870s proved that cooperation was possible.

A final cattle auction in the fall of 1991 signaled the official end of the stockyards in Kansas City, but, in truth, the yards began their decline several decades earlier. A devastating flood in July 1951 severely crippled the city's West Bottoms district, in-undating several packinghouses and nearby worker neighborhoods. House and yard managers did their best to reopen Kansas City's livestock trade, but at nearly the same moment, new technologies (like advanced refrigeration in interstate trucking), combined with the demand for lower labor and property costs, allowed urban pack-ers to move their operations to rural areas around the Midwest. By the mid-1950s, Kansas City's modern facilities were becoming increasingly outdated, and as a con-sequence animals were relocated closer to newer consolidated feedlots and regional auction houses. In the early 1960s, market conditions forced the stockyards to be-gin downsizing so that by the early 1990s, only a handful of employees remained. Today, evidence of the once massive stockyard footprint in the city is hard to find, but important legacies remain, none more significant than the political activism of packinghouse workers. The interracial and interethnic cohort of stockyard workers that coalesced in the 1930s remained largely in place throughout much of the 1940s and 1950s. That this coalition existed for so long required the continual integration of new workers into the union movement, a testament to the lasting commitment to worker solidarity and the city's claim to a progressive political tradition. Perhaps more significant still is that many of the key black packinghouse leaders of this era would remain politically active even as the yards began to decline, providing the African American community with experienced leadership in the civil rights struggle to come.

Notes

1. *Forty-Eighth Annual Live Stock Report of the Kansas City Stock Yards, Receipts and Shipments of Live Stock at the Kansas City Stock Yards for the Year Ending December 31, 1918* (Kansas City: Kansas City Stockyard Company, 1919), 1.

2. *75 Years of Kansas City Livestock Market History, 1871–1946: With Which Is Combined the 75th Annual Livestock Report for the Year Ending December 31, 1945* (Kansas City, Mo.: Kansas City Stock Yards Company 1946), 3.

3. A federal overview of the city's packinghouses in 1911 concluded succinctly, "in Kansas City, slaughtering and meat packing is not only the principal industry, but the only industry of importance." See US Senate, 61st Congress, 2nd Session, *Reports of the Immigration Com-mission*, Volume 13: *Immigrants in Industries, Part II: Slaughtering and Meat Packing* (Washington,

DC: Government Printing Office, 1911) (hereafter *Reports of the Immigration Commission*). This report, known informally as the Dillingham Commission, produced an enormous amount of data about the demographic profile of the Kansas City stockyards.

4. US Bureau of the Census, *Fourteenth Census 1920*, State Compendiums. See also *Kansas City Stockyards and Packing House Interests* (Kansas City, Mo.: Kansas City Stock Yard Company, 1899), 31.

5. William Cronon, *Nature's Metropolis: Chicago and the Great West* (New York: W. W. Norton, 1991), 219.

6. Charles N. Glaab, *Kansas City and the Railroads: Community Policy in the Growth of a Regional Metropolis* (Madison: The State Historical Society of Wisconsin, 1962).

7. See Joseph H. G. McCoy, *Historical Sketches of the Cattle Trade of the West and Southwest* (Kansas City: Ramsey, Millett, and Hudson, 1874).

8. There are many excellent studies of the Chicago stockyards, but for two examples, see Dominic A. Pacyga, *Slaughterhouse: Chicago's Union Stockyard and the World It Made* (Chicago: University of Chicago Press, 2015); and Wilson J. Warren, *Tied to the Great Packing Machine: The Midwest and Meatpacking* (Iowa City: University of Iowa Press, 2007).

9. Arthur Charvat, "The Growth and Development of the Kansas City Stockyards, 1871–1947: A History" (MA thesis, University of Kansas City, 1948), 5–6.

10. Daniel Serda, "Boston Investors and the Early Development of Kansas City, Missouri," speech transcript from the Midwest Research Institute's Midcontinent Perspectives program, January 23, 1992.

11. "Phil Armour and His Works," *Kansas City Star*, May 27, 1892.

12. *75 Years of Kansas City Livestock Market History*, 35–36. For more information on the early history of the stockyards, see Cuthbert Powell, *Twenty Years of Kansas City's Live Stock Trade and Traders* (Kansas City, Mo.: Pearl Printing Company, 1893).

13. See "Kansas City Stockyards," *Kansas City Times*, January 1, 1893. The second quote comes from "What We Have to Offer," *Kansas City Daily Journal*, March 31, 1893.

14. US Department of Commerce, *Report of the Commissioner of Corporations on the Beef Industry*, March 3, 1905 (Washington, DC: Government Printing Office, 1905), 7. See also articles on the meatpacking industry in the *Kansas City Star*, especially September 28, 1901. On the early history of the stockyards, consider G. K. Renner, "The Kansas City Meatpacking Industry before 1900," *Missouri Historical Review* 55 (October 1960): 22–29. In 1880, Kansas City processed 588,000 animals. Twenty years later that number had jumped to 4,556,000.

15. "Where By-Products Make the Profits," *Official Journal of the Amalgamated Meat Cutters and Butcher Workmen of North America* 6, no. 11 (September 1905): 2–3.

16. Ibid., 3–4.

17. Quoted in Robert M. Farnsworth, ed., *Caviar and Cabbage: Selected Columns by Melvin B. Tolson from the Washington Times, 1937–1944* (Columbia: University of Missouri Press, 1982), 246.

18. Rick Halpern, *Down on the Killing Floor: Black and White Workers in Chicago's Packinghouses, 1904–54* (Champaign: University of Illinois Press, 1997), 12–13, 17–19, 24–25; and

Roger Horowitz, *Putting Meat on the American Table: Taste, Technology, Transformation* (Baltimore: Johns Hopkins University Press, 2006), 26–39.

19. David Brody, *The Butcher Workmen: A Study of Unionization* (Cambridge: Harvard University Press, 1964), 7.

20. "Where By-Products Make the Profits," 3.

21. Quoted in Brody, *Butcher Workmen*, 4.

22. Reports of worker injuries were often carried in the local press. See, for example, one representative article from the *Kansas City Evening Star*, September 7, 1882: "Saturday was an unlucky day at Armour's": One worker "had his right hand laid open by accident, the cleaver of his companion descending upon it . . . another man was struck in the chest by a plank he was putting through the saw mill," a third worker had his thigh "crushed" and remains in "critical condition," and a fourth, a carpenter, "fell into a vat where three feet of hot water received him and scalded his limbs till the skin peeled off."

23. Quoted in Charles N. Glaab, "Meatpacking in Kansas City," 37. Working paper, n.d., Andrew Theodore Brown Collection, Folder 1, State Historical Society of Missouri, Kansas City Research Center, Kansas City, Missouri.

24. *Reports of the Immigration Commission*, 89.

25. See Serda, "Boston Investors," 5–6, and James R. Shortridge, *Kansas City and How It Grew, 1822–2011* (Lawrence: University Press of Kansas, 2012), 34–38.

26. *Reports of the Immigration Commission*, 308–309.

27. Darryn Snell, "Meat-Packing, Race, and Unionization in Kansas City, 1880–1904," in *Global Humanization: Studies in the Manufacture of Labour*, ed. Michael Neary (London: Mansell Publishing, 1999), 127–163.

28. *Reports of the Immigration Commission*, 285. The reports made no mention of Mexican workers, although Valerie Mendoza found references to Mexican immigrants working in meatpacking, especially after World War I. See her work in Chapter 11, as well as Valerie M. Mendoza, "Beyond the Border: Gender and Migration to Mexican Kansas City, 1890–1940" (manuscript in progress).

29. *Reports of the Immigration Commission*, 275–280; US Bureau of the Census, *Special Reports: United States Occupations: Slaughtering and Meatpacking* (Washington, DC: Government Printing Office, 1900), 585; and Sherry Lamb Schirmer, *A City Divided: The Racial Landscape of Kansas City, 1900–1960* (Columbia: University of Missouri Press, 2002), 60. The percentage of black laborers in Kansas City meatpacking varied slightly by plant. For example, 38 percent of Armour's hourly workers in 1935 were African American.

30. Asa E. Martin, *Our Negro Population: A Sociological Study of the Negroes in Kansas City, Missouri* (Kansas City, Mo.: Franklin Hudson, 1913), 52.

31. "Recent Industrial Strikes and the Negro," *Kansas City Sun*, September 22, 1917.

32. Brody, *Butcher Workmen*, 7.

33. Quoted in Snell, "Meatpacking, Race, and Unionization," 141. For more information on packinghouse outreach to the African American community, see Rick Halpern, "Race, Ethnicity, and Union in the Chicago Stockyards, 1917–1922," *International Review of Social History* 37 (1992): 25–58.

34. For more information, see *The Negro Worker of Kansas City: A Study of Trade Union and Organized Labor Relations* (Kansas City, Mo.: Urban League of Kansas City, 1939).

35. Quoted in Roger Horowitz, *"Negro and White, Unite and Fight!": A Social History of Industrial Unionism in Meatpacking, 1930–90* (Champaign: University of Illinois Press, 1997), 87.

36. *Reports of the Immigration Commission*, 285.

37. Snell, "Meatpacking, Race, and Unionization," 139–142.

38. "Beef Trust Employees to Strike," *San Francisco Call*, July 12, 1904. In addition to their other demands, union leaders requested 20 cents an hour for laborers. The packers countered with 17 cents, and when no agreement was reached, the strike was called.

39. See "Strike Breakers Hired in Kansas," *Kansas City Star*, July 22, 1904; "Packers Ask Police Protection for New Workers," *Kansas City Star*, July 23, 1904; "Strike Here Seems Broken," *Kansas City Star*, July 28, 1904; and "Strikes Here Turbulent," *Kansas City Star*, July 20, 1904. This is only a sampling of the local press stories on the strike. The events at the packinghouses remained front-page news for much of the summer.

40. Schirmer, *A City Divided*, 59.

41. "To Fight Big: Chicago Strike to Bitter End," *Labor World*, September 3, 1904, and "One Meat Strike Off," *Chicago Tribune*, September 4, 1904. See also "Unknown Negro Badly Beaten," *Kansas City Star*, July 27, 1904; and "Shot at Chicago Strikers," *Kansas City Star*, July 29, 1904.

42. "Raised the Race Issue," *Kansas City Star*, August 18, 1904.

43. Ibid.

44. See Chapters 1, 2, and 9 in this volume by John W. McKerley, Jeffrey L. Pasley, and Henrietta Rix Wood, respectively, for discussions of African American participation in electoral politics and political activism, and Chapters 10 and 12 by Jason Roe and Marc Rice, respectively, for discussions of African American associations and institutions.

45. Horowitz, *"Negro and White,"* 89.

46. *Kansas City Journal*, September 7, 1917; "Cudahy to Standstill," *Kansas City Star*, September 6, 1917; "Kansas Side into Strike," *Kansas City Star*, September 7, 1918; "Can't Meet in Cudahy Strike," *Kansas City Star*, September 8, 1917; and "More Packinghouse Men Are Out," *Kansas City Star*, September 10, 1917. On the issue of war profits, workers had a legitimate claim. In 1916, Armour and Swift made more than $20 million each in profit, up from $6 million and $9 million, respectively, prior to the war. See Halpern, *Down on the Killing Floor*, 47.

47. Quoted in Schirmer, *A City Divided*, 61. See also accounts in the local press, *Kansas City Times*, September 8, 1917; and *Kansas City Journal*, September 9, 1917.

48. Brody, *Butcher Workmen*, 75–83.

49. *Kansas City Sun*, September 22, 1917. See also William Z. Foster, *The Great Steel Strike and Its Lessons* (New York: B. W. Huebsch, 1920).

50. Quoted in Horowitz, *"Negro and White,"* 92.

51. Ibid.

52. There are many sources on the Wagner Act, but for one example with a midwestern focus see Lizbeth Cohen, *Making a New Deal: Industrial Workers in Chicago, 1919–1939* (New York: Cambridge University Press, 2008).

53. Rick Halpern and Roger Horowitz, *Meatpackers: An Oral History of Black Packinghouse Workers and Their Struggle for Racial and Economic Equality* (New York: New York University Press, 1999), 9.

54. Ibid., 73.

55. "An Armour Sit Down," *Kansas City Star*, September 9, 1938; "Fail in Armour Truce," *Kansas City Star*, September 10, 1938; "No Move at Armour," *Kansas City Star*, September 11, 1938; "In a Strike Plea," *Kansas City Star*, September 12, 1938; "Back to Armour," September 12, 1938; and *The Negro Worker of Kansas City*, 17.

56. Horowitz, "*Negro and White*," 97; and Halpern and Horowitz, *Meatpackers*, 74.

57. Horowitz, "*Negro and White*," 84.

CHAPTER SEVEN

The Bitterest Battle

The Effort to Unionize the Donnelly Garment Company

Kyle Anthony

The history of the Donnelly Garment Company and its battle with the International Ladies' Garment Workers Union (ILGWU) is one that defies conventional understandings of American life in the Great Depression.[1] It is a story of a female entrepreneur succeeding in an era of economic paralysis, and one of a union failing to organize a factory in a period when workers won substantive rights. ILGWU president David Dubinsky, garment manufacturer Nell Donnelly Reed, and Senator James A. Reed were the principal figures in a dispute to organize a single garment factory, a legal battle that came to represent much larger questions. What responsibility did employers have for their employees? To what extent would women, having recently won voting rights, take on a prominent role in the world of business and work? Was the federal government's support of unions allowing foreign radicalism to seep into American free markets? In assessing these questions, an exploration of what ILGWU president David Dubinsky referred to as "the bitterest battle," a battle that culminated in several courtroom trials, reveals how a reputable and respected union leader, a uniquely self-made female entrepreneur, and a retired senator in his twilight years came to embody the strains of Depression-era politics and society.[2]

While the market crash of October 1929 is often generalized as the origination of the Great Depression, for the textile industry the Depression began several years prior. The industry was identified by historian Irving Bernstein as "sick" in the 1920s, and Dubinsky described the competitive textile marketplace as a "rag jungle."[3] The textile industry's numerous problems included domestic and foreign competition that lowered prices, overproduction, and a decrease in demand. Following the end of World War I, England revived its lagging textile industry, and

Garment manufacturer
Nell Donnelly (Reed),
c. 1920s–1930s. Courtesy
of the State Historical
Society of Missouri, Kansas
City Research Center.

Asian nations began to invest in the field. Several American manufacturers, especially those dealing in cotton, responded to the poor conditions by moving their companies from the Northeast to the American South to take advantage of cheaper labor, land, and production costs. In 1927, 300,000 of the 1.1 million workers in cotton textiles in the United States lived in the South, with the large majority concentrated in the Piedmont region of southern Appalachia. Yet, moving to the South did not save the industry. By 1930, only one-quarter of firms were profiting, and the Depression accelerated dire conditions in the textile industry, culminating in failed strikes in the Piedmont region.[4] Because of overproduction that led to the average price of a housedress dropping from $9 in 1930 to as low as $3 by 1933, as well as a divided ILGWU membership, workers began to be laid off or face wage cuts.[5]

Yet for Kansas City, the garment industry was anything but sick, and the interwar period hastened growth in garment production. The first garment factories arrived in Kansas City in the 1880s, when Kansas City was growing into a railroad hub and a centralized access point for southern cotton. By the 1920s, national retailers, including J. C. Penney; Sears, Roebuck, and Company; and Montgomery

Ward, had distribution centers in Kansas City, making the city an attractive location for garment producers. Employment had averaged around 1,400 workers from 1880 to 1920, and garment production blossomed. By 1940, over 4,000 workers found jobs in the industry, which meant that only the stockyards employed more Kansas Citians. The city's Garment District expanded and eventually encompassed the area from Sixth to Eleventh Streets and from Wyandotte to Washington Streets in downtown Kansas City, Missouri.[6]

The district included many midsize companies owned by Jewish entrepreneurs who had relocated to the region. In 1918, an estimated 15,000 persons of the Jewish faith resided in the Kansas City metropolitan area; that number increased to over 28,000 in the metropolitan area by 1937.[7] Hyman Brand and Harry Puritz moved their ladies' coat and suit manufacturing business from New York City in an attempt to cut costs by relocating closer to the distribution warehouses of national retailers. Stern, Slegman, and Prins Company also moved to the city and made over 600 ladies' coats per week in the 1930s. Alexander Gernes, who began his career in the industry as a traveling salesman in 1904, established the Gernes Garment Company (which later merged with Hyman Gordon's garment outfit) in 1920. Gernes produced the fashionable Gay Gibson line, and of her father's company, DeSaix, Evans Gernes recollected, "I sometimes think my family's garment business was the story of the American dream," revealing one resident's belief in the strength of this industry.[8]

For these entrepreneurs, the Great Depression seemed to be something that negatively impacted other people while their businesses thrived. Francis Gaw, a civil servant, reported that in 1945 there were "over 80 busy garment factories doing an annual business estimated at between 75 and 100 million dollars," which led to the city being ranked seventh in the United States for the amount of clothing made for men, women, and children. Garment production had become the city's third-highest-grossing industry, after livestock and grain.[9] Historians Jeannette Terrell and Patricia Zimmer support this outlook, arguing that Kansas City "suffered extensively" from the Depression, but the garment district remained relatively unscathed because it made essential and affordable apparel items.[10] What accounted for the region's rapid success in the early 1930s was more than likely a function of a lack of unionization in Kansas City and, by proxy, cheap labor costs. Chicago was the second-largest textile manufacturer in the post–Civil War period, but it was largely unionized by 1919, which stunted its growth in the interwar period. Not all Kansas Citians shared in the prosperity of the growth of the garment district, however. During the critical year of 1933, the wages of employees in the textile industry in Kansas City declined from $12 per week to $6–10 per week in most factories, and as low as $2–3 per week in the sweatshops. According to the 1927 census, unionized workers in New England textile companies had earned a weekly average of $19.16.[11]

The company that came to dominate Kansas City's garment industry was always an outlier, not only in its physical space that resided outside the district at 1828 Walnut Street, but also by the mere fact that its founder, Ellen (Nell) Quinlan Donnelly Reed, was a woman. Biographies of Nell Donnelly Reed tend to tilt toward triumphalism. Terence Michael O'Malley, her great-grandnephew, produced a 2006 film that describes her story as "the stuff of legend." Edie McGinnis, a columnist for the *Kansas City Star*, contended she was "far ahead of her time." Margot Ford McMillen and Heather Roberson's *Called to Courage: Four Women in Missouri History* profiled Donnelly Reed in a volume centered on "extraordinary women" who "[experienced] success when they faced hardship and adversity in their lives."[12] As historians have suggested, her accomplishments were quite noteworthy in a time when few women succeeded as business executives.

Yet, Nell Donnelly Reed's business practices reveal more complexity than this mere story of exceptionalism suggests. Born Ellen Quinlan in 1889 in Parsons, Kansas, she was the twelfth child of Irish immigrants. After learning stenography at Parsons Business College, she moved to a boarding house in Kansas City at the age of sixteen. A year later, she had married a stenographer, Paul Donnelly, who helped to further advance her education by paying $900 to enroll her at Lindenwood College in St. Charles, Missouri. In 1916, when she was twenty-seven years old, Paul gave her a $1,270 loan from his personal savings to start a garment company that she molded into a multimillion-dollar business. When Paul returned from World War I, he quit his job as a credit manager to become president of the Donnelly Garment Company.

While Paul Donnelly managed finances, Nell Donnelly ran the factory, and in doing so, she displayed acumen for her business. Her entrepreneurial instincts recognized a gap in women's wear between fashionable and cheap housedresses. Prior to the Civil War, both men's and women's clothes were often produced through the "putting out" system, in which women were subcontracted to construct pieces of garments via seasonal work, typically in their own homes. By the 1840s, after the invention of the sewing machine, the "putting out" system began to fade in the production of men's clothing and was supplanted by centralized production in factories. Due to seasonal variations and changes in fashion, women's garments tended to resist mass manufacturing until late in the nineteenth century. Additionally, women who could afford expensive imported fabrics often hired skilled dressmakers to sew their garments by hand to fit their body type, rather than purchase a dress that was mass-produced in factories. Thus, the innovations of Donnelly's "section system" assembly line were designed to centralize and mass-produce fashionable, affordable housedresses for the average American woman. When economic crisis paralyzed the country, the Donnelly Garment Company continued to thrive, bolstered by the popularity of its Handy Dandy apron. Donnelly avoided widespread layoffs for the duration of the Great Depression and consistently maintained a factory with over 1,000 full- and part-time employees.[13]

The secret to Nell Donnelly's success also rested in a cognizant understanding of the limitations of the Kansas City labor market. Kansas City had few skilled tailors and relied mostly on an unskilled labor force in textiles. Donnelly's solution was the section system, in which each worker had one responsibility, such as sewing a pocket or snapping on buttons. She testified in court that, to maintain consistent quality, she "started having to teach my own operators." She established a training section in which operators learned at least three different types of assembly so that if the company was short on work in one area, the operator could move to a different section. Her testimony reveals that the company would "weed out" operators if they "were not adaptable or they were not good enough in any one particular way to make them valuable," which she justified by claiming that the clothes must meet her high standards. Donnelly's flexible solutions to cope with the inexperienced labor pool in Kansas City showed her talents not only in design but also in management, which led to more than 5,000 of the "Nelly Don" brand of dresses coming off the assembly line daily.[14]

Despite her company's expansive growth and well-designed model, Donnelly rejected the notion that she was a revolutionary—a uniquely successful, self-made, female millionaire. Yet she employed 900 women and 100 men in 1932 and provided upward mobility for female employees. A notable example is Elizabeth Gates Reeves, who began working at the Donnelly Garment Company as a clerk in the payroll office in 1921. After six years in this position, Reeves earned a promotion to production manager in which she oversaw all production in the factory.[15] Rose Mary Todd, glowingly described by Donnelly as "my all around man," filled numerous roles in the factory, bringing her aggregate salary to $195 a month in 1937, while minimum-wage operators could expect to earn $60 per month. While women clearly had opportunities in her company, Donnelly resisted the claim that she supported the position of radical women reformers, tersely noting in a magazine interview, "We simply pick the person who is available, and who we believe can do the job. If that person's a woman, well and good."[16]

In her management style, Nell Donnelly advocated what is commonly referred to as welfare capitalism, or programs that offered health care, athletic teams, vacations, and social events. Employers designed these programs in the 1920s to instill worker loyalty to the company and limit the potential of labor unions to organize. According to historian Anthony Badger, when the Depression struck, welfare programs were among the first items eliminated by most businesses. The Donnelly Garment Company continued to do well during the Great Depression, and so it never retreated from company standards of implementing programs to benefit workers. Donnelly encouraged socialization and fraternization among employees by hosting Christmas parties, summer picnics, and other company-sponsored recreation events. She established a residence close to Swope Park for company recreation and gatherings. The company paid for a physician to provide care for workers for one

Interior of the Donnelly Garment Company, revealing working conditions that were well-lit and ventilated from open windows and ceiling fans. Also shown is the section system of production, 1937. Courtesy of the National Archives at Kansas City, Kansas City, Missouri.

afternoon each week, and she later extended medical service to families of employees. She offered paid company vacations up to twelve days per year and even started a credit union for employees for the purposes of borrowing and investment. In her mind, "she adopted all the benefits that a union would offer."[17]

Among her employees, Donnelly attempted to position herself as their primary caretaker, thus, from her perspective, negating the need for unions or the federal government to step in and provide security in the form of wage protection mandates. In preparing for the first trial against the ILGWU in 1937, various workers wrote letters that testified to Donnelly's caring treatment of her employees. Lois Hall recalled that "the hospital and medical care given to us are the very best," and Gladys Wilson testified that Donnelly ensured that every child of an employee received a Christmas gift at the annual party. Additionally, pictures of her factory reveal bright lights and proper ventilation with ceiling fans and long open windows, indicating the sanitary conditions of her shop. Even ILGWU regional director Meyer Perlstein admitted that the Donnelly Garment Company was "a fine shop with regard to cleanliness and lighting."[18]

Donnelly's actions and the conditions of her factory can be interpreted as an expression of her commitment to providing for her workers. In a biographical feature in *Independent Woman* titled "Women Executives Are Just People," she denied being a radical female reformer. The interviewer referred to her as "distinctively feminine," described her modest clothing, and reported that Donnelly stated, "I don't approve of women getting off by themselves and trying to work out their destiny like hermits." Donnelly had become a woman of power and wealth yet still operated with her husband as the legal owner of the business, which was socially acceptable for women. She offered public statements that adhered to a traditionally conservative mindset with regard to gender. From her perspective, she brought nurturing instincts from the cult of domesticity into the world of business and produced dresses for the modest housewife, not for scandalous flappers. Above all, she claimed to take care of her employees, which won her respect and admiration from the women who worked under her.[19]

Donnelly's self-construction as a maternal executive also served the function of creating an entrenched loyalty to her, keeping unions out of her shop. She showed ruthless calculation in growing and developing her business, especially by creating a powerful political alliance with a marriage to three-time US senator James Alexander Reed, also from Kansas City, Missouri. Reed professed himself to be a Jeffersonian Democrat, and over the years he developed a reputation as a small government advocate. Opponents in Congress vilified him for being an obstructionist opposed to most government legislation. After a failed attempt to win the presidential nomination from the Democratic Party in the 1928 election, he came back to Kansas City in 1929 to reestablish his law practice.

Although they did not marry until December 1933, it is clear that Donnelly and Senator Reed developed an intimate relationship as they worked in concert to protect her company. Reed was still married to his wife, Lura Reed, and Donnelly was still married to Paul Donnelly when the two seem to have started a relationship in conjunction with a lawsuit in 1927. Reed, a talented lawyer, successfully won a case for the Donnelly Garment Company, which had sued the R. Lowenbaum Manufacturing Company of St. Louis for stealing the Handy Dandy apron design. He proved his mettle in court, as the *St. Louis Globe Democrat* reported: "Only lacking his famous cigar tilted at a rakish angle, the silver-haired orator occupied himself intently on every technical detail of designing and manufacturing of aprons." Shortly thereafter, Paul and Nell Donnelly moved behind Reed's magisterial house on Cherry Street, and the former senator and Nell Donnelly embarked on an extramarital affair.[20]

As Donnelly's business prospered, her home life came under strain. At one point, her alcoholic husband threatened to commit suicide if she ever bore her paramour's child. In 1931, a pregnant Nell Donnelly briefly moved to Chicago, where she gave birth to a boy, David. Upon her return to Missouri, she claimed the child was adopted, but in reality, David was James Reed's son. The dramatic relationship between Reed and Donnelly suffered another hardship when she was kidnapped two months after her return from Chicago. In response, Senator Reed threatened Johnny Lazia, a Kansas City Mafia leader, that he would release evidence of Lazia's relationship with the Pendergast machine unless she was returned safely. Although the Mafia had not kidnapped Donnelly, Mafia members quickly located and returned her to her home in just over a day. When James Reed's wife died in October 1932, Donnelly filed for divorce from her husband a month later, bought him out of the company, and married Reed in December 1933, becoming Nell Donnelly Reed.[21]

In their partnership, the couple forged a formidable opposition to the ILGWU and the federal government, which was seeking to reform business practices through the National Industrial Recovery Act (NIRA) in 1933. Prior to their marriage in early 1933, and during a Codes of Fair Competition hearing between the National Recovery Administration (NRA) officials and the Donnelly Company, Senator Reed presented himself as a disinterested observer because his romantic relationship with Donnelly was not yet public knowledge. The hearing was based on how much cotton or silk was used in Donnelly Company apparel, which was important because silk workers could expect to earn 21 cents more per hour under federal code. The NRA ruling gave the company a recommendation that 85 percent of its work fell under the cotton code, whereas David Dubinsky felt that it should have been only 71 percent. After the Reed-Donnelly relationship became publicly known, Dubinsky later claimed that Reed had used his political weight to influence the ruling and had been quite deceptive since he had a personal stake in acquiring a favorable result for Donnelly's company to keep its wages low.[22]

While Donnelly established and protected her lucrative business, the ILGWU neared collapse. The union's most recognizable moment involved the 1910 uprising of 20,000 textile workers in New York City, which was followed by the Triangle Shirtwaist Factory fire in 1911. After the fire, the ILGWU protested unsafe factory conditions, leading to a host of changes in state safety codes. By 1920, the ILGWU had 105,400 members and appeared healthy coming out of World War I. However, when the Russian Civil War ended with a Bolshevik victory, the Communist Party of the United States of America (CPUSA), under William Z. Foster, developed its strategy of "boring from within" by getting communist members in positions of leadership within established trade unions. The ILGWU was one union targeted by the CPUSA. By the late 1920s, the ILGWU was on its deathbed as a new leader, David Dubinsky, took on the task of saving the union from its communist contingent.[23]

Born in Brest-Litovsk, Russia, in 1892, Dubinsky spent his early years as a delivery boy and baker. Within this industry, he became a committed trade unionist and socialist, but after he was arrested a few times as a teenager, he fled czarist Russia and emigrated to America, where he began working as a garment cutter. Although he still held on to his socialist beliefs into the 1920s, Dubinsky realized that the only way to save the ILGWU was to oust communist members from the union, which came at great cost to the union's finances as membership fell to 32,300 by 1930. Dubinsky won the union's presidential election in 1932, a position that he would hold for thirty-four years. In time, he would turn the ILGWU into what an issue of *Current History* magazine called "America's best union." Despite his accomplishments, at the onset of the Depression few contemporaries believed that the ILGWU and the garment industry had entered a golden age.[24]

The ILGWU owed its recovery in part to the NIRA, a bill that allowed companies to opt into established industry-wide codes, with the condition that organized labor be allowed in the shop. Within months of the bill's passage in 1933, the ILGWU experienced immediate growth, and membership rose over 200,000. Historian Anthony Badger credits the New Deal with "the largest ever growth in union membership in a single decade in both absolute and relative terms." By 1945, 25 percent of the nation's workforce was unionized. As a result of Democratic support for collective bargaining through New Deal legislation, unions, which had tended to be nonpartisan, became one of the Democratic Party's primary sources of financial contributions in the 1940 election. For his part, Dubinsky wanted his union to be viewed as respectable, and he sought to accomplish that by stabilizing cutthroat competition in the industry so that both employer and employee benefited and a "sick" industry could be made well.[25]

The ILGWU decided to come to Kansas City in 1933 after a report compiled by the National Women's Trade Union League indicated that conditions in Kansas City garment factories were "appalling." While not singling out specific companies, the report designated the factories in Kansas City as "sweat shops." The report claimed that the Kansas City garment industry offered low pay, unsanitary conditions, and a "speed-up system" to reach daily quotas that left women fatigued.[26] Management at the Donnelly Company consistently denied that they employed a speed-up system and instead pointed to in-house nurses and a "rest" room that allowed fatigued employees to take breaks and get water as needed. Ellen Fry, a Donnelly employee who joined the ILGWU in 1934 and was promptly laid off as a result of that decision, testified about her work as a tucker, which she referred to as an "unusually tedious job." It involved making ten tucks for each dress in order to match lengths, punch holes, and stitch the seams. Fry was paid 25 cents per dozen dresses, and an individual tuck took about twenty seconds, meaning that, in ideal conditions without any restroom breaks or broken threads, a tucker could tuck about eighteen dresses per hour for a weekly wage of $15, which was the established minimum wage for all employees in the Donnelly factory. Nell Donnelly Reed defended the system, claiming that employees who earned a weekly wage of $15 were only operating at 75 percent efficiency; she was adamant that her model incentivized her workers to produce in a mutually beneficial relationship. Fry countered that she left work so exhausted that she did not have the energy to eat supper. Other employees agreed: Lottie Conroy complained to Fry that the work was killing her; then in March 1934, Conroy fainted on the job and was taken out on a stretcher. A few days later, the girls in the section learned that Conroy had died. Fry implied in court testimony that work had killed her. Donnelly Company lawyers, led by William Hogsett, countered Fry's testimony, producing a death certificate to prove that Conroy had died of second- and third-degree burns when her dress caught fire on a gas stove in her own home. While Fry's testimony lacked the evidential weight to prove that the speed-up system was detrimental to the health of employees, certain operators came to believe that the assembly-line work was damaging their health.[27]

Company management resisted the ILGWU's efforts to unionize the Kansas City garment factories. They formed company-owned unions, hired strikebreakers, and employed detective agencies such as the Ahner Detective Agency of St. Louis as "protection." In one instance in September 1936, an officer with the ILGWU, Samuel White, was "brutally assaulted" by Ahner's detectives before being kidnapped, driven into Kansas, and told not to return to Missouri. The most notorious episode of the early unionization efforts occurred when the ILGWU organized a strike at the Gordon Brothers, Gernes, and Missouri garment companies in March 1937, which resulted in violence when a strikebreaker stabbed a union officer with a pair of scissors. The violence that erupted in labor disputes in Kansas City's Garment District paled in comparison to the level and intensity of violence during ILGWU strikes in other cities, most notably St. Louis and Memphis, yet enough violence was observed for a federal judge, Andrew Miller, to later criticize the Kansas City police for failing to maintain law and order.[28]

These labor strikes provided ammunition for Donnelly Garment Company in preparing for the "bitterest" legal battle with the ILGWU. The union's attempt to organize this factory lasted almost forty years, until 1971, fifteen years after Nell Donnelly Reed sold all of her company stock. The first conflict between the two parties involved the ILGWU's attempt to force the Donnelly Garment Company to abide by the production codes set forth in the NIRA. Once the Supreme Court ruled the NIRA to be unconstitutional in 1935, the company sued for an injunction against the ILGWU after Dubinsky and Meyer Perlstein, a regional director of the ILGWU, called for a boycott of the company's housedresses. The injunction was designed to prohibit the ILGWU from administering a secondary boycott by pressuring retailers to stop carrying Nelly Don dresses. In all, Dubinsky devoted a "war chest" of over $100,000 toward the union's efforts to unionize Donnelly's company.[29]

The bitter legal battle exemplified several conflicts that shaped the 1930s. First, the hostility that ensued between Dubinsky and the Reeds was an outgrowth of nativist and antiradical fears prevalent in post–World War I America. After Senator Reed, a talented wordsmith, left politics in 1929, notable writer H. L. Mencken wrote a glowing tribute to Reed's oratorical talents and his ability to kill "sham" government legislation: "He is the supreme artist in assault. . . . The stone ax is not his weapon, but the rapier; and he knows how to make it go through stone and steel. . . . He was, it appears, a purely destructive force."[30] Since Dubinsky was Russian-born, Reed employed his oratorical talents to position Dubinsky as a foreign radical. In an oft-repeated exchange, Dubinsky stated to the press that Reed "dares to pose as an American patriot" and shrewdly asserted that "it will be the object of our union to teach him a lesson in real Americanism."[31] Reed countered: "He has the nerve to talk about Americanism, although he was born in Russia, and has only been in this country a few years!" Not one to back down, Dubinsky responded, "On the basis of this test of Americanism, we must be permitted to believe that Reed, when he was about to be born, decided to choose America as the place of birth, while I, given the same free selection, happened to pick Russia."[32] This grandstanding on the part of both Dubinsky and Reed shows how they each sought to define the concepts of true Americanism and Bolshevism in order to fulfill political goals.[33] This exchange also reveals the intensity of conflicting ideological beliefs that had been percolating since the end of World War I. In the years 1919–1923, the US government used excessive force, intimidation, and legal proceedings to imprison and deport radicals in a period generally known as the Red Scare. In a 1919 speech in Des Moines, President Woodrow Wilson intimated that Bolshevism is "a negation of everything that is American."[34] Nell Donnelly Reed, for her part, also produced a few jabs at Dubinsky, claiming that she would resist all efforts by any "-sky" to unionize the plant and, at one moment, disparagingly referred to him as "butt-insky."[35]

Anti-Semitic remarks further framed the Reeds' demonization of Dubinsky and the ILGWU. Meyer Perlstein wrote Dubinsky to inform him that Donnelly Reed and her supervisors brought the Kansas City ILGWU chairwoman and vice chairwoman into her office, where they intimidated and harassed the union members by asking them "what in the world they have in common with these little fat Jews." Perlstein also claimed that Nell Donnelly Reed tried to buy off the chairwoman with a "steady weekly position."[36] Senator Reed received letters from his supporters that further conflated being Jewish with political radicalism, including one from attorney Evan Hammett that stated, "It is getting high-time that this country rid itself of Communistic Jews and Jewish labor agitators. I extend you my full support in your gallant efforts to quell the Jew, Dubinsky."[37] Historian Laurel Wilson has argued that the majority of Kansas City garment companies encouraged "cooperation between Jewish and Gentile companies" and that the garment industry, with exceptions, was "integrated in terms of ethnicity, religion, and race." Yet the payroll sheets of the Donnelly Garment Company contain mostly anglicized names, indicating that Reed tended to hire non-Jewish workers when possible.[38]

Yet ILGWU supporters also made anti-Semitic comments. Clara Bagley, a Kansas City garment worker and member of the ILGWU, wrote to Dubinsky requesting that he replace local organizer Abraham Plotkin, who was Jewish, because the dressmakers desired a "Gentile . . . who would talk in plain, rough middle-Western English." Bagley asserted that the chief obstacle that local unionists found in gaining support was that Christian women on the shop floor could not relate to Jewish union organizers.[39] Even though Dubinsky was dismissive in his response to

Bagley, her suggestion certainly resonated with the union. In 1938, the *Kansas City Journal-Post* ran a feature titled "Garment Workers Play" that profiled union women participating in various events, such as tennis, ballroom dancing, basketball, bowling, and acting. Not only was this a part of the ILGWU's recreational program to combat the amenities offered by the Donnelly company, it was also designed to win the hearts and minds of native-born Kansas Citians. Upon receiving his copy of the *Journal-Post* with the feature, N. I. Stone, a New York–based consultant for the union, sent a telegram to Dubinsky offering a "hearty congratulations," stating, "The fine educational and recreational activities of the ILGWU should prove a strong drawing card for the American native element."[40]

Within this context, nativist sentiments empowered antiradicalism, and in court, Senator Reed and his colleagues invoked fears of foreigners by displaying lurid images of physical and sexual violence during strikes in order to encourage Americans to be wary of invasive aliens. Throughout the trial, especially during the hearing in 1939 in which he was pitted against ILGWU lawyer (and future secretary of state), Dean Acheson, Reed contended that the union waged aggressive destruction on American companies and women. Even though strikes in the Kansas City Garment District, such as the one at the Gordon Brothers, Gernes, and Missouri garment companies, involved relatively minimal violence, Reed attempted to position the violence perpetrated by ILGWU members as representative of how the union operated. In arguing for the injunction against the ILGWU, the former senator referenced cases from Dallas, Texas, in which Perlstein was briefly arrested for contempt of court, as well as a nationally recognized case from Memphis, Tennessee, in which a strikebreaker named Velma Dowdy was accosted by strikers who "mauled her and stripped virtually all her clothing from her." Photographs of Dowdy's torn shirt, exposing her bra, were reprinted in the *New York Sunday News*, which Reed offered as evidence of the ILGWU's debasement of female purity.[41]

Since there was a limited amount of violence at the Kansas City strikes, Reed instead produced a wealth of documented evidence that offered salacious details of prior ILGWU strike activities in other cities: the spanking of female workers, the stripping off of their clothes, and the throwing of acid in St. Louis, as well as the removal of all clothes but shoes of a strikebreaker in the presence of "two Negro porters" in Dallas. Reed screened motion picture clips and waved photographs of women in their undergarments during ILGWU strikes. He exclaimed: "If the devil scraped the caldrons of hell, and out of the scum created a sensate being, he would not be as vile as this man [pointing his cane at Acheson] who comes here to defend stripping women naked in the streets of this city." Essentially, the senator styled himself as a watchman of fading chivalric values in the post-flapper age and depicted the ILGWU members as hypersexualized brutes desirous of ruining the virtue of wholesome midwestern girls. In trial speeches, Reed appeared to be engaging in a rhetorical tactic typical of the Democratic Party in the era before the

Minor violence occurred during the Gernes, Gordon Brothers, and Missouri garment companies' strikes in March 1937. Courtesy of the National Archives at Kansas City, Kansas City, Missouri.

New Deal, which was the protection of womanhood from sexual violations by those designated as outsiders.[42]

Within this convergence of violence and the "otherness" of Jewish, eastern labor organizers, the senator wholly embraced the ideological remnants of nativism that persisted after World War I. The defense of Nell Donnelly Reed's company existed as a defense against an invasion of their conception of traditional American values: deregulated, laissez-faire capitalism, traditional femininity, and state-sponsored protection of American corporations from radical labor organizations. Historian Erica Ryan noted of this era, "In the view of . . . men of power and wealth, hierarchies of citizenship inscribed with patriarchal power and authority had been rocked with uncertainty," thus they sought "to refashion fading Victorian gender roles and exert social control over modernizing sexual desires and behavior." In the midst of these uncertainties, Reed assumed a defensive posture and became a self-appointed patriarchal and moral watchman, protecting women from a mythical trope of the sexually depraved, Bolshevik, Jewish unionists.[43] Despite this extremist rhetoric, union activity at the Donnelly factory was relatively benign. With no actual examples of violence on or near the property, Judge Nordbye ultimately ruled against Reed's injunction in 1942.

Although the ILGWU won the legal battle, they lost the war with the company. The victory rested in how the Reeds insulated their company from outsiders. The ILGWU's defeat can be attributed not only to the virulent rhetoric expressed by company management, but also to company policies that combined intimidation and incentives to preserve loyalty to Nell Donnelly Reed. Victory also rested in the company's establishment of its own union. Even though the National Labor Relations Board eventually disbanded the Donnelly Company union in 1948, during the tumultuous trials that lasted from 1937 to 1942, the company union served as a barrier to entrance for the ILGWU. Initially referred to as the Donnelly Garment Company Loyalty League, it was founded in March 1934, when supervisor Rose Mary Todd called for a company-wide meeting to announce, "We do not need the help of outsiders." The meeting was timely because Dubinsky was in the city that month to give a speech, which had contributed to the decision by fifteen Donnelly factory workers to join the union. By 1937, a National Labor Relations Board report essentially declared that the Loyalty League was in violation of law in that it denied the ILGWU access to Donnelly workers, and in response the Loyalty League rebranded itself the Donnelly Garment Workers' Union (DGWU).[44]

The Loyalty League and its offshoot, the DGWU, created a culture of loyalty to and dependence on Nell Donnelly Reed. Certainly, many women were legitimately grateful to have such an employer during the midst of the country's worst financial depression. The company unions capitalized on those sentiments by organizing letter-writing and Christmas card campaigns. During the 1937 trial, 1,016 Christmas cards were sent to Nell Donnelly Reed, many of which, beyond wishing her a Merry Christmas, expressed their gratitude for having such a wonderful employer. Additionally, the senator collected hundreds of letters in 1937 that stressed employees' loyalty to his wife, which often included messages similar to Mae Harcum's note indicating, "I . . . write this of my own free will."[45] The ILGWU's trial strategy brought women to the stand who had been fired or harassed on the job for joining the union. ILGWU members Fern Sigler and Sylvia Hull testified that loyal Donnelly employees shouted and sang at them as middle management looked on, implicitly supporting such intimidation tactics. Management further intervened by sending union members home without a definitive statement of when they could return to work. Although union members were eventually allowed to come back to their jobs, not all employees opted to return. As Nell Donnelly Reed fostered a sense of loyalty among her workers, the ILGWU found it difficult to find support inside the factory.[46]

In evaluating the legacies of Dubinsky and the Reeds, it is reasonable to conclude that each contended with the larger forces that were shaping American history during the Depression era. Dubinsky had earned respect and admiration in much of the business community. He could proudly show that formerly ardent anti-union men like Kansas City garment factory owner Frank Prins had become converts. Prins, in a letter to Dubinsky, which was duplicated and used as propaganda for the ILGWU, stated, "The day of unorganized labor is passing rapidly. Yet with it, contrary to past precedent, is going the long bitter antagonism of the employer towards unionism; the feeling that capital is capital and labor is labor and never the twain can meet on common ground is also disappearing."[47] No finer commentary can be produced in revealing Dubinsky's ultimate aims. He sought to save his industry and union from bankruptcy while working with owners to provide security in a competitive marketplace.

Yet despite the optimism of Prins and Dubinsky, the success of the ILGWU in unionizing much of the Kansas City Garment District had a relatively short shelf life in Kansas City. The city, which now produces hardly any clothing at all, was once home to one of the largest textile industries in America, as boosters promoted in the interwar period that one out of every seven American women wore a garment made in Kansas City. The district progressed into its own golden age of production and profits in the 1950s. By the end of the 1970s, the garment industry had essentially vanished from the city. Rising labor costs precipitated the outsourcing of the industry from American cities, and most of the preeminent owners had either passed away or retired from the field. Today, a museum dedicated to the district and a solitary sculpture, *The Needle*, remain at the intersection of Eighth and Broadway, which marks the area where garment workers used to disembark from streetcars to arrive to work at the dozens of factories scattered throughout the district. The sculpture exists as a "tribute to the entrepreneurs whose genius and dedication is a Kansas City legacy to tell to oncoming generations."[48]

But what is that legacy? Certainly, Nell Donnelly Reed leaves a lasting impression as a dedicated and innovative entrepreneur, yet the bitter battle between the Reeds and Dubinsky reveals a larger truth: that despite cooperation between unions and most garment factories in Kansas City, in the Donnelly Company, nativism and fears of labor radicalism, bolshevism, and violence remained. Conservative voices, represented by the Reeds, abandoned the Democratic Party under Franklin Delano Roosevelt and emerged as hostile opponents to federal intervention by declaring their intentions to continue free-market capitalism and business-run welfare programs. The legacy to reflect on regarding Kansas City's once-acclaimed status as a high-volume producer of clothing is that the relationships between employer and employee, between industry and the federal government, and between the liberalization of women's roles in business and an unstable male-dominated capitalist system remained unsettled and contested ground.

Notes

1. The author would like to express his sincere gratitude to Cheryl Beredo, the director of the Kheel Center for Labor-Management Documentation and Archives, and her hard-working staff for the hours that they spent making copies of much needed archival material. Additionally, Michael Sweeney, senior research specialist, at the State Historical Society of Missouri, Kansas City Research Center was of invaluable help to the creation of this essay.

2. David Dubinsky and A. H. Raskin, *David Dubinsky: A Life with Labor* (New York: Simon and Schuster, 1977), 170.

3. Irving Bernstein, *The Lean Years: A History of the American Worker, 1920–1933*, updated ed. (Chicago: Haymarket Books, 2010), 3; Dubinsky and Raskin, *David Dubinsky*, 7.

4. Anthony J. Badger, *The New Deal: The Depression Years, 1933–1940* (New York: Noonday Press, 1989), 19–20. Bernstein, *The Lean Years*, 1–43.

5. "The N.R.A Codes," *Christian Science Monitor* (1933), reprinted in Leon Stein, ed., *Out of the Sweatshop: The Struggle for Industrial Democracy* (New York: Quadrangle/New York Times Book Company, 1977), 229.

6. Ann Brownfield and David Jackson, *We Were Hanging by a Thread: Kansas City Garment District Pieces the Past Together* (Kansas City: Orderly Pack Rat Publishing, 2014), 7.

7. The Bureau of Jewish Social Research, "Statistics of Jews," *American Jewish Yearbook*, 1920–1921, 373, http://www.hillel.org/docs/default-source/historical/american-jewish-year-book-(1920–1921).pdf?sfvrsn=2, and *American Jewish Yearbook*, 1940–1941, 660, http://www.ajcarchives.org/AJC_DATA/Files/1941_1942_9_Statistics.pdf.

8. Edie McGinnis, *A Bag of Scraps: Quilts and the Garment District* (Kansas City, Mo.: Kansas City Star Books, 2012), 14; Laurel Wilson, "Kansas City's Garment Industry," in *A Perfect Fit: The Garment Industry and American Jewry, 1860–1960*, ed. Gabriel M. Goldstein and Elizabeth G. Greenberg (Lubbock: Texas Tech University Press, 2012), 163, 168–171; Sara DeSaix/Gay Gibson, Box 001, Folder 11, Laurel E. Wilson (1947–) Papers (K0594), State Historical Society of Missouri, Kansas City Research Center (hereafter Wilson Papers).

9. Francis Gaw, "Report No. 5, 1945," Research and Information Department, City Hall, Kansas City, Missouri, Box 001, Folder 21, Wilson Papers.

10. Jeannette Terrell and Patricia Zimmer, *The Economic Base of Greater Kansas City* (Kansas City, Mo.: Economic Research Department, Federal Research Bank, 1949), 25, Box 001, Folder 37, Wilson Papers.

11. Phyllis Dillon, "German Jews in the Early Manufacture of Ready-Made Clothing," in Goldstein and Greenberg, *A Perfect Fit*, 68; Donna Swisher, "A Tough Nut to Crack: Unionization and the Donnelly Garment Company," *Kawsmouth: A Journal of Regional History* 4, no. 1 (Summer–Autumn 2002), 20; Bernstein, *The Lean Years*, 10–11.

12. Terence Michael O'Malley, *Nelly Don: A Stitch in Time* (Kansas City, Mo.: Covington Group, 2006), 22; McGinnis, *A Bag of Scraps*, 20; Margot Ford McMillen and Heather Roberson, *Called to Courage: Four Women in Missouri History* (Columbia: University of Missouri Press, 2002), 127–178.

13. Dillon, "German Jews in the Early Manufacture of Ready-Made Clothing," 70; McMillen and Roberson, *Called to Courage*, 100–105.

14. McGinnis, *A Bag of Scraps*, 17–18; Judy Ancel, "The Garment Workers: Talk for Kansas City Labor History Tour," October 17, 1992, Institute for Labor Studies, http://kclabor.org/garment_workers.htm; Direct Examination of Mrs. James A. Reed, Case File 2924, Box 484, Folder 20; Equity and Law Cases (1913–1938), Western District of Missouri, Western Division, Kansas City, Missouri, Records of the US District Courts, Record Group 21, National Archives and Records Administration—Kansas City, MO (hereafter *Donnelly v. ILGWU*).

15. Direct Examination of Mrs. Elizabeth Gates Reeves, Case File 2924, Box 484, Folder 19, *Donnelly v. ILGWU*.

16. McMillen and Roberson, *Called to Courage*, 121–122; Swisher, "A Tough Nut to Crack," 21, 27.

17. Badger, *The New Deal*, 34; William Worley, "Kansas City Made: The Garment Industry Era, 1915–1975," Jackson County Historical Society Educational Forum, April 18, 1996, Box 001, Folder 7, Wilson Papers.

18. Copies of Letters by Donnelly Garment Co. Employees, July 1937, Box 034; James Alexander Reed (1861–1944) Papers (K0443), State Historical Society of Missouri, Kansas City Research Center (hereafter Reed Papers); Direct Examination of Meyer Perlstein, Case File 2924, Box 485, Folder 22; *Donnelly v. ILGWU*.

19. Dora Albert, "Women Executives Are Just People," *Independent Woman* 10, no. 1 (January 1931): 13.

20. "Spectators Throng to Court to Hear Reed in Apron Patent Suit," *St. Louis Globe Democrat*, July 7, 1927 in "Clippings," Box 031, Reed Papers.

21. Gary Pomerantz, *The Devil's Ticket: A Night of Bridge, a Fatal Hand, and a New American Age* (New York: Crown Publishers, 2009), 94–99, 204–210.

22. Swisher, "A Tough Nut to Crack," 20.

23. Bernstein, *The Lean Years*, 85; Dubinsky and Raskin, *David Dubinsky*, 56–60.

24. Herbert Harris, "America's Best Union," *Current History*, January 1938, 50; Bernstein, *The Lean Years*, 85.

25. Badger, *The New Deal*, 118.

26. Ancel, "The Garment Workers."

27. Regarding Fry's employment, she implied that she lost her job because she joined the ILGWU, whereas Elizabeth Reeves, the production manager, testified that Fry did not maintain the quality of standards needed to be an employee at Donnelly. Missouri State Board of Health: Death Certificate, Case File 2924, Box 485, Folder 25, and Direct Examination of Ellen Fry, Case File 2924, Box 488, Folder 38, both in *Donnelly v. ILGWU*.

28. Ancel, "The Garment Worker"; "A Strong Order," *Kansas City Star*, April 27, 1939.

29. For an in-depth narrative of the Donnelly Garment Company's legal battles with the ILGWU, consult Donna Swisher, "A Tough Nut to Crack."

30. H. L. Mencken, "Editorial," *The American Mercury* 16, no. 64 (April 1929): 410–412.

31. "Campaign Grudge," *Buffalo (NY) Express*, May 17, 1937, Scrapbook, Box 038, Reed Papers.

32. "Dubinsky Flares Back at Reed," *St. Louis Globe Democrat*, May 12, 1937, Scrapbook, Box 038, Reed Papers.

33. Erica J. Ryan, *Red War on the Family: Sex, Gender, and Americanism in the First Red Scare* (Philadelphia: Temple University Press, 2015), 15.

34. "Says the World Waits for America to Act: Wilson Suggests that Bolshevism May Spread Here Unless Delay Is Ended," *New York Times*, September 7, 1919.

35. Dubinsky and Raskin, *David Dubinsky*, 170; United States of America National Labor Relations Board: Case No. C-1382, 1939–45, ILGWU, David Dubinsky, President's Records, 1932–1966, 5780/002, p. 27, Box 58, Folder 1a, Jt. Bd. and B.C.: Kansas City Jt. Bd., Kheel Center for Labor-Management Documentation and Archives, Martin P. Catherwood Library, Cornell University (hereafter Dubinsky Papers).

36. Letter, Meyer Perlstein to David Dubinsky, December 21, 1934, 1934–35b, Box 57, Folder 3b, Dubinsky Papers.

37. Letter, Evan Hammett to Hon. James A. Reed, May 12, 1937, Box 001, Folder 24, Ellen "Nell" Quinlan Donnelly Reed (1889–1991) Papers (K0444), SHSM-KC.

38. Payroll from Oct. 30, 1936–Oct. 22, 1937, Case File 2924, Box 486, Folder 31, *Donnelly v. ILGWU*; Wilson, "Kansas City's Garment Industry," 179.

39. Clara Bagley, Letter to David Dubinsky, August 16, 1934, p. 4, 1934–35b, Box 57, Folder 3a, Dubinsky Papers.

40. "Garment Workers Play," *Kansas City Journal-Post*, September 25, 1938; N. I Stone to David Dubinsky, Oct. 4, 1938, 1934–35b, Box 57, Folder 2a, Dubinsky Papers.

41. "Supreme Court Refuses Habeas Writ," *Dallas Journal*, October 1, 1935; Donnelly Garment Company v. David Dubinsky, Case No. 2924, Box 487, Folder 035, *Donnelly v. ILGWU*.

42. "Brief for Plaintiffs and Proposed Findings of Fact and Conclusions of Law," District Court of the United States for the Western Division of the Western District of Missouri, Case No. 2924, pp. 14–15, 17, 71–72, Box 035, Reed Papers. See Ellen "Nell" Quinlan Donnelly Reed Papers, Folder 24; James Chace, *Acheson: The Secretary of State Who Created the World* (New York: Simon and Schuster, 1998), 70. For background information on the Democratic Party and use of sexual politics, see Joel Williamson, *A Rage for Order: Black-White Relations in the American South since Emancipation* (New York: Oxford University Press, 1986).

43. Ryan, *Red War on the Family*, 9–10.

44. McMillen and Roberson, *Called to Courage*, 116–117; Swisher, "A Tough Nut to Crack," 21–23, 32.

45. Mae Harcum, Letter, July 15, 1937, in "Copies of Letters by Donnelly Garment Co. Employees, July 1937," Box 034, Reed Papers.

46. Swisher, "A Tough Nut to Crack," 21–23, 32.

47. Frank Prins, Letter to Kansas City Joint Board, March 6, 1937, Local 250, Kansas City, Mo.: 1935–38, Box 97, Folder 7, Dubinsky Papers.

48. Garment Industry History Project of Greater Kansas City, Box 001, Folder 3, Wilson Papers.

CHAPTER EIGHT

Morally and Legally Entitled

Women's Political Activism in Kansas City

K. David Hanzlick

"Maisie [sic] Jones Ragan. Who wants to vote for a colored woman on the council?" proclaimed the handbill distributed by the Pendergast machine on the morning of the municipal elections of Tuesday, November 3, 1925. The elections took place under the new Kansas City charter approved in February of that year. The new charter replaced a two-chamber city governance structure of thirty-two elected representatives with a single council of nine people. Other handbills made similarly distorted claims. Ragan, in fact, was not African American, but rather a white woman with a long history of activism in the community. Although her candidacy in 1925 was unsuccessful, it reflected the aspiration of middle- and upper-class women to gain electoral victory and participate in the governance of their city, which was susceptible to appeals to racial prejudice.[1]

These Kansas City women—members of organizations such as the Athenaeum and the Woman's City Club—sought to assert power in their community and beyond. Coming from Republican and independent Democratic backgrounds and abhorring the influence of the Democratic machine, these women embraced a progressive spirit and revered a vision of good government. Their experiences reflected the difficulties that remained for women's political participation even after gaining the vote in 1920. At the local level, women's campaigns for city offices and the school board in the interwar period often united, but occasionally divided, progressive Republican and anti-machine, independent Democratic women. Likewise, African American women's groups often acted in collaboration with the white clubs while working-class women affiliated with machine politics worked at cross-purposes with their progressive sisters. This examination of the diversity of views across party, race, and class among women in Kansas City adds nuance to the scholarly view that after gaining the vote in 1920, women struggled for cohesiveness and the political power that accompanied it. Historian Nancy Cott notes, for example, that in the 1910s women united, despite racial, class, regional, political, and strategic differences, to advance the common cause of female suffrage. Their extant, disparate interests, Cott argues, caused divisions to resurface and unity to unravel once women obtained the vote.[2] With the defeat of Masie Jones Ragan for city council in 1925, women remained active in politics, but met with limited success in claiming political office.[3]

The women's club movement provided the necessary organizational structure to support activist goals. Women's clubs in Kansas City were among the thousands of local clubs affiliated with the national General Federation of Women's Clubs (GFWC), founded in 1890. By 1892, 20,000 women belonged to the GFWC, and by 1900, 150,000 women had joined. As with the Woman's Christian Temperance Union (WCTU), founded fifteen years earlier, the clubs provided a forum for women to pursue their interests in community improvement and to think and act collectively. While historian Ruth Bordin asserts that the GFWC nationally focused on "education, self-improvement, and sociability, rather than an activist program," women's clubs in Kansas City acted vigorously on a wide range of local, state, and national political issues.[4]

African American women also participated actively in the women's club movement and regularly interacted with white women's organizations in at least two ways. First, the General Federation of Women's Clubs admitted black clubs beginning in the early 1900s, but did not allow black members to attend the national convention. Second, the black Young Women's Christian Associations (YWCAs) operated as branches of the white central organization. A representative of the white central YWCA served on the branch board. Decisions of the branch were subject to approval by the central organization.[5]

This chapter primarily draws on the records of the large and venerable Kansas City Athenaeum, a women's club organized in 1894, and on those of the newer but equally large and influential Woman's City Club, founded in 1917.[6] While the Athenaeum scrapbooks from 1917 to 1939, with their committee lists and newspaper clippings recounting teas, dances, and plays staged by members, primarily reflect the prevailing constructions of middle- and upper-class womanhood, the clippings from the 1920s also demonstrate the club women's political aspirations internationally, nationally, and locally. These clippings discuss women's success in gaining power in European nations, the potential for women to serve abroad as US consuls, and broad support for the Kansas City charter of 1925, including a list of organizations that endorsed the move. In contrast to the gendered activities described in most of the scrapbooks, the minutes of the membership forums and board of managers' meetings more often dealt with the substantive political issues addressed by the organization in the early to mid-1920s and the late 1930s.[7] The local newspapers provided far more extensive coverage of the Athenaeum's political activities from the 1910s through the early 1920s and in the late 1930s than the Athenaeum's internal records.

The Woman's City Club, another large and politically active club in the community, was founded in 1917 in downtown Kansas City, Missouri, and sought to serve "women of various vocations and women of no vocation." The downtown location of the club highlights the presence of women in professions such as real estate, law, and medicine in the city's commercial district. The Woman's City Club emphasized the discussion of public affairs and featured prominent speakers, much like the downtown men's clubs and in contrast to traditional women's study clubs. John D. Rockefeller Jr. and Mrs. Dwight Morrow figured among the first speakers.[8]

The African American community also featured women's clubs that participated in public debate, as recounted in the pages of *The Call*, the city's African American newspaper. These organizations included the City Federation of Clubs, the YWCA, the Kansas City Association of Colored Women, the National Junior League, social sororities, masonic auxiliaries, and social and study clubs, among others. Even the Pleasure Seekers Art and Study Club, a name that suggested a purely social function, engaged in politics by hosting a lecture by Ida B. Wells-Barnett in 1925. Women in the black community continued their activism throughout the period. As John W. McKerley illuminates in Chapter 1, black Kansas Citians constituted an increasingly important voting group in this period.[9]

Activism, the Athenaeum, and the Woman's City Club

The importance of the activism of women's clubs cannot be overstated. While the General Federation of Women's Clubs, to which the Athenaeum belonged, did not embrace suffrage until the 1910s, the Athenaeum had long advocated an array of public issues related to municipal housekeeping in Kansas City. Achievements included, among others, the creation of public playgrounds, public kindergartens, the juvenile court, parent-teacher associations, the placement of a matron at the city jail to oversee female inmates who had previously been overseen by male jail attendants, advocacy for pure milk regulations, and the suppression of vice, among many other causes. The Club also took progressive stances on social issues such as holding husbands financially responsible when they abandoned their wives, ensuring better wages and working conditions for laundry workers, and supporting prohibition.[10]

At the national level, the Athenaeum clashed vigorously with the Democratic US senator from Missouri and former Kansas City mayor James A. Reed. In Chapter 2, Jeffrey L. Pasley highlights the pervasive influence of Reed in Kansas City during this period, and in Chapter 7 Kyle Anthony examines Reed's later career and marriage to the prominent Kansas City dress manufacturer, Ellen "Nell" Donnelly Reed. The Athenaeum's dispute with Reed centered on the Sheppard-Towner Infancy and

Maternity Protection Act of 1921, a pioneering piece of social legislation that provided prenatal care to mothers and continuing care and education to new mothers and infants. The conflict between the Athenaeum and Reed, however, had deeper roots. Club members retained vivid memories of Reed's vocal opposition to female suffrage, a position that earned him few friends among progressive women and their supporters. A leader of the club, Phoebe Jane Ess, spouse of prominent lawyer Henry N. Ess, spoke in favor of renewing Sheppard-Towner for another five years, and the Athenaeum sent a telegram to Reed to that effect. Ess and other members knew that Reed vehemently opposed the act but raised their voices nonetheless. Reed viewed the act as an invasion by the government into private life. Women's clubs supported Sheppard-Towner because it provided needed care for women and children and because the program was operated and administered largely by professional women under the auspices of the federal Children's Bureau. As such, the act empowered middle-class professional women. Reed subjected proponents of the act to public ridicule. The disagreement with the Athenaeum members helps explain why Reed won reelection to the US Senate in the next election but failed to carry his hometown of Kansas City.[11]

The two clubs' interactions and alignment with prominent political and cultural figures of the day reflected their influence. Henry J. Allen, the progressive Republican newspaper publisher and future Kansas governor and US senator, spoke to the Athenaeum in January 1918.[12] In 1922, Jeannette Rankin, the first woman elected to the US House of Representatives and the only member of Congress to vote against US entry into both world wars, spoke at a dinner at the Athenaeum about the living wage law or minimum wages that applied to women and men, and about women in industry.[13] The Woman's City Club also invested in a study of the conditions in the juvenile justice system in Jackson County. The club's influence and reach were reflected in the engagement of an outside investigator, Charles L. Chute, secretary of the National Probation Association. The study recommended reforms that received the endorsement of Jackson County juvenile court judge E. E. Porterfield, a nationally prominent advocate for mothers' pensions and aid to widows who were "morally and legally entitled" to assistance. The club also sponsored a speech by suffrage leader Carrie Chapman Catt in which she discussed world peace and asserted that US policy undercut peace efforts.[14]

While overwhelmingly middle and upper class, white and Protestant, the Athenaeum and Woman's City Club counted among its members both Republicans and independent Democrats who were not affiliated with the machines and interacted with other religious, ethnic, and racial groups in the community. They had Jewish members and collaborated with the National Council of Jewish Women on the use of silver nitrate to prevent blindness in newborns.[15] The Athenaeum also interacted with the black federated women's clubs, which played a prominent role in middle- and upper-class black society. The Athenaeum president addressed one such meet-

Masie Jones Ragan, 1925 candidate for city council, as she appeared in the 1921 Kansas City School of Law yearbook. Courtesy of the Missouri Valley Special Collections, Kansas City Public Library.

ing in 1919, which was attended by other members of the Athenaeum. African American women's clubs had deep roots in Kansas City by this time. Prominent Kansas City educator Josephine Silone Yates, spouse of the well-known principal of the Wendell Phillips School, W. W. Yates, had led the National Association of Colored Women nearly two decades earlier, having defeated Margaret Murray Washington, the wife of Booker T. Washington, for the presidency of the national organization in 1901.[16]

Masie Jones Ragan and the Council Race of 1925

Masie Jones Ragan became a flashpoint in efforts by the Athenaeum and other progressive women to elect a woman to the nine-member city council created under the new city charter of 1925. Ragan embodied not just the political but also the professional aspirations of her sex. She took up the study of law late in life. She was a grandmother when she graduated summa cum laude from the Kansas City School of Law, along with five other women in the class of 1921. In an article about her in the *Kansas City Times*, she explained that she became a lawyer because she had long handled real estate transactions and had consulted with attorneys. She decided to become one.[17] Following graduation, she served as the attorney for the Athenaeum and in 1923 was elected to represent the organization on the Water and Charter Committee to help write a new city charter.[18] She was elected to the upper house of the city council in 1924.[19] By 1927, Ragan served as the state vice president for Missouri of the National Association of Women Lawyers.[20]

Ragan's status as a prominent Athenaeum member, lawyer, member of the city council's upper house, and candidate for the nine-member council was made even more unusual by the fact that she was divorced in an era when society viewed divorced women in a negative light. According to her application for a passport to attend a convention of lawyers in London and travel throughout Europe in 1924, she had married physician Romulus "Ralph" C. Ragan in October 1887. The couple had two children and divorced more than ten years later in January 1898. Despite her divorced status, Ragan had earned the respect of her fellow Athenaeum members, lawyers, and Kansas Citians.[21]

Yet, Ragan's election to the city council in 1924 and candidacy for that body under the new charter in 1925 were not the first forays by women into local elective politics. Both political parties knew that the votes of the recently enfranchised women would be essential to their electoral success and included women in their governing structures and as candidates for office in the 1922 elections. The Republicans, in fact, nominated just two women for offices during that election cycle— Mrs. Bessie M. Elliott for city treasurer and Mrs. Carolyn M. Fuller for the school board. Fuller, the wife of a banker, distinguished herself as a past president of the Athenaeum from 1915 to 1918.[22] The local Republican Party also included women in its finance committee by naming eleven women to this group that numbered just over fifty people and fourteen women to positions on the sixty-one-member advisory committee. The Young Republican Club elected Miss Marjorie Hires as the vice president and only female officer in its five-person executive committee.[23] The Republican auxiliary of the Tenth Ward held a tea in honor of Elliott and Fuller on March 7, 1922. The tea drew more than 100 women.[24]

Not to be outdone in the competition for women's approval and their votes, the Democratic Party nominated three women for office—two for upper-house and one for lower-house alderman. The Democrats faced far greater complexity in their nomination process than the Republicans. To arrive at a list of candidates, three factions had to be considered: the Goats led by Tom Pendergast, the Rabbits led by Joe Shannon, and the independent Democrats who did not fall in line behind either of the machines. The process of nominating candidates for office in 1922 benefited from an agreement between Pendergast and Shannon on the slate.[25] Independent

A political cartoon demonstrates that politicians sought the women's vote. *Kansas City Journal-Post*, February 28, 1922.

Democrats who affiliated with neither machine faction were also included among the nominees. Emma Longan, an independent Democrat, received the nomination for a seat in the upper house of aldermen. Longan had a distinguished record of service in the community, was the wife of a former school district administrator and an expert on parliamentary procedure, and had founded an eponymous women's club.[26] The other two female Democratic nominees were less well known: Margaret Doherty Shepard, wife of Pendergast-affiliated judge James J. Shepard, as the second Democratic candidate for the upper house of aldermen, and Lucile Tappan Moreland for the lower house.[27]

Women played an integral role in the Democrats' nomination proceedings in Kansas City that year. The Kansas City Democratic Committee caucus, for example, created a forty-eight-member body composed of two men and one woman for each of the wards. While the committee structure included women, it clearly valued them half as much as men. With these actions, the newspaper reported that the women were nonetheless "pacified"—suggesting that the newly enfranchised women had demanded and received a role in the party.[28]

In the municipal elections of 1922, the first following the adoption of women's suffrage, the *Kansas City Journal* betrayed low expectations for women's ability to function as full participants in the democratic process. The paper declared that women had "voted intelligently without asking questions," a fact that clearly surprised the paper, which further noted that both white and black women appeared alone at the polling places and did not need assistance. Women also worked at the polls as clerks and challengers and were credited with helping to keep the election clean. Two Democratic women, Longan and Shepard, were elected to the upper house of aldermen. In addition, former Athenaeum president Mrs. Carolyn M. Fuller became the first woman to be elected to the Kansas City School Board.[29]

The municipal elections of 1924 provided an opportunity for the Republicans to sweep out of office the Democrats who were elected in 1922, a goal the party pursued with vigor. In addition to Masie Jones Ragan, the Republicans nominated another woman, Rose Ludlow, for a seat in the upper house of aldermen and nominated an African American clergyman, the Reverend J. W. Hurse, pastor of St. Stephen Baptist Church, for the city council as well. The Democrats nominated one woman for the upper house.[30] To achieve victory, the Republican women pioneered an electoral strategy for the party's candidates that would prove useful in later campaigns. In anticipation of the April elections, the women held 177 meetings across Kansas City, and all but one ward recorded a total attendance exceeding 5,000 voters. The campaign included organizing cars and drivers to take women to the polls—because many women did not have access to a car or did not drive—and a telephone campaign to ensure that every Republican woman voted.[31] Kansas City voters rewarded Republican tenacity. Republicans, including mayoral candidate Albert I. Beach, swept the city offices with the exception of the city treasurer's position, which continued to be held by a Democrat. The two Republican women candidates, Ragan and Ludlow, were each elected to the upper chamber, while Reverend Hurse did not fare as well and was defeated. Republican women received credit for organizing the Republican turnout.[32]

Even with the Republican sweep in the municipal elections of 1924, pressure continued to mount from the business community, good government advocates, women's clubs, and other opinion leaders for a simplified city council with an appointed professional city manager to replace the two-chamber alderman system. Inspired by Progressive Era zeal for businesslike efficiency in government, the new charter sought to remove politics from city government and, instead, focus on professional administration. Confident that the real motivation of reformers was to devise a structure to strip the political machines of influence in city government and, thereby, advantage white Anglo-Saxon Protestants over Irish Catholics for positions of leadership in the city, the Pendergast and Shannon machines had defeated each previous attempt at charter revisions.[33] Work on the 1925 charter began in 1923 with the appointment of the Water and Charter Committee, composed of 125 organizational delegates and individuals, including Masie Jones Ragan as a representative of the Athenaeum.[34]

To great fanfare and high expectations, a new city charter went before the voters on February 24, 1925, with the full support of the women's clubs. Advocates advanced the utilitarian view that the structure of city government affected policy outcomes and that city government would be made more efficient by concentrating more power into fewer—presumably progressive—hands. *The Call* dismissed opposition to the new charter as ill-founded.[35] Meanwhile, opposition from the Pendergast machine failed to materialize as Tom Pendergast came to the realization that formal political structures mattered little if he had the votes to control a majority of the seats on the new council. The new charter easily won voter approval.[36] The elections to be held under the new city charter were scheduled for November 3, 1925, when the voters were to elect a mayor, nine council members, and two municipal judges and to vote on the issuance of city bonds for a variety of city improvement projects. *The Call* strongly supported the Beach ticket, with the exception of the reelection of municipal judge Ira S. Gardner, who had convicted a young black man of rape, a conviction that was subsequently overturned. *The Call* also endorsed the bonds, which white and African American women's clubs actively supported.[37]

The new charter eliminated the political affiliations of candidates from the ballots, thus removing the voters' "obligation to follow party lines," in the naive or perhaps tongue-in-cheek language of the *Kansas City Star*.[38] The reality of the elections that followed soon after the charter's adoption, however, was far different. Masie Jones Ragan secured the nomination for an at-large council position from the Republicans with the support of the Athenaeum. Yet the desire of the progressive women to claim a higher level of power through a seat on the newly reconfigured council clashed directly with the imperative of the progressives led by Mayor Albert I. Beach to deprive the machine of a majority of seats. On election day, the bonds passed, but Ragan lost the race to machine Democrat Ira B. Burns by a margin of 55,045 to 51,746 votes. Whether Ragan's loss was attributable to her being a woman, her divorce, or the machine's false assertion that she was African American is impossible to discern. She ran a competitive race but still lost by the widest margin of any of the four at-large candidates. While any of those elements may have played a role in her loss, Marjorie Beach, the wife of Mayor Beach, blamed the handbills. The progressive Republican mayor faced a five-to-four majority of Democratic machine politicians on the council, which would hire the powerful city manager.[39]

The progressives' loss was the machine's long-term gain. Pendergast won political control of city government and held it for the next thirteen years. The Call lamented the internal divisions that prevented African Americans from exercising power in the election. The loss of control of the council also was due, in part, to a female candidacy that squelched enthusiasm for women candidates among the Republicans and independent Democrats in future elections. The machine Democrats no longer needed to nominate female candidates to compete with Republicans and independent Democrats as they had in the 1922 and 1924 elections. While women had tried to exercise power in city government and briefly succeeded, participation in municipal governance eluded their grasp after 1925 and reverted to the male sphere. No woman would serve again on the city council until the 1950s. With the defeat of the sole female candidate on the municipal ballot in 1925, women's political participation would change in form over the next fifteen years but not diminish in its intensity as they engaged in the political process prior to the fall of the Pendergast regime.[40]

Women on the Kansas City School Board

Women's quest for power in the community succeeded, however, in the arena of education. This success was due, at least in part, to society's view that children's and women's issues were an appropriate domain for women's involvement.[41] As early as 1897, the Missouri Federation of Women's Clubs discussed the possibility of women's service on local school boards. Women's involvement, the federation said, would usher in an era of compulsory education, kindergartens, and manual training.[42]

In a political mix of Republicans and independent Democrats who often collaborated, and the Pendergast and Shannon machines that occasionally went to war but sometimes cooperated, the school board held a unique position. The political machines that dominated other governmental units in Kansas City and Jackson County left the school district largely untouched. At school board elections, each

APR. 1928

Edwin C Meservey
PRESIDENT

Bryce B. Smith
VICE PRESIDENT

Carolyn Farwell Fuller

Charles Baird

J. Roy Smith

Annette Moore

C. W. Allendoerfer
TREASURER

George Melcher
SUPERINTENDENT

J. B. Jackson
SECRETARY

BOARD OF DIRECTORS,
OFFICERS AND SUPERINTENDENT
The School District of Kansas City, Mo.
As organized April 5, 1928.

Carolyn Fuller and the Kansas City School Board shown as organized on April 5, 1928.
Fuller was the first woman elected to the Kansas City School Board. Courtesy of the
Missouri Valley Special Collections, Kansas City Public Library.

party nominated a candidate—always white—for one of the two available seats. The candidates did not face opposition. In the April 1924 election, for example, Republican Edwin C. Meservey and Democrat J. C. Nichols were both elected.[43]

This largely hands-off approach by the machines flies in the face of both logic (the school district controlled hundreds of jobs that were the stock-in-trade of political machines) and historical precedent in other machine-controlled communities such as Chicago and New York, where the schools were an important source of patronage.[44] The reasons for this unusual arrangement are at least twofold. First, the members of the school board were prominent figures within the Kansas City business establishment.[45] They offered their service as a gift to the community, and their social and economic standing served to insulate the school district from encroachment by the machines. Second, the Pendergast machine did not establish firm control over city politics until well after the tradition of uncontested school board races had been firmly established. The machine chose not to challenge this practice, which would have required taking on senior-level community leaders. This nomination-cum-election process also made the path to a board seat easier for women to achieve. Once nominated, they would run unopposed; their challenge was to secure their party's nomination.[46] The women thus demonstrated their ability to work through the two parties to secure nomination and subsequent election to school board seats.

Women were routinely elected and reelected to the school board, unlike their short-lived experience with electoral success in city council races. Carolyn Fuller's election signaled the start of what became a long tradition of service by women on that body. In 1926, Miss Annette Moore, a law school contemporary of Masie Jones Ragan at the Kansas City School of Law and a Democrat, was elected to the board. Between 1926 and 1945, at least two and sometimes three of the seven board members were women at any one time. Despite the electoral success of these four women and their status as elected officials, none of them advanced beyond committee chair and vice president to lead the board as its president. While the parties and the electorate clearly welcomed the participation of women in the operation of the school district, societal views of appropriate gender roles limited their ability to claim the highest level of power, authority, and visibility on the school board.[47] At the same time, this unusual electoral arrangement did not serve the interests of African Americans, who had no school board representation even though the board provided employment for educated African Americans as teachers and staff within the segregated Kansas City schools.

Women's Involvement in Democratic Machine Politics

Unlike the middle- and upper-class women who sought political office, the working-class women who worked in Democratic machine politics played the far less seemly role of operatives in perpetrating election fraud. Some of the women held positions of authority and directed fraudulent activities. Most of the women, however, acted out of loyalty to the machine or feared the repercussions of not cooperating. Their fear was not unfounded. Machine-inspired fraud reached unprecedented levels in the elections of 1934, when machine-instigated violence against the anti-boss Citizens Fusion reformers, a coalition of reform-minded Republicans and independent Democrats, resulted in the deaths of five people. A federal grand jury empaneled in 1935 failed to return indictments, saying that the city was so "infested with . . . lawlessness . . . that citizens are afraid to tell the truth."[48]

Less violence, but no less corruption, accompanied the elections of 1936. The *Star* declared that "an honest election here . . . is an utter impossibility" because of the fraudulent placement of names—known as ghosts—on the voting rolls. Estimates placed the number of ghost voters in the election at between 50,000 and 60,000. The fraudulent voting practices varied. For example, Helen Honeyman informed authorities that she had voted a straight Republican ticket, but two ballots were on file under her voting number—both a straight Republican and a straight Democrat ballot. Other voters, including two whites and twenty-two African American men and women, also described voting irregularities, including that ghost voters had been added to the list of voters in their neighborhood.[49]

Unlike the election of 1934, however, the election fraud of 1936 did not transpire without repercussions or indictments. From 1937 to 1938, 278 women and men were indicted for voter fraud.[50] The court proceedings illuminate the role of women in conspiring to deprive voters of their rights through such actions as falsely counting the ballots. The names included precinct judges, clerks, and captains. Bail for men was set at $2,000, and for women, reflecting their lower level of risk or perhaps importance, at $1,500.[51]

The party label in the case of the indicted Republican clerks and judges cannot be construed as denoting loyalty to the Republican Party and its candidates. For example, lifelong Democrat Myrtle Middleton spent the morning of the election rounding up Democrats to go to the polls. Over the noon hour, she was approached by two Democratic operatives to serve as a Republican judge in the Twenty-Eighth Precinct of the Twelfth Ward. Middleton replaced Charles Ellis, the Republican judge who had been "run out" of the polling place by the same operatives.[52] Because the fraud took place primarily in working-class wards, the occupations of those indicted were also working class. Many of the women were married to public employees who feared the loss of a job if they refused to participate in the fraud. Alice M. Froeschl, for instance, worked as a cashier at the Jones Store. Her husband was a firefighter.[53]

Most women indicted on voting fraud charges were portrayed by the press as meek, attractive, and even fashionable. Mrs. Ruth Hagedorn, for example, broke down in tears on the stand as she recounted fraudulently affirming the vote count in exchange for a bribe. A *Star* reporter described Alice Froeschl as "an attractive brunette [who] wore a green hat and black dress with a row of green buttons as a contrasting note." Witnesses such as Democratic election judge Samuel J. Clark testified to the tyrannical atmosphere at his polling place, where female poll workers received threats from machine operatives. The prosecution, defense, and media cast most of the women as passive players in a larger drama.[54]

Feminine passivity does not, however, describe Twelfth Ward Democratic committeewoman Frances Ryan. The daughter of a Pendergast lieutenant, Ryan established herself as a person of substance in the community as early as the mid-1920s, when her name appeared as a signatory in an advertisement supporting the Democratic ticket in the elections of 1925. Other signatories included J. C. Nichols, William T. Kemper, John B. Gage, and Phoebe Jane Ess, among others. At the time of the 1936 election, Ryan served as the superintendent of the Jackson County Parental Home, which functioned as the juvenile detention center, and as ward boss. US prosecutor Maurice Milligan described Ryan as the mastermind of the voter fraud in the ward. As such, Milligan charged that Ryan gave instructions to the precinct election officials to count "just so many" ballots for the Republican candidates.[55]

For their fraudulent activities, women generally received one year of probation for their roles as accessories. Men, who were viewed as perpetrators, received far more severe sentences—up to five years in the federal prison. Frances Ryan and Marie Ogden, who also played an active role in directing fraud, received lengthy prison sentences of two three-year prison terms and one four-year term, respectively. Ryan made her influence felt even after her conviction by engineering the appointment of her sister, Gertrude Kennedy, to replace her as superintendent of the county juvenile home to the consternation of the women's clubs and other reform groups.[56]

Women's Activism after the Fall of Pendergast

After suffering a substantial loss of power in part due to Democratic governor Lloyd C. Stark's break from it, the Pendergast machine suffered its coup de grace on April 7, 1939, when "Boss" Tom and former state insurance superintendent R. Emmet O'Malley were indicted on federal income tax evasion charges. The indictments stemmed from funds they received through exercising influence in an insurance settlement.[57] The business community, given the opportunity to envision a future for the city that did not include Tom Pendergast, quickly coalesced to form the Forward Kansas City Committee.[58]

Progressive women with both Republican and independent Democrat affiliations added their organizational skills and time to the business community's enthusiasm for fundamental change in the administration of city government. They followed the patterns of electoral activism the Republican women had pioneered during the election of 1924. While the usual narrative of the cleanup campaign emphasizes middle- and upper-class women uniting to bring honesty to government, a more nuanced telling cannot omit the fact that other women—those affiliated with the Pendergast machine—lost power. The women who lost were more likely to have Irish surnames, come from working-class backgrounds, and practice the Catholic faith.

The women who gained power generally bore Anglo-Saxon surnames and adhered to Protestant Christianity. At the same time, the female advocates of city reform were often characterized in a pejorative sense as "south siders," a term that connoted wealth and privilege. While the south side had also been home to Tom Pendergast, Robert Mehornay, and other people friendly to the machine, that label did not describe all of the women reform leaders. The Athenaeum president, Elsie Child, who was married to Harry C. Child, the proprietor of an electroplating business, was from the east side, a much more modest part of the city. By the end of May 1939, the Forward Kansas City Committee included representatives of the Parent-Teacher Association (PTA), the Visiting Nurse Association, the League of Women Voters, the University Women's Club, the Athenaeum, and the African American community, among other groups.[59] By June, the *Kansas City Star* reported that "thousands of . . . women have pooled their resources and experiences in a determined drive for good government."[60]

Claude Gorton, a south sider, Democrat, longtime community leader, and spouse of plumbing supply owner George H. Gorton, led the women's participation through the Women's Forward Kansas City Committee, a separate entity from the Forward Kansas City Committee. The existence of a separate women's committee reflected widespread enthusiasm and unity for the task on the part of middle- and upper-class women, but also the gendered nature of their involvement.[61] By early 1940, the various entities—the Forward Kansas City Committee, the Women's Forward Kansas City Committee, the Charter Party, and others—operated collaboratively as the United Campaign to amend the city charter through the February election. The primary charter revisions reduced the terms of sitting council members from four years to two years, provided for two-year terms for the city council members, the mayor, and two municipal judges, and required that elections be held for a new council in early April of that year. While business leaders and club women were both heavily represented in the coalition, representatives of labor, immigrant communities, and the working class were largely absent.[62]

Just as white women acted as a separate group within the larger Forward Kansas City campaign, so too did African American men and women activists coalesce in support of municipal reform. While women's organizations such as the YWCA had remained active and held conferences on topics such as anti-lynching, housing, and jobs legislation, women's political activity in municipal reform reflected a partnership with men. Elmore Williams, manager of the People's Finance Corporation and president of the local chapter of the National Association for the Advancement of Colored People (NAACP), served on the executive committee of the Forward Kansas City Committee, a move lauded by *The Call* as a step forward for the African American community. Williams and other men and women used the opportunity to form the Citizens Movement within the larger municipal reform initiative, proposing a ten-point platform that called for fairness in the treatment of African Americans in public employment, housing, education and training, juvenile and adult corrections, and representation on the school board, among other grievances. By August 1939, the Citizens Movement claimed 1,000 members and had a goal of enlisting 5,000 members. A woman served on the executive committee of the Citizens Movement, and women served in committee roles as well.[63]

For the charter election on February 13, 1940, Claude Gorton and the Women's Forward Kansas City Committee fielded 1,500 women who were assigned to polls, 500 women who worked the telephones, and another 500 women who provided transportation for voters. Many others prepared lunches for the election judges and clerks.[64] They faced less opposition than expected when the machine's forces reversed their prior opposition to the charter amendments and then announced their support.[65] Few surprises occurred on election day other than the lopsided victory of the charter amendment campaign, which prevailed by a margin of six-to-one.[66]

The United Campaign and women's committee intensified their efforts in preparation for the municipal elections on April 2, 1940, in which they supported independent Democrat John B. Gage as the United Campaign's candidate for mayor. Claude Gorton continued to serve as a visible spokesperson for the campaign just as she had for the campaign for the charter amendments. The campaign also included endorsements by Marjorie Beach, wife of the late mayor Albert Beach, and longtime anti-machine crusader Rabbi Samuel S. Mayerberg. Prominent black community leader and undertaker T. B. Watkins served as chairman of the African American division of the Charter Party, one of the entities pushing for new city leadership. The NAACP appointed a committee of men and women to call on independent Democrat John B. Gage and machine Democrat Flavel Robertson to "ask them to state their policy toward Negroes." Each candidate also appeared separately before what was then called the Negro Chamber of Commerce. The audience at each session included both men and women.[67]

Under Gorton's leadership, the women's campaign grew to 7,500 active volunteers. On election day, they served as telephone coordinators, drivers, and babysitters and as poll observers. The press offered what it thought was the ultimate affirmation of their value when it described the women as being "as serious as any man could be." Their success and that of the United Campaign resulted in a comfortable win for Gage and considerable plaudits for their efforts.[68]

The triumph of the United Campaign, the defeat of the last vestiges of machine control, and the prominent role of middle- and upper-class Protestant women underline the arc of women's activism in Kansas City. These women negotiated the boundaries of electoral office, meeting with success in city and school board elections in 1922 and 1924, and in the years after they found sustained success only in school board elections. They remained united in activism, which found effective expression in educational policy and municipal reform once their contest for power in the male-dominated realm of city politics had been rebuffed. African American women often joined in common cause, whether through their club ties or working in concert with black men as in the Citizens Movement and the Forward Kansas City Committee. Working-class Democratic women's political participation, publicly characterized by their involvement in voter fraud, tended to be far less laudable. While women in Kansas City remained politically active across class and racial lines after the advent of women's suffrage, they were no longer united in a single cause.

Notes

1. Marjorie M. Beach, *The Mayor's Wife: Crusade in Kansas City* (New York: Vantage Press, 1953), 141–151.

2. Nancy F. Cott, *The Grounding of Modern Feminism* (New Haven: Yale University Press, 1987), 10–30. See also Dorothy Sue Coble, "More Than Sexual Equality: Feminism after Suffrage," in *Feminism Unfinished: A Short, Surprising History of American Women's Movements,* Dorothy Sue Cobble, Linda Gordon, and Astrid Henry (New York: Liveright Publishing, 2014), 12–13.

3. The effective struggle for power was not limited to upper- and middle-class women. For an example of the effective organizing of working-class women, see Dorothy Sue Cobble, *Dishing It Out: Waitresses and Their Unions in the Twentieth Century* (Urbana: University of Illinois Press, 1991).

4. Ruth Bordin, *Women and Temperance: The Quest for Power and Liberty, 1873–1900* (Philadelphia: Temple University Press, 1981), 149; William E. O'Neill, *Feminism in America: A History,* 2nd rev. ed. (New Brunswick, NJ: Transaction Publishers, 1989), 85–86.

5. O'Neill, *Feminism in America,* 87; Nancy Marie Robertson, *Christian Sisterhood, Race Relations, and the YWCA, 1906–46* (Urbana: University of Illinois Press, 2007), 32.

6. K. David Hanzlick, *Benevolence, Moral Reform, Equality: Women's Activism in Kansas City, 1870 to 1940* (Columbia, Mo.: University of Missouri Press, 2018).

7. Athenaeum Scrapbooks, Series 1, and books of minutes, Kansas City Athenaeum Collection (SC 160), Missouri Valley Special Collections, Kansas City Public Library, Kansas City, Missouri (hereafter Athenaeum Collection).

8. Woman's City Club Scrapbook, newspaper article, vol. 1, 1917; Scrapbook, vol. 1, 1920; 1922 Bulletin, Scrapbook, vol. 1, 1922; Board minutes, 1-11-1938, Box 1, Folder 10; Scrapbook, vol. 1, 1922; Woman's City Club Collection (KC 257), State Historical Society of Missouri, Kansas City Research Room (hereafter Woman's City Club Collection). In this chapter I also use newspaper articles from the clipping file at the Kansas City Public Library

(hereafter Clipping File) in addition to articles from the *Kansas City Star*, the *Kansas City Journal-Post*, and other sources.

9. "The Proposed Charter," *The Call*, February 13; *The Call*, February 20; and "Women Work for Passage of Bonds," *The Call*, October 23, 1925. For a discussion of African American enfranchisement in Missouri, see Chapter 1.

10. See Chapter 1 for information about the 1905 workhouse scandal in which an African American guard allegedly abused a white female inmate.

11. For more on Reed and the Sheppard-Towner Act, see Theda Skocpol, *Protecting Soldiers and Mothers: The Political Origins of Social Policy in the United States* (Cambridge, Mass.: Belknap Press of Harvard University Press, 1992), 501, 508–510; and Robyn Muncy, *Creating a Female Dominion in American Reform, 1890–1935* (New York: Oxford University Press, 1991), 112–132. On the election of 1922, see Linda Harris Dobkins, "What Men Expected, What Women Did: The Political Economy of Suffrage in St. Louis, 1920–1928," *Missouri Historical Review* 109 (October 2014): 1–17. Athenaeum Membership Forum minutes, Athenaeum Collection, December 16, 1925; January 6, January 27, February 10, and February 24, 1926.

12. "Allen at the Athenaeum Tomorrow," *Kansas City Star*, January 22, 1918.

13. "Host to Ex-Congresswoman: Kansas City W.C.T.U. Will Entertain Jeannette Rankin," *Kansas City Star*, April 22, 1922. For information about the living wages, see Skocpol, *Protecting Soldiers and Mothers*, 407–412.

14. Scrapbook, vol. 1, December 1923; Scrapbook, vol. 2, December 1924; Scrapbook, vol. 2, February 1925; Woman's City Club Collection. "Clubwomen Reticent on Chute Report: Porterfield Agrees with Official in Survey Recommendations," *Kansas City Journal*, February 20, 1925.

15. "Guard Baby's Sight," *Kansas City Star*, March 12, 1915, 6. "Work for Woman's Club," January 29, 1917, Clipping Files. "Mrs. George Curtis to Speak Today," *Kansas City Times*, April 20, 1919.

16. "Defeated Mrs. Washington," *Kansas City Star*, July 14, 1901, 1. For more on the remarkable life of Josephine Silone Yates, see Gary R. Kremer and Cindy M. Mackey, "'Yours for the Race': The Life and Work of Josephine Silone Yates," *Missouri Historical Review* 90, no. 2 (January 1996), 199–215. See also Mia Bay, *To Tell the Truth Freely: The Life of Ida B. Wells* (New York: Hill and Wang, 2009), 222–225. For a discussion of Ida B. Wells's interactions with Yates, see Ida B. Wells, *Crusade for Justice: The Autobiography of Ida B. Wells*, ed. Alfreda M. Duster (Chicago: University of Chicago Press, 1970), 267–268.

17. "L. L. B. to a Grandmother," *Kansas City Times*, June 7, 1921, 2.

18. A wide range of organizations sent representatives to serve on the committee, including the Kansas City Business Women's Club, the Chamber of Commerce, the Good Roads Association, the Society for the Suppression of Commercialized Vice, the Consumers League, the Jackson County Medical Society, the Stereotypers and Electrotypers Union, and the Switchmen's Union. Athenaeum Executive Board/Board of Managers minutes, December 21, 1921, and February 12, 1923. Undated newspaper article, Athenaeum Scrapbooks, Series 1, Athenaeum Collection.

19. City Directory, 1924, microfilm, Missouri Valley Special Collections, Kansas City Public Library.

20. *Women Lawyers Journal* 15 (1927): 1.

21. US Censuses of 1920 and 1930, and passport application, Ancestry.com, accessed December 6, 2015.

22. "History of the Kansas City Athenaeum," *Kansas City Journal*, November 15, 1920.

23. "Organize, Foster Basis of Victory; Primary Spurned [sic]," *Kansas City Journal*, February 21, 1922; "Delano Chooses Committees for G.O.P. Campaign," *Kansas City Journal*, March 3, 1922.

24. "Tea Party and G.O.P. Meeting Are Combined," *Kansas City Journal*, March 8, 1922.

25. "Slate Is Ready for Convention of Democrats," *Kansas City Journal*, March 11, 1922.

26. Jane Fifield Flynn, *Kansas City Women of Independent Minds* (Kansas City, Mo.: Fifield Publishing, 1992), 106–108. The Longan Study Club ceased operations in 1983. While Flynn's work is useful as a general resource, the information she provides is occasionally lacking in accuracy and completeness. For example, she stated that Emma Longan was the first woman elected to city government. In fact, she was one of the first two women elected to the upper house.

27. "Cromwell Is Nominee of Democrats," *Kansas City Journal*, March 12, 1922.

28. Ibid.

29. "The Vote," *Kansas City Journal*, April 5, 1922. George Fuller Green, *A Condensed History of the Kansas City Area, Its Mayors, and Some V.I.P.s* (Kansas City, Mo.: Lowell Press, 1968), 141; Fuller Green incorrectly recorded Longan as Logan.

30. "Residential Tidal Wave Sweeps Republican Nominee into Office; G.O.P. Wins All Upper House," *Kansas City Journal*, April 9, 1924; US Census, 1920. For more information on Reverend Hurse and the 1924 election, see Chapter 2 in this book.

31. "Republicans Hurl Fire at $5000 Check," *Kansas City Journal*, April 6, 1924.

32. "Residential Tidal Wave Sweeps Republican Nominee," *Kansas City Journal*, April 9, 1924; Larry Grothaus, "Kansas City Blacks, Harry Truman, and the Pendergast Machine," *Missouri Historical Review* 69 (October 1974): 65–82.

33. For more on the operation of the council-manager system since its adoption in 1925 in Kansas City, see Max J. Skidmore, "Kansas City, MO: The Experience of a Major Midwestern City under Council Manager Government," *Journal of American and Comparative Cultures* 24 (Fall–Winter 2001): 81–91; Beach, *The Mayor's Wife*, 136–137.

34. Woman's City Club Scrapbook, Volume 1, Woman's City Club Collection. Undated newspaper article from 1923, Series 1, and Athenaeum Board of Managers minutes, February 12, 1923, Athenaeum Collection.

35. "City to Adopt New Charter Today, Belief [sic]," *Kansas City Journal*, February 24, 1925; "The Proposed Charter," *The Call*, February 13, 1925.

36. William M. Reddig, *Tom's Town: Kansas City and the Pendergast Legend* (Philadelphia: J. B. Lippincott, 1947), 117.

37. "Charter Wins by 28,223; North Side Aids in Triumph," *Kansas City Journal*, February 25, 1925. "Women Work for Passage of Bonds," *The Call*, October 23, 1925; "It Is Fair," *The Call*, October 30, 1925.

38. "On a Nonpartisan Ballot," *Kansas City Star*, November 2, 1925, 1.

39. Beach, *The Mayor's Wife*, 142–154; "The Outstanding Candidates at Today's Election," *Kansas City Star*, November 3, 1925, 1; "The New City Officials," *Kansas City Star*, November 4, 1925, 1.

40. Beach, *The Mayor's Wife*, 142–154; "The Outstanding Candidates at Today's Election," *Kansas City Star*, November 3, 1925, 1, and "The New City Officials," *Kansas City Star*, November 4, 1925, 1; Reddig, *Tom's Town*, 122; A. Theodore Brown, *The Politics of Reform: Kansas City's Municipal Government, 1925–1950* (Kansas City, Mo.: Community Studies, 1958), 1–4; "Voters Fail in Chance to Show Power," *The Call*, November 6, 1925; Fuller Green, *A Condensed History of the Kansas City Area*, 141.

41. Robyn Muncy, *Creating a Female Dominion in American Reform, 1890–1935* (New York: Oxford University Press, 1991), 112–132.

42. "Work Is Well Under Way," *Kansas City Star*, January 20, 1897, 2.

43. "Residential Tidal Wave Sweeps Republican Nominee," *Kansas City Journal*, April 9, 1924.

44. Jim Carl, "Good Politics Is Good Government: The Troubling History of Mayoral Control of the Public Schools in Twentieth-Century Chicago," *American Journal of Education* 115, no. 2 (2008), 305–336; Diane Ravitch, *The Great School Wars: A History of New York Public Schools* (Baltimore: Johns Hopkins University Press, 2000), 92–99.

45. Dick Fowler, *Leaders in Our Town* (Kansas City, Mo.: Burd and Fletcher, 1952), 297–299.

46. Manual and Directory of Public Schools of Kansas City, Mo., 1922–1960, Missouri Valley Special Collections, Kansas City Public Library, Kansas City, Missouri (hereafter Manual).

47. Manual, 1922–1944; Manual, 1959. The Pandex (Kansas City School of Law yearbook) 1924, vol. 20, 107, Dr. Kenneth J. LaBudde Special Collections, University of Missouri–Kansas City, Kansas City, Missouri.

48. "Kansas City Jurors Indict 36 in Fraud," *New York Times*, January 10, 1937, 41. For more information on the 1934 election, see Reddig, *Tom's Town*, 237–242.

49. "Fraud Rolls On," *Kansas City Star*, November 1, 1936, 1; "'Ghosts in Court,'" *Kansas City Star*, May 27, 1937, 1. For a discussion of the relationship between the African American community and the Pendergast Machine, see Grothaus, "Kansas City Blacks, Harry Truman, and the Pendergast Machine," 65–82.

50. "Fraud Rolls On," *Kansas City Star*, November 1, 1936, 1. "Indicts in Vote Fraud [sic]," *Kansas City Star*, January 9, 1937, 1. Reddig, *Tom's Town*, 287–290.

51. "Firm In Vote Cases," *Kansas City Star*, January 11, 1937, 1; and "Tyranny at Polls," *Kansas City Star*, June 23, 1937, 1.

52. "Tyranny at Polls," *Kansas City Star*, June 23, 1937, 1.

53. "Touched Only One Ballot," *Kansas City Star*, March 13, 1937.

54. Hagedorn and Froeschl mentioned in "'Magic' in Voting," *Kansas City Star*, March 11, 1937, 2; "Touched Only One Ballot," *Kansas City Star*, March 13, 1937.

55. Reddig, *Tom's Town*, 293–294; "'Saw Vote Fraud,'" *Kansas City Star*, March 17, 1937;

"Vote Guilty Plea," *Kansas City Star*, May 17, 1937, 1; "'Czar' at Polls," *Kansas City Star*, May 18, 1937, 1; "Tyranny at Polls," *Kansas City Star*, June 23, 1937, 1.

56. "To Prison in Fraud," *Kansas City Star*, February 25, 1937, 1; "Graves Still Silent," *Kansas City Star*, June 3, 1937, 1; "Two More Guilty," *Kansas City Star*, June 24, 1937; "Three to Prison in Vote," *Kansas City Star*, June 29, 1937. Reddig, *Tom's Town*, 293–294. Woman's City Club scrapbooks, newspaper clippings, scrapbook vol. 9; minutes April 18, 1939, KC 257 Box 1, Folder 10, Woman's City Club Collection.

57. Reddig, *Tom's Town*, 323–331. See also Lawrence H. Larsen and Nancy Hulston, *Pendergast!* (Columbia: University of Missouri Press, 1997), 130–151.

58. Brown, "The Politics of Reform," 7, 136–137, 337; Reddig, *Tom's Town*, 333, 337–338.

59. Board of Managers minutes, May 22, 1939, Athenaeum Collection; US Census, 1940, Ancestry.com, accessed December 6, 2015.

60. Clipping Files [no headline], *Kansas City Star*, June 4, 1939, June 15, 1929, September 26, 1939, Clipping Files.

61. Reddig, *Tom's Town*, 363–364.

62. Ibid., 359–362; "Kansas City Beats Machine by 6 to 1," *New York Times*, February 14, 1940, 1; Brown, "The Politics of Reform," 139–141.

63. "Citizens Movement Reaches 1,000 Mark in Membership," *The Call*, August 11, 1939; "N.A.A.C.P. to Confer with Candidates on Both Tickets," *The Call*, March 15, 1940, 1.

64. "Home Vote Rises," *Kansas City Star*, February 13, 1940.

65. "Eye on Machine," *Kansas City Star*, February 12, 1940, 1.

66. "Kansas City Beats Machine by 6 to 1," *New York Times*, February 14, 1940.

67. Albert Beach (July 30, 1883–January 21, 1939). "Ticket in Review," *Kansas City Times*, March 23, 1940, 1; "A Local City Manager," *Kansas City Times*, March 22, 1940; "To Peak Tonight," *Kansas City Times*, March 30, 1940, 1; "1000 Democrats for Gage and Entire United Ticket," *Kansas City Times*, April 1, 1940, 1. For information about the relationship between the African American community and the Pendergast machine, see Grothaus, "Kansas City Blacks, Harry Truman, and the Pendergast Machine," 65–82. For more on Mayerberg, see Reddig, *Tom's Town*, and Larsen and Hulston, *Pendergast!* "N.A.A.C.P. to Confer with Candidates on Both Tickets," *The Call*, March 15, 1940; "John B. Gage Is Speaker at C. of C. Lunch," *The Call*, March 22, 1940; "C. of C. Hears Democratic Candidates," *The Call*, March 29, 1940.

68. "Brooms Do a Job," *Kansas City Times*, April 3, 1940, 1. The Kansas City election board was reorganized by state directive in 1937 under a system of permanent voter registration, in which voter registration remained in force from one election to another. The police force was placed under state control in 1939 due to the corruption of local control. Under the new electoral structure, voter registration dropped from 263,000 to 203,000. "In Nation's Eye," *Kansas City Times*, April 4, 1940, 1. For more information on the electoral and police department reforms, see Reddig, *Tom's Town*, 301, 333.

CHAPTER NINE

Collaborative Confrontation in the "Persistent Protest"

Lucile Bluford and the Kansas City *Call*, 1939–1942

Henrietta Rix Wood

On February 3, 1939, subscribers to *The Call* opened the weekly African American newspaper and scanned the front page. The national edition of *The Call* reached a wide audience of both black and white readers, perhaps as many as 100,000 throughout Missouri, Kansas, and thirteen other states. At first glance, the reports seemed typical: The National Association for the Advancement of Colored People (NAACP) had rejected a federal anti-lynching bill as inadequate; heavy-weight boxing champion Joe Lewis had recently defeated challenger John Henry Lewis at Madison Square Garden in New York City; the presiding bishop of the African American Methodist Episcopal Church had died; and black Republicans had met in Kansas.[1]

As readers continued to peruse the front page, however, they saw six remarkable stories gathered under a single banner headline, "M.U. Rejects Woman Student." Positioned prominently was a first-person account by Lucile Bluford, the twenty-seven-year-old African American managing editor of *The Call*, about her attempt to enroll in classes of the graduate program in journalism at the racially segregated University of Missouri (MU) in Columbia. The headline of Bluford's report read: "Nothing Will Happen When Negro Student Is Admitted to M.U." In the first paragraph, she argued, "Those who fear trouble if a Negro student attends the University of Missouri may rest at ease—there will be no trouble, no violence of any kind. That is the one significant thing that my attempt to enroll brought out." Reassuring African American readers who anticipated hostile reactions to her appearance at MU, she also defied the expectations of some whites with her assertion. Bluford's second story appeared in the lower right corner of the front page, next to a column, "Why I Applied to Missouri U." A conventional news story and two other short items about the incident provided more details on the front page. On an inside page of this issue was a final story, "Desired to Enter M.U. Long Time."[2] In an era when reputable newspapers rarely featured first-person stories or reports with bylines, this series was extraordinary. In trying to persuade readers to support the national campaign for educational equity, Bluford and *The Call* carried on the tradition of African American women journalists and the black press that had long advocated for racial rights.

That larger campaign was well under way when Bluford made headlines in *The Call*—the paper had already chronicled other African Americans who were challenging the racist policies of institutions of higher learning during the 1930s. Before Bluford tried to cross the color line at MU, Donald G. Murray of Baltimore had attempted to enroll in the University of Maryland Law School, and Lloyd L. Gaines of St. Louis had sought admittance to the University of Missouri Law School. Although *The Call* and other African American newspapers such as the *Baltimore Afro-American* and the *Chicago Defender* documented the actions of Murray and Gaines, the coverage differed dramatically from Bluford's first-person accounts. For example, *The Call* began reporting on Murray's legal case against the University of Maryland Law School on April 26, 1935, with a five-paragraph wire story buried deep in the paper that did not quote Murray. Similarly, the first story about Murray in the *Baltimore Afro-American*, on April 27, 1935, was a conventional report that noted NAACP lawyers had filed a petition on Murray's behalf, but the article appeared on page twenty-three of the twenty-four-page newspaper and did not carry a byline or quote Murray. The *Baltimore Afro-American* continued to cover Murray's case with standard stories through late January 1936, when the Maryland Court of Appeals ruled that the university must admit him as a student. Another major African American newspaper, the *Chicago Defender*, also began covering Murray's case in April 1935. Its first story was a one-column report on the front page of the national edition that identified Murray and his lawyers but did not carry a byline or quote Murray. The *Chicago Defender* took the same approach through January 1936, when it published an editorial that saluted the actions of the Maryland Court of Appeals.[3]

The *Call*, the *Baltimore Afro-American*, and the *Chicago Defender* also covered Gaines's effort to enter the University of Missouri Law School in 1935. *The Call* devoted extensive coverage and editorial comment to the case from January 1936 to January 1939, but the newspaper never published a first-person account by Gaines. The Baltimore and Chicago newspapers kept readers informed of the Gaines case with standard reportage. Ascertaining whether any African American who tried to enter segregated institutions of higher education wrote first-person accounts for black newspapers before Bluford is beyond the scope of this project, but her role as a journalist adds an important, if often overlooked, dimension to civil rights activism in the period.[4] Bluford's action may be unique, but still, by capitalizing on her capabilities as a reporter and *The Call*'s capacity to serve as an argumentative forum, this young journalist and the newspaper collaborated to deliver *confrontative rhetoric*, a form of persuasive discourse used by individuals and groups promoting social change. In so doing, Bluford and *The Call* participated in what historian Leslie Brown termed the "persistent protest," the crusade for African American rights that began decades, if not centuries, before the civil rights movement of the 1950s. Brown contends that the civil rights movement was a phase of the persistent protest, and other scholars concur that the movement did not emerge from a void in the 1950s.[5]

This chapter fills a gap in both the historical and rhetorical narratives of Bluford and *The Call* by analyzing her reporting on her effort to enter MU, her commentary on her failed civil lawsuit in May 1942, and the announcement of the newspaper's fundraising campaign for African American education in May 1942. Scholars of journalism have examined the press coverage of Bluford's activities, but few have considered Bluford's reportage as a rhetorical performance or *The Call* as a persuasive podium. The facts of Bluford's three-year crusade to enroll at MU (repeated attempts to register and three separate lawsuits) are well known, but how she and *The Call* collaborated to influence readers' responses to the quest for African American educational rights is not.[6] Informed by archival research, interdisciplinary methodology, and the work of feminist scholars of the history of women and rhetoric such as Shirley Wilson Logan, my investigation also contributes to conversations about women in African American print culture.[7]

By the time that Bluford made news in 1939, she was already a civil rights advocate and experienced journalist. Growing up in Kansas City, she attended NAACP meetings with her father, John H. Bluford, who was a teacher at Lincoln High School, the only public high school for African Americans in the city until 1936. Bluford went to Lincoln in the 1920s, where she was an officer of the junior branch of the NAACP and an editor of the school newspaper. In 1926, she wrote a signed editorial for the Lincoln newspaper that called for a new African American high school and questioned the Kansas City board of education for failing to build it. Barred from attending racially segregated MU, Bluford studied journalism at the University of Kansas (KU) in Lawrence and reported for the KU student newspaper as well as *The Call* during her summer breaks.[8]

At *The Call*, Bluford worked with the publisher, Chester A. Franklin, and the

Staff of *The Call*, with Managing Editor Lucile Bluford shown fourth from left in the back row, October 5, 1935. Courtesy of the American Jazz Museum, Kansas City, Missouri.

news editor, Roy O. Wilkins. A native of Texas, Franklin helped his family run a newspaper in Denver before he moved to Kansas City and founded *The Call* in 1919. Scholarly assessments of him vary. Historian Sherry Lamb Schirmer refers to him as "the spokesman for race men and women in Kansas City," characterizing him as a leader of those who identified themselves "proudly as Negroes" and "defined themselves by their deeds." Thomas D. Wilson asserts that Franklin "believed civil rights depended on economic success, and economic success depended on the Protestant work ethic. When African Americans failed to display this ethic, he chastised them." Wilson also contends that Franklin regularly took issue with the stances promoted by the NAACP in its publication, *The Crisis*. Historian Charles E. Coulter maintains that in the early years of the newspaper, Franklin was often more conservative than many of his readers. He tended to favor running sensational stories of sex and scandal in the early 1920s that boosted readership. During his tenure at *The Call*, Roy Wilkins served as secretary of the Kansas City chapter of the NAACP, and he joined forces with Franklin's wife, Ada Crogman Franklin, to convince Franklin to report on politics and serious issues. Wilkins left the paper in 1931 to become assistant secretary of the NAACP in New York, and Bluford replaced him as news editor when she began working full-time for the newspaper in 1932 after she graduated from KU.[9]

Despite his conservative reputation and penchant for profit as editor and publisher of *The Call*, Franklin endorsed the progressive statement that appeared on the editorial page in 1936: "The Call believes our country can lead the world away from racial and national antagonisms when it accords Negroes their human and citizen rights. Hating no man, fearing no man, this paper strives to help every man, because we believe all are hurt so long as anyone is held back."[10] The use of "man" in the statement was standard for the day but ironic given that Bluford, a woman, would soon lead the way for legal rights. Gender may have been an asset to Bluford's campaign: historians speculate that she may have thought it would be safer for a woman to challenge MU. Given the fact that African American women frequently were the victims of white violence, this point is debatable, but regardless, gender would remain a part of Bluford's fight for educational opportunity.

Franklin also authorized *The Call's* coverage of Lloyd L. Gaines, who wanted to pursue legal training in Missouri, which did not have a law school for African Americans. Gaines applied to the University of Missouri Law School in August 1935 and a month later, MU advised Gaines to seek out-of-state scholarships to attend a law school that would admit African American students. Gaines then sought help from the NAACP, which was assisting other African Americans who were trying to enter whites-only educational institutions. A NAACP team began legal action, and eventually, the Gaines case became the first of its kind to go to the US Supreme Court. In December 1938, the Court ruled that MU must admit Gaines or that the state of Missouri must provide a law school for him in the state. The Missouri legislature passed a bill to enable Lincoln University, the public university for African Americans in Missouri, to establish a law school. During the course of further legal action, Gaines disappeared in the spring of 1939, but his NAACP lawyers did not know that he was missing until October 1939 and had to drop his case. Gaines was never seen nor heard of again, but as scholars such as legal historian Mark V. Tushnet note, Gaines helped to erode the principle of separate but equal education in the United States.[11]

The first article about Gaines in *The Call* appeared on January 31, 1936. A conventional news story that reported Gaines had filed suit to enter MU, it summarized his actions to date and noted that the NAACP was supporting his case. This story established the newspaper's approach to Gaines's case for the next two years. A week after the first story about Gaines, *The Call* ran an editorial, "Separate Schools," that referred to the Gaines case, a rhetorical gesture that linked this commentary to the initial news story.[12]

In August 1937, Bluford became managing editor of *The Call*, and she supervised the continuing coverage of the Gaines case that culminated in a front-page spread in the national edition of the newspaper on December 16, 1938, after the Supreme Court announced its decision.[13] The banner headline, "Victory in Missouri U. Case," appeared above a report on the Supreme Court majority opinion, which was reprinted next to the story. In adjacent boxes were the names of the six Supreme Court justices who had voted in favor of Gaines and the two who had voted against him, a review of the main points of the ruling, and a timeline of the case. Another front-page story proclaimed: "The winning of the Gaines case is a new feather in the cap of the National Association for the Advancement of Colored People." To illustrate the series, *The Call* published a photo of Gaines and a

Lucile Bluford, civil rights activist and managing editor of *The Call*, 1946. Courtesy of the LaBudde Special Collections, University of Missouri–Kansas City.

photo of Sidney R. Redmond, one of the three NAACP lawyers who handled the case. On an inside page, the newspaper reprinted the opinion of the dissenting Supreme Court justices. *The Call* then commented on the Gaines case in an editorial that concluded the right to equal education is the "foundation of all equality."[14] Although the Gaines coverage was extensive, none of the stories had bylines and Gaines was never quoted.

In contrast, Bluford and *The Call* made the most of the rhetorical occasion that she created when she attempted to enroll at MU. Despite speculation that she was a pawn of the NAACP, Bluford acted on her own in applying to MU. She sent her application in early January 1939 and was provisionally admitted because the registrar did not know that she was African American.[15] On January 30, 1939, Bluford arrived on campus and then recounted her experience for *The Call* on February 3, 1939. She reported, "After spending two hours on the M.U. campus as a prospective student, I am thoroughly convinced that the students are not perturbed over a Negro's entrance. I found the students no different from those at K.U., where I was a student for four years. Some are friendly, most of them indifferent. I found no animosity." Bluford described her meeting with the dean of the University of Missouri School of Journalism, who told her that she had the prerequisites to begin a master's program but lacked permission to enroll in classes. She then noted that the registrar's office refused to grant her permission to register for classes.

Bluford also informed readers that she spoke to several white journalism students and a white faculty member. The students and instructor did not object to her efforts to enroll, she explained, and one student told her that he regularly read *The Call*, which he described as "the best weekly in the state." Using these sources to support her argument that there would not be "trouble" if an African American student went to MU, Bluford provided reasons for her actions:

> After being "in the field" for five years, I think it time to "brush up" in my profession. That's why I planned to return to school. My logical choice is M.U. Missouri has the strongest school of journalism in the country. It was the first established in the United States. Students come from all over the world to study journalism in Missouri. While I was waiting in the registrar's office, I saw students from many foreign countries receive their permits to enroll. There was one boy from Portugal who wanted to study journalism. He was admitted.

Bluford then cited statistics about the MU student body, observing that students from eleven different countries, every state of the United States, and every county in Missouri attended MU. She concluded matter-of-factly: "They come from everywhere to Missouri U. I live in Missouri."[16] Compiling a remarkable collection of evidence, Bluford and *The Call* tried to convince readers, both black and white, that African Americans could challenge segregated education.

In the process, Bluford and *The Call* created a case study of confrontative rhetoric. Rhetorician Robert C. Rowland observes that confrontative rhetoric ignores Aristotle's time-honored advice that successful rhetors must adapt to the attitudes, beliefs, and values of their audiences. Instead, Rowland views this kind of rhetoric as a strategy for individuals or groups that seek significant change or are outside the social system, such as radical environmentalists or gay rights advocates during the 1950s. Confrontative rhetors, people who use this form of persuasion, rely on a variety of strategies to appeal to two primary audiences: an internal audience within an organization or social movement and an external audience encompassing the broader society. The two goals of confrontative rhetors for the internal audience are to convince members that change is possible and to help them redefine their identities as oppressed individuals. To influence the external audience, Rowland concludes, confrontative rhetors seek to publicize their movement and create guilt or challenge the assumptions of members.[17]

Readers of *The Call* included members of the internal audience as well as members of the external audience. In 1939, the newspaper had 19,020 subscribers and published different editions that reached readers in Missouri, Kansas, Colorado, Oklahoma, Texas, and Wyoming.[18] The internal audience of *The Call* included African Americans who supported the campaign for educational equality, as well as African Americans who supported racial justice initiatives but did not always agree about the best way to challenge discrimination. The external audience encompassed African Americans who did not regard themselves as part of an African American social justice movement. Although it is impossible to determine how many whites read *The Call* in 1939, many did. In his autobiography, Roy Wilkins reported that by 1931, the circulation of *The Call* was 20,000 copies a week. Since there were only about 14,000 black families in Kansas City at that time, the newspaper must have reached every black household and many white readers as well. Wilkins also noted sympathetic whites in Kansas City, such as Burris Jenkins, the white pastor of Linwood Christian Church, who criticized Jim Crow codes from his pulpit and invited Wilkins to speak to his congregation in 1929. When African American activist Walter White of the NAACP spoke in Kansas City in 1926, Wilkins reported that 1,000 whites were in the audience.[19]

In her effort to persuade readers that diverse audiences supported the quest for educational equity, Bluford suggested that *The Call* had white readers by documenting the comments of the white MU student in her front-page reports in 1939. During her testimony at a hearing in the Boone County Circuit Court in February 1940, Bluford claimed that *The Call* had "a large number of white readers" that included subscribers and Kansas City reporters for other newspapers, as well as social workers, members of juvenile court staffs, and "persons interested in learning the problems of the whole community."[20] Consequently, whites constituted two other factions of the external audience: whites who were sympathetic to the African American campaign for equal education, such as the students and faculty whom Bluford met at MU, and whites who alternately opposed or ignored the campaign. The front-page placement of Bluford's first-person stories and the scope of the coverage of her experience at MU signals that *The Call* intended to persuade both African American and white supporters of integrated education that change was possible. The publicity of Bluford's actions served the confrontative goal of informing the external audience about the growing educational equity movement.

Characterizing the audience of *The Call* in the 1930s before the advent of sophisticated market analysis is challenging (indeed, gauging audience reception remains one of the most difficult aspects of any rhetorical analysis). But even without a complete profile of *The Call*'s readership, some generalizations are relevant. Economist and sociologist Gunnar Myrdal asserted that the majority of African American readers of black newspapers in the mid-twentieth century were members of the middle class and "the upper layers of the lower class." In his landmark study, *An American Dilemma: The Negro Problem and Modern Democracy* (1944), Myrdal defined the "Negro press" of this era as "a fighting press," "an educational agency," and "a power agency." Noting that upper-class African Americans wrote and published newspapers and tried to influence the opinions of lower-class blacks, he observed, "*The* [black] *press defines the Negro group to the Negroes themselves.* The individual Negro is invited to share in the sufferings, grievances, and pretensions of the millions of Negroes far outside the narrow local community. This creates a feeling of strength and solidarity. The press, more than any other institution, has created the Negro group as a social and psychological reality to the individual Negro" (italics in original). He concludes that "the importance of the Negro press for the formation of Negro opinion, for the functioning of all other Negro institutions, for Negro leadership and concerted action generally, is enormous." Charles H. Loeb, an African American journalist who was Myrdal's contemporary, concurred. "There can be no question today of the enormous importance of the Negro Press in forming Negro opinion, in the improvement of educational opportunities for Negroes, in the field of interracial relationships, and in the elevation of the Negro people toward incontestable equality with their fellow citizens of other races."[21] Significantly, both Loeb and Myrdal describe the African American press as a shaper of opinion, but Myrdal raises the important issue of class differences among the producers and the consumers of African American newspapers.

Class differences among African Americans and the consequences of those differences for the black community of Kansas City are noted by Wilkins in his autobiography. Reflecting on his eight years of living in Kansas City and working for *The Call* in the 1920s and early 1930s, Wilkins wrote:

> Deep divisions separated the town's [African American] social classes. At the bottom was a floating world of hustlers, torpedoes, fly-by-night artists, and easy women. The center was held by solid workingmen, railroad porters, hod carriers, and truck drivers, a labor force that was far larger than anything I had seen in St. Paul. At the top was a prosperous upper middle class of doctors, lawyers, dentists, pharmacists, teachers, school principals, and a scattering of businessmen.

Wilkins refers to professional gunmen as "torpedoes" and alludes to his upbringing in St. Paul, Minnesota, where he lived in a racially integrated neighborhood. What he calls the "top" of the black Kansas City community was small. Kansas City historian Charles E. Coulter calculated that only 3 percent of African Americans could be classified as middle class during this time and that "the foundations for the political and economic success for black elites lay in the trials and triumphs of the black working class" that constituted the majority of the black community. Wilkins claims that most of the "elite, middle-class" African Americans with whom he associated in Kansas City were not committed to change and "were content to live with what they already had." Frustrated by what he perceived to be widespread African American acceptance of Jim Crow codes and the low status quo of blacks in Kansas City among all classes, Wilkins proved the power of the black press in small ways. For example, in 1930 he organized and publicized in *The Call* a boycott of a white-owned local bakery that depended on black consumers but refused to hire black truck drivers. The boycott reached its goal when black shoppers responded by refusing to buy the bakery's bread, forcing the company to employ black drivers.[22] Despite these isolated successes, the divisions in the African American community challenged blacks who wanted to inspire change and collective action.

Nine years later, it was just this problem that Bluford and *The Call* tried to address head-on by appealing to different audiences of the newspaper, including African Americans who questioned the emphasis on education by black elites. This group of readers was represented by D. A. Holmes, a prominent African American minister in Kansas City. Shortly after *The Call* began to cover the Gaines case, Holmes wrote "An Open Letter to *The Call*," published in the city edition on February 21, 1936. In this essay, he wrote:

> In Kansas City, the Negro needs everything, "from the hat down and from the overcoat in," as the song expresses it. Rich man, poor man, beggar man, thief are making a clamor for what they want. Why shall not we? Negro citizens in our home town ought to at least tell what they want. That I am endeavoring to do, Mr. Editor, both to get an outlet for my pent-up feelings and to make all of your readers think about what they need.

Holmes continued by citing the poor lighting and damaged sidewalks and roads in African American neighborhoods and business districts, comparing the condition of these areas to the well-maintained Country Club Plaza and other areas for whites. Complaining that there was no public meeting place for African Americans or effective representation on the Kansas City council, Holmes then posed a provocative question: "What's the use of the National Association for the Advancement of Colored People coming to Missouri to fight in the courts for equal education when death-dealing unsanitary buildings, expressing only landlord greed, are allowed to stand?" Although Holmes was active in the Kansas City chapter of the NAACP in the 1920s and 1930s, he took issue with the focus of the NAACP on education during the deprivations of the Depression, which exacerbated racial inequities in Kansas City.[23]

To accommodate the resistant members of the internal audience that Holmes represented, readers who believed that addressing the economic plight of African Americans during the Depression was more important than advocating the integration of public universities, Bluford and *The Call* used the account of her trip to MU to encourage what Rowland describes as a "rhetorical redefinition of self."[24]

Whereas Holmes defined African Americans as victims of white Kansas City officials who ignored the needs of the black community and of unscrupulous property owners who took advantage of tenants, Bluford defined herself as a rational and qualified applicant pursuing her right to equal education following the Supreme Court ruling on the Gaines case. In other words, Holmes emphasized the passive helplessness of blacks, and Bluford advocated their active agency to effect change. She reinforced this message with her short article, "Why I Applied to Missouri U," which enumerated her reasons: "1. I am a resident of the state of Missouri. 2. Missouri U. has the best school of journalism in the country. 3. Fees are lower in your own state than in another state. You don't have to pay out-of-state tuition." Countering suspicion that she was a troublemaker or agent of the NAACP, Bluford portrayed herself as a reasonable person appealing to the common sense of readers.[25]

Bluford further emphasized her rationality in her second first-person story, "Missouri U. Not Ready for Negro." Calmly narrating her experience at the registrar's office, she observed:

> The University of Missouri found a loop-hole Monday to prevent me from
> enrolling in the school of journalism for graduate work. A week before I came
> to Columbia, my credits from the University of Kansas, where I received my
> A.B. degree in journalism, had been accepted and the registrar had told me by
> letter that my credits were sufficient for admittance to the graduate school. He
> sent me a registration blank and told me to come by his office when I arrived
> in Columbia to receive my permit to enroll.

To prove her point, Bluford then quoted from the registrar's letter before resuming her account. Instructed to stand in line for her permit, she claimed:

> When I joined the line, there was not a ruffle of excitement. Students who
> came in the office after I did stood behind me waiting their turn, paying
> no more attention to me than they would any other new student enrolling.
> No one in the line said anything to me. There were no comments about my
> presence, no demeaning glances at one another. The students chatted about
> "dates" and the courses they planned to take.

Continuing the account, Bluford reported that a secretary escorted her to the office of Silas W. Canada, MU's registrar, where he read a prepared statement from the MU Board of Regents that indicated the university was contesting the decision of the Supreme Court on the Gaines case. "After hearing the statement, I asked Mr. Canada how the Gaines case could go back to the Missouri supreme court after the United States supreme court already had ruled on it. He said, 'I really don't know. I'm not a lawyer and am not familiar with all the legal angles.'" Rather than chastise Canada in print for his remark, Bluford concluded this first-person story by noting that she and the registrar "chatted for quite a while" and he suggested that "the matter" might be straightened out by September and then she could enroll at MU.[26] Ending on an optimistic note, Bluford implied that her efforts were not necessarily in vain.

Of course, the matter of Bluford's admittance to MU was not straightened out by September 1939, and she repeatedly tried to enroll at MU while her NAACP lawyers pursued legal action through the early 1940s. *The Call* continued to confront readers by reporting on Bluford's court appearances, responses by MU, and the efforts of the Missouri legislature to circumvent the Supreme Court ruling. Bluford did not, however, write any more first-person stories until May 1, 1942, after she lost her second civil damage suit against the MU registrar. That day, *The Call* published her column, "How I Feel About Missouri U. Case," on the front page. Seeking to stir both sympathetic and resistant members of the internal and external audiences, Bluford declared:

> The most brazen, impassioned appeal to race prejudice that I have ever heard
> was made by William S. Hogsett, attorney for the University of Missouri in my
> damage suit against the university registrar tried in federal court at Jefferson
> City last Thursday and Friday. "We speak Anglo-Saxon," he bellowed in his
> closing argument to the 12 white Missourians on the jury. "We understand
> each other. If this colored girl wants to study journalism let her go to Kansas."
> Hogsett, a reputable Kansas City lawyer, knew in his heart that he had lost the
> case. The law and the facts were clearly against him and in our favor. In dignity
> of presentation, eloquence of expression, brilliance of mind, and depth of soul,
> Hogsett was overshadowed by our lawyer, Charles H. Houston, who came from
> Washington to prosecute the case. Thus defeated, Hogsett then took the only
> course open to him—a direct plea to the jury to act as *white* men and put in her
> place a Negro who dared sue the state for her rights as a Missouri citizen.[27]

Positioning herself again as a reasonable rhetor, Bluford encouraged both the internal and external audiences to judge rather than merely accept Hogsett's racist tactics and arguments. Quoting Hogsett's offensive comments, she also tried to create guilt in the external audience, swaying African Americans who did not support the campaign for educational rights, whites who did, and whites who opposed this crusade. Like other confrontative rhetors, Bluford depended on myth. As Rowland notes, "Movement leaders often draw on myth to energize their followers."[28] Here, however, Bluford created myth by praising Houston, the NAACP lawyer, as superior to Hogsett. Suggesting that Houston's skill forced Hogsett to ignore the law and facts of the case and pander to the presumed prejudice of the white jury, Bluford transformed Houston into a mythical hero of the persistent protest.

A week later, Chester Franklin confronted readers about Bluford's case. In an editorial published on the front page of *The Call*, Franklin wrote:

> To every Public-Spirited Negro Citizen of Missouri, especially to Ministers, Teachers, and CALL agents. Dear Fellow Missourians: The outrageous verdict in the Bluford case, tried in the federal court in Jefferson City on April 23 and 24, is a blow to Negro education everywhere in Missouri. . . . We must not let the Bluford case be the end of our fight for equal education. . . . To raise a "FIGHT FOR JUSTICE" fund, I am giving the first $1 and have deposited it in the People's Finance Corporation of Kansas City. I call upon you to help raise the $2,000 needed. What I ask of you, you can do quickly. Tell of this need to everybody in your community. Tell them all. Methodists and Baptists, Republicans and Democrats. Tell white people who believe in fair play. The important thing is not how much each gives but that this appeal represent [sic] all of us. No one person gives a large amount. Let everybody give.[29]

Vowing to print the names and hometowns of contributors in the newspaper, Franklin urged the internal and external audiences to redefine themselves as active agents of change, not passive spectators of racial injustice, and to recruit whites to a new phase of the persistent protest for African American rights. And while Franklin had an overt agenda of soliciting local financial support for the campaign to end segregated education, he astutely did not call his fund the "Fight for Equal Education" and thus offend African Americans who considered jobs more important than college degrees. Seeking to appeal to audiences with varying priorities, he linked equal education to the broader concept of "justice."

Fifteen years after Bluford and *The Call* collaborated to pursue equal education for African Americans, the US Supreme Court struck down racially segregated education in *Brown v. Topeka Board of Education* (1954). Soon after this landmark decision, Bluford became editor of *The Call*, and she continued to deliver confrontative rhetoric on local issues, such as the Kansas City department store diner boycott in 1959, as well as national civil rights campaigns. In 1989, fifty years after Bluford tried to enroll at MU, the university awarded her an honorary doctorate. Bluford accepted the degree "not only for myself, but for the thousands of black students" that MU had barred for years. Although Bluford was known as the "conscience" of Kansas City until her death in 2003, her rhetorical performance and historic collaboration with *The Call* in 1939 to promote the persistent protest for African American rights has never been properly recognized.[30] She did not, like more famous African American women journalists, such as Ida B. Wells-Barnett, write an autobiography that could have cemented her legacy, but that is not unexpected. For Bluford the journalist wanted the facts, as she documented in her first-person accounts for *The Call*, to speak for themselves. A middle-class, well-educated activist who was part of what Gunnar Myrdal identified as the "fighting press," she capitalized on her skills and access to the persuasive forum of *The Call* to challenge the complacency of blacks and whites in Kansas City. Although she lost her battle to cross the MU color line, she continued to confront all of the audiences of *The Call* to stand and speak up for racial justice throughout her long career.

Notes

1. Lucile Bluford provided this information about the circulation of *The Call* during her testimony at a hearing that began on February 9, 1940, in the Boone County Circuit Court in Columbia, Missouri. See "No. 37449, in the Supreme Court of Missouri, Division No. 1, May Term, 1941, State Ex Rel. Lucile Bluford, *Appellant*, v. S. W. Canada, Registrar of the University of Missouri, *Respondent*," 55–56, Missouri State Archives, Jefferson City, Missouri; *The Call*, February 3, 1939. For this chapter, I reviewed microfilm of *The Call* from 1935 to 1942 that is held by the Kansas City Public Library. I am grateful to the library and to Jenn Salvo-Eaton of the Miller Nichols Library of the University of Missouri–Kansas City for assistance in accessing these sources.

2. Lucile Bluford, "Nothing Will Happen When Negro Student Is Admitted to M.U.," *The Call*, February 3, 1939.

3. "Student Barred from Law School Sues Maryland," *The Call*, April 26, 1935; "Bill to Break U. of Md. Jim Crow Is Prepared," *Baltimore Afro-American*, April 27, 1935; "Fights U. of Maryland Law School Ban," *Chicago Defender*, April 27, 1935; "We Salute Maryland's Court of Appeals," *Chicago Defender*, January 25, 1936.

4. See Mark V. Tushnet, *The NAACP's Legal Strategy against Segregated Education, 1925–1950* (Chapel Hill: University of North Carolina Press, 1987).

5. Leslie Brown, "Long before 'The Movement': Persistent Protest," address at the Annual Richard D. McKinzie Symposium, Kansas City Public Library, Kansas City, Missouri, March 1, 2013. Historian Darlene Clark Hine notes that black professionals led "proto–civil rights campaigns" from 1890 to 1950 that "helped lay the foundation for the classic civil rights movement of the 1950s and 1960s"; see Darlene Clark Hine, "Black Professionals and Race Consciousness: Origins of the Civil Rights Movement, 1890-1950," *Journal of American History* 89, no. 4 (March 2003): 1,281. Sociologist Aldon D. Morris describes the "persistent struggle" of Africans Americans, citing slave revolts, the antebellum Underground Railroad, Marcus Garvey's Universal Negro Improvement Association during the 1920s, and the March on Washington Movement in 1941; see Aldon D. Morris, *The Origins of the Civil Rights Movement: Black Communities Organizing for Change* (New York: Free Press, 1984), x. Historians Vicki Crawford, Jacqueline Rouse, and Barbara Woods catalog the importance of African American women in the "ongoing struggle for freedom and equality," noting that women organized and led campaigns for anti-lynching laws, suffrage, and fair housing in the late nineteenth and early twentieth centuries; these scholars conclude that "the civil rights movement of the fifties and sixties is merely the continuation of a long-standing tradition"; see "Editors' Introduction," *Women in the Civil Rights Movement: Trailblazers and Torchbearers,*

1941–1965, ed. Vicki L. Crawford, Jacqueline Anne Rouse, and Barbara Woods (New York: Carlson, 1990), xix.

6. Diane E. Loupe, "Storming and Defending the Color Barrier at the University of Missouri School of Journalism: The Lucile Bluford Case," *Journalism History* 16, nos. 1–2 (Spring–Summer 1989); Aimee Edmondson and Earnest L. Perry Jr. discuss the coverage of the *Columbia Missourian* and the *Columbia Daily Tribune* in "Objectivity and 'The Journalist's Creed': Local Coverage of Lucile Bluford's Fight to Enter the University of Missouri School of Journalism," *Journalism History* 33, no. 4 (Winter 2008): 233–240. Noel Avon Wilson notes Bluford's first-person reports for *The Call* but does not analyze them extensively in his dissertation, "The Kansas City Call: An Inside View of the Negro Market" (PhD diss., University of Illinois, 1968), 357–360. See also Robert McLaran Sawyer, "The Gaines Case: Its Background and Influence on the University of Missouri and Lincoln University, 1936–1950" (PhD diss., University of Missouri, 1966), 209–241.

7. Shirley Wilson Logan, *"We Are Coming": The Persuasive Discourse of Nineteenth-Century Black Women* (Carbondale: Southern Illinois University Press, 1999). Women of color have influenced journalism, but until recently, historical narratives have neglected them. Bluford, for example, is mentioned briefly in *The Black Press in the South, 1865–1979, The Black Press, U.S.A.,* and *A History of the Black Press,* which noted that her MU suit led to the establishment of the journalism department at Lincoln University in Jefferson City, Missouri; see George Everett Slavens, "Missouri," in *The Black Press in the South, 1865–1979,* ed. Henry Lewis Suggs (Westport, Conn.: Greenwood, 1983), 241; Roland E. Wolseley, *The Black Press, U.S.A.,* 2nd ed. (Ames: Iowa State University Press, 1990), 264; and Armistead S. Pride and Clint C. Wilson II, *A History of the Black Press* (Washington, DC: Howard University Press, 1997), 148. As Maurine H. Beasley and Sheila J. Gibbons comment, "Black women journalists have had to contend with twin barriers: discrimination based on race as well as gender. Their achievements, often overlooked in the general field of journalism history, are now being chronicled by African-American scholars and others interested in the ways a group of unusually strong women have used their journalistic skills to fight for social change"; see Beasley and Gibbons, eds., *Taking Their Place: A Documentary History of Women and Journalism* (Washington, DC: American University Press, 1993), 147. Rodger Streitmatter identifies Maria W. Stewart as the first woman of African descent to use print as a podium through her antislavery essays published in the *Liberator* beginning in 1832. Mary Ann Shadd Cary established an antislavery newspaper, the *Provincial Freeman,* in 1853. From the early 1870s to the end of the nineteenth century, Gertrude Bustill Mossell encouraged black readers nationwide to pursue racial reform and new occupations. The best-known African American woman journalist of the late nineteenth and early twentieth centuries is Ida B. Wells-Barnett, who led a long campaign in print and person against the lynching of African Americans. In 1890, Josephine St. Pierre Ruffin founded *Woman's Era,* a national newspaper for the black women's club movement. Roger Streitmatter calls Charlotta A. Bass, editor and publisher of the *California Eagle* from 1912 to 1951, a "radical precursor of the Black Power Movement"; see Rodger Streitmatter, *Raising Her Voice: African American Women Journalists Who Changed History* (Lexington: University Press of Kentucky, 1994), 5, 38, 49–52, 62, 95. Other

scholars charting the achievements of African American women journalists include Noliwe M. Rooks, who discusses Katherine E. Williams, the founder of *Half-Century Magazine* in Chicago, which was published from 1916 to 1925 and claimed 75,000 readers in the early 1920s; see Rooks, *Ladies' Pages: African American Women's Magazines and the Culture That Made Them* (New Brunswick, N.J.: Rutgers University Press, 2004). Amy Helene Forss documents the work of Mildred Dee Brown (1905–1989), the co-founder of the *Omaha Star* in Nebraska, the longest-running black newspaper founded by an African American woman in the United States; see Forss, *Black Print with a White Carnation: Mildred Brown and the Omaha Star Newspaper, 1938–1989* (Lincoln: University of Nebraska Press, 2013). James McGrath Morris chronicles the career of Ethel Payne, who was a reporter for the *Chicago Defender* during the 1950s, 1960s, and 1970s and was one of the first black journalists in the White House press corps; see Morris, *Eye on the Struggle: Ethel Payne, the First Lady of the Black Press* (New York: Amistad/HarperCollins, 2015). Bluford, who worked as a reporter, editor, and eventually publisher during her sixty-nine-year career at *The Call*, merits inclusion on the roster of important African American women journalists.

8. Loupe, "Storming and Defending the Color Barrier," 22; "N.A.A.C.P. Club," in the *Lincolnian* [yearbook], 1928, 66, Dr. Kenneth J. LaBudde Special Collections, University of Missouri–Kansas City, Kansas City, Missouri; Bluford, "New Schools," *The Lincolnite* [newspaper], November 4, 1926, Missouri Valley Special Collections, Kansas City Public Library, Kansas City, Missouri.

9. Charles E. Coulter, *"Take Up the Black Man's Burden": Kansas City's African American Communities, 1865–1939* (Columbia: University of Missouri Press, 2006), 107–110; Sherry Lamb Schirmer, *A City Divided: The Racial Landscape of Kansas City, 1900–1960* (Columbia: University of Missouri Press, 2002), 148, 177; Thomas D. Wilson, "Chester A. Franklin and Harry S. Truman: An African American Conservative and the 'Conversion' of the Future President," in *Kansas City, America's Crossroads: Essays from the Missouri Historical Review, 1906–2006*, ed. Diane Mutti Burke and John Herron (Columbia: State Historical Society of Missouri, 2007), 223–224, 232; Roy Wilkins with Tom Mathews, *Standing Fast: The Autobiography of Roy Wilkins* (New York: Viking, 1982), 56–59, 91, 107–108.

10. *The Call*, January 31, 1936.

11. Lucile H. Bluford, "The Lloyd Gaines Story," *Journal of Educational Sociology* 32, no. 6 (February 1959): 242–246; Jessie P. Guzman, "Twenty Years of Court Decisions Affecting Higher Education in the South, 1938–1958," *Journal of Educational Sociology* 32, no. 6 (February 1959): 248–249; Sawyer, "The Gaines Case," 152–195; Tushnet, *The NAACP's Legal Strategy*, 70–75.

12. "Lloyd Gaines of St. Louis Is Applicant," *The Call*, January 31, 1936; "Separate Schools," *The Call*, February 7, 1936.

13. State Ex Rel. Lucile Bluford, *Appellant*, v. S. W. Canada, 50–51.

14. "Victory in Missouri U. Case," *The Call*, December 16, 1938.

15. Court records show that Bluford wrote the registrar on January 4, 1939, to request a catalog and application form for the graduate program in journalism. On January 11, 1939, she notified the MU registrar that she had asked KU to send her undergraduate transcript.

On January 19, 1939, the MU registrar advised Bluford to go to Columbia to obtain her permit to enroll in classes. It was not until January 25, 1939, however, that Bluford wrote to NAACP lawyers for advice about how to proceed because she had realized that MU did not know she was African American. In the Boone County Circuit Court hearing in February 1940, Bluford testified that she began thinking of going to graduate school at MU two years after she earned her bachelor's degree at KU, which would have been in 1934. At that same hearing, Dorothy Davis, a reporter at *The Call*, testified that Bluford began talking to her about applying to MU when Davis began working at the newspaper in 1937; Ada Franklin, the wife of publisher Chester Franklin, testified that Bluford began talking to her about MU in 1939; see State Ex Rel. Lucile Bluford, *Appellant*, v. S.W. Canada, 57, 60–64, 106–109, 384, 387. On May 2, 1942, Bluford reviewed her lawsuits against MU in a column for *The Call* and stated she sought help from the NAACP after she applied to MU; see Bluford, "How I Feel About Missouri U. Case," *The Call*, May 1, 1942. In 1987, Dorothy Davis, who had remarried and changed her name to Dorothy Johnson, reiterated in a documentary that it was Bluford's idea to apply to MU; see Dorothy H. Johnson interview in *Writing for Rights: The Lucile H. Bluford Story*, VHS (MT Productions, 1987). In a 1989 interview, Bluford said that she decided to apply to MU in early 1939 because she was "curious about what the university would do"; see Fern Ingersoll, "Interview with Lucile H. Bluford, Kansas City, Missouri, May 15, 1989," in Beasley and Gibbons, *Taking Their Place*, 148. Court records confirm that the NAACP encouraged Bluford to go to MU to enroll in classes. On January 27, 1939, NAACP lawyer Charles H. Houston wrote Bluford that she should try to register for classes at Columbia to generate publicity and to influence the Missouri legislature as it took steps to start a law school at Lincoln University; see State Ex Rel. Lucile Bluford, *Appellant*, v. S. W. Canada, 109. These sources suggest that the NAACP did not ask Bluford to apply to MU, but clearly she and the organization colluded after she took the important first step. One scholar offers what could be interpreted as a refutation of this evidence, if it is not read carefully: Diane E. Loupe noted that during an interview with Bluford in November 1988, Bluford admitted "that her case was directed by the NAACP, which wanted to integrate the University of Missouri more than she wanted to attend graduate school"; see "Storming and Defending the Color Barrier," 24. Loupe does not quote Bluford nor specify what she means by the phrase, "her case," and I deduce that after Bluford applied to MU and was rejected, her action became a "case" that then was directed by the NAACP. I do not think this point contradicts my assertion that Bluford initially acted on her own by applying to MU.

16. Bluford, "Nothing Will Happen."

17. Robert C. Rowland, *Analyzing Rhetoric: A Handbook for the Informed Citizen in a New Millennium*, 4th ed. (Dubuque, Iowa: Kendall Hunt, 2012), 215–216, 220–222.

18. J. Percy H. Johnson, ed., *N. W. Ayer and Son's Directory of Newspapers and Periodicals, 1939* (Philadelphia: Ayer, 1939), 497 (hereafter *Ayer*); Slavens, "Missouri," 233. In contrast, the *Baltimore Afro-American* was published on Tuesdays and Fridays and had a circulation of 52,621 in 1939; see *Ayer*, 379. *Ayer* does not list circulation figures for the *Chicago Defender* in 1939, but the weekly claimed 97,000 readers in 1938, according to *N. W. Ayer and Son's Directory of Newspapers and Periodicals, 1938* (Philadelphia: Ayer, 1938), 203. The 1939 edi-

tion of *Ayer* reported that there were 309,879 readers of the daily evening *Kansas City Star* and 318,089 readers of the Sunday edition; the *Kansas City Times* morning newspaper had 306,313 readers every day other than Sunday (circulation figures for the *Star* and *Times* on *Ayer*, 498).

19. Wilkins, *Standing Fast*, 89–90, 107.

20. State Ex Rel. Lucile Bluford, *Appellant*, v. S. W. Canada, 53–54.

21. Gunnar Myrdal, *An American Dilemma: The Negro Problem and Modern Democracy*, vol. 2 (New York: Harper, 1944), 908, 911, 917, 920–921, 923. Charles H. Loeb, "Introduction," in *The Negro Newspaper*, ed. Vishnu V. Oak (Yellow Springs, Ohio: Antioch, 1948), 26.

22. Wilkins, *Standing Fast*, 72, 74, 76, 99; Coulter, "*Take Up the Black Man's Burden*," 8.

23. D. A. Holmes, "An Open Letter to *The Call*," *The Call*, February 21, 1936; Coulter, "*Take Up the Black Man's Burden*," 87–89, 128.

24. Rowland, *Analyzing Rhetoric*, 221.

25. Bluford, "Why I Applied to Missouri U.," *The Call*, February 3, 1939.

26. Bluford, "Missouri U. Not Ready for Negro," *The Call*, February 3, 1939.

27. Bluford, "How I Feel About Missouri U. Case," *The Call*, May 1, 1942.

28. Rowland, *Analyzing Rhetoric*, 224.

29. C. A. Franklin, "Letter to Missourians," *The Call*, May 8, 1942.

30. Jacqueline Jones, Peter H. Wood, Thomas Borstelmann, Elaine Tyler May, and Vicki L. Ruiz, *Created Equal: A Social and Political History of the United States*, 2nd ed. (New York: Pearson, 2006), 852–853; Coulter, "*Take Up the Black Man's Burden*," 114; Carlynn Trout, "Lucile Bluford (1911–2003)," *Historic Missourians*, https://shsmo.org/historicmissourians /name/b/bluford/ (accessed May 31, 2013); Mary Beveridge, "Biography of Lucile H. Bluford (1911–2003), Journalist and Former Owner/Publisher of 'The Call' Newspaper," *KCHistory.org*, http://www.kchistory.org/content/biography-lucile-h-bluford-1911-2003-jour nalist-and-former-ownerpublisher-call-newspaper (accessed February 5, 2018).

CHAPTER TEN

"As Good as Money Could Buy"

Kansas City's Black Public Hospital

Jason Roe

"They did not try to build something 'good enough for Negroes' but something as good as money could buy." This is how Chester A. Franklin, the Republican founder of *The Call* newspaper and one of Kansas City's most prominent black leaders, greeted the newly constructed seven-and-a-half-story building that housed General Hospital No. 2, serving the indigent African American population of Kansas City.[1] When the new building opened on March 2, 1930, national public health experts joined the local black and white communities in considering the new facility to be the finest black public hospital in the nation, even rivaling some of the best white public hospitals with its state-of-the-art equipment and modern architecture.

Kansas City's new General Hospital No. 2 replaced a dilapidated fifty-year-old building that had previously served as the city's segregated black public hospital. Highly unusual, and perhaps unique nationally in 1930, the city's black patients now had access to municipally funded care at a newly constructed hospital building, staffed and supervised completely by black physicians, nurses, and administrators. In both 1931 and 1932, the National Negro Health Contest rated Kansas City as the top city for black health.[2] The moment of the hospital's opening marked a point of pride for the black community and promised to usher in a golden age of public health and improved living conditions. But despite being "the best money could buy," with a new building, modern equipment, the promise of racial equality in a segregated facility, and public fanfare, the new construction obscured several institutional weaknesses that reflected Kansas City's contentious racial and community politics. Even as the new General Hospital No. 2 swept up accolades, it also reached its apex of patronage appointments, corruption, and political interference from the local Democratic machine controlled by Thomas J. Pendergast. The machine's influence, combined with concerted lobbying from black leaders, ensured unprecedented political and financial support for the health needs of a disadvantaged population, but these reforms came with limitations and could not overcome the inherent effects of racial discrimination and political bossism.[3]

Well before the Pendergast machine gained power, Kansas City's white and black public hospitals already fit into a national trend of deficiencies among public hospitals. In most cities, public hospitals were the largest ones and primarily focused on treating indigent patients, typically providing care from an all-white staff on a racially segregated basis in one facility. Categorically, public hospitals shared an unfortunate history of patient neglect, overcrowding, and political scandal. The counterpart to public hospitals, private hospitals, often admitted a share of poor patients on a charitable basis, especially to ensure a higher volume of patients for teaching purposes. But compared to public hospitals, the private facilities typically offered a higher standard of care, increased creature comforts, and privacy for middle class or wealthier patients.[4]

Kansas City hardly diverged from national trends when it opened its first city hospital in 1873, at present-day Twenty-Second Street and Kenwood Avenue. For decades, the public—white and black—had little trust in the institution. A 1913 bulletin from the Jackson County Medical Society (JCMS) acknowledged past mistakes, the long-standing existence of "prejudice against the General Hospital," and the need to establish "a change of feeling on the part of the public toward the hospital."[5] As the city's population exploded, the facility became overcrowded, requiring beds to be set up in hallways, and sometimes two patients shared one bed. Black patients received treatment from an all-white staff on a segregated basis, and in later years, an article in the *Jackson County Medical Journal*, the publication of the JCMS, acknowledged that black patients "took what treatment they could get." African American doctors and nurses were legally barred from working in the hospital, cutting them off from their patients who had been hospitalized and precluding opportunities for professional development. In 1908, hospital spending each day for white patients more than doubled that for black patients in the same facility. Combined with poor living conditions, the lack of care contributed to blacks in Kansas City dying at a much higher rate than whites, including an infant mortality rate two times greater.[6]

A catalyst for change occurred in 1903, when the city suffered a debilitating flood that overwhelmed the capacity of the municipal hospital, which was originally constructed when the city's population was just one-seventh its size at the time of the flood. The downtown Convention Hall served as an emergency hospital, with black patients segregated under the care of Dr. Thomas C. Unthank, who had earned his medical degree at Howard University and set up practice in Kansas City five years earlier. The 1903 flood convinced the city to build a new public hospital, and Unthank took the lead in advocating that the old city hospital building be converted into a separate hospital for minorities and that it should be staffed at least in part by black doctors and nurses.[7] The new white hospital became known as General Hospital No. 1, while the old building became the "colored division" of the city hospital, or General Hospital No. 2, opening in 1908. Overcoming resistance from members of the white community who did not believe blacks could be competent medical practitioners, the hospital started hiring black physicians, interns, and staff in 1911. Dr. William J. Thompkins, an African American doctor who would eventually gain influence in the Missouri Democratic Party, became the hospital's superintendent in 1914. By 1924 it had an all-black staff and administration. (Officially, the hospital remained the "colored division" of the city hospital, and white physicians continued to serve as "supervisors" or consultants for each department.)[8] Despite these gains for black patients and staff, though, Thompkins continued to describe the hospital under his own authority as a "dirty, dangerous and filthy hole."[9]

For all the difficulties entailed in establishing General Hospital No. 2, and despite its subpar conditions, the fact that Kansas City supported a standalone black municipal hospital, with African Americans making up a growing portion of its staff, placed it near the leading edge of the national black hospital movement. With the establishment of separate black private or public hospitals, that movement sought to escape the neglect or potential abuse suffered at the hands of the white-dominated medical profession. Separate black hospitals had a number of positive implications for black professional development in the medical field, for community uplift and pride, and for the overall confidence of black patients in the care they received. The allocation of taxpayer dollars to medical care for black patients—always a tricky proposition politically—received a boost from certain white medical practitioners, civic leaders, and reformers, even if many of them had less than virtuous motives and often described blacks as vectors of disease who could spread germs to the white population if they went untreated.[10]

Black patients who could afford treatment from private physicians or hospitals had additional (but still segregated) options besides the charitable public hospitals. Nationally, about 3,500 black physicians had received training by 1920, and in Kansas City a few dozen had established private practices.[11] Shut out from practicing in whites-only hospitals and highly unlikely to treat white patients in general, some established their own private hospitals intended specifically for minority communities.[12] In Kansas City these included Dr. John Edward Perry's Sanatorium, Dr. Unthank's Lange Hospital, and the Douglass Hospital in Kansas City, Kansas. Architecturally, these facilities tended to be little more than repurposed houses, but in one case, the Provident Association, a charitable organization run by white Kansas City businessmen, took over management of Perry's Sanatorium and merged with the Phyllis Wheatley Association, a national young African American women's club similarly organized to the Young Women's Christian Association (YWCA), to form

Wheatley-Provident Hospital, which occupied a former parochial school at 1826 Forest Avenue in 1918 and remained in operation until the opening of the Truman Medical Center in 1971. These private hospitals offered charitable services and partnered with community organizations, such as the Guadalupe Center detailed in Chapter 11 in this volume, to offer free health and social service clinics but could not meet the full health needs of the minority population. The decision to build separate hospitals was echoed by other disenfranchised or minority groups in Kansas City. Outraged by the systematic removal of Jewish medical practitioners from the JCMS and Kansas City's public hospitals, for example, the Jewish community established Menorah Hospital in Kansas City in 1931. Similarly, the German Hospital (later renamed Research Hospital) and the Swedish Hospital served their respective communities.[13]

General Hospital No. 2, more so than private black hospitals, tended to be overcrowded but offered municipally funded care for a larger number of blacks, Mexicans, and other nonwhite residents of Kansas City, Missouri, who could not afford care at Wheatley-Provident or another private facility. Originally, No. 2 offered free care to all patients without any attempts to determine their financial status, but after July 1923, it admitted only those patients deemed to be indigent (an inexact and inconsistent determination in practice), or wealthier patients needing emergency care. Also in the 1920s and 1930s, as both white and black municipal hospitals faced growing costs for increasingly sophisticated medical equipment and trained professionals, the hospitals experimented with various "part-pay" schemes whereby their "social investigators" attempted to bill patients according to their financial means. Another major policy change occurred in 1924, when General Hospital No. 1 began admitting other patients of color, further segregating General Hospital No. 2 to only African American patients.[14]

By 1922, General Hospital No. 2 had attained the highest (Class A) accreditation from the American Medical Association, the black National Medical Association, and the American College of Surgeons.[15] It had also become a center of black medical training for newly minted doctors. Only 125 black doctors were graduating in the United States per year in the mid-1920s, with many coming out of the largest black medical schools of Howard University and Meharry Medical College in Nashville, Tennessee. For these doctors, fully half of all accredited internships in the mid-1920s were offered in Kansas City or St. Louis.[16] These statistics underscored the unusual achievements of General Hospital No. 2. As a fully segregated black hospital, it managed to offer an internship program accredited by white professional organizations. Not long after Kansas City established General Hospital No. 2, black reformers in St. Louis lobbied for their own hospital in a similar vein, and City Hospital No. 2 (later renamed the Homer G. Phillips Hospital) opened in a repurposed building in 1919.[17]

Defining a Political Space

The construction of the new General Hospital No. 2 in 1930 stemmed in large part from the growing political influence of the African American population of Kansas City, which gradually shifted its support from the Republican Party to the Democratic Party and its local political machine led by "Boss" Tom Pendergast. The moment closest to a tipping point realignment of political allegiances occurred around the 1924 elections, as described in Chapter 2 in this volume. The Democratic Party in Missouri distanced itself from the resurgent Ku Klux Klan and entered the earliest stages of building a labor-oriented, racially liberal coalition that would come to define the national Democratic Party through the remainder of the twentieth century. The state party followed the lead of Democratic machine bosses in St. Louis and Kansas City, who had associated themselves with immigrant and minority communities, as well as Irish and Italian Catholic leaders and interests who were opposed by the Klan.[18] In the local medical field, a Republican overreach that followed the party's electoral victories in 1922 helped hasten the backlash against the Republicans in 1924. The prominent Democrat and superintendent of General Hospital No. 2, Thompkins, lost his appointment in 1922, and in the words of another doctor at the hospital, "all the other top flight Negro democratic politicians [were] pushed . . . gradually out of the picture."[19] Dr. James F. Shannon, a black Republican and (it should be acknowledged) a respected physician, took Thompkins's place in the sweep of black and white Democratic hospital administrators. Republicans statewide alienated themselves from African Americans to such a degree that by 1930, Chester A. Franklin, himself an outspoken black Republican and the publisher of The Call, accused the Republicans of actively working with the Klan and being complicit with police brutality in Jackson County.[20]

Of course, political interference and racialized politics were nothing new to the medical scene in Kansas City. Dr. Milton C. Lewis, a graduate of Howard University who came to General Hospital No. 2 as an intern in 1920 and continued on the regular staff, observed that black physicians who wanted a successful career had to do more than possess medical skill; they had to navigate the city's political environment. The superintendent of the hospital, by Lewis's description, "was appointed by the head of the party which won the city election and was responsible to this man and to a lesser degree to the Hospital and Health board." For all physicians, white or black, achieving success required joining the JCMS, itself divided by political loyalties and disputes. For black doctors to succeed, they additionally needed to "be [recommended] by a white doctor, call in a white doctor, or be exceptionally good."[21]

Perhaps because physicians did not want to admit the influence of political affiliations or petty rivalries on their profession, it is rare to see a candid acknowledgment of these political divisions in the historical record. In a brief memoir, however,

Lewis described a local black medical profession polarized into two groups, which "were constantly at each others [sic] throats engaged in bitter personal, medical and political feuds." The first group consisted of Republicans, or the "majority of the better class Negroes," as he described them. He elaborated that this first group "had the ear of [the] white people. They had the [confidence] of the public." The second group, "composed principally of politicians," in his view, was made up mostly of Democrats. Lewis claimed to belong to a third group of younger doctors who attempted to avoid entanglements with the other two groups.[22]

It was the Democratic doctors who prevailed after the adoption of a new city charter in 1925. The Pendergast machine co-opted the new reform government by capturing five of the nine city council seats, giving the machine control of the hiring of the city manager. The machine selected Henry F. McElroy, who took charge in April 1926 and wasted no time in establishing authority over the city's director of the Health Department. Publicly, McElroy disagreed about the color of paint that Dr. E. W. Cavaness had selected for the nurses' quarters at General Hospital No. 1, and the city council soon had Cavaness removed by a five-to-four margin. The real conflict was likely about Cavaness's refusal to fill job openings with Pendergast's political appointees, but the "paint color" dispute sent an irrefutable message about the machine's power. In just six months, 42 percent of Kansas City's municipal employees were replaced.[23]

As this transition in city government occurred, Lewis described a new alliance forming between General Hospital No. 2's Democratic physicians and his own cohort of younger doctors, who had supposedly remained neutral in hospital politics. Whatever his misgivings about the Democrats being "politicians," Lewis described them as being "on the whole of good caliber."[24] The Democrats and young doctors captured the positions of staff president and secretary of the staff, with Lewis assuming the latter position. The old guard Republican faction maintained control of the surgical service, but was otherwise marginalized in hospital authority. Confirming other accounts, Lewis observed that "politics entered more and more into the affairs of the city hospital and a point was reached where the superintendent could not fire [an] orderly without the consent of some political boss."[25] Corroborating Lewis's account, the *Jackson County Medical Journal* claimed in 1933 that doctors had "to go to a political boss to gain his support before being considered eligible for appointment . . . [and] the candidate's real or imagined control of a block of votes [was] the chief consideration for appointment."[26] White and black doctors, it seemed, needed to promise to deliver the votes of their patients in addition to healing them.

Even before the machine established full control over the city's health board, it had moved to build a new black hospital, among several other public health facilities. A bond in the amount of $1.2 million passed by the end of 1925, but plans for construction were delayed until a location suitable to all interests could be found.[27] Kansas City's Democrats linked the Klan and police brutality to the Republican Party with such success that in 1926 the Republican-leaning *Call* endorsed several Democratic candidates, including Casimir "Cas" Welch, who had recently allied with Tom Pendergast and controlled "Little Tammany," consisting of thirty-six precincts east of downtown. Thompkins, who had risen in the ranks of regional Democratic politics, was appointed assistant health commissioner in a newly established hygiene department.[28] With Pendergast's backing and in partnership with Felix Payne, Thompkins began publishing a Democratic rival to *The Call*, named the *Kansas City American*, in 1928.[29] A growing portion of Kansas City's African American community had entered into an arrangement with the Pendergast machine, with the proposal for a new hospital emerging as a leading mutually beneficial development. The stakes were high; by 1930, General Hospital No. 2 accounted for 95 percent of all professional and semiprofessional black employees of the municipal government of Kansas City, Missouri, making it the city's most fertile ground for political patronage in the black community of some 40,000 persons.[30] Excluding volunteers, the hospital employed an all-black staff of 292 individuals, including 72 professionals made up of doctors, dentists, and nurses.[31] A full 70 percent of Kansas City's black physicians—thirty-five in all, and all well-to-do community leaders—served as staff members for General Hospital No. 2 on a full- or part-time basis.[32]

The New Building

Notwithstanding machine politics, the need for a new General Hospital No. 2 would have been obvious to any nonpartisan observer. As early as 1923, a committee of white civic leaders, including the anti-machine philanthropist William Volker and several doctors, formed to advocate for a new black hospital. In a report, they described the conditions at the fifty-year-old building: "Mental patients there must be chained to their beds to protect other patients. The building is dilapidated. It has been patched up time after time and it is simply worn out."[33] That same year, a committee of the JCMS noted that wall plastering was falling off and that the building was "infested with rats and vermin." Interns lived "in an attic," and nurses lived in a "frame building in a miserable state of repair with leaking roof and inadequately heated and terribly over-crowded."[34] The committee concluded that the building was "in a wretched state of repair" and was "so old that constant repairs are necessary. Floors, stairways, and walls are in bad condition."[35] The JCMS chastised the city, adding that "any Christian community" should treat its black citizens better.[36] Presciently, as it would turn out, the committee also warned of a "very great fire hazard."[37]

The successful 1925 bond issue did not move the project along very quickly. The original site proposed for the hospital was at the present-day Nelson C. Crews

A photograph from the *Jackson County Medical Journal* shows the newly constructed, segregated General Hospital No. 2, October 8, 1932. Courtesy of the Missouri Valley Special Collections, Kansas City Public Library.

Square, just north of Spring Valley Park near Twenty-Seventh Street and Euclid Avenue. This location was at the extreme southern point of black residence in Kansas City, prompting objections from the Linwood Improvement Association, which represented hundreds of white homeowners residing south of Twenty-Seventh Street. The association claimed "a legitimate right to protect values of property that have been honestly earned," and feared that construction of the hospital nearby would encourage blacks to take over Spring Valley Park, move into homes south of Twenty-Seventh Street, and depress property values.[38] Their opposition forced a relocation of the planned hospital, but some years later, Dr. Samuel U. Rodgers noted that resisting the black hospital made little difference in the long run, as the "Negro belt," as he called it, ended up extending all the way south to Sixty-Third Street by 1962.[39]

The black community soon blamed McElroy for the construction delays.[40] In his capacity as assistant health commissioner of the hygiene department, Thompkins completed a study of health conditions, housing, and sanitation in the city.[41] His publicized findings underscored the need for a new hospital, and his connections to the Pendergast machine and the national Democratic Party lent weight to the campaign for a new hospital. Numerous appeals were made to the Pendergast machine, and in the end, the *Kansas City American* and other sources credited Tom Pendergast with moving the project forward personally.[42]

What finally spurred construction plans, though, was a fire that spread through the existing building in July 1927. It endangered the lives of sixty patients and caused $30,000 of damage. The outdated design and poor state of maintenance made the hospital susceptible to fire, and the patients were lucky to escape alive. The city finally approved plans for construction in 1928, with the building to be sited near the old one and General Hospital No. 1, at what is still known as Hospital Hill.[43] Built at a cost of $300,000, it was located at 600 East Twenty-Second Street and opened on March 2, 1930, to great fanfare.[44]

If the new hospital relieved the white community of a sense of Christian guilt, it promised to be a lifesaver for African Americans who had long suffered in the decrepit old facilities. Aside from *The Call* labeling it the "best money can buy," the paper lauded it as the "most modern public hospital in the country now ready for occupancy," presumably even in comparison with white municipal hospitals. The facility was "spic and span" and had "the most modern design" and "the best equipment available."[45] In addition to details about various medical resources, the *Jackson County Medical Journal* proclaimed, "Everything has been done to make the new General Hospital for Colored Patients, cared for by Colored Physicians and Attendants, a pleasant and inviting haven of refuge for the indigent sick, a pride to the city, and a boon to its colored citizens." The building was supposedly fireproof, with concrete or tile floors. The journal set the scene: "The new building is situated on the north slope of 'Hospital Hill' with a panorama to West and North, including the Liberty Memorial, the Union Station, and the City's magnificent sky line." The building "is seven and one-half stories high, the material brick relieved by bands of stone and terra cotta, with an approach and entrance in the best taste." Upon entering the new hospital, "the entrance hall and adjacent rooms are beautifully decorated in marble and ornamental plastering, giving an effect of dignity and refinement and diffusing a pleasant atmosphere for the entering patients."[46]

Another local article promised an end to overcrowding and declared that innovative measures would be taken to improve patient comfort, including a system for dimming the electric lights at night. There was even a new system allowing each patient to push a button, triggering several lights that would alert nurses that the patient needed assistance. The new facility would have a modern, well-lit, and comfortable mental health ward, unlike the unfortunate arrangement at the old hospital, which was described as a "cell" by one doctor who worked there. A reporter described the previous mental health ward in darker terms: "At the end of the hall, under a stairway, is a locked door. Moans and screams were heard behind it."[47] The new General Hospital No. 2, by contrast, was an unquestionable improvement, and Kansas City's residents from all backgrounds expected it to be among the best in the nation, perhaps even equal to white public hospitals.

Deficiencies, Political Patronage, and Corruption

Unfortunately, beneath the shiny façade of a new building and apparent support from the Pendergast machine, countless problems lurked. Political patronage and corruption at General Hospital No. 2 was not a new development with the Pendergast machine. As noted, a change in superintendents and other key positions had regularly coincided with elections prior to 1925.[48] But through McElroy, the Democratic machine tightened its grip, maintained control for thirteen years, and ultimately proved to be a mixed blessing for black medical care and public health.

Alongside machine support and the headline project of a new building, a pattern of chronic deficiencies in medical supplies and staffing plagued it, a pattern that fit well within the national trend of black public hospitals being shortchanged relative to white hospitals.[49] In his memoir, Lewis initially concurred with all of the fawning publicity, writing that the "new hospital had been built fully equipped." But, he added, "before long the whites at No. 1 had eased a [quantity] of [essential] equipment from No. 2. Nothing was done about it."[50] While it does not appear that this equipment was anything as expensive or obvious as an x-ray machine, oral histories have established that the black hospital suffered from a chronic shortage of day-to-day supplies such as needles or syringes, even years after the machine fell.[51]

Some of the initial problems resulted from machine infighting that took place about six months after the new building opened. Cas Welch had allied with Tom Pendergast in 1925, but in August 1930, he managed to have Dr. Howard Smith, the hospital's superintendent and a Pendergast appointee, removed and replaced by Dr. D. M. Miller, who besides being a loyal Democrat was best known for a scandal wherein he physically abused residents at the Home for Aged Negroes. *The Call* reported a decline in the quality of medical services, bedpans sitting unattended for twenty-four-hour periods, hospital staff demanding what amounted to bribes from patients, and a payroll that had been padded in the amount of $40,000. Pendergast did not reassert control of the hospital until late 1932, reportedly restoring some measure of competency to the hospital administration but not abandoning other corrupt practices.[52]

Deficiencies at No. 2, as well as at No. 1, extended beyond a rogue political boss. According to interviews with Dr. J. Harvey Jennett (the superintendent of General Hospital No. 1 from 1932 to 1936), the superintendent had no authority to hire staff. Only the director of the Health Department could do so. In practice, though, the health director answered to McElroy, the city manager who had appointed him. Approval for much of the hiring, down to the lower-level jobs, went all the way up to Tom Pendergast himself. The machine claimed to allow the superintendent to fire incompetent employees, but once dismissed, those workers frequently politicked their way back into new jobs at the hospital. At times, hospital payrolls included a handful of "employees" who had never worked in the hospital.[53] Again focusing on General Hospital No. 1, an editorial in the *Jackson County Medical Journal* complained about previously demoted staff members being reinstated without consultation with the staff, about newly hired staff not only being unqualified but also totally unknown, and about long-serving, competent staff members being dismissed for no substantive reason. Among the accusations, "at least three outstanding clinicians have been demoted to make way for men who have never done anything for scientific medicine."[54]

Meanwhile, McElroy maintained a baseline level of support from the JCMS by conceding to allow them an up-or-down vote on the city health director he appointed, by nominating a popular director for this initial appointment, and by giving the JCMS new organizational headquarters as a part of the city's Ten-Year Plan. Passed in the early 1930s as a form of relief during the Great Depression, the plan called for a total of around $50 million of bond issues for civic improvements, including a new wing for General Hospital No. 1. McElroy allotted the third floor of the new wing to the JCMS for offices, a new medical library, and a 400-seat auditorium.[55]

Beyond the distractions of political interference from Henry McElroy and the Pendergast machine, General Hospital No. 2 also suffered from numerous design flaws. The architectural layout—widely praised in newspapers and considered the best in the nation for a black public hospital—nonetheless received harsh criticism from a health and hospital survey conducted for the Chamber of Commerce in 1931. The survey found that "throughout the building there are many evidences that the hospital was not planned by one familiar with the administration of a hospital." Hot steam from exposed radiators threatened patients in the psychopathic ward, and privacy partitions for toilet facilities had already been ripped down by violent patients. Worse still, the space reserved for the morgue had no ventilation and had to be abandoned. As a result, "it is necessary to transport the bodies of deceased patients across the lawn, down a flight of steps into the basement of a building which also serves as [the] nurses' dwelling." That space, located in the old black hospital building, was also unventilated, making it "probable that unpleasant odors arising during post-mortem examinations will penetrate into the nurses' living quarters." To avoid overcrowding, which affected both the black and white public hospitals, the survey found that the new building should only have held 110 beds, not the 179 it had.[56] Patient demand eclipsed the hospital's resources, and some patients had to be kept in the hallways of both the white and black hospitals.[57]

For black nurses and doctors alike, segregation and other restrictions imposed on hospital operations limited their opportunities for professional development and their effectiveness in treating patients. It was widely known that patients were sometimes transferred to General Hospital No. 1 for advanced surgeries, certain x-rays, or consultations with white specialists, although that was apparently not official policy. Sometimes patients were transferred underground through a steam and maintenance tunnel that connected the two buildings. Likewise, black physicians and nurses who wanted to observe surgeries or access training opportunities had to seek them out informally at No. 1.[58] As Lewis observed at the beginning of his memoir, a black physician could not succeed without the patronage of a sympathetic white doctor. But such support existed only on an individual basis, not as any sort of official policy. As noted previously, the hospital was a national leader in the training of black interns and nurses, but its residency program struggled to maintain accreditation, and it could not expand into a full teaching hospital, partially because of its lack of an affiliation with a four-year medical school; the University of Missouri medical school barred blacks from studying there. With few opportunities for residencies, black doctors found it nearly impossible to specialize in certain fields, even as the medical profession focused more on specialization.

Although General Hospital No. 2 was an acknowledged national leader in black internships, the program still only offered twelve internships in 1930. The internships lasted one year, received supervision from just two black physicians, and spent six weeks on each of the following specialties: eye, ear, nose and throat; orthopedics; dermatology; pediatrics; genitourinary (specialization in genital and urinary systems); outpatient departments; and roentgenology (radiology). Black interns could not work in the tuberculosis clinic because it was operated by a separate organization, the Tuberculosis Society. They also lacked the opportunity to study under or collaborate with the more thoroughly trained white physicians and white interns at No. 1. The superintendent of No. 2 complained of staff shortages in the outpatient, orthopedic, and neurological departments, limiting the effectiveness of training in those fields. The JCMS agreed that there was a lack of medical, nursing, and social services staff throughout the hospital. The x-ray equipment was modern but operated by only one part-time roentgenologist and his assistants. The hospital was similarly well-appointed with modern laboratory equipment, but there was only one part-time pathologist available to oversee the labs.[59] In addition to paid

A general laboratory at General Hospital No. 2, showing staff and modern equipment, October 8, 1932. Courtesy of the Missouri Valley Special Collections, Kansas City Public Library.

interns, administrators, nurses, and physicians, many white and black doctors in private practice volunteered on an unpaid basis for the charitable cause of treating indigent patients.[60]

The 1931 survey also observed irregularities in the payroll, wherein certain employees had been officially reclassified into different positions from their actual jobs. The report concluded that the "present situation in regard to salaries and positions might bring considerable criticism and subsequent embarrassment to the present administration." The survey also criticized the practice of designating white supervisors for each department on an unpaid basis, when in reality they were usually only consulted when called in by the black doctors who were the de facto chiefs of their departments. The report concluded that the system was "not functioning," adding that white supervisors should actually be in charge and be held accountable for their departments, or else be removed from responsibility altogether.[61]

Political corruption and patronage continued to overshadow medical concerns, while some individuals benefited greatly from machine connections. In 1932,

Thompkins served as president of the National Colored Democratic Association, backing Franklin Delano Roosevelt for the presidency. In return, President Roosevelt made Thompkins the recorder of deeds of Washington, DC.[62] At General Hospital No. 2, irregularities and corruption persisted. The superintendent's wife received the title of "matron" and a stipend equal to 50 percent of his annual salary.[63] Citywide, some 1,700 people were on the payroll but not actually employed by the city. In exchange for patronage, the machine expected reciprocation. During campaigns, appointees had to give a bribe, or "lug," of 20 percent of one month's salary to the machine. In order to make up for deficits created by McElroy's "country bookkeeping," each year all city employees were expected to request a pay reduction of between 25 and 50 percent for several months. Officially the funds were supposed to be repaid, but they were not.[64] In the "bloody election" of 1934, in which ballot boxes were stuffed and four people killed at polling stations, the machine released a number of city employees to turn out the vote or otherwise influence the election. Dr. Arthur E. Wells, a candidate for the city council who opposed machine involvement in the city hospitals, was beaten up on election day, just as the machine had threatened.[65] As easily as the machine could give jobs for its own advantage, it could take jobs away from individuals who defied it or who were no longer useful.

The Pendergast machine eventually collapsed in 1939, with Tom Pendergast sent to jail for tax evasion. Because the machine had exerted influence over the city government, municipal courts, and police department, McElroy managed to build up a secret deficit of $19,453,976 in general accounts, plus fraudulent spending of more than $11.4 million out of the Ten-Year Plan funds (paid without contracts or competitive bidding). In the same year, the American Medical Association revoked its accreditation for internships at General Hospital No. 2. The number of interns had already dropped off dramatically to just one individual the prior year. Meanwhile, the new reform government swept out McElroy's appointed health director, Dr. Edwin H. Schorer.[66]

The hospital quickly reformed its internship program and regained accreditation for internships from the American College of Surgeons in 1941. Black interns' studies were aligned more closely with those of the white interns, and racially integrated training and medical conferences were held, but all of the instructors were now white physicians. Black interns then received something closer to the training of white interns, and the program numbers immediately rebounded to eleven interns and two residents, mostly from Howard University and Meharry Medical College. Although the hospital had residents, that program still lacked accreditation. Black physicians still headed up most of the departments, but they were general practitioners; none were trained in the specialties of the departments they supervised.[67]

The city's reform government set up a bipartisan governing body in 1942, but General Hospital No. 2 continued to suffer from a scarcity of supplies and train-

Physician staff posing in front of General Hospital No. 2, with Dr. William Thompkins shown fifth from right in the front row, October 8, 1932. Courtesy of the Missouri Valley Special Collections, Kansas City Public Library.

ing opportunities. In 1946 and 1947, black doctors protested the supply shortages and, while not going so far as declaring a general strike, refused to perform elective surgeries or other nonemergency services. The city acquiesced to some of their demands, and the American Medical Association renewed its accreditation for the hospital in several areas of practice. In the same years, the city issued bonds to construct new wings at both public hospitals, finally addressing the overcrowded conditions. Staff shortages at No. 2, however, were more difficult to resolve because of an ongoing national shortage of black doctors.[68]

In some respects, then, it was business as usual at General Hospital No. 2, but Lewis reflected that the fall of the machine "was the beginning of the end for all Negro doctors as far as the hospital was concerned[,] for the Negroes could once get political aid but those days are gone." The hospital increasingly relied on white doctors as attending chiefs of service instead of supporting the professional development of black doctors. Writing sometime after 1947, Lewis bemoaned twenty-five years of "poor leadership" and stated that, "The Negro medical profession is at the lowest depth since 1925."[69] Lewis's perspective emphasizes that the reforms made to restore the internship and residency programs may have made those programs more rigorous and improved outcomes for black patients, but it came at a cost for black physicians already established in practice, whose opportunities for specialization and other professional development dwindled. Corruption, incompetence, and neglect abounded at General Hospital No. 2 under the Pendergast machine, and it ultimately failed the black medical profession, patients, and community. But the machine's need for votes from the black community had at least ensured a degree of patronage to loyal physicians and a great deal of financing for construction projects and modern equipment that black, and even some white, city hospitals elsewhere could never hope to receive. As the machine collapsed, so did the aspirations for a stand-alone black public hospital administered by an all-black staff.

Increasing costs and political pressures amid the civil rights movement of the 1950s ultimately made it difficult for Kansas City to sustain two separate facilities for whites and blacks. In 1957, the city council decided to consolidate General Hospitals No. 1 and No. 2, and black patients and staff moved into No. 1 in 1959.[70] In 1962, the city continued to provide funding for the hospital, but it turned over management to a nonprofit organization that renamed it General Hospital and Medical Center.[71] In the early 1970s, General Hospital was replaced by the Truman Medical Center, which still operates on Hospital Hill today.

Conclusion

If the history of General Hospital No. 2 in the 1920s and 1930s is considered alongside black public hospitals in other American cities, the arrangement between the Pendergast machine and the black medical community appears to have worked to the advantage of the black community. The public praise heaped on General Hospital No. 2, especially for the efforts of its staff and administrators, as well as for the newly constructed building in 1930, seems understandable when one considers the difficulties of black city hospitals nationwide. Ground-up construction of a new hospital built specifically for black patients and staffed almost entirely by African Americans was unprecedented. Largely outside the public view, there were considerable organizational issues and shortages of staffing and supplies, but staff and patients had access to superior buildings and equipment compared to segregated black hospitals in other cities. Indigent black patients maintained deeper trust for the care they would receive from doctors and nurses of their own race, and they typically did not have to wait in line behind white patients for treatment. Hospitals are often not at the forefront of discussion about community formation and uplift, but in General Hospital No. 2, African Americans had successfully lobbied for an institution that they could be proud of and, at least in comparison to most other cities, rely on for their medical needs. When considering that the new building for General Hospital No. 2 opened in the midst of the Great Depression in 1930, numerous economic benefits undoubtedly accrued to the hospital's staff and the indigent black patients who could receive free surgeries and outpatient services.

None of these positive developments, of which black medical professionals and the black community were justifiably proud, suggest that black patients received care equal to that given white patients at General Hospital No. 1, or that black physicians had opportunities for professional growth equal to those for white doctors. Even under the best of circumstances, with political support from the Pendergast machine and its highest levels of funding, the experiment faltered in the space of a decade and the program was restructured in a way that left local black doctors excluded from the professional opportunities available at the white hospital. In 1930, General Hospital No. 2 inspired hope with its large new building and modern equipment, with nothing being handed down from the white hospital. But within a year, its facilities, staffing shortages, and internship programs were excoriated by the Jackson County Medical Society, and by the time the machine fell, the hospital had lost accreditation and its physicians were marginalized in the reform efforts and hospital administration. General Hospital No. 2 probably was the "best money could buy," as originally described in The Call, but only in an ironic sense. Increased funding, political support, and industrious physicians could not compensate for the effects of political corruption, mismanagement, and overtly racist policies against black doctors and patients.

Notes

1. Charles E. Coulter, "Take Up the Black Man's Burden": Kansas City's African American Communities, 1865–1939 (Columbia: University of Missouri Press, 2006), 213.

2. Sidney L. Bates, "Medicine without Method: Kansas City, Missouri's General and Allied Hospitals under the Department of Health, 1870–1962" (MA thesis, University of Missouri–Kansas City, 1972), 51.

3. The administrative records of General Hospital No. 2 have been lost, as have those of most black hospitals, but scattered newspaper articles, oral histories, career memoirs, medical society publications, commissioned studies, and correspondence survive.

4. Paul Starr, The Social Transformation of American Medicine: The Rise of a Sovereign Profession and the Making of a Vast Industry (New York: Basic Books, 1984), 171–172.

5. Jackson County Medical Society, Weekly Bulletin of the Jackson County Medical Society, April 5, 1913, James L. Soward Collection, Box 3, Folder 12, State Historical Society of Missouri, Kansas City Research Center, Kansas City, Missouri (hereafter SHSM-KC).

6. Bates, "Medicine without Method," 36, 45, 51.

7. "Dr. Thomas Conard Unthank: The 'Father' of Kansas City's Negro Hospital," Jackson County Medical Journal 26, no. 41 (October 8, 1932): 27.

8. Samuel U. Rodgers, MD, "Kansas City General Hospital No. 2: A Historical Summary," Journal of the National Medical Association 54, no. 5 (September 1962): 525–527; Mary Cecile Sutton, "A History of the Kansas City, Missouri, General Hospital" (MA thesis, University of Chicago, 1946), 67–70; Committee on Administrative Practice of the American Public Health Association and Kansas City Public Service Institute, Health and Hospital Survey, Kansas City, Missouri (Kansas City: Lechtman Printing, 1931), 290–291, Missouri Valley Special Collections, Kansas City Public Library, Kansas City, Missouri (hereafter MVSC).

9. "Dr. Thompkins Says Reform, Soap, and Brushes Are Needed," Kansas City Sun, April 19, 1924, 8, SHSM-KC.

10. Vanessa Northington Gamble, Making a Place for Ourselves: The Black Hospital Movement, 1920–1945 (New York: Oxford University Press, 1995), 7–11.

11. Ibid., 11.

12. The public isolation hospital for tuberculosis patients at Leeds, on the eastern outskirts of Kansas City, accepted mostly white indigent patients, until a wing for black patients was added in 1928, but white patients protested at being treated by black nurses. The *Jackson County Medical Journal* speculated that white nurses feared working with contagious patients, leading the hospital to employ black nurses instead. See Bates, "Medicine without Method," 60.

13. Barbara M. Gorman, Richard D. McKinzie, and Theodore A. Wilson, *From Shamans to Specialists: A History of Medicine and Health Care in Jackson County, Missouri* (Kansas City: Jackson County Medical Society, 1981), 105, 111, 151; Menorah's origins are also described in Milton C. Lewis, M.D., p. 1, Milton C. Lewis Collection, 2011, Box 65, Truman Medical Center Archives, Kansas City, Missouri (hereafter TMC).

14. Bates, "Medicine without Method," 72–73; Sutton, "A History of the Kansas City, Missouri, General Hospital," 90–92.

15. "Dr. Thompkins Says Reform, Soap, and Brushes Are Needed," SHSM-KC, 1.

16. B. I. Burns, "The Municipal Hospitals of Kansas City, Missouri," 9, "General Hospital History" folder, TMC.

17. Mitchell F. Rice and Woodrow Jones, *Public Policy and the Black Hospital: From Slavery to Segregation to Integration* (Westport, Conn.: Greenwood Publishing, 1994), 58.

18. Larry Grothaus, "Kansas City Blacks, Harry Truman and the Pendergast Machine," *Missouri Historical Review* 69, no. 1 (October 1974): 70–73; "Dr. Thompkins Says Reform, Soap, and Brushes Are Needed," 1.

19. Milton C. Lewis, p. 4, TMC.

20. Grothaus, "Kansas City Blacks," 75–76.

21. Milton C. Lewis, p. 2, TMC.

22. Ibid.

23. Bates, "Medicine without Method," 94–96.

24. Milton C. Lewis, p. 2, TMC.

25. Ibid., 4–5.

26. Sutton, "A History of the Kansas City, Missouri, General Hospital," 21.

27. Bates, "Medicine without Method," 49.

28. Grothaus, "Kansas City Blacks," 73; Coulter, *"Take Up the Black Man's Burden,"* 211.

29. Gary R. Kremer, "William J. Thompkins: African American Physician, Politician, and Publisher," in Gary R. Kremer, *Race and Meaning: The African American Experience in Missouri* (Columbia: University of Missouri Press, 2014), 191.

30. Harry F. Dowling, *City Hospitals: The Undercare of the Underprivileged* (Cambridge, Mass.: Harvard University Press, 1982), 159. Historian K. David Hanzlick establishes in Chapter 8 in this volume that professional black teachers at the city's segregated schools were employed by the Kansas City School District, a separate entity from the city government, and that the Pendergast machine generally did not interfere with school district operations.

31. Rodgers, "Kansas City General Hospital No. 2," 530.

32. Sutton, "A History of the Kansas City, Missouri, General Hospital," 71.

33. "Set Out Hospitals Needs: Physicians Declare the City Has Outgrown General," *Kansas City Times*, November 28, 1923, James L. Soward Collection, Box 3, Folder 8, SHSM-KC.

34. Gorman, *From Shamans to Specialists*, 152.

35. "This Is Health Week! Attention Called to Hospital for Colored People," *Kansas Citian* 12, no. 50 (December 11, 1923), 1078, James L. Soward Collection, Box 5, Folder 23, SHSM-KC.

36. Gorman, *From Shamans to Specialists*, 152.

37. "This Is Health Week!," *Kansas Citian*.

38. "An Improvement Association Writes of Its Aims," *Kansas City Star*, January 23, 1927, James L. Soward Collection, Box 3, Folder 17, SHSM-KC.

39. Rodgers, "Kansas City General Hospital No. 2," 528.

40. Grothaus, "Kansas City Blacks," 77.

41. Kremer, "William J. Thompkins," 191.

42. Grothaus, "Kansas City Blacks," 77.

43. Rodgers, "Kansas City General Hospital No. 2," 528; "A Fire at Negro Hospital," *Kansas City Times*, July 11, 1927, James L. Soward Collection, Box 3, Folder 8, SHSM-KC.

44. James L. Soward, *Hospital Hill: An Illustrated Account of Public Healthcare Institutions in Kansas City, Missouri* (Kansas City, Mo.: Truman Medical Center Charitable Foundation, 1995), 95.

45. Rodgers, "Kansas City General Hospital No. 2," 528–529; "Most Modern Public Hospital in Country Now Ready for Occupancy," *The Call*, February 28, 1930.

46. Clyde Reed Bradford, MD, "Kansas City General Hospital: Colored Division," *Jackson County Medical Journal* 26, no. 41 (October 8, 1932): 10, 15.

47. "Better Care for Negro: New City Hospital Will Be Open in Sixty Days," newspaper article from unknown source, circa 1930, 1930s–1940s folder, TMC.

48. Rodgers, "Kansas City General Hospital No. 2," 529.

49. Dowling, *City Hospitals*, 159.

50. Milton C. Lewis, p. 5, TMC.

51. Kevin Willmott, *From Separate to Equal: The Creation of Truman Medical Center* (Truman Medical Centers and Ninth Street Studios, 2011), 57 min., 23 sec., http://www.kcpt.org/health/from-separate-to-equal-the-creation-of-truman-medical-center/ (accessed November 1, 2016).

52. Sherry Lamb Schirmer, *A City Divided: The Racial Landscape of Kansas City, 1900–1960* (Columbia: University of Missouri Press), 164.

53. Gorman, *From Shamans to Specialists*, 128–129.

54. E. P. H., "The New Deal at General Hospital," *Jackson County Medical Journal* 27, no. 30 (July 29, 1933): 7–8, James L. Soward Collection, Box 3, Folder 12, SHSM-KC.

55. Gorman, *From Shamans to Specialists*, 129–130.

56. Committee on Administrative Practice, *Health and Hospital Survey*, 279–280, 284.

57. Gorman, *From Shamans to Specialists*, 142.

58. Willmott, *From Separate to Equal*.

59. Sutton, "A History of the Kansas City, Missouri, General Hospital," 70–75, 92–94; Bradford, "Kansas City General Hospital," 10.

60. Gorman, McKinzie, and Wilson, *From Shamans to Specialists*, 129–130.

61. Committee on Administrative Practice, *Health and Hospital Survey*, 287, 290–291.

62. Kremer, "William J. Thompkins," 192–194.

63. Rodgers, "Kansas City General Hospital No. 2," 530.

64. Bates, "Medicine without Method," 96.

65. Andrew E. Naylor, Community Studies, "A History of the General Hospital, Kansas City, Missouri," 29–30, "General Hospital History" folder, TMC.

66. Sutton, "A History of the Kansas City, Missouri, General Hospital," 75–76; Bates, "Medicine without Method," 105; Soward, *Hospital Hill*, 89.

67. Soward, *Hospital Hill*, 97–98; Sutton, "A History of the Kansas City, Missouri, General Hospital," 75–76, 80–81.

68. Ibid.

69. Milton C. Lewis, p. 5, TMC.

70. Gorman, *From Shamans to Specialists*, 171.

71. Bates, "Medicine without Method," 115.

CHAPTER ELEVEN

Kansas City's Guadalupe Center and the Mexican Immigrant Community

Valerie M. Mendoza

The Agnes Ward Amberg Club 1931 Annual Report prominently featured its work with the Guadalupe Center. "Social Case Work," it noted, "has as its objective the aiding of Spanish speaking immigrants with their problems of adjustment to a new culture and new conditions. This includes much interpreting and close co-operation with both public and private educational and welfare agencies, as well as with the Federal Immigration Service and local courts." The report went on to list other types of services offered to the Mexican community through the Guadalupe Center, such as child welfare stations and dental clinics. In addition, the center offered recreational and educational activities, including a library, game room, and playground.

The Guadalupe Center, a settlement house serving Mexican immigrants, began its operations during the summer of 1919 under the auspices of the Agnes Ward Amberg Club of Kansas City. The club's purpose was to "care for the spiritual, as well as the physical, welfare of those in less fortunate circumstances."[1] By 1925 the club had opened the doors to the physical space of the Guadalupe Center, a house purchased in the heart of the Westside Mexican neighborhood, and its initial $500 budget had exploded to over $13,000.[2] In 1936, the center expanded once again when executive director Dorothy Gallagher and her family donated the land for the current-day building to accommodate its ever-increasing activities.[3] Since its origins in 1919, the Guadalupe Center has been a mainstay of the Mexican and Mexican American community in Kansas City.

The Guadalupe Center offered services similar to those offered by other settlement houses throughout the country; however, it differed in three important respects. First, unlike Hull House and other settlement houses in the East and Midwest, the Guadalupe Center sprang up specifically to serve Mexican, not European, immigrants. Second, from its outset the Guadalupe Center affiliated itself with the Catholic Church, unlike most other settlement houses, which were officially secular but culturally Protestant or whose aims were outright missionary.[4] Third, the Guadalupe Center offered both community-based activities and individual casework services. In this respect, it emerged as a unique hybrid between the settlement house model, where reformers lived among their clientele and worked for the betterment of the community, and the charities model, in which outsiders came into impoverished neighborhoods to see who needed and, in their view, was deserving of services.[5] This chapter discusses the development of Kansas City's Mexican community during the Pendergast era and how immigrants adapted to their new home. I argue that the Guadalupe Center first arose to meet the concerns of the greater Kansas City Anglo community regarding the "Mexican problem." It did this mostly through Americanization programs. However, Mexican immigrants themselves began to request services to meet their own needs, and in the process the center became a means to "Mexicanize" their Kansas City environment.

Migration to Kansas City

Mexicans from the agricultural states of Guanajuato, Jalisco, and Michoacán in west-central Mexico began arriving in large numbers in Kansas City around 1910 due to the chaos and economic upheaval caused by the Mexican Revolution.[6] These Mexican states experienced high population densities and the policies of overthrown dictator Porfirio Díaz left many rural dwellers from this region landless and unable to make a living. Railroad agents for the Atchison, Topeka, and Santa Fe Railway Company recruited men from these areas to come to Kansas to work and the company soon grew to be the largest employer of Mexicans in the region.[7] The railroad sought workers because of labor pressures created by World War I. The war affected the labor force in two ways. First, it virtually halted immigration from Europe and the unskilled laborers who would normally take railroad and meatpacking jobs, and second, and most importantly for Kansas City, it diverted men from the workforce to the armed services. Mexican workers were attractive because the United States did not restrict migration from Mexico as it did migration from other places, such as China, Japan, and European countries.[8]

The initial Mexican settlement in Kansas City consisted mainly of men who migrated by themselves in order to provide for their families left behind in Mexico, creating a bachelor society of Mexican men.[9] The men typically lived in boarding and rooming houses rather than single-family dwellings, and restaurants, pool halls, and drinking establishments, such as the Hotel Paraiso (controlled by Tom Pendergast), sprang up to accommodate them. As a result, Mexican men often attracted the attention of the police, who clamped down on perceived lawlessness, and reformers who wanted to help the community.[10]

Although most immigrants were working-age men, World War I also brought appreciable numbers of women and children from Mexico to Kansas City. Railroads and packinghouses needed a steady labor force, and believing that men with families present would be more likely to remain on the job, they actively encouraged Mexicans to bring their wives and children. Over time, the skewed sex ratio began to even out.[11] According to historian Sherry Lamb Schirmer, approximately 7,000 persons of Mexican descent settled in Kansas City between 1910 and 1925, with 10,000 calling the area home by 1930.[12] This change in demographics allowed for the creation of a Mexican space in Kansas City, and this Mexican space eventually included the Guadalupe Center.

Many Mexican immigrants felt out of place in their new home, and the Guadalupe Center helped to make Kansas City a welcoming environment for them. Because most came from a rural, agricultural environment, the hustle and bustle of city life and industrial labor itself proved foreign. They left mountain villages filled with forests for an urban environment where they lived in and near railroad tracks and packinghouses. The noise and stench of both trains and cattle replaced fresh air and quietude, and smoke and soot assaulted their senses. The security of extended family and friends met at the market, town square, or church was also gone.

In addition to encountering an alien environmental landscape, immigrants also experienced an alien social landscape in their new home. Kansas City had no prior permanent Latina/o presence until the large influx of immigrants during the World War I era. Mexicans carved out community by establishing physical spaces in which to live and opening stores that catered to their countrymen and women. These establishments provided familiar goods and services to Mexican immigrants in order to make Kansas City seem more like home. This included foods such as chorizo to spice up their meals or cornmeal for making tortillas.

Neighborhood demographics during the second decade of the twentieth century illustrate a boomtown among Mexicans, as evidenced by the rapid arrival of newcomers, the temporary character of housing (boxcars and rooming houses), population transience, and short-lived businesses. As more women and children arrived, Mexican immigrants settled into three distinct neighborhoods—Argentine, Armourdale, and the Westside corridor of Twenty-Fourth Street—with several smaller ones in outlying areas, near places of employment, mainly railroad tracks and packinghouses.

One of the earliest Mexican communities was known as Argentine. Located in Kansas on the south side of the Kansas River near the Atchison, Topeka, and Santa Fe railroad tracks, the Argentine district began to take shape around 1915 and consisted of just over 300 Mexican immigrants.[13] Well over 200 of these were men over the age of sixteen who worked for the railroad. Large groups of *Mexicanos* either lived in boxcars provided by the Santa Fe Railroad or roomed in private boardinghouses.[14]

The Westside was another neighborhood where Mexicans began to reside around 1915, although they shared the neighborhood with a smaller Swedish community.[15] The immigrants who lived there, on the Missouri side of the Kansas River near the West Bottoms, worked for various railway companies and labored at downtown hotels. A few also secured employment with the packing companies. The Twenty-Fourth Street artery of the Westside proved to be the main business district in this neighborhood, with at least eighteen different types of services catering to Mexicans, such as Cecil Hernández's grocery store, El Buen Gusto restaurant, and Mike Parra's barbershop. Mexicans owned or operated at least a third of these businesses.[16]

By 1920, one other distinct neighborhood could be found near the packinghouses. Known as Armourdale and located on the Kansas side of the river, it was bound by railroad tracks, stockyards, and the Kansas River. This *colonia* consisted mainly of families who lived in rented homes or apartments and worked for the packing companies, although a large number also found employment with the railroads.

By 1930, these latter-day colonias were characterized by a large degree of home-ownership among the Mexican population.[17] This in turn reflected permanence and financial stability.

Kansas City and the "Mexican Problem"

Mexican immigrants encountered a foreign physical and social landscape in their new home, but Kansas City's Anglos also had little prior knowledge of Mexicans. These two groups were relative strangers to one another and, therefore, often operated on stereotypes and assumptions. For example, local newspapers castigated Mexicans as "greasers" and "chili con carnies," and cast the entire Mexican community of Argentine as "trouble for the police department."[18] Mexican immigrants to Kansas City represented the largest group of foreign-born in Kansas City during this time period, which cast them in the position of racialized "other."[19]

One stereotype of Mexicans in particular and immigrants in general centered on the belief that they were inherently inferior and needed to be uplifted to American standards. In the United States these notions focused on class and nationality, with the latter racialized. Reformers found one solution to this so-called immigrant deficiency in the settlement house movement. This movement began in England in the late nineteenth century and was brought to the United States by Jane Addams, whose Hull House in Chicago was arguably the most famous of all settlement houses in the country. Settlement houses offered social services to the poor and underserved, and targeted immigrants. For example, Hull House initially catered to Italian, Polish, and Jewish immigrants. The settlement house in general also infamously served as a source of Americanization for these newcomers. According to settlement house workers, immigrants needed to be taught proper notions of cleanliness, sanitation, and nutrition. The idea quickly spread to other cities and became a way for middle- and upper-class Anglo women to respectably enter the workforce, which was the case for Guadalupe Center director Dorothy Gallagher.

Gallagher, who eventually became executive director of the Guadalupe Center, was born in 1894 to a wealthy Kansas City family. In 1918, she decided to put her time to worthwhile use by joining the Agnes Ward Amberg Club, a Catholic women's charitable organization, and became so enthusiastic about the work that she attended the New York School for Social Work. She also was active in other charitable groups, such as serving as president of the Sionian Charity Club, another Catholic organization serving the Mexican community. The Guadalupe Center became nationally known under her leadership. In fact, Gallagher believed in the value of social work so much that she served as director of the center on a voluntary basis until 1944, when she left to aid war-torn France in its recovery efforts. She was beloved by the Mexican community and known as the "Godmother of Guadalupe." After her return from Europe, she taught classes at the University of Kansas and the College of St. Teresa, known today as Avila University.[20]

Settlement houses in the Northeast and Midwest catered to the large number of European immigrants. The Guadalupe Center fell out of this purview and more closely resembled southwestern settlement houses, whose sole focus was Mexican Americans and Mexican immigrants. For example, in El Paso, Texas (the Mexican equivalent of Ellis Island, according to one scholar), the Rose Gregory Houchen Settlement House and its health center coordinated a variety of Americanization activities for Mexican immigrants from 1920 to 1960.[21] Los Angeles also proved to be a city with a large number of Anglo reformers who targeted Mexican-origin peoples.[22] Historian George J. Sanchez notes that reformers established programs specifically for Mexican women in order to change their cultural values, and American studies scholar Stephanie Lewthwaite has this to say about Los Angeles: "Reform was not simply about social or humanitarian impulses, but about planning, redesigning, and restructuring landscapes, community units, living spaces, lifestyles, and mentalities in a way that materially and socially reshaped the Mexican population."[23]

The founders of the Guadalupe Center also embraced Americanization and reform. For most, these were the first Mexicans they encountered, and Anglo Kansas Citians showed them little empathy. One landlord commented that his Mexican tenants treated his property roughly. According to him, "they pile wood and coal against the plaster in the kitchen instead of in the box provided outside." He complained of having to repaper after each tenant.[24] In other words, Mexicans were uncouth and dirty, and they kept their homes in that state as well. Anglo residents also blamed Mexicans for the spread of the influenza epidemic in 1918.[25]

A variety of organizations carried out Americanization programs throughout

Kansas City. In 1926, the Council of Social Agencies devoted an entire issue of its bulletin to Mexican relief, noting that "the best policy for Kansas City seems to be to accept the Mexicans and extend a friendly hand to them and try to help them become good substantial self-supporting and semi-respecting members of the community."[26] Members of the council believed Mexicans could never become full-fledged members of the Kansas City community, only "semi-respecting" ones due to their ethnicity. Even providing a bathhouse for Mexican immigrants was seen as being a "stimulus to become good citizens."[27] Here again we see the emphasis on Mexicans being dirty and uncouth.

The early 1920s saw a focus on a "Mexican problem" in Kansas City for several reasons. First, the economy suffered a postwar economic downturn, and Americans feared that immigrants would take their jobs. Second, the severe winter of 1920–1921 left many Mexicans unemployed and destitute. In order to combat this and keep Mexicans from using relief services, Kansas City chose to send them back to Mexico and repatriated several hundred immigrants. A harsh winter occurred again in 1925–1926, and the city looked into whether the immigrants could be deported at the expense of the federal government rather than the city this time.[28] Social service agencies throughout the city policed who was deserving of their services and who was not. Those deemed undeserving received no services. An early incident illustrates this point. Kansas City's Spanish-language newspaper *El Cosmopolita* reported that well-known merchant Lázaro Gándara left his wife and six children for another woman. As a result, his wife and children were found "in grave condition."[29] Rather than sending the family to receive aid from city services, the community *mutualistas* (mutual aid societies) took care of the family because they deemed the family respectable and worthy of financial assistance.

Americanization and the Agnes Ward Amberg Club

The Guadalupe Center began its operations during the summer of 1919 because of the efforts of eighteen Catholic young women, who volunteered to organize a Mexican summer school. This group of women named themselves the Agnes Ward Amberg Club and stated that the purpose of their organization was to "care for the spiritual, as well as the physical, welfare of those in less fortunate circumstances."[30] As noted in its first annual report, "the club is fortunate in having some very talented members, especially some experienced and successful social service workers."[31] While the club received the blessing of the formal Catholic structure in the city (churches and their affiliated priests), members themselves originated, planned, and delivered the programming.

Women in Kansas City had actively participated in the city's civic life since the years after the Civil War with the founding of the Women's Christian Association. According to Chapter 8 in this volume, women claimed space in the public sphere

Sewing class for girls at the Guadalupe Center summer school, 1924. Courtesy of the Missouri Valley Special Collections, Kansas City Public Library.

through activism in the form of benevolence and reform.[32] Women's reform efforts included forming local chapters of national organizations, such as the Woman's Christian Temperance Union, the General Federation of Women's Clubs, and the Catholic Women's Association. The broader goals of these organizations (for example, their focus on developing good citizens) aligned with those of the Agnes Ward Amberg Club. For the most part, those involved in the Amberg Club were young, single, middle- and upper-class Anglo women. Club membership grew to over 100 women within the year. These women recognized what devout Catholics the members of the Mexican community were and were moved by the extreme poverty of the immigrants.

The Agnes Ward Amberg Club was aided in its ministry by its affiliation with Our Lady of Guadalupe Parish, located on the Westside at Twenty-Third Street and Madison. Father José Muñoz ministered to this flock until 1926 and supported the work of the women of the Amberg Club. In its first year, the club "engaged in many lines of social service work," including a night school for adults, a sewing school for Mexican girls, a Sunday school, and a summer school attended by over fifty Mexican children daily.[33]

From the beginning, the Amberg Club and the Guadalupe Center exhibited a unique hybrid of social services—the settlement house and charities models. On the one hand, the community classes followed the settlement house model "to eliminate the sources of distress and to improve urban living" and tried to improve immigrants through programming. Additionally, Gallagher herself lived in the neighborhood, consistent with the goals of the settlement house model. On the other hand, the charities model relied on friendly visits by Anglo reformers to potential aid recipients' homes in order to distinguish between those worthy and unworthy of services.[34] These early activities focused on women and children in particular. Reformers targeted women because of their importance in the home and to raising children, and they hoped their efforts would most benefit children.[35] When Mexican women resisted the efforts of reformers by not attending classes and events designed for them, settlement workers set their sights on children and adolescents, whom they viewed as more malleable. The wording of a club pamphlet hints that the night school for Mexican adults was not nearly as popular as the summer school for children, describing the former as "well attended" (the numbers were unspecified because they were small), whereas the summer school for Mexican children had "over 50 participants daily."[36]

At the summer school volunteers taught the children English and took them for a picnic in Penn Valley Park, where "the joy they showed upon being able to have a change of scenery would cause one to want to give them a trip to the woods quite often."[37] From the reformers' point of view, an outing at the park encouraged Americanization by engaging in an acceptable form of leisure. It also showed that club members espoused the thinking of the day regarding immigrants and the poor: the circumstances of their everyday lives were due to their own lack of effort rather than segregation or discrimination. If one tried or expressed the will, park outings were within reach and could be made regularly.[38] This type of thinking, however, discounts the day-to-day lives and living conditions of the Mexican community. Residents lived near the railroad tracks and stockyards on the Westside of Kansas City, Missouri, and in the Argentine and Armourdale districts (also among the stockyards and railroad tracks) on the Kansas side of the state line. They lived either in railroad boxcars or with multiple family members in small, rented housing in order to make ends meet. Most worked ten- to twelve-hour days, six days a week and, therefore, did not have the time or energy for park outings and lacked the means of transportation to get there even if they did. The overcrowded industrial nature of their living conditions made the trip to Penn Valley Park overlooking Union Station all the more special.

Amberg members also engaged in friendly visits, which formed the core of the charities model of social services. According to one scholar, friendly visitors intervened in the lives of the poor based on "presumed wisdom and superiority," and "friendly visiting assumed the right and duty of intervention in the lives of the poor by their social and economic betters."[39] The outright disregard for or lack of understanding of Mexican immigrants' circumstances and any attempts at Americanization occurred through these "friendly visits." This type of work proved so popular with club members that eight to ten women enrolled in a course on social service work given by the Provident Association, a charitable organization founded by prominent Kansas Citians that focused on providing relief to families and individuals in need. The women attended lectures by Mrs. Ream, field supervisor of the Provident Association, on social service work, and upon completion of the course, they were assigned a Catholic family "to visit and care for."[40] Friendly visits assumed that immigrants wanted moral guidance and that "the right and duty of intervention in the lives of the poor [rested with] their social and economic betters."[41]

The Amberg Club members began friendly visits in order to augment their services to the Mexican community. According to the club's 1919 annual report, members visited the homes of those "absent from the Parochial school and also the sick."[42] Jose Martinez and his family represent the type of people club members tried to reach. Martinez, his wife Lena, and their four children ranging in age from seventeen to four migrated to Kansas City in 1917. He worked as a section hand for the railroad, and the family lived in a railroad car on the Westside along with two male boarders. Amberg Club members, such as President Marguerite Sullivan, likely would have been concerned about the poor living conditions of this family and would have instructed Lena Martinez in how to keep her bunk car home clean and how to cook proper meals for her children.[43]

By 1925 the club had expanded its Americanization and charity services through the purchase of a two-story home that it named the Guadalupe Center. Located at 907 West Twenty-Third Street, next door to Our Lady of Guadalupe Church, the center became the headquarters for the Agnes Ward Amberg Club. The women adopted a motto for the settlement house: The House of the Good Neighbor. The center possessed the distinct advantage of being associated with the Catholic Church, which served to legitimate it within the Mexican community. It also achieved legitimacy through the adoption of Guadalupe Center as its name. Our Lady of Guadalupe is the patron saint of Mexico, and all Mexican immigrants (whether religious or not) instantly recognized the name. The naming of the settlement house after both the saint and the church next door used Mexican culture as a way to draw Mexican immigrants into the center's services. It also gave the impression of being friendly to the community. The center, along with the church, served as a safe public space for an immigrant group that was ostracized by large segments of Kansas City's Anglo community, as evidenced by the community's segregation into distinct neighborhoods and the education of its children in Mexican-only elementary and middle schools.[44] The club moved from working *in* the Mexican community to the center being *part* of the Mexican community.

The purchase of a permanent building allowed the club to add a medical clinic to aid clientele, expanding the services previously offered and also striking a blow in the sectarian rivalry between Protestants and Catholics. The Protestant Mexican Christian Institute, also located on the Westside, had operated a clinic since 1917. The institute, however, focused on proselytization and "religious and moral uplift."[45] The Guadalupe Center wanted to curb "defection" to Protestantism and began to offer medical services in the heart of the community.[46] During the clinic's first year of operation, it treated 1,733 patients, fewer than the Protestant clinic but very respectable for its first year of operation, especially as the Guadalupe Center offered fewer medical services.[47] By 1931, use of the Guadalupe Center clinic by its Mexican clientele exploded to over 3,000 patients, and the center itself boasted an attendance of over 21,000 patrons at its organized meetings that year.[48] This large number accounts for community members who attended multiple events, but it nonetheless suggests the growing popularity of center programming.

In these early years, the center clearly espoused a patronizing attitude toward the immigrants. For example, the women's sewing class taught expectant mothers how to make a "proper" layette for their newborns, and reformers organized a mother's club "for better housekeeping and care of children." A kindergarten also taught youngsters "proper American customs, habits, and language." Additionally, executive director Dorothy Gallagher noted in her 1926 report on the center that the Mexicans' "ignorance of proper standards of living could be changed by a trained sympathetic Spanish-speaking housekeeper who would visit, teach and inspire them to make efforts to improve their home life."[49] From the Anglo point of view Mexican women did not cook nutritious meals, keep clean homes, or raise their children to be industrious citizens. The irony here is that Mexican women prided themselves on their housekeeping skills. Indeed, one of the main tenets of Mexican womanhood was a woman's ability to care for her family. Mexican women placed care of children and family before themselves, and the community recognized them as the moral center of the home.[50]

At the same time, however, the staff of the Guadalupe Center used Mexican culture to its own ends. First, due to the competing nature of social services, they wanted to attract as many Mexican clients as they could in order to continue receiving funding, which came in part from Amberg Club members' dues and donations. The staff did this by offering services that they thought would appeal to the Mexican community and by acquiescing to client requests, such as sponsorship of the J. W. Club started by Mexican girls in response to the boys' club known as the Knights of the Round Table.[51] According to one historian, this pattern proved typical of settlement houses, which after gaining the trust of the community would expand their activities.[52]

For example, beginning in 1926 the center organized a yearly fiesta in order to raise funds for a playground. The annual fiestas could be seen as demonstrating respect for and as a celebration of Mexican culture. After all, it allowed the Mexican

Performers in Spanish costumes at the first Gran Fiesta in mid-August 1926. Courtesy of the Missouri Valley Special Collections, Kansas City Public Library.

immigrants to show pride in their culture in a public setting. However, the yearly celebration also represented the beginning of the center's cultural programming and can be viewed from the lens of cultural appropriation. While it provided the vehicle for immigrants to publicly perform their Mexican-ness in a socially accept-able space among fellow countrymen and women, it also attracted a sizable crowd of Kansas City's Anglos who were curious about these newcomers. The fiesta was romanticized as "Spanish." Indeed, the mid-1920s marked the opening of J. C. Nichols's Spanish colonial–inspired Country Club Plaza shopping district, and a photo of performers from the 1926 fiesta certainly plays into this theme. It shows a couple in Spanish costume and an American flag in the background.[53] The Mexi-can community at once showed off its Spanish heritage, its love of the home coun-try of Mexico, and its adoption of its new country.

It is unclear whether the center itself or its Mexican clientele encouraged the Spanish theme. The 1930 program saw fiesta performers in merengue costumes, and center director Dorothy Gallagher described the Gran Fiestas as "such genuine folk expressions that they were hailed as 'events' throughout the city and attended by thousands from all neighborhoods."[54] Clearly, Gallagher viewed and tried to present her Mexican clients as quaint and possibly nonthreatening. Additionally, presenting this community as Spanish served to Europeanize the group, making it more respectable.

The Guadalupe Center and Mexican Immigrant Agency

By the mid-1930s, the focus of the center began to change from one of Americanization to one that celebrated Mexican culture for its own sake. The center listened to its clientele as they expressed their needs. In response to their continued presence in Kansas City and deliberate decision to settle permanently, the Mexican community began to ask for and receive services from the Guadalupe Center, partly because of increased need during the Great Depression and partly as a way to appropriate the Guadalupe Center space as their own. Rather than providing services from the top down, agency heads took into account the desires of the Mexican and Mexican American clientele.

The change in attitude on the part of reformers occurred for a variety of reasons. The Mexican community began to stabilize. Migration of Mexicans to Kansas City from Mexico and other parts of the United States virtually halted during the Depression, and a stable population of homeowners, who had American-born children, remained.[55] These children were raised in the United States so the need for Americanization lessened because they grew up more fully assimilated in the schools. The permanent residents, therefore, had proved their worthiness by settling down, owning homes (they were clearly trying to better themselves), and raising American citizens.

In 1936, in the midst of the Depression, the Guadalupe Center expanded once again when executive director Dorothy Gallagher and her family donated the land for a new building to accommodate the center's ever-increasing number of activities.[56] The building came about in part because the center outgrew its space due to increased demand from the Mexican community. As Dorothy Gallagher stated, "Neighbors began appealing for help. . . . Children came in to play in inclement weather. Older groups wanted to meet for their parties in the clinic room, 'the only big room in the neighborhood.'"[57] Gallagher herself drew up the initial building plans and hired the architect to complete her vision.[58]

The new building cost over $21,000 and was built in the Spanish-colonial style of architecture with a "stucco and adobe effect" and red tile roof.[59] According to Gallagher, the new building brought "the spirit of the Spanish Southwest" to Kansas City. Writing about the center in 1942, Sister Celine Vasquez noted that "the physical structure of the Center is important not only because of the immediate advantage in carrying out a program . . . but also in its psychological effect upon the people."[60] Evidently, Kansas City reformers such as Gallagher equated Spanish-style architecture with their Mexican clients. This ideal was characteristic of the time period, particularly in the Southwest when Californians imagined the Spanish foundational roots of their cultural heritage through Spanish-themed parties and parades and honored Spanish explorers.[61]

Evidence that the center took its programming seriously can be found in the use of space in the new building. The first floor contained offices, a large assembly room ("the living room of the neighborhood"), a kitchen and dining area, and another large room known as the all-purpose room, where the well-baby station was located and dances and meetings were held. The first floor also contained club meeting rooms and a gymnasium. The second floor housed two club rooms and a music studio in addition to the director's office, a library, and a small apartment for the caretaker. The basement housed equipment for wood and metalwork.[62]

The center's Mexican neighbors did indeed view the large room as the living room of the neighborhood and used it for such purposes as weddings and parties.[63] The Club Tepeyac organized a Halloween party in the large room in 1939, which included a costume contest and had over fifty-five people in attendance, and in 1940 the room was used for a Noche Buena party with an equally large number in attendance.[64] "Tepeyac" denotes the name of the hill where Juan Diego first came into contact with Our Lady of Guadalupe, so it had significant meaning to the Mexican population. Also notable is the use of the Spanish "Noche Buena" rather than the English "Christmas Eve." Additionally, women of the community used the kitchen to cook large quantities of food, such as tortillas, for various events. As Dorothy Gallagher commented, "For the past two years Mexican suppers at the Center have been a growing fad."[65] All of these events served as examples of greater respect that center staff afforded Mexican immigrants and the growing Mexican American population. The use of the center by the Mexican community for cultural events also shows their trust of the center and their staff. In essence, they were beginning to "Mexicanize" the Guadalupe Center.

That the Mexican community felt comfortable utilizing the center space and asking for resources to promote Mexican culture and community can be found in these two examples. First, the community created the space they needed. For example, boys from the neighborhood desired to play baseball and under the guidance of center volunteers cleared a vacant lot owned by the center for a field.[66] Second, in 1938 the center used its resources to take a group of folk dancers to the Fourth Annual National Folk Festival in Washington, DC. The group of eight men, four women, and two children participated in the program, including dance instructor Joe Lopez. The group performed for large crowds on May 6 and 7, and their photo appeared in the *Washington Post*.[67] The dance group proved popular in Kansas City, performing at the Hotel Muehlebach and El Torreon Ballroom, among other venues.[68] Whether the dancers themselves or the center initiated this once-in-a-lifetime

An adult English class at the Guadalupe Center, December 3, 1936. Courtesy of the Missouri Valley Special Collections, Kansas City Public Library.

opportunity is unknown; however, it brought great prestige and recognition to the group and the center alike.

In 1942, Sister Celine Vasquez noted that interested groups were organized according to demand and that an endeavor was made "to meet the needs of the people."[69] Center staff in particular strove to meet the needs of the youth of the community, as evidenced by the baseball field referenced above. They also hired a "boys' worker" to take charge of activities centered on this group, and sanctioned the formation of the *Knight's Spear*, a center newspaper written by children in the neighborhood. This publication appeared sporadically throughout the 1930s and chronicled important events in the lives of the children.[70]

The center had previously supported a club for boys known as the Knights of the Round Table, and in August 1931 the boys "entered into a new enterprise . . . of publishing a monthly paper not only for the community's welfare but also for theirs."[71] According to editor in chief Erineo Lopez, the goals of the publication included the following: "1. To create a brotherly feeling in the community. 2. Clean sportsmanship. 3. To spread the appreciation of old Mexico." Only three extant issues of the publication exist—the August and Christmas 1931 editions and one from May 1934. Each volume contained articles written only in English and exclusively by the children. The influence and importance of the center in the lives of these children permeated the issues. For example, the staff dedicated the first issue to "our true friend, Miss Dorothy Gallagher, who labors so unselfishly and cheerfully for our welfare."[72] Each issue also highlighted the interests of the children, such as the establishment of a playground at the corner of Twenty-Third Street and Summit down the street from the center, or a Christmas program performed at West Junior High and featuring groups from the Guadalupe Center such as the all-girls J. W. Club, whose members performed a play entitled *A Visit from Santa Claus*.[73]

Conclusion

The Guadalupe Center began under the auspices of the Agnes Ward Amberg Club in 1919 as a vehicle for charity services. Its affiliation with the Catholic Church made it a popular and trustworthy destination for Mexicans coming from a Catholic cultural tradition who attended mass with a Spanish-speaking priest at Our Lady of Guadalupe Church. The club opened the Guadalupe Center next to Our Lady of Guadalupe Catholic Church in 1925 and became a neighborhood center. It offered a unique hybrid of social services, comprising both the settlement house and charity models. As a center, it initially focused on Americanization and represented one way Anglo Kansas Citians responded to these foreign newcomers. In 1936, the center opened its current-day building. By this time, the stability of the community, combined with the fact that a Mexican American population of citizens was growing, forced the center to focus on the needs of its clients, as expressed by themselves.[74] The center became a Mexican space that was appropriated by the Mexican community to meet their own need to "Mexicanize" their new home.

The Guadalupe Center continues to serve the Mexican-origin community in its original 1930s building, and bills itself as "the longest continuously operating organization serving Latino/as since 1919," whose mission is to "improve the quality of life for individuals in the Latino/a communities of greater Kansas City."[75] The center accomplishes this through educational programs, health and social services, and promoting and providing Latino cultural enrichment events.

Notes

1. Agnes Ward Amberg Club Pamphlet, 1919, Guadalupe Center Collection, Missouri Valley Special Collections, Kansas City Public Library, Kansas City, Missouri (hereafter Guadalupe Center Collection).

2. Agnes Ward Amberg Club Annual Report, 1925, Guadalupe Center Collection.

3. Thesis, 1942, Box 5, Guadalupe Center Collection. While the thesis has no title page,

it is thought to be written by Sister Celine Vasquez for her master's degree in social work at St. Louis University.

4. See David Baldillo, "Incorporating Reform and Religion: Mexican Immigrants, Hull-House, and the Church," in *Pots of Promise: Mexicans and Pottery at Hull House, 1920–1940*, ed. Cheryl Ganz and Margaret Strobel (Urbana: University of Illinois Press, 2004).

5. The charities model developed in the late nineteenth century to prevent fraud and inefficiency in private and public charity institutions. See Walter Trattner, *From Poor Law to Welfare State: A History of Social Welfare in America*, 6th ed. (New York: Free Press, 1999), 93. This type of hybrid model appears to be unique to the Guadalupe Center. The closest type of institution is the urban mission geared toward African Americans in the late nineteenth century, such as the New York Colored Mission founded in 1865 by Quakers. See Ralph E. Luker, "Missions, Institutional Churches, and Settlement Houses: The Black Experience, 1865–1910," *Journal of Negro History* 69, nos. 3–4 (1984): 101–113. Luker argues that the urban missions served as a precursor to settlement houses for African Americans and traces their evolution. Mission functions, however, included home visits, which later settlement houses did not, save for the Guadalupe Center.

6. According to Sherry Lamb Schirmer, during the heyday of the Santa Fe Trail in the 1840s, several wealthy Mexican traders lived in Kansas City while trading their goods. However, no Mexican communities were established. She also found that in 1905 the Santa Fe railroad recruited 155 Mexicans, who resided in Kansas City, but this small population did not attract much attention from Kansas City's Anglo community. See Sherry Lamb Schirmer, *Historical Overview of Mexicans in Kansas City* (Kansas City: Pan-Educational Institute, 1976).

7. Schirmer, *Historical Overview of Mexicans in Kansas City*. According to historian Judith Fincher Laird, Mexicans who settled in the Argentine neighborhood of Kansas City were primarily from Tangancícuaro and Michoacán. Judith Laird, "Argentine, Kansas: The Evolution of a Mexican-American Community, 1905–1940" (PhD diss., University of Kansas, 1975). Mexican immigrants did not start working in the packinghouses in large numbers until after World War I.

8. The Chinese Exclusion Act excluded skilled and unskilled Chinese laborers. In the Gentlemen's Agreement of 1907, the United States allowed wives and children of Japanese men currently living in the country to immigrate, and in return Japan no longer issued passports for Japanese wanting to emigrate to the United States. The 1917 Immigration Act restricted "undesirables" from other countries and implemented an $8 head tax and a literacy test on immigrants over the age of sixteen. For additional information on the Chinese Exclusion Act of 1882, see https://www.ourdocuments.gov/doc.php?doc=47; on the 1917 Immigration Act, see US Immigration Legislation Online, University of Washington, Bothell Library, http://library.uwb.edu/static/USimmigration/1917_immigration_act.html, all accessed August 20, 2016.

9. Kansas State Census, Wyandotte County, Kansas, 1915; Bureau of Commerce, 14th Census of the United States, Wyandotte County, Kansas, and Jackson County, Missouri, 1920.

10. For Hotel Paraiso, see *El Cosmopolita*, April 29, 1916, and May 13, 1916, "Escandalos en el Hotel Paraiso"; for police harassment, see March 6, 1915, when the newspaper reported that a delegation of Mexican citizens went to the police commissioner to ask him to tell his officers to stop harassing Mexicans on Twenty-Fourth Street in the Westside district.

11. 1920 Federal Census, Wyandotte County, Kansas, and Jackson County, Missouri. For a discussion of the gendered nature of Mexican immigration to Kansas City, see Valerie M. Mendoza, "Beyond the Border: Gender and Migration to Mexican Kansas City, 1890–1940," (manuscript in progress).

12. Schirmer, *Overview of the Mexican Community*, 3. It is unclear whether Schirmer is referring to the Kansas City metropolitan area or Kansas City, Missouri, specifically.

13. Information regarding settlement patterns for 1915 pieced together from the Kansas State Department of Agriculture, 1915 Kansas State Census; *Gates 1915 Kansas City Directory and Business Catalog* (Kansas City: Gate City Directory Company, 1915); and *Kansas City El Cosmopolita*.

14. 1915 Kansas State Census. This area had previously been settled in the late nineteenth century by Belgian immigrants, who farmed the land but moved to Johnson County when the area became industrialized. Schirmer, *Overview of Ethnic Communities in Kansas City*.

15. Schirmer, *Overview of Ethnic Communities in Kansas City*.

16. The number of businesses in this area was derived from advertisements found in the 1914 and 1915 editions of *El Cosmopolita* and may not be inclusive, but are representative of the types of businesses serving the Mexican community. See also *Gates 1920 Kansas City Directory and Business Catalog* (Kansas City: Gate City Directory Company, 1920).

17. Ibid.

18. Robert Cleary, "The Education of Mexican-Americans in Kansas City, 1916–1951" (MA thesis, University of Missouri–Kansas City, 2002), 34–35.

19. The foreign-born made up 10.2 percent of Kansas City's population in 1910 and 6.0 percent in 1930. A. Theodore Brown and Lyle W. Dorsett, *K.C.: A History of Kansas City, Missouri* (Boulder, Colo.: Pruett Publishing, 1978), 183. According to Sherry Schirmer, between 1910 and 1930, there were "thousands of Italians" (she gives no exact number), 2,500 Greeks, 1,500 Belgians, 2,000 Croats, and 4,000 Czechs and Slovaks. See Schirmer, *Overview of Ethnic Communities*. Kansas City did have a sizable African American population as a result of the Great Migration. That group grew by 50 percent between 1910 and 1925, from 23,000 to 34,000. Mexicans were often lumped together with African Americans due to skin color.

20. Jason Roe, "The Godmother of Guadalupe," http://www.kchistory.org/week-kansas -city-history/godmother-guadalupe, accessed September 10, 2018, and Barbara Magerl, "Biography of Dorothy Gallagher (1894–1982)," http://www.kchistory.org/content/biography -dorothy-gallagher-1894-1982-social-worker, accessed August 18, 2016.

21. Vicki Ruiz, "Dead Ends or Gold Mines? Using Missionary Records in Mexican-American Women's History," *Frontiers: A Journal of Women Studies* 12, no. 1 (1991): 33–56.

22. One of the factors that distinguishes Mexican enclaves in the Southwest as opposed to the Midwest and Kansas City in particular is the fact that the southwestern states (California, Arizona, New Mexico, and Texas) had once been part of Mexico and, therefore, were home

to a sizable Mexican American population that strove to, in some cases, distance itself from the Mexican immigrant population.

23. George J. Sanchez, "'Go After the Women': Americanization and the Mexican Immigrant Woman, 1915–1929," in *Unequal Sisters: A Multicultural Reader in U.S. Women's History*, ed. Ellen Carol Dubois and Vicki Ruiz (New York: Routledge, 1990); Stephanie Lewthwaite, *Race, Place, and Reform in Mexican Los Angeles: A Transnational Perspective, 1890–1940* (Tucson: University of Arizona Press, 2009), 5.

24. Paul Schuster Taylor papers, BANC MSS 84/38 c, Bancroft Library, University of California, Berkeley.

25. Cleary, "The Education of Mexican-Americans in Kansas City, Kansas, 1916–1951," citing "The Influenza Situation," *Argentine Republic*, October 19, 1918, 1, 4. The article states that Mexicans live in "disease-ridden shacks" and that white children should not have to go to school with Mexican children.

26. "Social Planning: Bulletin of the Council of Social Agencies, March 1926," Guadalupe Center Collection.

27. Ibid.

28. Ibid. Laws numerically restricting immigration at this time did not apply to Mexicans. Notably, however, the 1924 Immigration Act created the Border Patrol, whose purpose was to prevent unauthorized entry to the United States, which at this time meant keeping out the Chinese.

29. *El Cosmopolita*, January 22, 1916.

30. Agnes Ward Amberg Club pamphlet, 1919, Guadalupe Center Collection. The club was named after a Chicago philanthropist who started a settlement house for the Italian community there.

31. Agnes Ward Amberg Club pamphlet, 1919, Guadalupe Center Collection. Walter Trattner notes that settlement houses began to decline in importance after World War I because of the turn to trained experts in social work and because it became difficult to find volunteers. That was not the case in Kansas City. See Trattner, *From Poor Law to Welfare State*, 185.

32. K. David Hanzlick, *Benevolence, Moral Reform, Equality: Women's Activism in Kansas City, 1870 to 1940* (Columbia, Mo.: University of Missouri Press, 2018).

33. Agnes Ward Amberg Club pamphlet, 1919, Guadalupe Center Collection.

34. Trattner, *From Poor Law to Welfare State*, 96, 163, and 169.

35. Sanchez, "Go after the Women."

36. Agnes Ward Amberg Club pamphlet, 1919, Guadalupe Center Collection.

37. Ibid.

38. Trattner, *From Poor Law to Welfare State*, 95.

39. Ibid., 98–99.

40. "The Agnes Ward Amberg Club," December 1919, Guadalupe Center Collection. See also Hanzlick, *Benevolence, Moral Reform, Equality*.

41. Trattner, *From Poor Law to Welfare State*, 98.

42. "The Agnes Ward Amberg Club," December 1919, Guadalupe Center Collection.

43. Department of Commerce, Bureau of the Census, Fourteenth Census of the United States (1920), Wyandotte County, Kansas. The Santa Fe railroad often provided railroad cars as a form of housing for Mexican immigrants. Boxcars measured fifty feet long and ten feet wide.

44. See Cleary, "The Education of Mexican-Americans in Kansas City"; and Mendoza, "From Mexican to Mexican-American in Kansas City, 1914–1940."

45. "The Mexican Christian Institute Annual Report (1925)," Box 5, Folder 3, Guadalupe Center Collection.

46. While Mexicans were admitted into General Hospital No. 2 southeast of downtown, the Guadalupe Center provided translators and was located in the heart of the Mexican community on the Westside.

47. Agnes Ward Amberg Club Annual Report, 1925, Guadalupe Center Collection.

48. Ibid., 1931, Guadalupe Center Collection. How these numbers were tallied is not mentioned. For example, the large number of attendees could be due to the fact that the same person was counted more than once if he or she attended multiple events.

49. "Social Planning: Bulletin of the Council of Social Agencies," Guadalupe Center Collection.

50. This ideal, known as *marianismo*, closely resembles the nineteenth-century "Cult of True Womanhood" explored by Barbara Welter, which had piety, purity, submissiveness, and domesticity as its main tenets. See Rosa Maria Gil and Carmen Vazquez, *The Maria Paradox: How Latinas Can Merge Old World Traditions with New World Self-Esteem* (New York: G. P. Putnam's Sons, 1996); and Barbara Welter, "The Cult of True Womanhood, 1820–1860," *American Quarterly* 18, no. 2 (1966): 151–174.

51. *Knight's Spear*, August 1931, Guadalupe Center Collection.

52. Trattner, *From Poor Law to Welfare State*, 176.

53. Photo Album 1, 25, Guadalupe Center Collection.

54. Photo Album 1, 48, and Dorothy Gallagher, "Mexican Welfare Work in Kansas City," *Catholic Action* (September 1937), 17, Scrapbook 5, Folder 8, Guadalupe Center Collection.

55. "Charities Fund News," Charities Bureau, Kansas City, Mo., February 1935, Guadalupe Center Collection.

56. Ibid.

57. Dorothy Gallagher, "Mexican Welfare Work in Kansas City," *Catholic Action* (September 1937), 17, Guadalupe Center Collection.

58. Magerl, "Biography of Dorothy Gallagher."

59. "Charities Fund News," Guadalupe Center Collection.

60. Thesis, 1942, Box 5, Guadalupe Center Collection.

61. Carey McWilliams, *North from Mexico: The Spanish-Speaking People of the United States* (Philadelphia: J. B. Lippincott, 1948). McWilliams argues that the Spanish fantasy heritage was used as a marketing tool to promote tourism but in doing so, it erased the brutality of the Spanish toward the indigenous communities and ignored the culture of Mexicans of mixed Spanish and Indian ancestry.

62. Ibid., 8.

63. Album 2, 76, Guadalupe Center Collection.

64. Album 2, 73 and 86, Guadalupe Center Collection. These were not the only events Mexicans used the room for but represent a range of activities.

65. Album 2, 75, Guadalupe Center Collection; and Gallagher, "Mexican Welfare Work in the City," *Catholic Action* (September 1937), Guadalupe Center Collection.

66. Album 2, 9, 77, 88, Guadalupe Center Collection.

67. Box 3, Folder 14, Guadalupe Center Collection.

68. *Knight's Spear*, May 1934, Folder 4, Guadalupe Center Collection.

69. Thesis, 1942, Box 5, Guadalupe Center Collection.

70. In addition, a photo of the *Knight's Spear* staff was taken in October 1939 and can be found in Photo Album 2, 66, Guadalupe Center Collection.

71. *Knights' Spear*, August 1931, Folder 4, Guadalupe Center Collection.

72. Ibid.

73. *Knight's Spear*, August 1931 and Christmas 1931, Folder 4, Guadalupe Center Collection.

74. According to Schirmer, the overall Mexican population in Kansas City shrank significantly during the Depression from roughly 10,000 to 2,500. However, the number of children of immigrants born in the United States began to increase as a percentage of the population, and it is these children who began to assert their rights as Americans. Schirmer, *Historical Overview of Mexicans in Kansas City*.

75. Guadalupe Centers, Inc. http://www.guadalupecenters.org/, accessed September 25, 2015.

PART THREE

Culture at an American Crossroads

CHAPTER TWELVE

"The Event of the Season"

Race, Charity, and Jazz in 1920s Kansas City

Marc Rice

Society is demanding higher standards in all of its social phases. Bennie Moten and his Musical Cohorts have raised the standard of Dance Pleasure and announce the lease of the Big Hall at Fifteenth and Paseo for the indulgence of Colored Devotees of Terpsichorean Delight. With the best possible dance floor, the best installed acoustics for carrying the best Music, a good time is assured at all times.

—"Something New!" *The Call*, March 14, 1924

This quote, announcing the opening of the Paseo Hall to African American patronage in 1924, illustrates the strong ties in the 1920s between Kansas City's black community and the development of the city's unique jazz and dance music. African American "Society" was demanding "higher standards" in music and dance entertainment, and bandleader Bennie Moten, an astute businessman, filled the need by shaping a band and leasing a ballroom that catered to the tastes of the middle and upper classes. When people think of Kansas City jazz in the 1920s and 1930s, certain images come to mind: political corruption, gangster activity, and music that catered to and benefited from this type of environment. All this was present, of course, during the time of our study, but believing that vice and corruption were the only contributing factors that made the city a center of innovative music is a mistake. This chapter tells another side of the story of Kansas City jazz, whereby the black middle and upper classes also supported the music and the musicians, at least until the Great Depression. Indeed, many musicians moved between these two social spheres—the political and corrupt, and the proper and refined. The story of jazz and the Pendergast regime has been told; instead, this is the story of jazz and the National Association for the Advancement of Colored People (NAACP), the Twelve Charity Girls, and the black Elks Lodge and many other such organizations.[1]

During the week of March 7, 1920, the midwestern lodge of the Improved Benevolent and Protective Order of the Elks of the World, an African American fraternal organization, held an event in Kansas City advertised as "The Big Rocky Gulch Frontier Days Celebration" that offered "the biggest shows ever presented of this kind by any organization." The event created a fictional town, "Rocky Gulch," modeled on "a Wild Western Town in the good old days of 1849," complete with lodge members playing deputies, jailers, and cardsharps, as well as a bank, a jail, a saloon, and "Calamity Jane's Dance Hall." Among the cast of characters were Bailey Handcock, who worked the checkroom, Dude Langford, a jailor, and "Benny" [sic] Moten, who appeared as "Two Gun Johnson."[2]

The significance for this chapter of the presence of Handcock, Langford, and Moten is that collectively they formed a jazz trio, the B. B. and D. Orchestra, three young men in their early twenties who were establishing professional connections with the many African American social and political organizations of Kansas City. Bennie Moten, in particular, would parlay his promotional abilities and sense of political acumen among the black social and professional elite of Kansas City as he established one of the most successful dance ensembles in the Midwest. B. B. and D. was just the beginning. Within a few years, black Kansas City would be a center for dancing, and most of the dance bands that catered to this community, including the Bennie Moten Orchestra, did quite well indeed.

The social and cultural dynamics of black Kansas City in the 1920s and their impact on music were shaped, at least in part, by a rapid population expansion. The city was one of the recipients of the Great Migration, the movement to the urban North of thousands of African Americans from the South. This is clearly revealed by the census figures. In 1910, the overall population of the city was 248,381, and the black population was 23,704, or 9.52 percent of the total. This figure rose to 30,893 by 1920. By 1930 there were 42,005 African Americans, who now constituted 10.5 percent of the total population.[3]

This population shift created a culture clash between an established, socially elite black population, and the new, poorer migrants from the South. The newcomers established different music and dancing styles, ways of entertaining, and social mores from those of the upper classes in Kansas City's African American neighborhoods. In the 1920s and early 1930s, the venues and occasions in which jazz was heard were governed by the separate needs of the distinct social classes, such that, as Katrina Hazzard-Gordon accurately summarizes, "in jooks and after-hours joints and at rent shouts, dance became a litmus test for sociocultural identity."[4] To be certain, the jazz musicians of Kansas City could move between these various social

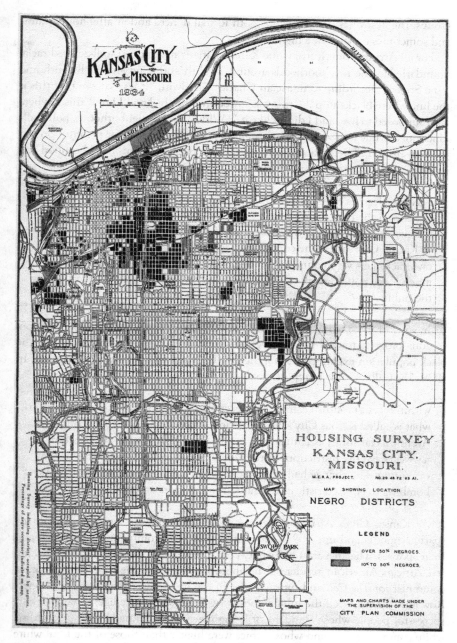

African American population centers depicted in a 1934 map of Kansas City. Courtesy of the Missouri Valley Special Collections, Kansas City Public Library.

groups; the best ones could play for both formal dances and at after-hours joints, and sometimes on the same night.

For all African Americans, white Kansas Citians maintained well-defined racial boundaries in the neighborhoods around Twelfth and Vine and Eighteenth and Vine Streets. According to musician Charles Goodwin, "It was known that this is the line where blacks stop . . . this was my boundaries [sic] and I know this is where I am supposed to live, and I didn't like it."[5] Within these neighborhoods, politically sanctioned crime and vice were prevalent.[6] A prominent place for prostitution was the area around Eleventh and Twelfth Streets on the Paseo. This neighborhood and its associated corruption were clearly described in an editorial from *The Call*:

> Because Negroes have the least financial and political weight, ties between the police and the racketeers endanger us most of all the elements that make up the city's population. As is typical of the American city, our residence district in Kansas City suffers the contamination of white vice resorts. In addition, our own racketeers very naturally bid for protection, and the double burden is too much if the police are more interested in getting money than in safeguarding the public.[7]

In spite of these many obstacles, the African American communities made continuous progress toward the destruction of racial barriers. Geographically, as the black population expanded during the 1920s, so too did black neighborhoods. In 1929, *The Call* was able to report that

> within recent months Negroes have occupied a considerable area to the east of what is called Kansas City's Negro section. They are now living on Brooklyn Avenue as far south as 25th street . . . this and the adjoining area is where a few years ago the restrictions were made by white owners against our buying or renting. The change had been made by mutual consent, and none of the bombing so characteristic of Kansas City a few years ago has occurred.[8]

As Kansas City's African American population grew in numbers and living space, a middle and upper class emerged, shaped by prominent businessmen and their spouses. The area around Twenty-Fourth Street and the Paseo was the wealthiest African American residential neighborhood during this time. Roy Wilkins, columnist for *The Call* and future leader of the NAACP, termed this area Society Row and characterized the inhabitants as "well educated, intelligent, hardworking successful people whose standard of living matched anything in the surrounding white community . . . and whose ethics were higher than those of the local white community."[9] Some of the most prominent African American businesses located here were Homer Roberts's car dealership, the T. B. Watkins funeral home, the offices of *The Call*, and the Monarchs baseball team. By the early 1920s this area was already a thriving African American commercial district, and the number of businesses increased substantially throughout the late 1930s.

As the black middle and upper classes grew, they built social and political organizations, and the goals of many of these groups were the betterment of black life in a segregated city and the improvement of prospects for the race in the country as a whole. The organizations to which the elite class of Kansas City belonged can be categorized as follows: large associations with national ties, such as the Urban League and the NAACP; fraternal lodges catering to the male economic elite, such as the Knights of Pythias and the Elks Lodge; ladies' auxiliaries, catering to the female economic elite, such as the Forget-Me-Not Girls; and clubs for young men, including the Cheerio Boys and the Beau Brummels. This study reveals that each of these organizations held dances and staged other musical events that employed jazz-influenced dance bands. For many bands and individual musicians, these events were important sources of income and offered a completely different performance atmosphere than the after-hours establishments that were connected with vice and political corruption.

The first mention of the word "jazz" in the Kansas City black press is found in the *Kansas City Sun* in 1917 and reveals that the music was beginning to be a part of polite black society. There was an announcement in September of that year for a dance to be held at the M. & O. Hall, which had been newly painted and wallpapered. The dance was for members of the Cosmos Club, who were implored to "make this the grandest affair in the history of this, the most famous dancing club of Greater Kansas City." And to make sure that proper decorum was kept, the article stated that dance instructor/moderator "Prof. Frank Buckner will lend the magic of his presence on the floor," and the "Cosmos Club orchestra will furnish both jazz and jizz for the occasion."[10]

The Elks Lodge discussed in this chapter's opening paragraph was just one of a number of Kansas City's African American fraternal lodges and male social groups that sponsored jazz dances. As historian Willard B. Gatewood illustrates, throughout the country the number of social clubs for the black upper class multiplied rapidly in the late nineteenth and early twentieth century.[11] The men's groups, including the Elks Lodge, the Masonic Lodge, and the Knights of Pythias, maintained a benevolent purpose and organized many fund-raising dances. For example, the Pythians were dedicated to "recognizing the universality of human brotherhood . . . to disseminate their great principles of Friendship, Charity, and Benevolence, nothing of a sectarian or political character . . . our noble order was instituted to uplift the fallen; to champion humanity, to be his guide and hope, his refuge, shelter and defense."[12] For these reasons, the placement of students in higher education was an important goal for the elite, for a strong educational background was an essential criteria for admittance to the upper class. William M. Brooks, the leader of the Elks'

Knights Templar Annual
Public Easter Family Party

Yourself, your family and your friends are invited by
Emanuel Commandery No. 25, to be present at

Labor Temple

14th and Woodland

Monday Night, Apr. 21

The Best Union Orchestra in the two Kansas Cities will furnish popular and Jazz music

Dancing

Continuous 8:00 p. m.
to 12:00 o'clock

No Drills—No Drilling

Refreshments

By the Ladies of the Heroines of the Crusader Guilds.

2 Prizes 2

No. 1, an Old Hen with 1 doz. chicks
No. 2, one Sack best Granulated Sugar

Come, bring your friends and enjoy an evening with us.

25 cents ———— Admission, ———— 25 cents

Sir Samuel C. Winston, E. C.
Sir William H. Brown, Recorder

Advertising for a Knights Templar Easter charity event featuring dancing and jazz music. *Kansas City Sun*, April 19, 1919.

midwestern lodge in 1929, stated before a fund-raising dance, "The Elks believe in education for the youth and charity for the needy. At the present time our order is maintaining 39 young Negro boys and girls in colleges and universities. . . . We need the whole hearted support of Greater Kansas City."[13]

By 1919 the fraternal lodges and benevolent groups were beginning to employ bands that played jazz-oriented dance music for fund-raisers and recruiting events. An advertisement from April 1919 shows the elaborate decorations typical of the largest events. Many charity dances were held around Easter, a time of year for nice weather and new clothing fashions. In the event advertised here, held by Kansas City's African American Knights Templar group with help from their female counterparts, the Ladies of the Heroines of the Crusader Guilds, dancing to an unstated jazz group and the awarding of prizes were the main attractions.

Also by 1920, the B. B. and D. trio began to work regularly with these groups, and their leader, Bennie Moten, started to parlay his connections among the black elite into expanding his own enterprise. Many of these dances were held at the Labor Temple, a community institution that was a meeting place for many of the city's labor unions, both black and white. As a member of the International Hod Carriers and Building Laborers' Union, and frequently in attendance at the temple's dances, Fred Hicks was quite familiar with the building. He recalled that the first floor was divided into rooms for union meetings, and that the "dance hall was kind of upstairs. . . . It wasn't too large but it was large enough to give a dance . . . all night dances. You'd like to go there about 12 o'clock, dance till about 5 in the morning. That's where the people went. *That* was a dancing hall [audible emphasis]."[14]

Advertisements in *The Call* indicate that by 1922, bands led by Bennie Moten were a regular feature at the Labor Temple. These dances were Moten's first performances for the elite class, who expected a different type of music than that of the brothel or gambling den. Moten's drummer Dude Langford recalled that dance lessons were announced in the window of the Labor Temple, and were featured during a night's entertainment.[15] Such an event was advertised in *The Call* in 1922, which stated, "All the latest dances [will be] introduced and featured. Special entertainment for those who do not dance. Profs. Buckner and Beach, floor managers."[16] In September 1922, a new dancing club was introduced in an advertisement with a caveat aimed at a specific, exclusive membership: "Opening Dance at the Labor Temple under the auspices of the New Way Dancing Club. Plenty of Soda Pop and good old punch. Note: We wish the patronage of respectable people only."[17] In February 1922, the African American order of the Knights of Pythias gave "A Grand Ball" featuring the "B. B. and B. Orchestra," with a 35 cent admission charge.[18] The orchestra also performed for the African American Elks annual "Priest of Pallas" Charity Ball at the Labor Temple, in both 1922 and 1923, by which time the group had received the title of the "Elks Official Orchestra."[19] And in October there was a "Halloween Dance" benefit for the Niles Home for Colored Orphans, held at Shriner's Hall in Kansas City, Kansas.[20]

As its popularity among black Kansas Citians rose in the early 1920s, the Bennie Moten Orchestra had its first opportunity to record. Most of the black Kansas City bands did not record, or only recorded a few songs, but the Moten Orchestra left a recorded legacy of 106 sides. From 1923 to 1932 the band recorded about every eight to twelve months, enabling scholars to chart its musical growth as its importance to the community grew, as its reputation spread, and as its fortunes waxed and waned. Although a comprehensive discussion of all of the Moten recordings is beyond the scope of this chapter, a comparison of an early Moten recording with one done several years later reveals the musical growth of the band and the influence that the musical tastes of the Kansas City audience had on the band's stylistic development.

In the autumn of 1923 the Moten Orchestra made its first recordings for Okeh Records. The event was announced in *The Call* on the first page, with a photo of

Bennie Moten's Victor Recording Orchestra, 1927. Courtesy of the Kansas City Museum and Charles Goodwin.

the band and an article detailing the titles of the recordings. At this point they were a six-piece ensemble, and the photo shows the band with record store owner/promoter Winston Holmes seated at center, and the two singers, Mary Bradford on the left and Ada Brown on the right, who were added for this first session:

> Bennie Moten's Kansas City Orchestra . . . is the first Kansas City organization to go away and make phonograph records. Three records made by them in the Chicago recording laboratories of the Okeh Company have already been released. They contain the following selections: "Selma Bama Blues," "Chattanooga Blues," "Break 'O Day Blues," "Evil Mama Blues," "Elephant's Wobble," and "Crawdad Blues." Next month the company will release the "Waco Texas Blues" and "Ill-Natured Blues." January records will be made by the orchestra in Chicago in December.[21]

The discovery by Okeh Records of the Bennie Moten Orchestra in 1923 was instigated by Kansas City businessman Winston Holmes. Holmes had a shop at the corner of Eighteenth and Highland, where he sold "race records," phonographs, and radios. He also had recording equipment and in 1925 formed his own label, the Merritt Recording Company, which specialized in blues singers and sermons by African American preachers. However, in 1923, the Moten Orchestra was a primary concern for Holmes, as *The Call* article concludes: "The management of the trip to Chicago and the recordings of the orchestra was under the direction of Winston Holmes, of the Winston Holmes Music company. . . . It was Mr. Holmes's original idea to have Kansas City talent record for the Okeh Company and it was solely through his efforts that negotiations were successfully completed for the trip."

The 1923 recording sessions produced eight sides, which show the influence of the two most popular styles of black vernacular music of the early 1920s. Two tunes, "Elephant's Wobble" and "Crawdad Blues," were instrumentals in a 2/4, "Dixieland" feel, akin to the collective improvisation of the New Orleans bands. Six sides were vocals for female blues singers. For their 1923 recording sessions Winston Holmes and the Moten Orchestra tapped into the popularity of the New Orleans musicians, who had recently migrated to other parts of the country, especially Chicago, and of the black female blues singers whose sudden popularity among African American record buyers was then changing the recording industry. Before 1920 the industry paid little attention to black artists, but in that year the surprising sales of Mamie Smith's "Crazy Blues" revealed to producers and executives that the new migrants to the urban North now had buying power. Indeed, throughout the early 1920s advertisements for recordings by Mamie Smith, Bessie Smith, and other blues singers can be found in *The Call*. Witnessing this, Winston Holmes connected the Moten Orchestra with singers Ada Brown and Mary Bradford and made the arrangements with Okeh for the first sessions.[22]

"Elephant's Wobble" is not exactly an exhibition of virtuosity, but it does reveal the youthful exuberance of the musicians and their audience. It is an instrumental, a series of 12-bar blues choruses beginning with collective improvisation in the New Orleans "Dixieland" fashion, followed by solo choruses for trombone, cornet, clarinet, and banjo. The outstanding soloist is the teenage cornetist Lamar Wright, whose rhythmic attack and melodic sense clearly emulate the master of Dixieland cornet, bandleader King Oliver. Another featured soloist is clarinetist Woodie Walder and his unique method of blowing his mouthpiece into a glass to create "novelty" squeaks, similar to those of Larry Shields in the Original Dixieland Jass Band, which had been recording since 1917. The 1923 Moten Orchestra recording is representative of the music popular with audiences at the various charity events frequented by Kansas City's African American upper and middle classes.

By the mid-1920s, formal dancing was one of the most popular forms of entertainment in black Kansas City and was also a means to raise money for charitable causes. In 1924 Bennie Moten began to lease the Paseo Hall, located at Fifteenth and Paseo, and opened it up to African American audiences. According to Fred Hicks, who attended many dances there, the Paseo Hall catered to the "elites," and one had to dress appropriately. There was a big crystal chandelier, and absolutely no vice, including alcohol consumption, was tolerated.[23] The men's lodges were active in sponsoring dances at the Paseo Hall, and many were quite elaborate. The

Elks were particularly active in using dance events to raise money and awareness. For the dance held in 1928, in support of a contingent they were about to send to a convention in Chicago, the Elks hired Chauncey Downs and His Rinky Dinks, as the Moten Orchestra was on tour. In addition to the Kansas City Elks, other lodges from towns in the region were also in attendance, bringing with them their own marching bands. And the marching parade, taking place before the dance, was done in a darkened Paseo Hall, with flashlights.[24]

One of the most elaborate charity events at this time was held the week of December 6, 1926, Monday through Friday, at the Lincoln Hall on Eighteenth and Vine. Sponsored by the black Masonic Lodge, this affair featured different types of entertainment each night. Monday was "Masonic and Suburban Night," Tuesday was a "Masked Mardi Gras," Wednesday was "Civic Night," Thursday was "All Fraternal Night," and on Friday prizes were awarded, including a "ton of free coal." The event featured most of the popular bands in the city, including those of George E. Lee and Maceo Birch, and Cooper's Military Band, in addition to the Moten Orchestra.[25]

In addition to the men's lodges, there were other types of African American social clubs formed by members of the upper class. Some of the most prominent clubs held regular dances, especially for fund-raising, which employed the Moten Orchestra or other jazz ensembles. These clubs and their activities were prominently featured in the pages of *The Call* throughout the 1920s and 1930s, for, as Gatewood writes, "The black press rarely had difficulty in placing clubs and societies on the proper rung of the social ladder and was quick to identify those at the top."[26] In particular, the announcements for benefit dances sponsored by the men's San Souci Club, the Beau Brummels, and the Cheerio Boys, and the women's Forget-Me-Not Girls, and the Nit Wit Club indicate that they were an important component of the entertainment life in black Kansas City during the 1920s.

The dances sponsored by these clubs were often charity benefits and, in the case of the Beau Brummels and the San Souci Club, annual events. They typically had elaborate themes and other types of entertainment besides music. In 1925, a "Vaudeville Review, Carnival [and] Dance," was given by the Beau Brummels and featured the Moten Orchestra, performing for the benefit of the Niles Home for Colored Orphans.[27] A 1928 show held at Paseo Hall combined dancing to the music of Chauncey Downs with a circus theme, for the benefit of a girl's home and an orphanage.[28]

Roy Wilkins called Kansas City's African American women's auxiliaries "brave little outposts of middle-class normalcy in a hostile white world."[29] In addition to having luncheons, teas, and card games, the women's groups also sponsored charity dances that employed the city's black dance orchestras. There were several dozen such groups that were organized by the City Federation of Clubs.[30] Some of the wives of jazz musicians were involved in these clubs; for instance, the wife of the Moten trombonist Thamon Hayes was a member of the Forget-Me-Not Girls.[31]

Six members of the Chauncey Downs Orchestra, date unknown. Courtesy of the Black Archives of Mid-America, Kansas City, Missouri.

The women's auxiliaries raised money for several charitable causes that benefited the black community, and one of their favorite fund-raising techniques was to sponsor a dance. Wheatley-Provident Hospital, located at Eighteenth and Forest, was often the beneficiary of charity dances. The hospital was not only a provider of health care but also played an important role in shaping the community's identity as the leading private hospital for black patients, staffed by black doctors and nurses. Thus, much planning went into making the Wheatley-Provident benefit dances elaborate, with special decorations for the hall and unique themes.[32]

Each spring, beginning in 1918, a fashion show was organized by a women's group in support of Wheatley-Provident Hospital. In 1920, it was held at the Labor Temple, with dancing featured after the show. The event raised $606, and the organizing auxiliary "wished to thank every citizen of Kansas City for helping to make this a record-breaker. Each lady of the Auxiliary put forth every effort to make the Fashion Show a success, and they feel proud of their effort." The president of the auxiliary was Effie Watkins, wife and sister-in-law of John T. and T. B. Watkins, black Kansas City's most successful funeral directors.[33]

The fashion shows continued into the 1930s and became more elaborate each year. The advertisement for the 1928 event showcased parades, men's fashions, and revues, followed by dancing to the Rinky Dinks. By 1930 the show drew "slightly more than 5,000 persons." Its theme was "Fashions in a Garden," and it boasted a fashion show, a circus, and a concluding dance with music by the Moten Orchestra. There were 137 models in the fashion show; 24 ballet, 10 soft shoe, and 25 toe dancers at the dance; and a snake charmer, tightrope walker, and bearded lady for the circus. The event was held at the Convention Hall, and admission was 50 cents.[34] And two months later, the Council of Men's Clubs sponsored another dance benefit for Wheatley-Provident, with four orchestras, including Bennie Moten's, providing the music.[35]

The fashion show was just one event of several dozen benefit dances that were sponsored each fall and spring. For example, in March 1925, the Moten Orchestra played a benefit for the Douglass Hospital and Orphan Children's Home of Kansas City, Kansas, sponsored by the Parliamentary and Culture Clubs.[36] They played a Barn Dance sponsored by the Harmony Literary Art Club at the Labor Temple in April.[37] Later that month the orchestra performed at an important event, a Charleston Wedding, given by the Twelve Charity Girls.[38]

The sorority Delta Sigma Theta, whose members were students at Lincoln University, also held events featuring jazz that benefited Wheatley-Provident. Lincoln, Missouri's historically black college located in Jefferson City, was a source of pride for African Americans throughout the state. The Call regularly featured stories on the matriculation of local students and ran editorials that discussed the university as a key part of racial uplift. One such editorial stated, Lincoln University "has caught the spirit of constructive change, and hold fast to what is good, they have wrought a wonderful improvement. With rare good judgment they have inspired the faculty so it is harnessed up to the bigger vision."[39]

An event organized in April 1926 was characteristic of Delta Sigma Theta's charity events. The sorority held a "carnival night" at the Labor Temple, featuring a dance accompanied by the Bennie Moten Orchestra. Advertising the event as "Restful, jolly, artistic, and beautiful," the women announced that "Bennie Moten's orchestra will tempt you to trip it lightly on your toes if you enjoy that form of recreation, or should you prefer to sit quietly enjoying the refreshments and graceful performances offered in the special features." There were elaborate table decorations and waitresses "eager to make your evening the best ever." Proceeds went to Wheatley-Provident.[40]

By the early 1920s the NAACP had become an important part of political expression in Kansas City's black community, and the group's meetings and rallies featured music by local bands. An editorial in The Call illustrates that the organization was seen as a powerful advocate in the fight to end racial discrimination, and it exhorted its readers to become involved:

> Except one hold himself cheaply, he will join the NAACP. It is less for the
> dollar membership fee, than for the force that each person gives the cause, that

all should join in the coming membership drive . . . it is because the NAACP has the desire to better the condition of the Negro in America, and because it has won some considerable successes, that the membership of us all in it is vital.[41]

In addition to the political meetings, the city's NAACP also sponsored musical events that raised money for the organization's national fund. One such affair, which occurred in 1931, was a "Cabaret Minstrel," a kind of variety show in which "one hundred or more people . . . entertained with pop songs and light classics." Some participants apparently wore minstrel cork and performed skits. These were not professional entertainers—there were no jazz musicians among them, but the performers instead were citizens affiliated with the organization, who for the most part came from the middle and upper classes of society.[42]

As jazz and dancing became more popular in the late 1920s, the local branch of the NAACP hired the city's jazz bands to play benefit dances. An advertisement for one such event, held at the Paseo Hall in 1927, announces a "Greenwich Village Dance" in solidarity with the authors and musicians of the Harlem Renaissance. There was also a costume element to the dance, as a rhyme in the advertisement indicates:

> Fifty cents only, a reasonable fee,
> Good 'cause you will be helping the NAACP.
> Everybody come, whate'er your size,
> The best costume there brings a grand prize.[43]

Another political group that used dances to organize and attract members was the Universal Negro Improvement Association (UNIA), the black nationalist group formed by Marcus Garvey. Garvey believed in racial unity, pride, and complete autonomy, and his activities, including marches and demonstrations, were well-chronicled in The Call during the 1920s. Indeed, pictures of Garveyite demonstrations and calls to action appeared frequently on the front page of the newspaper as a dramatic enticement to purchase the issue. In addition, one of the most prominent supporters of the Garvey movement in Kansas City was Winston Holmes, the music store owner and early promoter of the Bennie Moten Orchestra.[44]

A 1928 advertisement announced a meeting held by the Kansas City division of the UNIA at Lincoln Hall. Speaker W. A. Wallace was a former businessman and current state commissioner in Illinois. Oscar De Priest, also from Illinois, was waging what would be a successful campaign to become the first African American to be elected to Congress in the twentieth century. Two hours of speeches on behalf of the UNIA concluded with dancing to the Rinky Dinks.[45]

During the mid- to late 1920s, the Moten Orchestra continued to grow and to develop stylistically. Its final recording session was in December 1932. These sides are stylistically very different from those of 1923. By that time, the band had been established as Kansas City's premier black ensemble for several years. The orchestra could and did play refined dance music, featuring medium-tempo foxtrot rhythms and full arrangements, and by 1926 it was performing for white audiences and dance halls, as well as those in black communities. The band had grown from six pieces to fourteen, including the important additions of Walter Page, whose mastery of the upright bass transformed the rhythm section; Eddie Durham, a trombonist whose arrangements led to an expansion from three- to four-part harmony; and pianist Count Basie, who also served as an innovative arranger for the band. But the Bennie Moten Orchestra's final recording session revealed new and exciting musical developments that foreshadowed the faster, more virtuosic dancing of the swing era.

In the late 1920s the Moten Orchestra made several trips to the East Coast, where the members were introduced to the Lindy Hop dance, which featured faster rhythms and more improvisation for the musicians and dancers alike. The band's late style is revealed in the 1932 tune "Toby." Like several other sides from this recording session, it is very fast, influenced by the Lindy Hop and the swinging abilities of bassist Walter Page. The plodding 2/4 rhythm of Dixieland has been replaced by the lighter 4/4 feel of the newer dances. Unlike the 12-bar blues sides of the 1923 sessions, "Toby" and most of the other tunes on this session follow the 32-bar AABA popular song structure. The arrangement is much more sophisticated than anything on the 1923 sessions. "Toby" opens with a chorus for harmonized reeds, with a guitar solo by Durham on the bridge. Then follow solo choruses for trumpet and tenor sax, which are accompanied by harmonized reeds. The last choruses are interchanges of brief motives or "riffs" between harmonized brass and reeds, with solos for alto sax and trumpet on the bridge, which foreshadows the signature riffing technique of the later Count Basie Orchestra.

Dancing to African American orchestras reached a summit of popularity in Kansas City among both white and black audiences from the autumn of 1929 to the spring of 1932. During this period, there were always at least five or six bands working in the immediate vicinity. Because of fiscal corruption within city government and the approval of several municipal bonds for massive construction projects, the Great Depression did not hit white Kansas Citians as hard as their black counterparts until the mid-1930s.[46] Bandleader Andy Kirk recalled, upon his return from a tour in the autumn of 1931, that "there was no Depression. The town was jumping!"

Kirk likely was not referring to the dances held by the black elite.[47] Despite his remembrances, Kansas City's African Americans did lose much in the early 1930s. Local bands struggled, and a few, like the Moten Orchestra, disbanded. Two editorials from The Call paint a picture of declining fortune. The first, from January 1932, seems almost optimistic, as if the Depression were a learning opportunity:

The year 1932 will be better for everybody than 1931. It could hardly be worse.
. . . Just because it was possible for a day laborer to buy silk shirts at $10 in the
high price era that followed the World War, and because investments measured
in dollars were shooting skyward two years ago, we forgot that those were not
the normal conditions. . . . The net result of these demands and conditions is
a wiser use of money, which is another way of saying we will come out of the
Depression better off.[48]

The second editorial, from the following year, begins with unemployment figures
that, if true, were certainly bleak, and follows with determination in the face of
adversity:

What if ten or twenty or thirty per cent of us are not working? The rest, the
great majority, are. They are not only working, but they are demonstrating that
ability which has always characterized Negroes—they are keeping fat on what
would mean deprivation if they were not the world's best managers. Black-eyed
peas do not sound so aristocratic as mushrooms, but they are mighty filling![49]

In addition to the economic impact of the Depression, the elite dances were also
affected by changing musical tastes and the growing power of politicians and underworld figures over nightlife in the black neighborhoods. Beginning in the early
1930s in Kansas City, there was a transition in dance halls from the semiformal
ballroom style venues toward nightclubs, which offered floor shows in addition to
dancing. During the late 1920s, nightclubs, often sponsored by underworld figures,
had become very popular among white audiences. The Cotton Club in Harlem and
the Pekin Cafe in Chicago were two of the most famous examples. In Kansas City
in the late 1920s and early 1930s, the white El Torreon, the black Cherry Blossom,
and eventually the segregated Reno Club were established in imitation of nightclubs in other cities. Even Paseo Hall was transformed into such a venue.[50]

The economic decline of the African American community impacted charitable
giving and the benefit dances, and increased corruption and vice found a place in
the nightclubs. As Ronald Morris discovered, the big-city nightclubs in Chicago,
New York, and Kansas City attained prosperity as the power of their gangster owners grew.[51] Much to the dismay of at least some African Americans, many of the
nightclubs were placed in their own community, and some members of the community were in collusion with the criminal element, as a *Call* editorial stated:

Because Negroes have the least financial and political weight, ties between the
police and the racketeers endanger us most of all. . . . Our residence district . . .
suffers the contamination of white vice resorts. In addition, our own racketeers
very naturally bid for protection, and the double burden is too much if the

police are more interested in getting money than in safeguarding the public. The good citizen who has only his vote with which to win the attention of public officials . . . has been hopelessly displaced by the racketeer with his campaign gifts and herd of followers.[52]

Was the dance culture created by Kansas City's black elite "hopelessly displaced" by the racketeer? Perhaps, as with many newspaper editorials, this statement is a bit overly dramatic, but there is much true here as well. The popular notion of Kansas City jazz is that of the nightclub, the politician, and the gangster, not the charity event. Yet, for much of the 1920s, Kansas City's middle and upper classes were the primary economic supporters of the community's jazz musicians. Their dances provided the bandleaders with steady work and allowed the individual musicians to develop their technique and forge cohesive ensembles. The full story of Kansas City jazz cannot thus be told without acknowledging this contribution.

Notes

1. The connections between jazz and vice in Kansas City were first revealed in Franklin S. Driggs, "Kansas City and the Southwest," in *Jazz: New Perspectives on the History of Jazz by Twelve of the World's Foremost Jazz Critics and Scholars*, ed. Nat Hentoff and Albert J. McCarthy (New York: Holt, Rinehart, and Winston, 1959). Nathan W. Pearson Jr.'s *Goin' to Kansas City* (Champaign-Urbana: University of Illinois Press, 1994) is a trove of valuable interviews in which musicians discuss the gangsters who supported them. And in *Kansas City Jazz*, Franklin Driggs and Chuck Haddix provided a detailed account of the evolution of the music in conjunction with the vice and corruption of the Pendergast machine: Driggs and Haddix, *Kansas City Jazz: From Ragtime to Bebop—A History* (New York: Oxford University Press, 2006).

2. "Elks Big Frontier Days," *Kansas City Sun*, March 13, 1920, 4.

3. US Bureau of the Census, *Statistical Abstracts of the United States* (Washington, DC: Government Printing Office, 1930), 22–23. These statistics concern the city of Kansas City, Missouri, and do not include the surrounding area.

4. Katrina Hazzard-Gordon, *Jookin': The Rise of Social Dance Formations in African-American Culture* (Philadelphia: Temple University Press, 1990), 117.

5. Charles Goodwin, *Kansas City Jazz Oral History Collection*, folder K0012, State Historical Society of Missouri, Kansas City Research Center, Kansas City, Missouri.

6. In addition to profiting from illegal alcohol sales, the Pendergast machine either looked the other way or took kickbacks from the sale of drugs, gambling—including a popular dice game called "coon cans"—and prostitution.

7. "Killing the Graft," *The Call*, January 10, 1930, 6.

8. "Owners Improve Property," *The Call*, July 5, 1929, 6. The writer is referring to a series of bombings that occurred in these neighborhoods in the early 1920s, as the city's black population began its expansion during the Great Migration.

9. Roy Wilkins, *Standing Fast: The Autobiography of Roy Wilkins* (New York: Viking Press, 1982), 77.

10. "M. & O. Hall," *Kansas City Sun,* September 1, 1917, 1. There is no way to know exactly what the writer meant by "jizz," but, in the context of the article, it seems to mean something like "fun," used for its alliterative relationship to "jazz."

11. Willard B. Gatewood, *Aristocrats of Color: The Black Elite, 1880–1920* (Bloomington: Indiana University Press, 1990), 212.

12. E. A. Williams, S. W. Green, and Jos. L. Jones, *History and Manual of the Colored Knights of Pythias* (Nashville: National Baptist Pub. Board, 1917), v.

13. "Elks Annual Charity Ball," *The Call,* December 6, 1929, 7. For more information concerning the role of education among the elites, see Gatewood, *Aristocrats of Color,* 247–271.

14. Fred Hicks, personal interview, May 16, 1996. Mr. Hicks lived in the Eighteenth and Vine neighborhood for the entirety of his ninety-plus years. He worked as a hod carrier and was also the custodian of the building that housed the Musician's Local 627, now the Mutual Musician's Foundation at the corner of Nineteenth and Highland Streets in Kansas City.

15. Pearson, *Goin' to Kansas City,* 123.

16. "Dance Lessons at Labor Temple," *The Call,* January 21, 1922, 4.

17. "Opening Dance at Labor Temple," *The Call,* September 15, 1922, 7.

18. It appears as B. B. and B. Orchestra in the text. "A Grand Ball," *The Call,* February 11, 1922, 4.

19. "Elks 'Priest of Pallas' Ball," *The Call,* October 12, 1923, 7; "Elks Annual Charity Ball Thursday," *The Call,* December 6, 1923, 7.

20. "Halloween Dance," *The Call,* October 26, 1923, 7.

21. "Kansas City's Record-Making Orchestra," *The Call,* November 30, 1923, 1.

22. For more on this session, see Driggs and Haddix, *Kansas City Jazz,* 44–47.

23. Fred Hicks, personal interview.

24. "First Annual Flashlight Ball," *The Call,* March 30, 1928, 5.

25. "Let's Go! Mason Charity Fair," *The Call,* December 3, 1926, 7.

26. Gatewood, *Aristocrats of Color,* 211.

27. "Beau Brummel Vaudeville Review," *The Call,* May 17, 1925, 4.

28. "The Big Tent," *The Call,* April 20, 1928, 4.

29. Wilkins, *Standing Fast,* 77.

30. "City Federation Education Day," *The Call,* February 25, 1927, 3.

31. "Club Notes," *The Call,* January 31, 1930, 5.

32. For more on the health issues of the black community, see Chapter 10 in this volume.

33. "A Fine Report," *Kansas City Sun,* May 1, 1920, 4.

34. "Fashions in a Garden," *The Call,* May 18, 1930, 5.

35. "Benefit Dance," *The Call,* June 13, 1930, 5.

36. "'Spring Fashion Show' by Parliamentary and Culture Clubs," *The Call,* March 27, 1925, 5.

37. "Barn Dance and One Act Musical Show," *The Call,* April 3, 1925, 4.

38. "Charleston Wedding," *The Call*, April 24, 1924, 4.

39. "University Is Half Million Richer Now," *The Call*, April 11, 1922, 1.

40. "Carnival Night at Labor Temple," *Kansas City Advocate*, March 26, 1926, 1.

41. "Joining the NAACP Is Self-Preservation," *The Call*, February 27, 1925, 6.

42. "To Be Part of the NAACP Cabaret Minstrel," *The Call*, January 30, 1931, 3. This event raises many questions. Minstrel shows and black minstrel entertainers were popular among black audiences across the country at the turn of the century, but by the 1930s these types of shows were seen by younger blacks as outdated. Perhaps the organizers of the event, and the leaders of this NAACP chapter, were of an older generation.

43. "Greenwich Village Dance," *The Call*, April 22, 1927, 7.

44. Charles Coulter, *"Take Up the Black Man's Burden": Kansas City's African American Communities, 1865–1939* (Columbia: University of Missouri Press, 2006), 160.

45. "Big Mass Meeting," *The Call*, August 6, 1928, 5.

46. Andrew Theodore Brown, *The Politics of Reform: Kansas City's Municipal Government, 1925–1950* (Kansas City, Mo.: Community Studies, 1958), 26.

47. Andy Kirk, as told to Frank Driggs. "My Story," *Jazz Review* 2 (February 1959): 15.

48. "A Better New Year," *The Call*, January 1, 1932, 12.

49. "Keeping Fat, Thank You!" *The Call*, April 21, 1933, 11.

50. For a discussion of the transformation of Paseo Hall, see Driggs and Haddix, *Kansas City Jazz*, 123–125.

51. Ronald L. Morris, *Wait until Dark: Jazz and the Underworld, 1880–1940* (Bowling Green, Ohio: Bowling Green University Popular Press, 1981), 112.

52. "Killing the Graft," *The Call*, January 10, 1930, 11. Many of the jazz cabarets, even in black neighborhoods, were segregated. For more information concerning the Reno Club, see William Barlow, *Looking Up at Down: The Emergence of Blues Culture* (Philadelphia: Temple University Press, 1989), 242.

CHAPTER THIRTEEN

Radio Pioneers

The Coon-Sanders Nighthawks

Chuck Haddix

When Coon and Sanders start to play,
Those Nighthawk Blues you'll start to sway,
Tune right in on the radio, grab a telegram and say hello.

—Nighthawk Blues

Jazz was born in New Orleans, moved to Chicago in the early 1920s, and then came of age in New York and Kansas City during the 1930s and 1940s. Geographically isolated from the other cradles of jazz, Kansas City bred a distinctive hard-swinging style of jazz, distinguished by driving rhythm sections and a spirited call-and-response interplay between the instrumental soloists and the brass and reed sections.

Under the control of the Pendergast political machine, Kansas City was a wide-open town. During Prohibition, it was business as usual. The clubs never closed. Throughout the Great Depression, musicians from the economically hard-hit southwestern United States moved to Kansas City, where work was plentiful in the clubs and ballrooms scattered across the city from the Missouri River bottoms south to an unincorporated area outside the city limits referred to as "out in the county."

African American musicians who migrated to Kansas City settled in the Eighteenth and Vine Streets area. In the days of segregation, Eighteenth and Vine was the heart and soul of the African American community, a bustling community that provided residents the services and goods denied by downtown business owners. The list of musicians who worked and made their home in Kansas City during this golden age of jazz represents a veritable "Who's Who" of jazz: Count Basie, Mary

Lou Williams, Lester Young, Benny Moten, Walter Page, Jay McShann, Joe Turner, Pete Johnson, Julia Lee, Harlan Leonard, Andy Kirk, and Kansas City's most infamous son, Charlie Parker.

As African American bands playing near Eighteenth and Vine pioneered a new style of jazz, a number of white bands in downtown Kansas City were performing a style of hot jazz modeled after nationally popular white bands. Because of segregation, there was little interaction between white and black jazz musicians, and the separation extended to their union affiliation. White musicians were members of Musicians' Protective Union, Local 34, and their black counterparts belonged to Musicians' Protective Union, Local 627.

Ironically, while Kansas City became widely known for the great African American bands that barnstormed across the country, it was a white dance band, the Coon-Sanders Original Nighthawk Orchestra, that first established Kansas City's national reputation as a jazz center. The Coon-Sanders Nighthawk Orchestra was the most successful and influential of the early white bands to come out of Kansas City. Co-led by drummer Carleton Coon and pianist Joe Sanders, the Nighthawks performed novelty tunes, popular songs, and hot jazz featuring close vocal harmonies, syncopation, instrumental solos, and spread voicing of the three-member saxophone section. During the 1920s, the Nighthawks' popularity eclipsed the bands of Jean Goldkette and Ben Bernie, and rivaled the "King of Jazz," Paul Whiteman.

In 1922, the Nighthawks' late-night radio broadcasts—then a new phenomenon—from Kansas City over WDAF created a national sensation. In 1896, Guglielmo Marconi patented the technology to broadcast radio waves over great distances. Hobbyists picked up the technology and began broadcasting Morse code using wireless telegraphy. By the early 1920s, the technology to broadcast human voice and music using radio waves was widely available. In 1920, KDKA in East Pittsburgh, Pennsylvania, became the first radio station licensed by the government. The new media became a national craze. In January 1922, there were four licensed radio stations operating in the United States. Within a year, that number had leaped to 576.[1]

Located in the "Heart of America," WDAF's signal could be picked up across North America. Thousands of listeners tuned in to the Nighthawk's nightly broadcasts, making Kansas City a beacon of jazz. Throughout their careers, Coon and Sanders continued to pioneer trends in radio broadcasting, including becoming one of the first organized bands to broadcast nationally and the first to establish a radio fan club. Their broadcasts over the NBC network helped usher in the golden age of radio. The Nighthawks' broadcasts were so popular during the 1920s and early 1930s that they became known as the "band that made radio famous."[2]

The Origins of the Nighthawks

A fortuitous encounter launched Coon and Sanders's wildly successful association. They first met in 1918 at the J. W. Jenkins Music store in downtown Kansas City. According to Sanders, he was playing the piano and humming softly while auditioning some new sheet music when "I suddenly heard a voice join me. A lovely tenor quality proved to be possessed by Carleton A. Coon. . . . We met and Coon said he would try to get the union's permission to allow me to play a dance with him and a small band New Year's Eve."[3] Striking up a friendship, Coon and Sanders began performing around town as a vocal duo and with small bands.

Sanders, who had performed as a classical vocalist and pianist for numerous churches and civic events around town since he was a youth, was already highly regarded by Kansas City music fans. Blessed with an ear for a catchy phrase, he also composed popular songs. At the time, Coon was working as a milk inspector while launching his musical career by performing with vocal groups for social events and fund-raisers on the Kansas side of the metropolitan area. Although just two years older than Sanders and less accomplished musically, Coon assumed the role of senior partner.

On October 3, 1918, Coon and Sanders entertained a crowd of 13,000 attending a war bond rally led by former president Theodore Roosevelt at Convention Hall. They performed "Kick In," a song composed by Sanders for the campaign. The *Kansas City Star* reported, "Joseph L. Saunders [sic] and Carleton Coon entertained the waiting audience with singing patriotic songs, including 'Kick In,' one of the fourth [sic] Liberty Loan songs. The lilt of the tune and parts of the words were learned by the crowd, all joining in to help make the hall resound to the song of encouragement to 'Buy! Buy! Buy!'"[4] Following the sing-along led by Coon and Sanders, Roosevelt bounded on stage to address the roaring crowd and became the first of a string of luminaries whom Coon and Sanders would rub shoulders with during their careers. Shortly after the war bond rally, Sanders was drafted, ending his initial association with Coon.

After the war, Coon and Sanders reunited and formed a band that became one of the most popular dance bands of the 1920s. Their lives and music personified the exuberance and excesses of America during the Jazz Age. As a time of great social, cultural, and technological change, the Jazz Age ushered in the modern era. New media, including movies, radio, magazines, and records, created a popular culture shared by rural and metropolitan areas alike. The popularity of movies and stars of the silver screen, such as Jean Harlow (a Kansas City native), brought glamour to everyday life. The Nighthawks' popular radio broadcasts quickly established the band nationally, and sales of their records helped introduce jazz to far-flung audiences. The booming economy, fueled by the rising stock market, brought about shared national prosperity, and the Nighthawks flourished by playing for elite audiences in upscale hotels and ballrooms. The enactment of Prohibition in January 1920 inadvertently created a nation of lawbreakers, and gangsters made fortunes on bootlegging and operating speakeasies. The most notorious of the gangsters, Al Capone, was a big fan of the Nighthawks and lavished $100 tips on the band at the Blackhawk Restaurant in Chicago. When the Nighthawks played the Dells, a nightclub in Morton Grove, Illinois, Coon and Sanders played cards with Capone. Broadcasting from the top of the Hotel New Yorker, the Nighthawks also mingled with stars and celebrities. The proliferation of automobiles made the country mobile to an unprecedented degree, enabling the Nighthawks to tour extensively during summers when city clubs closed down. The ratification of the Nineteenth Amendment in 1920, giving women the right to vote, inspired young women to become liberated from traditional roles. Called "flappers," they shed societal taboos, bobbed their hair, raised their hemlines, and danced the Charleston, Black Bottom, and other dance crazes sweeping the nation. Stylishly dressed young men with slicked-back hair, sporting hip flasks, flocked to nightclubs to hear their favorite bands. The Nighthawks were the top band with college students. Then the Roaring Twenties came to a screeching halt with the advent of the Great Depression, triggered by the crash of the New York Stock Exchange in October 1929.

Like Nick Carraway, F. Scott Fitzgerald's narrator for *The Great Gatsby*, the novel most often associated with the 1920s, Coon and Sanders grew up in the Midwest and then moved to New York, where they enjoyed fame and ultimately experienced tragedy. Carleton Allyn Coon, who was affectionately known as "Coonie," was gregarious and happy-go-lucky. Coon was born in Rochester, Minnesota, on February 5, 1894. His mother abandoned the family when he was a child. In 1898, Coon and his father moved to Lexington, Missouri, a historic Civil War–era town nestled on the bluffs above the Missouri River. His father owned a hotel and sold Allen's Red Tame Cherry, a popular soda fountain syrup. A philanderer, Coon's father insisted that Coon refer to him in public as "uncle."

With little adult supervision, Coon spent considerable time hanging out on the docks on the Missouri River with stevedores and warehouse workers, picking up "bits and snatches of folk music and spirituals from black workers."[5] With their encouragement, Coon began playing bones, which soon led to the drums. Coon also was influenced by the drummers in the military bands at nearby Wentworth Military Academy. Coon would later include a pair of timpani and a wide range of percussion instruments in his drum set. When Coon was a teen, he moved with his father to Kansas City, Kansas, where he attended high school. During the evenings, he learned to entertain while leading the sing-along at the Electric Theater. After graduating from high school, Coon worked as a chief milk inspector for Kansas City, Kansas. He took his job seriously and publicly crusaded to ensure that the milk supply was safe. In his spare time, he learned harmony and melody while performing with vocal quartets for social groups and civic functions.

Jazz musicians Joe Sanders, *left*, and Carleton Coon, c. 1920. Courtesy of the Missouri Valley Special Collections, Kansas City Public Library.

Tall, handsome, and athletic, Joseph LaCeil Sanders was a gifted pianist, composer, and arranger. Sanders was born October 15, 1896, in his grandmother's hotel in Thayer, Kansas. He later mused that it "seems odd that I was born in a country hotel and have spent most of my life living and playing in hotels."[6] The family moved frequently, following the whims of the father, a hard-luck cattleman, land speculator, and oilman. When Sanders was five, his family moved to Belton, Missouri, located southeast of Kansas City, where his parents operated a hotel. A child prodigy, Sanders studied piano and voice. He began his musical career as a boy soprano at the Grand Avenue Methodist Episcopal Church, a prosperous congregation located on Ninth Street in downtown Kansas City. He became celebrated for his vocal range spanning two and a half octaves and his virtuosity at the piano.

In 1913, the Sanders family moved to Kansas City, where Joe attended Westport High School during his senior year. At night, he accompanied female cabaret singers at the Blue Goose Café, a popular nightclub located in the lower level of the Hotel White at Ninth and Wyandotte. At the time, downtown Kansas City sported many cabarets, saloons, taverns, and bars that featured live music, ranging from ragtime to popular songs of the day. Kansas City's other leading cabaret, the Jefferson Café, was in the basement of the Jefferson Hotel, the headquarters for the Democratic political machine headed by "Boss" Tom Pendergast. At the Jefferson, torch singers went from table to table singing mournful songs of love spurned.

Sanders's engagement at the Blue Goose paid in tips, which he split with the vocalists at the end of the evening. His brother Roy marveled at the mound of coins and bills piled up on his younger brother's dresser each morning. Suspecting that Joe had fallen in with the wrong crowd, Roy discovered the truth by following his younger brother to the Blue Goose. On July 25, 1914, the police raided the Blue Goose and the Jefferson Café. The Kansas City Star reported, "About a hundred men and women patrons of the Jefferson and Blue Goose cabaret cafés rode to police headquarters early this morning because neither they nor their hosts, the café managers, had taken seriously the police order that the drinking lid must go on at the closing hour, which is midnight on Saturday night."[7]

After graduating from Westport High School in 1914, Sanders joined the Kansas City Oratorio and Choral Society. In exchange for free voice lessons, he provided piano accompaniment for choir rehearsals. Sanders learned the art of arranging by orchestrating the various voices in the choir. He developed an ear for harmony while performing around town with vocal groups, including the Orpheus Quartet and the Collegians Male Quartet. (Later, Sanders's mastery of harmony and arranging would give the Coon-Sanders Nighthawk Orchestra an edge over other bands.) For the next two years, Sanders toured the United States with several vocal quartets and dramatic troupes.

Sanders was drafted into the army in October 1918, just before the armistice was signed between the Allies and Germany. He was stationed at Camp Bowie near Fort

Coon-Sanders Novelty Orchestra at the Gayety Theatre, Kansas City, Missouri, c. 1920. Joe Sanders is seated at the piano and Carleton Coon by the smaller drum. Courtesy of the Missouri Valley Special Collections, Kansas City Public Library.

Worth, Texas. Shortly after arriving at the base, Sanders participated in an amateur show, delighting his fellow recruits with his ragtime piano and vocals. Impressed by Sanders's talents, the company commander transferred him to Headquarters Company to entertain at the officers' mess. Sanders formed the Missouri Jazz Hounds, a four-piece jazz and ragtime ensemble that entertained officers and local society. The Jazz Hounds were so popular that after the conclusion of the war, the community offered the band long-term engagements, and officers at Camp Bowie delayed discharging band members to keep them in the area.

After Sanders was discharged from the service in early April 1919, he returned to Kansas City and resumed his partnership with Coon. The two formed a dance band and booking agency, known as the Coon-Sanders Novelty Orchestra, that played at country clubs, social events, dance halls, Electric Park and Edison Wonderland at Forty-Seventh and Paseo, and private parties for the city's elite. In early October 1919, the Coon-Sanders Novelty Orchestra opened at the Café Trianon in the Hotel Muehlebach. The twelve-story, 500-room Hotel Muehlebach at the southwest corner of Twelfth and Baltimore Streets had been a popular gathering spot for Kansas City society since it opened in 1915. Café Trianon, which could be reached by stairs leading from the lobby, was modeled after the salon in Marie Antoinette's summer home near Versailles. French gray with ornate relief of gold and ivory accented the café's Louis XVI motif. The band played daily for lunch and dinner dances and the Saturday afternoon Tea Dance. Travelers and Kansas City's social elite crowded the Café Trianon to dance to the Novelty Orchestra. With tight vocal harmonies, entertaining stage antics, and danceable music, the Novelty Orchestra quickly became Kansas City's most popular band.

In September 1920, the band switched to the Plantation Grille, located in the lower level of the hotel and decorated according to a southern antebellum theme. Murals depicting life from the veranda of a southern plantation lined the walls of the grille. In addition to dancing and music, it featured a small ice-skating rink and cooled air. The band played for lunch, dinner, and supper. After-theater crowds flocked to the grille for supper. Taking advantage of their popularity with after-theater audiences, the band began playing matinees at the Doric, Newman, and other grand theaters downtown.

Recordings "for Music Lovers All over the World"

The band's local celebrity led to a recording session in Kansas City for the Columbia label. Kansas City had long been a music publishing center. The number of music stores and publishing houses in downtown Kansas City grew from five in 1871 to twenty-four by 1916. In 1897, the Kansas City Talking Machine Company published "The Letter Edged in Black," a sentimental ballad that sold 300,000 copies nationally. The musicians who worked in the theaters and cabarets spread across downtown created a ready market for sheet music and musical instruments. Music stores also sold records and cylinders along with instruments, accessories, and sheet music. Columbia and other record labels were quick to cash in on the strong market for records in Kansas City and the surrounding area by opening branch offices in downtown Kansas City to facilitate regional sales of records and phonographs.

On March 24, 1921, Edward N. Burns, vice president of Columbia Records, came to Kansas City to personally supervise the Novelty Orchestra's recording session. Burns publicly praised the band in an article published in the *Kansas City Star*, stating, "We plan to make records of the Coon-Sanders Orchestra for music lovers all over the world, because this group of musicians has distinguished itself from all others in this country. . . . In my opinion, it is one of the few really great orchestras in America."[8] The session, held at the local branch office of Columbia Records, was reportedly the first local recording for national distribution by a major label. More than 100 musicians and record dealers gathered around the cutting lathe to witness the historic event. Four songs were recorded, with one novelty selection, "Some Little Bird," issued to modest success. In 1924, Coon and Sanders signed with Victor Records. They went on to become one of Victor's best-selling bands.

Coon and Sanders quickly took advantage of another emerging media that would catapult them to national prominence—radio. The station WDAF, which was licensed to the *Kansas City Star*, signed on in May 1922. WDAF was one of a handful of 500-watt stations stretching from the East Coast to the Midwest. Most of these early high-powered radio stations were licensed to newspapers in major cities. Radio was a new and expensive technology, so newspapers in smaller markets deferred on embracing the new media. Because WDAF was centrally located in Kansas City and had little interference from other radio stations, its broadcast signal could be picked up from Maine to Hawaii and Canada to Mexico when atmospheric conditions were right. Emphasizing radio's reach, the *Kansas City Star* published letters received from listeners in Bermuda, Hawaii, Mexico City, Canada, Nicaragua, and Cuba.

Like other early radio stations, WDAF broadcast civic events, lectures, a cappella vocal renditions of popular standards, band concerts, classical recitals, coverage of sporting events, and other programming intended to culturally elevate and inform listeners. Coon and Sanders, with their on-air antics and danceable music, brought entertainment and hot jazz to the WDAF schedule and airwaves nationally. On September 22, 1922, the Coon-Sanders band made its debut on WDAF as part of a broadcast of the stage show at the Newman Theater. The broadcasts from the Newman became so popular with listeners that WDAF offered Coon and Sanders their own program. On Monday, December 4, 1922, the Coon-Sanders band launched a nightly "midnight radio program" broadcast over WDAF, between 11:45 p.m. and 1 a.m., from the Plantation Grille. The *Nighthawk Frolic*, as the program became known, was the brainchild of Leo Fitzpatrick, the chief announcer and radio editor for WDAF. In the early days of radio, the engineer would shut off the microphone between numbers, so the studio noise would not go out over the air. For the new Coon-Sanders program, however, Fitzpatrick decided to include the atmosphere of the grille to bring the listener into the broadcast. "I got the idea of why not let the public listen to some of the atmosphere," Fitzpatrick recalled:

> The hottest thing in town at that time was the Coon-Sanders Orchestra, playing at the local Newman Theatre and the Hotel Muehlebach. We installed microphones in the hotel, and the next night we were up on the air. . . .
> The listeners had their first taste of transferring a night club into the ether where they heard the chatter of the dancers, the playing of the orchestra and such popular pieces of the day as "Gallagher and Shean," "Runnin' Wild," "Maggie," "Yes Ma'm—Come Upstairs," and others.[9]

During the first broadcast, Fitzpatrick, who became known as the "Merry Old Chief," commented to Coon and Sanders that "nobody will stay up to hear us but a bunch of night hawks [sic]."[10] His off-the-cuff remark sparked an immediate reaction from listeners across the country. During the following week, 5,000 listeners from Canada, Mexico, and thirty-seven states in the United States responded by letter or telegraph that they were indeed Nighthawks.[11] Realizing a good thing, Coon and Sanders changed the name of the band to the Coon-Sanders Nighthawk Orchestra.

The Coon-Sanders Nighthawks created the first radio fan club and issued membership cards, c. 1922–1924. Courtesy of the Missouri Valley Special Collections, Kansas City Public Library.

Sanders composed a new theme song, "Nighthawk Blues," encouraging listeners to "tune right in on the radio, grab a telegram and say hello." They also formed the first radio fan club, the Nighthawk Club, which Coon and Sanders deftly used to promote the band and radio as an entertainment platform. The Nighthawks issued cards and inducted each new member on the air by reading their name and hometown to the ceremonious clank of a cowbell. Listeners across the country phoned in and wired their requests and appreciation. The Western Union and postal telegraph offices rushed the telegrams to the Plantation Grille to be read over the air by Fitzgerald, Coon, and Sanders. During the first year, 37,000 listeners, known as the "Enemies of Sleep," joined the club.[12]

The *Nighthawk Frolic* was reportedly the first regularly scheduled radio program hosted by an organized band to be heard nationally. These pioneering broadcasts intimately connected listeners from across the country as no other media had before. One fan explained, "Between hilarious and roof-rocking numbers, the boys used the mike [microphone] to convey friendly greetings and messages of cheer to hospitalized shut-ins and to loyal correspondents listening on battery-powered sets at points ranging from a lonely Canadian rancher's hut to a ship off the Virginia coast."[13]

A railway hub for the nation, Kansas City had long been a regional destination for commerce and entertainment. The Nighthawk broadcasts established Kansas City as a music mecca for tourists nationally. Responding to the clarion call of the *Nighthawk Frolic*, fans from across the country flocked to Kansas City to experience the music and mirth emanating nightly from the Plantation Grille. The *Kansas City Star* reported:

> National interest in The Star's Nighthawk Club is shown by the assembling in Kansas City lately of many of the club's members from every part of the country. From North, East, South and West they gather in the Plantation grill [sic] of the Hotel Muehlebach each midnight to become acquainted with the Nighthawk entertainers who produce music for the world-wide programs. Friday night probably had the largest delegation of members. More than twenty out-of-town Nighthawks came to the grill solely to hear the program, not through ear receivers, but straight from the musicians' instruments. . . . One member from Saskatchewan, Canada was on his way to New Orleans. He came out of his way to attend the program at the hotel.[14]

The Nighthawks after Kansas City

The band's broadcasts and popularity caught the attention of club and resort owners across the Midwest. In the summer of 1923, the band played an extended engagement in the dance pavilion at the newly opened Springlake Amusement Park in Oklahoma City. In the closing weeks of the band's 1924 season at the Plantation Grille, Jack Huff, the owner of the Lincoln Tavern located just north of Chicago, sent the band a letter offering them a summer engagement. Thinking the letter was a joke, Joe responded in kind. About a week later, Huff visited the grille and made the band an offer in person.

In the summer of 1924, the Nighthawks played a three-month engagement at the Lincoln Tavern, a roadhouse in Morton Grove located twenty miles north of Chicago. When Prohibition was enforced after January 1920, Chicago clubs were increasingly under scrutiny by federal law enforcement agencies. Circumventing the law of the land, a number of roadhouses sprang up in the northern and western suburbs of Chicago, where law enforcement was lax. College students and well-heeled patrons from the Chicago area piled into automobiles and drove to the roadhouses in the surrounding suburbs, where they could drink, gamble, and dance the night away. The roadhouses varied in sophistication from rustic bars where patrons danced to records to spacious resorts that featured floor shows and bands. The Lincoln Tavern and its nearby neighbor, the Dells, were the two biggest resorts in the area.

The Coon-Sanders Nighthawk Band was the first big-name band to play the Lincoln Tavern. A spacious white frame building, the tavern was located a few hundred feet off Dempster Road, the main east-west thoroughfare traversing Morton Grove. A large semicircular parking lot that could accommodate 100 cars greeted visitors. The Tavern boasted two dining rooms, one that measured 250 feet by 75 feet with a polished wood dance floor in the center. The band's nightly broadcasts over KYW, a Chicago station owned by Westinghouse Electric Corporation, attracted fans from across the region.[15]

While at the Lincoln Tavern, the Nighthawks were approached by optometrist Jules Stein, who wanted to start a booking agency but lacked the necessary venture capital. Coon and Sanders agreed to let Stein book a thirty-two-day tour for the Nighthawks, starting on Labor Day of 1924. The tour was a success, and Stein used his profits to found the Music Corporation of America, with the Nighthawks as his first and most important client. Out of gratitude, MCA booked extended summer tours of plum venues and increasingly prestigious engagements for the Nighthawks. With the Nighthawks on MCA's roster, Stein managed to sign other top-shelf bands, and MCA quickly emerged as one of the most prominent booking agencies in the country.

That summer, Jack Huff had introduced Coon and Sanders to H. L. Kauffman, the manager of the stately Congress Hotel in Chicago. Impressed by the band's strong draw at the Lincoln Tavern, Kauffman offered the band an engagement later in the fall at the hotel's cavernous Balloon Room. Located on South Michigan Avenue across from Grant Park, the Congress featured 871 rooms and suites. Like the Hotel Muehlebach in Kansas City, the Congress was a gathering spot for the city's social set.

On opening night, the Nighthawks sold out the Balloon Room at $15 per plate. The band formed a new radio club, the *Insomnia Club*, and broadcast nightly from midnight to 2:30 a.m. over KYW. Its signal, like WDAF's, could be picked up across the country. Management of the Congress capitalized on radio as a new advertising media by installing a studio for KYW on the top floor of the hotel. KYW broadcast from the hotel's three music venues: the Pompeian Room, the Louis XVI Room, and the Balloon Room, billed as the "world's most beautiful supper club." The immensity of the Balloon Room dwarfed the bandstand nestled at one end of the semicircular dance floor. Sanders later marveled how during the opera season the Balloon Room was "ablaze [sic] of color and dazzling jewels."[16] A stream of celebrities stopped by the Balloon Room, including Ignacy Jan Paderewski, Sergei Rachmaninoff, and Tito Schipa.

In the summer of 1925, the band toured from the Midwest to the East Coast, opening new territory for MCA, which was still building its roster of bands. Heading east, the band played a string of engagements, leading to a six-week engagement at Young's Million Dollar Pier in Atlantic City, New Jersey. Extending 1,775 feet into the ocean, Young's multilevel glittering pier boasted the world's largest ballroom. Dancers crowded the ballroom floor to dance the Charleston, a new dance craze sweeping the nation. Al Jolson and other celebrities stopped by nightly to enjoy the music of the already legendary Nighthawks. Sanders spent his afternoons comparing notes with songwriters Irving Berlin, Gus Khan, and Walter Donaldson. After closing out at the Million Dollar Pier, the Nighthawks returned to the Balloon Room for the 1925–1926 season. They resumed broadcasting over KYW and continued attracting record crowds to the Balloon Room. Offers flooded in from clubs across the nation, but the Nighthawks decided to maintain their base in Chicago.

Although the Nighthawks had established Chicago as their new headquarters, they remained associated with Kansas City. Magazine articles about the Nighthawks often touted the band's legendary broadcasts from Kansas City. Coon maintained a home for his family there, and he and Sanders often returned during breaks in their busy schedule. Kansas City fans lamented losing the Nighthawks to Chicago but continued following the band's broadcasts. For their part, Chicago fans proudly adopted the Nighthawks, who emerged as the city's favorite band. Trombonist Rex Downing proudly recalled the Nighthawks as "the number one band in Chicago as far as the dancing public was concerned and as far as the young were concerned, we were number one straight across the country."[17]

During the previous year, MCA had expanded its network of theaters, nightclubs, ballrooms, and roadhouses, creating new territory for Coon-Sanders and other bands in their roster. In the summer of 1926, the Nighthawks traveled 18,198 miles by railroad and car, playing one-night stands across the Midwest and East Coast. Also over the summer, Sanders negotiated with the Congress Hotel for a return engagement for the 1926–1927 season. Having played two successful seasons at the Balloon Room, Sanders felt the band deserved a raise. Negotiations fell through when H. L. Kauffman told Sanders that since playing the Balloon Room had "made the band," they should play for the same money. Sanders declined Kauffman's counteroffer, and with the help of MCA, switched the Nighthawks to the Blackhawk Restaurant, located in the Chicago Loop at the corner of Wabash and Randolph.

Well-known for its good food, the Blackhawk also featured music on special occasions. Jules Stein, Karl Kramer, and other MCA employees often had lunch at the Blackhawk, which was located a block and a half from MCA's offices. Kramer became friendly with Otto Roth, the owner of the Blackhawk, and convinced him to book the Nighthawks for the season. Roth agreed and remodeled the restaurant to accommodate the band.

In September 1926, the Nighthawks opened at the Blackhawk Restaurant. The band broadcast nightly from the Blackhawk over WBBM. On Wednesday, Saturday, and Sunday, the Nighthawks were featured on a late-night program, the *Nutty Club*. The *Evening Independent*, a St. Petersburg, Florida, newspaper, reported:

Two of the best known sleep eliminators in the country have joined hands. One is the Nutty Club of WBBM, the Stewart-Warner Air Theater, known coast to coast for its "Cuckoo Signal," and the other is an orchestra that has made insomnia a famous indoor sport—Coon-Sanders Original Nighthawk Kansas City Orchestra. Under an arrangement just completed this orchestra is to broadcast exclusively over WBBM by remote control from the Blackhawk Grill, Chicago.[18]

For the next four years, the Nighthawks maintained their home base at the Blackhawk.

During the summers, the Nighthawks played at the Dells, a roadhouse across the street from the Lincoln Tavern. According to Rex Stout's wife, Florence Stout, "they had a machine gun on the roof and 2 'hoods' patrolling the grounds."[19] The band was so celebrated that during their opening night 1,200 cars were turned away. During breaks the band played cards with Al Capone, their biggest fan and local protector. Hailing from Kansas City, the home of "Boss" Tom Pendergast, they were perfectly at home sitting down for a friendly game of cards with one of the most notorious gangsters of the 1920s. When Coon was robbed of his treasured watch and diamond-studded pinky ring, Capone's henchmen located the culprits and returned the purloined jewelry with a note of apology from Capone, declaring the culprits had been "taken care of."[20]

During a 1927 winter tour of the Midwest, the Nighthawks returned to Kansas City for the grand opening of El Torreon ballroom. With the advent of the Jazz Age, the nation had become dance crazy, creating a demand for dance halls and ballrooms. Throughout the 1920s, grand ballrooms opened across the country: New York's Roseland Ballroom opened in 1919, the Graystone Ballroom in Detroit opened its doors in 1922, and Chicago's palatial Aragon Ballroom made its debut in 1926.

During the winter of 1927, in Kansas City, the Pla-Mor and El Torreon ballrooms opened within a month of each other. The Pla-Mor, known as the "Million Dollar Ballroom," opened on Thanksgiving evening 1927. The wildly popular Jean Goldkette Orchestra presided over opening night festivities. Located at Linwood and Main Streets, the Pla-Mor featured an indoor ice hockey rink, a bowling alley on the ground floor, and a spacious ballroom upstairs. The ballroom's spring-loaded dance floor could accommodate 3,000 dancers. On December 15, 1927, El Torreon Ballroom opened at Thirty-First Street and Gillham Road, a few blocks east of the Pla-Mor. El Torreon sported a Spanish Mission motif with arched doorways and a vaulted ceiling. An enormous crystal ball adorned with 100,000 mirrors hung over the dance floor, which could accommodate 2,000 dancers. A balcony surrounded the dance floor on three sides.

After closing out at the Chase Hotel in St. Louis, the Nighthawks drove to Kansas City two weeks ahead of opening night at El Torreon. The next day, they hauled their bags to Union Station for the celebration of their "official" arrival. They were met in the vast marble lobby of Union Station by a bevy of local officials, who gave them the key to the city, and a huge crowd of fans. Band members then piled into new Fords for a motorcar parade that snaked through downtown to the Pantages Theater at Twelfth and McGee Streets, where they played a weeklong engagement.

The next week, the Nighthawks opened at El Torreon on a double bill with the El Torreon Orchestra, directed by Phil Baxter. The orchestra opened the night's festivities with "El Torreon," a new theme song composed for the new ballroom by Phil Baxter. That night, the 3,000 dancers and onlookers that crowded El Torreon gave Baxter and the El Torreon Orchestra a warm welcome, and then went wild and surged forward when the Nighthawks hit the stage. After closing out the weeklong engagement at El Torreon, the Nighthawks stayed in Kansas City through Christmas, celebrating with relatives and friends. Oddly, years later, Sanders recalled the shows at the Pantages and El Torreon as "the biggest flop we ever took." He went on to complain bitterly that "strangers always appreciate us more than the old home-towners" and "too much was expected of us." The Nighthawks sporadically visited Kansas City afterward, but never played their hometown again.

After wrapping up their winter tour in Kansas City, the Nighthawks returned to the Blackhawk Restaurant in Chicago. In 1928, the Nighthawks switched from WBBM to WGN, which was licensed to the *Chicago Tribune* in an arrangement similar to WDAF's licensing to the *Kansas City Star*. WGN's call letters were drawn from the *Tribune*'s claim to be the World's Greatest Newspaper. Listeners coast-to-coast tuned into the band's nightly remotes from the stage of the Blackhawk. On Saturday nights, the band was featured on the program *Knights and Ladies of the Bath*, so named because in those days most people bathed once a week—on Saturday night. Western Union and postal telegraph machines were installed on stage, and so many requests and dedications came in that by the end of each broadcast the stage was covered by a blizzard of paper.

The popularity of the Nighthawks' broadcasts from the Blackhawk attracted the attention of several corporations, including Florsheim Shoes. Seeking to cash in on the popularity of radio, corporations began sponsoring shows on radio stations and newly formed radio networks. In early 1930, the Nighthawks launched their first network program, the *Florsheim Shoe Frolic*, broadcast Tuesday nights from the National Broadcasting Company (NBC) studios on Michigan Avenue.

Florsheim promoted the *Shoe Frolic* with full-page advertisements in magazines and trade publications nationally. The ads prominently touted the popularity of Coon and Sanders:

Florsheim, seeking the best in entertainment, selected the Coon Sanders
Dance Orchestra because of its tremendous popular appeal, and because
Carleton Coon and Joe Sanders are two outstanding radio personalities. Both

Coon and Sanders are possessed of such irresistible personalities and have such a knack of instilling their enthusiasm into their radio appearances that they are distinctive among orchestra leaders on the air. Their playing of popular songs, played according to their own transcriptions, are always in dance tempo and have such an individuality that they are instantly recognized by radio listeners. Both Coon and Sanders sing each in his own inimitable way, and Sanders has composed many famous song successes. Florsheim presents this famous dance band for the first time on a nation-wide broadcast.[21]

Although Coon and Sanders had been broadcasting nationally over radio stations that could be picked up nationally, like WDAF, the *Shoe Frolic* was their first program broadcast over a network. Networks were a fairly new development in radio. NBC was established in 1926, followed by the Columbia Broadcasting System (CBS) in 1928.[22] At the time, most stations were independent and not affiliated with a network. NBC and CBS scrambled to expand their networks by adding new affiliates. As a network affiliate, stations received programming generated by other stations and the network. This expansion of the networks created a demand for programming for the networks to distribute to member stations. Coon and Sanders were more than happy to contribute to that effort. For two seasons, the Nighthawks hosted the *Florsheim Shoe Frolic*, broadcast by stations across the nation over the NBC network.

The Great Depression that followed the stock market crash of 1929 devastated the entertainment industry. Record sales plummeted from a record high of 104 million in 1927 to 6 million in 1932. During the same time, production of phonographs dropped from 987,000 to 40,000.[23] While sales of records and phonographs floundered, the radio industry boomed. Destitute families would sell everything but their radios, which kept them entertained and connected to the world. Clubs and ballrooms across the country closed, and theaters cut back on entertainment, leaving many leading bands struggling. Due to Coon and Sanders's popularity on radio, however, the Nighthawks managed to continue recording and move up to more prestigious engagements, even during the depths of the Great Depression.

In 1931, MCA arranged an eleven-month engagement for the band at the New Yorker Hotel's Terrace Room. Located across from Pennsylvania Station, the forty-three-story, 2,500-room hotel dominated New York's skyline. Art deco flourishes highlighted the tiered setbacks on the top floors. According to Sanders, "Our opening on Wednesday night, October 7, was the most sensational of the year—and one of the most successful little old New York had *ever* seen. Every 'big name' in show business was present."[24]

The Nighthawks broadcast locally over WMCA and nationally over the NBC network. On Saturday nights, the band formed a new radio club, the *Nite Riders*, which was broadcast over WMCR from 12 p.m. to 2 a.m. The band also appeared regularly on the *Lucky Strike Hour*, which was hosted by syndicated newspaper gossip columnist Walter Winchell. Sponsored by Lucky Strike Cigarettes, the program featured a short gossip report by Winchell, guest appearances by stars like Jean Harlow and William S. Hart, and remote broadcasts by bands from across the country. Sanders reported, "The band gained steadily in popularity and we were soon doing the business of the town—we had 'arrived' on Broadway—or, to speak correctly—west of Broadway."[25]

After hours, Coon and Sanders frequented the Cotton Club and other nightclubs in Harlem, making friends with Cab Calloway, Duke Ellington, and other African American bandleaders. Calloway once confessed that Coon and Sanders influenced his vocal style and the Nighthawks were one of his favorite bands. Coon and Calloway formed a mutual admiration society, exchanging Christmas cards. Duke Ellington was also an admirer of the Nighthawks. Years later, Ellington informed Coon's son John that he based his classic "The Mooche" on the theme from the Nighthawks' "The Wail."

Just as the Nighthawks reached the pinnacle of success, though, disharmony between Coon and Sanders and a medical emergency brought the group tumbling down. Coon and Sanders had long been heavy drinkers. Since 1930, Coon's excessive drinking caused him to be unreliable and flub the lyrics of songs he knew well. Sanders grew to resent covering for his old partner. Compounding matters, both men grew to dislike New York and longed to return to Chicago. Sanders's homesickness for the Midwest was reflected in his composition, "I Want to Go Home," which was recorded during the Nighthawks last session for Victor on March 24, 1932. The same weariness that had settled on the country from the Great Depression affected the band.

Sanders and other band members' spirits were briefly elevated by their return to Chicago for an engagement at the College Inn, opening on Friday, April 8, 1932, but their exuberance was short-lived. On April 30, 1932, Coon entered the hospital in critical condition, suffering from blood poisoning from an abscessed tooth. The Coon-Sanders Nighthawk Orchestra essentially died with Carleton Coon on May 4, 1932. Coon's body was returned to Kansas City for burial at Mount Moriah Cemetery. His funeral was one of the biggest that Kansas City had ever witnessed, with a procession that stretched for miles on Holmes Road south of 105th Street. Sanders continued to lead the group as Joe Sanders's Nighthawk Orchestra, but the magic of the Coon-Sanders Original Nighthawk Orchestra was gone. Joe disbanded the group on Easter Sunday in 1933 and relocated to Hollywood for a short time, writing movie scores without much success. In 1934, he formed a new group, Joe Sanders and His Orchestra. Sanders recorded for the Decca label and remained popular in the Midwest, but he never enjoyed the national success he achieved as co-leader of the Nighthawks. In 1953, he disbanded the group and retired to Kansas City, where he died on May 14, 1965.

Notes

1. Thomas Streissguth, *The Roaring Twenties: An Eyewitness History* (New York: Facts on File, 2007), 126.

2. See Fred W. Edmiston, *The Coon-Sanders Nighthawks: "The Band That Made Radio Famous"* (Jefferson, N.C.: McFarland, 2003).

3. Joe Sanders, "The Coon-Sanders Story (Part II)," *Jazz Notes Published by the Indianapolis Jazz Club, Inc.* 6, no. 1 (1961): 3.

4. "T. R. Talks to 13,000," *Kansas City Star*, October 3, 1918, 1.

5. Joe Popper, "America's Band," *Kansas City Star*, July 9, 1989, *Star Magazine*, 10.

6. Joe Sanders, "The Coon-Sanders Story," *Jazz Notes Published by the Indianapolis Jazz Club, Inc.* 6, no. 2 (1961): 2.

7. "Raid the Jefferson Café," *Kansas City Times*, July 26, 1914, 1.

8. "Phonograph Records Made by K.C. Talent," n.d., Joe Sanders Collection, Scrapbook #11, Missouri Valley Special Collections, Kansas City Public Library, Kansas City, Missouri (hereafter MVSC).

9. William James Ryan, "Kansas City Broadcasting: The First 65 Years," 38, unpublished manuscript, William James Ryan Papers, K0457, State Historical Society of Missouri Kansas City Research Center, Kansas City, Missouri.

10. Ibid.

11. "'Nighthawks Defy Sleep," *Kansas City Star*, December 10, 1922, 6B.

12. Popper, "America's Band," 26.

13. Ryan, "Kansas City Broadcasting," 39–40.

14. "Nighthawks Visit Here," *Kansas City Star*, January 7, 1923, 15.

15. Charles A. Sengstock Jr., *That Toddlin' Town: Chicago's White Dance Bands and Orchestras, 1900–1950* (Chicago: University of Illinois Press, 2004), 139.

16. Joe Sanders Collection, Box 4, Scrapbook A, 47, MVSC.

17. Bob Harrington, "Tales of Coon-Sanders," *Mississippi Rag* (April 1991): 12.

18. *Evening Independent*, December 1, 1926, 2.

19. Harrington, "Tales of Coon-Sanders," 11.

20. Ibid., 12.

21. Florsheim Shoe advertisement featuring Coon-Sanders Dance Orchestra, Carleton Coon Collection, Box 1, Folder 10, Dr. Kenneth J. LaBudde Special Collections, University of Missouri–Kansas City, Kansas City, Missouri.

22. Christopher Sterling and John Kittross, *Stay Tuned: A Concise History of American Broadcasting* (Belmont, Calif.: Wodsworth, 1978), 510.

23. Roland Gelatt, *The Fabulous Phonograph* (New York: Collier Books, 1977), 255.

24. Sanders, Scrapbook, 168, MVSC.

25. Ibid., 170, MVSC.

CHAPTER FOURTEEN

Thomas Hart Benton and Kansas City's "Golden Age"

Henry Adams

In 1935 Thomas Hart Benton angrily departed from New York amid a storm of controversy. He announced that he was moving back to Kansas City, in his home state of Missouri, to paint a mural for the State Capitol and to become head of the painting department at the Kansas City Art Institute, a nationally recognized college of art and design. His bigger goal, however, was to create an American Athens in the Midwest. During his time in Kansas City, Benton did in fact complete his now-famous Missouri mural, which he regarded as his masterpiece. He also completed his best-known easel painting, *Persephone*, produced major accomplishments as a writer and musician, and staged a show of his students' work from the Art Institute that won national acclaim. But within a decade he had once again stirred up enough conflict that he was fired from the Kansas City Art Institute and ostracized from the city's upper crust. For Benton, it was an especially painful moment as he could no longer dream of Kansas City as a thriving center of American Regionalist painting—and regionalist culture in general—under his guidance.[1]

The common denominator of Benton's New York and Kansas City activities is that they were intensely controversial. More intriguing, however, is that the attacks against him came from opposite directions. In New York, he was criticized by the leftist crowd, who viewed him as a reactionary; in Kansas City, he was deemed too irreverent, too outspoken, perhaps even too populist by the conservative establishment. Indeed, to view Benton in the context of Kansas City is to discover a new Thomas Hart Benton, one significantly different from the image he projected in New York. What is notable is that during this period, Benton's achievements and missteps both drew upon the peculiarities of Kansas City culture. The period between the wars, arguably the time of the city's greatest cultural influence, was also one filled with curious contrasts, discordances, and contradictions.

Regionalist artist Thomas Hart Benton posing with his painting, *Rape of Persephone*, date unknown. Courtesy of the Missouri Valley Special Collections, Kansas City Public Library.

In the minds of most Americans, Missouri is not often associated with high culture, but if we list the artists and statesmen linked with the region, the accounting is impressive. It is the state that produced perhaps the greatest American novelist, Mark Twain, and most influential American poet, T. S. Eliot. It is home to the composer Scott Joplin, whose introduction of the regularly syncopated beat, an African device, changed the history of American music, as well as the statesman Harry S. Truman, whose presidential legacy has been judged overwhelmingly positive. Two painters of national distinction, George Caleb Bingham and, of course, Thomas Hart Benton, complete this roster of achievement. In fact, during this period, Missouri was a state that more than any other epitomized the cultural tensions of America, as it sought to find a balance between the cultures of North and South, of East and West. Artists such as Benton, who in his work and personal life embodied these tensions, could produce regional art that spoke to the nation as a whole.

In the space of a few decades beginning in the late nineteenth century, Kansas City grew from a frontier "cowtown," with gambling and open prostitution, into a "true" city. By the turn of the century, local visionaries and reformers like William Rockhill Nelson, the owner of the *Kansas City Star*, proposed that the city should have all the accoutrements of civilized locales—parks, fountains, boulevards, and museums—like London, Berlin, and Paris. Although many parts of the community retained a raw frontier flavor, Benton arrived just as the earliest foundations of these cultural refinements were laid.

Despite this increasing cultural maturity, the dichotomies within Missouri politics and society gave life in Kansas City a somewhat schizophrenic quality. One side of Kansas City society was rather prudish and conservative. In fact, the realtor J. C. Nichols, discussed in Chapter 3 in this volume, would drive through the neighborhoods he had developed and send homeowners admonishing notes if their properties did not fit the expected norm. Leaving a garage door open or the lawn untidy was sure to receive a rebuke. Such commitment to uniform expectations also pervaded the city's social scene. Prominent events, such as the Jewel Ball, a debutante pageant still staged annually at the Nelson-Atkins Museum of Art, dictated social hierarchies for the upper-class denizens of the city as rigidly as Ward McAllister had once done for Mrs. Astor in New York City in the days of "The 400." Such convention occasionally took unexpected forms, as this was the exact period when Laurence Sickman, curator of "Oriental" art (as it was referred to at the time) at the Nelson-Atkins Museum of Art and only the second student of Chinese language at Harvard, assembled one of the finest collections of Chinese paintings in the United States. At this same moment, however, many downtown restaurants and nightclubs offered titillating entertainment, prostitution was unregulated, and an often-corrupt political machine dominated city government. Most famously, of course, this was the period when jazz thrived in the nightclubs and dives of the black section of town, and produced "Kansas City jazz"—a distinct category of the jazz art form.

To a remarkable degree, then, Thomas Hart Benton embodied the different extremes of the city itself. It was unclear whether he fit in with the rough manners of the working class or the refined practices of the city's cultural elite. Local businessman George O'Malley vividly illuminated this divide when describing his first meeting with Benton in 1935. O'Malley's mother lived next to the Kansas City Art Institute, and O'Malley was looking for someone to mow the grass. As he recalled:

> I saw these people that looked like they were yard men out just beyond the property line and I thought, well, I'll go over and negotiate a contract for them to cut her grass. . . . So I walked up to what I thought was a strange and unique-looking person. He needed a haircut and he had holes in the sleeves of his tweed coat. So I said, "Are you the new gardener?" and he took off on me. He said, "I am, like hell!" He said, "I'm Thomas Hart Benton, the new head of the painting department at the Art Institute."[2]

This episode marked the beginning of a friendship that lasted for the next forty years, but it also provides a revealing glimpse into how Thomas Hart Benton even in appearance defied the usual social frameworks of Kansas City—or at least cut through them in surprising and fascinating ways. A congressman's son, he grew up with wealth and privilege and mixed easily with powerful men, yet with his unruly haircut, rough dress, and profane demeanor, he could also pass for a workman.

Benton, for his part, reveled in his ability to pass through the fabric that was the American class structure. One of Benton's pupils from Kansas City Art Institute, Ray Ottinger, later reminisced:

> Mr. Benton loved scenes from American life, the more passionate and uniquely American the better. He encouraged his students to seek out those scenes as sources of personal and professional inspiration. I recall three places that he recommended to his students. The first was the Blue Room near 45th and Main. It was full of hard drinking men and women. . . . The second was the Metropolitan Church of God at 13th and Garfield. It was Old Time Religion at its finest. The worshippers wore their Sunday best and the singing was spectacular. . . . The third place . . . was the Folly Theater Burlesque at 12th and Central. I recall one evening there with a group of Benton students . . . [when] a dancer with an extremely enthusiastic smile pranced to center stage, and, as the momentum from her shimmy worked its way up her torso, her false teeth popped out of her mouth. She caught them on the fly and reinserted them without missing a bump or grind. Benton would have loved her.[3]

Yet the same Benton who applauded the burlesque was also close with politicians and diplomats, like his friends Harry Truman and the famed African American

Thomas Hart Benton on KMBC radio with artists John Steuart Curry, Grant Wood, and Reeves Lewenthal of the Associated American Artists, March 5, 1938. *Left to right:* Reeves Lewenthal, Thomas Hart Benton, Neal Gordon Keehn (KMBC interviewer), John Steuart Curry, and Grant Wood. Courtesy of the Thomas Hart Benton Home and Studio State Historic Site, Kansas City, Missouri.

scholar Ralph Bunche. He befriended Norman Thomas, the perennial socialist candidate for president, the architect Frank Lloyd Wright, and the painters Boardman Robinson, John Steuart Curry, and Grant Wood.[4] He also entertained African Americans in his home and welcomed a range of students, models, and artists into his social circle. As such narratives illustrate, Benton's range of acquaintances was large, and he anchored himself to local society in unexpected ways.

In his manners, too, Benton was a man of surprising contrasts. He could be quite profane, and I think this was one of his techniques for bonding with members of the working class. He could set new acquaintances at ease by dispensing with the traditional hallmarks of genteel society, but in proper social settings, he displayed impeccable manners. Another of his Art Institute students, for example, was Margot Peet, the wife of the wealthy soap manufacturer who lived in the city's most prestigious neighborhood, in a huge medieval-style mansion that resembled a set for a Douglas Fairbanks movie. Peet came to Benton because she had a daughter who was very ill, and in an attempt to find some release from the stress of her care, she enrolled in his classes as a kind of therapy. Art became her salvation, and to show thanks for pulling her from despair, she frequently invited Benton to visit the

Peet home and to attend social events she sponsored. Although she was a woman of genteel restraint, Peet's eyes would famously flash at any suggestion that Benton was ever less than a perfect gentleman.

Benton incorporated this duality into the active scene that revolved around his home. The parties at the Benton house were legendary for their unusual collection of guests. For example, the artist Roger Medearis, who arrived in Kansas City as a first-year student at the Art Institute in 1939, later wrote of his experiences at the Benton home:

> Beginning [in 1940] . . . I was in the Benton home with increasing frequency, and came to associate the place with the rich aroma of spaghetti and green salads and red wine and the mellow notes of TP's [Benton's son] flute descending from above. . . . The Saturday night parties, filled with the voices and laughter and clinking glasses of a bizarre assortment of people—intellectuals from the university, possibly a priest, a writer from France, a neighbor, a lawyer, musicians from the Philharmonic, art students, etc. The music varied from hillbilly tunes to Mozart, Bach and Brahms. . . . With a glass of bourbon and water in hand, Tom would tell his stories in language that mixed graceful phrasing with plain Missouri dialect. His talk was punctuated now and then by verbal chuckles and profanity or, once in a while gross vulgarities. . . . Occasionally Rita [Benton's wife] would interrupt to confirm his stories, or add to them in her distinctive Italian–New York accent, cigarette bobbing in her lips as she spoke, wisps of smoke drifting upward. There were also times when she would challenge his facts—or he, hers. He, voice rising, would insist, and she would shout indignant protest, and he would respond in kind, until finally a sort of compromise would be reached. His outrageous vulgarities were always followed as if on cue by Rita's reprimands—enough to make it seem that she was forever surprised by such obscenity. . . . It seemed to me that Tom had the knack of turning everything about him into art. It seemed that whatever might be his current interest—literature, social speculation, travel, music, whatever—it would somehow be reflected in the formation of his art.[5]

The divided nature of Benton's character also extended to the two most prominent citizens of the city—the political boss Tom Pendergast and the visionary developer J. C. Nichols. These men represented the two poles of Kansas City culture, and yet the malleable Benton was able to bridge the space between. The well-known Pendergast political machine had its roots in an Irish saloon located in the working-class West Bottoms section of Kansas City, near the stockyards. Tom Pendergast started from this base and, by the mid-1920s through 1939, had almost complete control of the politics of the city. He did not hold political office himself but rather from a second-floor office in a small yellow-brick building on Main Street after 1927, he maintained his power as chairman of the local Jackson Democratic Club. From 1925 to 1939, Pendergast effectively ruled the city, determining who was elected to office and siphoning off large amounts of public money into his own coffers through a cement company that won nearly all the major government contracts. Around 1936, however, his reign began to unravel, in part because of a conflict with the Republican governor, Lloyd Stark, and in part because of the increasingly flagrant nature of his activities, including extensive gambling debts to a local gangster, John Lazia. In 1939, he was convicted of income tax evasion and sentenced to fifteen months in federal prison.

Benton, the son of a populist Democrat, a social reformer, and a follower of William Jennings Bryan, would appear to have little patience for boss politics. Indeed, in the early twentieth century, Benton flirted with both communism and socialism and voted for the labor leader Eugene Debs. In the 1930s, he morphed into an avid New Dealer and voted the straight Democratic ticket. Given this history, Benton's political allegiances leaned toward the progressives, including the young Democrats dedicated to overthrowing the Pendergast machine. Yet, like many elements of his life, Benton's relationship with the Kansas City machine was complicated. In 1924, when Benton was living in New York, his father developed throat cancer. Despite being estranged from his father for several years, Benton returned to Springfield, Missouri, to be with him. At that same moment, the annual state Democratic Convention in Springfield was in progress, and a steady string of delegates came to the hospital to pay respects to Benton's father. Among these visitors was Tom Pendergast. As Benton recalled:

One day a Kansas City group headed by Tom Pendergast, then in his stalwart prime, came to see the dying man. They were a silent lot going into his room one by one to shake his hand. Pendergast was the last. When he came back into the anteroom he reached a big half-closed fist out to me. When I grasped it I felt a hard object left in my palm. "This is from his friends for any little things he might need," Pendergast said and walked out. The hard object was a tight roll of bills, eight hundred dollars in all.[6]

Benton later conjectured that the ease with which his contract for a mural for the State Capitol building passed through the state legislature was connected to a political debt to his father—now paid off to his son. In a sign of political loyalty, Tom Pendergast also allowed Benton to come to his office on Main Street to make a portrait sketch from life, so that Pendergast could be included in the Kansas City panel of the mural. It is not clear whether Benton intended this portrait as a tribute to Pendergast or an attack on his regime, but he remained in the final painting, a source of considerable controversy.[7]

Next to "Boss" Tom, the most influential figure in Kansas City of the age was the stout, balding, affable, but relentlessly forward-pushing J. C. Nichols, the developer of the Country Club District and the Country Club Plaza.[8] In addition to the construction of his real estate empire, Nichols played a key role in creating the institutions that remain central to Kansas City's cultural life. In these endeavors, he showed a remarkable gift for drawing social and business rivals together into civic projects. He was, for instance, one of the principal figures behind the construction of the Liberty Memorial across from Union Station. He was instrumental in the creation of the Midwest Research Institute and the founding of the University of Kansas City. He took on the presidency of the Kansas City Art Institute when it was a shoestring operation and developed it into a nationally significant art school. Nichols also contributed, as the leader of the trustee board, to the Nelson-Atkins Museum of Art. He supervised the construction of the building, the hiring of its professional staff, and the early formation of its great art collection. He also supported Benton, which was crucial to the artist's survival, especially during his early years in Kansas City. When that support was withdrawn, it would have major consequences for Benton's career.

The revitalized city that Nichols intended to create intersected with Benton's world in profound ways. Even in the depths of the Great Depression, Kansas City in the 1930s went through a remarkable renaissance, creating new social institutions that helped to define the role of art in civic life. In that decade, the city created three great institutions: a university, a philharmonic orchestra, and a museum. Benton's social and artistic activities were closely tied with all three.

Benton was especially drawn to the newly founded University of Kansas City and its president Clarence Decker, whose circle of friends and supporters closely overlapped with Benton's. Born in Fargo, North Dakota, Decker lost his father as an infant and spent much of his childhood in various locations around the United States. He enrolled in a series of private and military schools—some good, others grim, sadistic, and worthy of the pen of Charles Dickens. By the time he arrived in Kansas City, Decker had an MA from Carleton College and a PhD from the University of Chicago. He had taught at a string of universities and had solid business experience from managing a large bookstore in Chicago and overseeing production for one of America's largest printers, R. R. Donnelley and Sons. Along the way, he rode freight cars, was jailed as a vagrant, crossed to Europe on a cattle boat, and studied for a year in Berlin, where his apartment was only a short distance from Nazi Party headquarters and where he had witnessed the outrages of fascism first-hand. Like Benton, then, Decker arrived in the city with experience in the school of hard knocks.[9]

Decker came to Kansas City to serve as chair of the English Department at the university, but after the abrupt resignation of the then president, John Duncan Spaeth, Decker took over and did a remarkable job of strengthening its faculty and building its cultural life through publications, lectures, concerts, and other activities. Under his administration the university increased sixfold in enrollment, land, budget, and endowment and effected a merger with the Kansas City School of Law. Decker, also like Benton, was socially progressive. One result was that the University of Kansas City became one of the first establishments of higher education in Missouri to accept African American students and to admit Japanese Americans when they were banished from California upon the outbreak of World War II.[10] Unconventional, irreverent, and often bombastic, Decker became a regular at Benton's social gatherings.

Through Decker, Benton befriended faculty members at the university, some of whom were quite distinguished. It was through Decker, for instance, that Benton became friendly with André Maurois, the accomplished biographer, scholar of letters, and member of the Académie Française, who because of his Jewish origins spent the war years in exile in Kansas City. Maurois later wrote with great fondness of Kansas City, declaring: "Who in Europe, or America, for that matter, knows that Kansas City is one of the loveliest cities on earth? And yet it is true."[11] In addition to expanding his circle of friends, Decker also enabled Benton to give public lectures and, through the *University of Missouri Review*, to publish essays on art and contemporary events. And, naturally enough, Benton found ways to repay Decker's favors. For example, he lent his early mural cycle, *The American Historical Epic*, to hang in Haag Hall at the university.

Benton was also closely associated with the Kansas City Philharmonic and its conductor, Karl Krueger. Raised in Atchison, Kansas, Krueger studied a number of subjects in Europe, including law and philosophy, but he was especially drawn to music. He served as guest conductor of the Chicago Symphony, as conductor at the Vienna Imperial Opera, and from 1926 to 1932, as the principal conductor of the Seattle Symphony Orchestra. In 1933, Krueger was lured to Kansas City to preside over the newly formed Kansas City Philharmonic. Despite his classical training, Krueger was an outspoken populist, very much in the Benton vein. He once declared:

The greatest fallacy in connection with music is the belief on the part of many laymen that only the listener who understands the mechanics of the music can get enjoyment from hearing it. Nothing could be further from the truth, and it is deplorable that the misconception has prevented many persons from feeling the deep joy that great music imparts. Wagner never tired of insisting that the public should not be aware that anything technical exists in music.[12]

The Kansas City Philharmonic had more than ninety musicians, and during the 1930s and 1940s, members of the orchestra were regular attendees at the parties at the Benton home, often performing small, intimate chamber concerts in the artist's house. The Benton home was very musical because in the late 1930s, Benton's teen-age son, Thomas Piacenza Benton, or "T. P.," took up the flute and became serious about music. T. P. would eventually become a professional musician, performing with the Miami Symphony Orchestra. Benton's relationship with Krueger and the philharmonic was further supported by Decker, a violinist with a great enthusiasm for classical music.

One of the major results of this interaction was a record that Benton produced for Decca, recorded in the fall of 1941. Benton performed on the harmonica with T. P. on the flute and backing provided by members of the Kansas City Philhar-monic, including the oboist Lloyd Rathbone, his wife Betty, and Hale Pharis. Many of the arrangements were produced by Benton's close friend and composer, Ed Robinson, who also wrote trios for Benton, Rita, and T. P. for the harmonica, re-corder and guitar. I must confess that I find this record, a period piece of American folk tunes in classical guise, a bit too sweet, even schmaltzy, but the project indicates the seriousness with which Benton pursued his musical interests and those of the Kansas City community. In his autobiography, Benton recalled the high times in his home during the late 1930s and early 1940s:

> We had a lot of fun. This fun went a little beyond music, however, especially for our listeners, and my liquor bills began to take on extensive proportions. We'd have twenty or twenty-five people for dinner and maybe fifty or more after and though none of the musicians drank much, the other folks did. It began to be like the old days in New York where we never knew who'd be sleeping on the living room couch when morning came.[13]

There was an emotional motive for these gatherings as well. During this period, many philharmonic performers in Kansas City were Jewish refugees from Germany. A common complaint for these musicians was the cultural adjustment required by life in the American Midwest. As one of Benton's students, Bill McKim, discussed with me at length, Benton was profoundly troubled by their trials. He bemoaned the sad irony that transformed skilled professionals into exiles from the very culture they celebrated with their music, a condition all too familiar to Benton. He did all he could to take them in, make them feel welcome, and to provide them a home away from home.

His support of Jewish musicians did not come without some social cost, how-ever. It was clear that Benton belonged to a slightly different social set than the WASP crowd that populated the Kansas City Country Club and controlled the Nelson-Atkins Museum of Art. Indeed, in some quarters of local society, Benton was increasingly suspect because of his close allegiance with the Jewish community and his distance from the city's traditional Protestant elite. Yet Benton's Jewish friends did not just link him to the social groups surrounding the university and the philharmonic but also formed a core constituency of his artistic patronage.[14] In fact, the exact circle of Jewish businessmen who supported the university and the philharmonic also gave Benton his strongest allies. Among the key figures in this cohort of Jewish intimates were Bernie Hofmann, the owner of a chain of clothing stores, frequently described as one of Benton's closest friends; the five brothers (particularly Samuel) of the prominent Sosland family; Arnold Adler, owner of a clothing store on the Country Club Plaza and Benton neighbor; and Rabbi Samuel Mayerberg, a socially progressive (and sometimes controversial) figure who played a central role in bringing down the regime of the political boss Tom Pendergast. For many of these people, Benton became a virtual member of the family—even if as a sort of eccentric uncle—and a regular participant in family events such as birthdays and holiday celebrations. When Arnold Adler died, for instance, Benton served as a pallbearer at his funeral.

Given these close ties, it is not surprising that Benton's most important commission of the 1940s—from Jewish businessman Lester Siegel for the Harzfeld's Department store in downtown Kansas City—came from this community. (Benton's 1947 mural, *Achelous and Hercules*, now belongs to the Smithsonian Institution's American Art Museum.) From the early years of the decade forward, something approximating half of the sales of Benton's paintings went to Kansas City Jewish families. Benton's Jewish patrons were not put off by the irreverent subject matter of his work that often offended the city's elite. In New York, one of the charges against Benton was anti-Semitism. He was no friend of what he described as the Stalinist Left, many of whose supporters were of the Jewish faith. But in Kansas City, Benton was portrayed as an ally of the Jewish faith. Benton was an outsider, but in Kansas City, so too were many Jewish families—a bond that brought both together.

Benton's relationship with the third cultural pillar of the community—the Nelson-Atkins Museum of Art—is more complex. It is not uncommon in new museums for there to be a conflict between those who conceive of the young enterprise as a world-class institution that should, as a result, acquire classic works of art from everywhere else, and those who believe that community organizations should patronize local art. In Kansas City, this recurrent drama of museum practice was carried out in an unusually colorful fashion.

The Nelson-Atkins Museum combined two bequests, that of William Rockhill Nelson and that of Mary Atkins, an unobtrusive spinster, who made wise investments in a cement company at the time when the city changed from wooden board-walks to cement sidewalks. These combined sums were then augmented by bequests from Nelson's daughter, Laura Kirkwood, and his lawyer, Frank Rozelle. It took a decade to bring these different bequests together and to construct an impressive classical building, which opened in 1933, with the largest interior volume of any building in Kansas City. By the will of William Rockhill Nelson, the museum was controlled by just three trustees, and one of them, J. C. Nichols, played the central role. Once the building was built, the trustees set out to hire a staff and build a collection. To fulfill these basic goals, Nichols went first to Harvard University, where he found key advisors, such as Langdon Warner, who was a consultant for the Oriental collection, and two key staff members, Paul Gardner, who became the director, and Laurence Sickman, who was hired as curator of Oriental art.

Interestingly, William Rockhill Nelson was never a serious art collector, although he did commission a series of copies of famous master paintings that he lent to the public library. His belief was that since most citizens of the region would never travel far from Kansas City, these quality copies could provide them with an introduction to high culture. Nelson was also committed to "the tried and true." His will dictated that artists must be dead for at least fifty years—to have passed the test of time—before their work could be added to the collections of his namesake museum.

Benton, of course, had a very different idea of what museums, especially local museums, should do. He saw no more lofty purpose than the display of his work—or that of his pupils and friends. This tension, which colored conversations about the role of art and the artist in Kansas City, was all the more acute because of the resentment Benton had felt since childhood toward those who disparaged the Midwest. One of the most intense loci of his resentment was Harvard University, the epitome of East Coast snobbishness. Benton's views may appear extreme, but this was, after all, the period when Paul Sachs, director of the Harvard University's Fogg Museum of Art, provided training in the pretentious British accent and social mannerisms that conveyed an aura of European sophistication. Paul Gardner, director of the Nelson-Atkins from 1933 to 1953, was the product of this training. The Boston-born Gardner had lived in Europe and spoke several languages, but from Benton's standpoint, it did not help that he was gay and had danced with the Ballets Russes.

A certain level of conflict was perhaps inevitable, although in the early 1930s it was staved off by a group of Benton's friends in Kansas City, who formed the Friends of Art, a group specifically created to circumvent Nelson's will and acquire contemporary art for the permanent collection. Several of Benton's friends held active roles in this society, among them Henry Haskell, brother-in-law to the Wright brothers, and Dan James.[15] James was related to the famous bank robber Jessie James but came from a more respectable branch of the family that had established a profitable china company in Kansas City. Haskell wrote art criticism for the *Kansas City Star* and both men had literary and artistic interests. Due to their ministrations, and no doubt those of other Benton friends, one of the first purchases of the Friends of Art was a major painting by Benton, a portrait of the modernist composer Carl Ruggles. The Friends of Art was also behind a Nelson-Atkins 1939 preview of a Benton retrospective scheduled for the Associated American Artists gallery. Behind the scenes, however, stress was building, especially because Benton believed that Paul Gardner was making disparaging remarks about his paintings to Kansas City matrons.

The conflict burst onto the public stage not over the purchase of a Benton piece, but because of controversy surrounding his teaching position at the Kansas City Art Institute. Benton had been subject to public rebuke before. In the late 1930s, Howard Huselton, a Kansas City businessman and one of the first directors of the Kansas City Art Institute, had attempted to push Benton from the faculty. Huselton waited until Benton was out of town on a sketching trip and then launched an attack on the artist's moral character based on his irreverent interpretation of Missouri history in his mural in the State Capitol. Huselton also was offended by what he saw as immoral passages in Benton's 1937 autobiography, *An Artist in America*. To support his case, Huselton underlined the offensive passages in red pencil and made sure each trustee of the Art Institute received a copy. In their early discussion of the matter, the board members of the Art Institute failed to renew Benton's contract, but the local press took up his cause, and his contract was eventually renewed in a closed-door meeting of the Art Institute board. Benton's ally, J. C. Nichols, leveraged behind-the-scenes support for Benton and enlisted Richard Fillmore, founder of the Unity School of Christianity, to vouch for the artist's moral character.

Unfortunately, Benton did not embrace caution after this initial episode, and while he got on well with the director of the Kansas City Art Institute who had initially hired him, Rossiter Howard, he did not with Howard's successor, Keith Martin, who took over the presidency of the Art Institute in 1939. It did not help that Martin was a graduate of Harvard, where he had managed the Glee Club, and was friendly with Paul Gardner. Benton's criticism of the school president was constant and cutting. A society portrait painter, Martin hung some of his own works in the main building of the Art Institute, and when Benton encountered them he remarked: "What the hell are these doing here? I thought this was supposed to be an art school."

The fatal moment occurred on April 4, 1941. At a press conference accompanying a show of his work in New York, in a back room of the Associated American Artists gallery, Benton, while sipping bourbon from a leaky paper cup, launched an attack on the stuffiness of art museums. He declared that he would rather have his paintings hang in saloons and brothels than American museums. Unfortunately, he also launched into a denunciation of homosexuals, in which he made unmistakable references to specific staff members of the Nelson-Atkins Museum of Art. Apparently, Benton had made previous statements of this sort, but the press had charitably failed to record them. In this instance, however, his words were quoted by Floyd Taylor in the *New York World-Telegram*. Benton declared:

> Do you want to know what's the matter with the art business in America? It's the third sex and the museums. Even in Missouri we're full of them. We've got

an immigration on out there. And the old ladies who've gotten so old that no man will look at 'em think these pretty boys will do. Our museums are full of ballet dancers, retired businessmen, and boys from the Fogg Art Institute at Harvard, where they train museum directors and artists. They hate my pictures and talk against them.[16]

It is hard to defend Benton's remarks, which have a nasty homophobic character, although it is also true that the people in question had said unflattering things about Benton's work and attempted to sabotage his career. The reference to ballet dancers, of course, was a direct link to Paul Gardner. One of the ironies of the episode is that despite having legitimate complaints about how many in the art world viewed his work, Benton's real trouble came because he touched on many of the social hypocrisies of the era.

One purpose of Benton's diatribe was to ridicule the pretensions of high culture, somewhat in the mode of Mark Twain in works like *The Innocents Abroad*. Underlying his harsh remarks, one can sense Benton's desire to present himself as possessing a manly frontier character, of the sort more likely to visit a saloon or brothel than an art museum. He also tried to draw on a tradition of humorous exaggeration that was a hallmark of frontier humor, as found in Davy Crockett's amazing stories of his hunting exploits. Unfortunately for Benton, however, his frame of reference was an outmoded one, not in tune with the pretensions of elite Kansas City, or even with the looser morality of Kansas City nightclubs and jazz clubs. He may have thought he was among friends, speaking to the figures of his father's generation or to the Missouri pioneers who would have supported Andrew Jackson. Instead, he was speaking before Americans of the modern age. Rather than make excuses or see humor in his remarks, genteel Kansas City properly felt threatened and took action accordingly.

For a month, the controversy simmered throughout the community. Benton was interviewed by journalists and seemed mildly contrite. His students marched to save his job, and one of his colleagues, printmaker John De Martelly, resigned in support. Benton's standing in American art ensured that his case would receive a wide hearing, and the nationally known art critic, New York's Thomas Craven, issued a statement on Benton's behalf. Despite all this activity, on May 5, 1941, the board of the Art Institute voted unanimously to fire Benton. As it happened, Benton's nemesis, Keith Martin, was sick with the measles and did not attend the meeting, but significantly, J. C. Nichols, who had rescued him the first time, voted to dismiss.

Benton's removal puts a dark coda on one of the most productive and notable periods of his career. His now-famous statehouse mural and several of his easel paintings had established Benton as a force in American art. His work had also helped put Kansas City before a national audience as his art and the city's cultural renaissance conveniently joined together. It is also striking, however, that the point at which he was fired from the Art Institute marks not only the high-water mark of his reputation but also the moment when Kansas City lost the opportunity to become a center of artistic engagement. For Benton to be earthy and forthright in his statements about himself was evidently acceptable, but he was no longer allowed to upset the balance of Kansas City's social and cultural life. For six years, Benton had bridged the chasm between upper-crust society and the colorful denizens of a wide-open frontier town, but at this point, the gap became too much to sustain. Perhaps Benton had not noticed that after this remarkable period of change, the city was now different. When he aired his complaints, he did so before a New York audience. Benton and his allies may have viewed the coastal establishment as pretentious outsiders, but their opinions still mattered. In response, the city closed ranks, defended its reputation, and left Benton on the outside.

Notes

1. Biographical information on Benton that is not footnoted is sourced in my two books, Henry Adams, *Thomas Hart Benton: An American Original* (New York: Alfred A. Knopf, 1989); and *Thomas Hart Benton: Discoveries and Interpretations* (Columbia: University of Missouri Press, 2005).

2. See the Ken Burns interview with George O'Malley, typescript, 2. Copy in the possession of Florentine Films, Walpole, New Hampshire.

3. Gregg Ottinger, letter to Marianne Beardi (with a transcript of Ottinger's father's memories), January 27, 1992.

4. Henry Adams, "Thomas Hart Benton as a Teacher," in Marianne Berardi, *Under the Influence: The Students of Thomas Hart Benton* (St. Joseph, Mo.: Albrecht-Kemper Museum of Art, 1993), 16.

5. Roger Medearis, *Student of Thomas Hart Benton*, 1986, typescript, 35–36. Excerpts of this manuscript were published in Roger Medearis, "Student of Thomas Hart Benton," *Smithsonian Studies in American Art* (Summer–Fall 1990): 46–61.

6. Thomas Hart Benton, "The Thirties," unpublished typescript, Benton Trust, copy in the Nelson-Atkins Museum of Art, 50. It was later published as Benton, "The Thirties: Critical Desires," in *The Regionalist Myth* (Kansas City, Mo.: Kansas City Artist Coalition, c. 1989).

7. For example, Benton's inclusion of Pendergast was criticized at some length in the savagely critical review of Benton's mural in the *Tulsa Tribune*, reprinted in Thomas Hart Benton, *An Artist in America* (Columbia: University of Missouri Press, 1981). Harry Truman, who rose to power as Pendergast's protégé and was the only political figure to attend his funeral, was also one who took serious offense at this portrait, feeling that it libeled his former political mentor. In 1939, when Pendergast was convicted of tax evasion, some prankster broke into the House Lounge and painted a jail number on the back of Pendergast's coat. Truman thought that Benton was somehow complicit in this, and it became an impediment when Benton was first proposed to produce a mural for the Truman Library in 1959—an obstacle that was fortunately overcome when the two met face-to-face and quickly hit it off as

two enthusiastic history buffs who also liked the same brand of bourbon. The Kansas City panel of the statehouse mural serves as the artwork for the cover of this volume.

8. Dick Fowler, *Leaders in Our Town* (Kansas City, Mo.: Burd and Fletcher Company, 1946), 329–332.

9. For a biography of Decker, see ibid., 93–96. Decker also wrote a memoir of his years in Kansas City. See Clarence R. Decker, *A Place of Light: The Story of a University Presidency* (New York: Hermitage House, 1954).

10. See "Dr. C. R. Decker Dies in New York: Former President of Kansas City University was 64," *Kansas City Star*, November 22, 1969, 2. Harold Holliday was the first African American student accepted into the University of Kansas City School of Law in 1948. The university had enrolled over 150 African American students by 1950. See Christopher Wolff, *A Pearl of Great Value: The History of UMKC* (Kansas City, Mo.: UMKC Alumni Association, 2016), 54.

11. This quotation from Maurois is frequently quoted in books on Kansas City and is cited in Jack Kolbert, *The Worlds of Andre Maurois* (London: Associated University Presses, 1985), 59.

12. For a history of the Kansas City orchestra, see William Everett, *Music for the People: A History of the Kansas City Philharmonic, 1933–82* (Kansas City, Mo.: Kansas City Star Books, 2015).

13. Benton, *An Artist in America*, 287. The late 1930s was a period of particularly intense pursuit of these musical interests, as is suggested by a sketchbook found in a funeral home in Greenfield, Missouri, which is filled with sketches for Persephone and Susanna and the Elders, as well as with music that Benton had transcribed. Benton apparently played the harmonica with Dan Green, the funeral home's proprietor.

14. Fowler, *Leaders in Our Town*, 96.

15. For information on Henry Haskell, see Harry Haskell, *Boss Busters and Sin Hounds: Kansas City and Its Star* (Columbia: University of Missouri Press, 2007).

16. Floyd Taylor, "Thomas Hart Benton Says Art Belongs in Clubs and Barrooms, Not Museums," *New York World-Telegram*, April 5, 1941, 1, 4.

CHAPTER FIFTEEN

From Proscenium to Inferno

The Interwar Transformation of Female Impersonation in Kansas City

Stuart Hinds

The Orpheum Theater, the most opulent playhouse in Kansas City, opened the day after Christmas in 1914.[1] The exterior of the new show palace on Baltimore Avenue, just south of Twelfth Street, was wrapped in terra-cotta formed to resemble Tennessee marble and inset with panels depicting symbols of music and dance. The same terra-cotta arched over the grand lobby's mosaic marble floor. Guests sat in leather-upholstered mahogany seats arranged underneath a forty-foot dome painted to mimic the star-filled sky.[2] Enormous columns supported the main auditorium, and every seat had an unobstructed view of the stage.

The rarefied venue drew a correspondingly exclusive crowd of civic and cultural leaders. The tony Kansas City Club reserved the entire sixth row for its members every season. Much of the entertainment was vaudeville, as the national Orpheum circuit was one of the country's leading vaudeville producers. Treading the boards alongside the bumbling comics, lovelorn songsters, and sleight-of-hand magicians regularly performing at the Orpheum was another, perhaps more unexpected, act: female impersonators. These colorful characters were a holdover from the earliest days of minstrelsy, but during the heyday of vaudeville, a number of female impersonators enjoyed impressive careers and became household names across the country.[3] During Prohibition, the tradition expanded into nightclubs and cabarets and drew enormous crowds in large cities like New York and Chicago. In the late 1920s and early 1930s, the arrival of popular radio dramas, big bands, and motion pictures increased competition for American entertainment tastes, and in many areas of the country female impersonation disappeared from "legitimate" stages throughout the United States. But in wide-open Pendergast-era Kansas City, female impersonators remained popular until the late 1930s.

Vaudeville theater was a reaction to the bawdy, boisterous, adult-oriented entertainments found in nineteenth-century American music halls. Industrialization led to widespread relocation of rural families to urban centers, and theater producers hoped to tap this growing market for family-friendly fare. Tony Pastor is often credited as the "father of vaudeville," launching his Opera House in New York in 1865 with shows advertising "fun without vulgarity." Pastor, the son of an immigrant musician, came of age in music halls and bars and was seemingly destined to become an actor and master of ceremonies. His enormous success with the Opera House led other theatrical entrepreneurs to follow his lead, and by the mid-1880s vaudeville was an established American entertainment style. Pastor and his competitors were influenced by the efficiencies and standardization of Gilded Age manufacturers and the scientific management craze. They created theater-management systems that were unique to vaudeville; they treated the show as a business. Their employment infrastructures, booking and management methodologies, and networks of circuit touring were new to the industry. These nimble techniques enabled them to react quickly and decisively to changing audiences' demands.[4]

Given that the primary emphasis of vaudeville was "good clean fun," regularly featured female impersonators might surprise modern readers, but these impersonators occupied a world apart from twenty-first-century drag queens.[5] Their performances were typically incorporated into skits or longer theatrical pieces that ranged from exaggeratedly comic to empathetically tragic. Many of these actors were excellent singers, and with circuit system houses in cities across the country, these impersonators became well-known figures in American society. Histories of vaudeville record more than 135 entertainers who were female impersonators, and of that number, nearly three dozen performed in the Kansas City circuit.[6] Female impersonation was not limited to the city's Orpheum Theater, as these actors appeared in a number of houses, including the Ninth Street Opera House, Coates House, Doric, Empress, Gillis, Globe, Grand, Loew's, Majestic, Orpheum, and Shubert.[7] The range of styles of these impersonators was as broad as the theaters in which they appeared, including actors who donned dresses for short bits to those who were onstage in female clothing for the entirety of a show. They were such a regular presence that noted local theatrical photographer Orval Hixon regularly included them in his portfolio.[8] Kansas City theatergoers were fortunate to have experienced shows that featured the two most famous female impersonators of the day, Julian Eltinge and Bert Savoy. These two actors were enormously talented and represent the diverse and contradictory facets of the art and culture of impersonation.

Julian Eltinge (1881–1941) trained as a dancer in the Boston area. His extraordinarily graceful movements and style led his instructor to encourage his entrance into professional impersonation. In the early twentieth century, impersonators fell

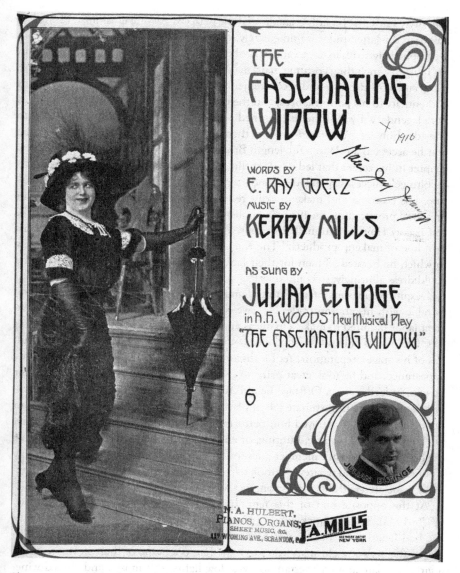

Sheet music cover for the musical *The Fascinating Widow*, featuring photographs of female impersonator Julian Eltinge, 1910. Courtesy of the LaBudde Special Collections, University of Missouri–Kansas City.

into two camps: the broadly comedic and the perfectly passing illusionist. Eltinge focused on the latter and was immediately successful, performing costumed and choreographed vignettes in large vaudeville shows. He polished every detail to maintain his illusions, including costume, hair, makeup, and movement. He also spent enormous sums on clothing and accoutrements. His natural soprano vocal talents lent authenticity to his performances, and the quality of his illusions and performances were legendary. By 1910 he had reached a peak in vaudeville, leading one critic to consider him "as great a performer as there stands on the stage today."[9] That same year he accepted a role in a full-length Broadway musical comedy, launching a new chapter in his career that led to silent films in Hollywood.[10]

Eltinge's success expanded beyond stage and screen into popular consumer culture. His costume and makeup skills resulted in women seeking his expertise in dress and presentation. In 1913, he published the short-lived *Julian Eltinge Magazine and Beauty Hints*, a nationally distributed fashion magazine.[11] He soon added his own line of makeup products.[12] The *Kansas City Star* featured him in an interview in which he berated women for their lack of fashion sense. He claimed that if he could dress alluringly, so could they.[13]

Despite his mastery of an illusory feminine ideal, Eltinge was markedly uncomfortable with his chosen trade. He gave several interviews complaining about the great labor required to make a living as an impersonator. A large man—he stood six feet, two inches tall and weighed 240 pounds—it is easy to understand the difficulties of his stage preparation. Yet his discomfort extended beyond the change in his appearance, and he took great pains to ensure that his audiences understood that he was, indeed, acting. Offstage he affected the demeanor of a paragon of masculinity stuck in the unfortunate job of playing a woman. Eltinge staged many photo opportunities that portrayed him performing quintessentially masculine acts such as chopping wood, fishing, hunting, or engaging in fistfights. When stagehands or the occasional audience member questioned his masculinity, he was quick to throw a punch. Eltinge did whatever it took to distance himself from the perceived effeminacy associated with his profession, lucrative as it may have been.[14]

At the opposite end of this feminine/masculine dichotomy was Bert Savoy (1876–1923). Savoy's shtick was to play the dim but witty woman repeating gossip she had heard from her friend "Margie" to her stage partner, Jay Brennan, who played the act's straight man in more ways than one. One of their stories featured a girl on a date at a chic restaurant with low lights, soft music, and chilled wine. Her date noted, "I've never been in a place like this before." Savoy retorted, "My God! I'm out with an amateur!" A second oft-repeated anecdote included a noted showgirl who, having recently seen the latest Hollywood version of *The Three Musketeers*, spied a copy of the book in a shop window and exclaimed, "Ain't the printing press wonderful—they've got the book out already." Savoy also had a supply of stock phrases that were long associated with his character, such as "You *must* come along,"

"You don't know the *half* of it, dearie," "My nerves is all unstrung," "You slay me," and "You *must* come over"—idioms that would also find their way into the classic characters of American actress Mae West. While clearly more lowbrow than Eltinge, Savoy's comic stylings were just as attentive as his famous competitor's to wardrobe and other components of illusion. But unlike Eltinge, Savoy's outlandishness extended to his off-stage persona as well. He regularly employed feminine pronouns when referring to himself and his cadre of like-minded friends and he frequently remained in costume and in character offstage. Even the end of his life came in a masterfully ironic moment of camp bravado. On June 26, 1923, Savoy and a colleague were strolling on Long Beach in California when a thunderstorm erupted. After an exceedingly loud clap of thunder, Savoy was reported to declare, "Mercy, ain't Miss God cutting up something awful?" An immediate bolt of lightning struck both Savoy and his companion dead, ending an illustrious career in style.[15]

Of the two performers, Julian Eltinge was more popular with Kansas City audiences. He appeared onstage in Kansas City four different times between 1913 and 1921.[16] At one point a local theater gossip columnist asked readers, "Are you a partisan in the bitter costume rivalry between Dorothy Jardon's 'dazzling array of gowns' at the Orpheum and the 'wardrobe of ultra-latest models in gowns' worn by Julian Eltinge at the Shubert this week?"[17] Following his migration to motion pictures, Eltinge's films enjoyed long runs at movie theaters throughout the city, including one continuous nine-month streak in 1917–1918.[18] In contrast, Savoy and Brennan appeared in Kansas City only once, at the Orpheum in February 1917.[19] The piece they presented, "On the Rialto," contained the line, "You can do things in Greece that you can't get away with here." This prompted one print critic to comment: "We don't know what they meant, but we have an idea and are glad we are in America. The act is just one of those coarse, vulgar things with which vaudeville audiences must be afflicted semi-occasionally, and which spoil so many good shows."[20] Despite this writer's distaste for the antics of the comedy team, opportunities for female impersonation in the Savoy vein expanded throughout the 1920s, beyond the vaudeville stage and onto the floors of the speakeasies and cabarets that blossomed across the country during Prohibition.

Despite the restrictions of the Eighteenth Amendment, a large percentage of urban America ignored the ban on alcohol consumption. Of New York City during this period, for example, historian George Chauncey noted, "The proliferation of illegal speakeasies and nightclubs after Prohibition led to the wholesale corruption of policing agencies . . . more distressingly . . . the popular revolt in New York against the aims and tactics of Prohibition undermined the moral authority of such policing altogether."[21] The loosening of moral restrictions spread to the consumption of alternative nightlife as well. Club goers were increasingly more receptive to alternative forms of entertainment. This was particularly evident in the popular acceptance of gender impersonation.

New York was the center for the most visible manifestations of drag in cabaret society. Masquerade balls, known colloquially as "drags," had been a staple of the city's homosexual underground since the late nineteenth century. They grew more popular among broader audiences and evolved a cachet during the open years of the 1920s, especially in Greenwich Village and Harlem. By the latter years of the decade, enormous balls were held every other month throughout midtown Manhattan.[22] In Harlem, the drag balls were known for the diversity of races, classes, and sexual orientations of their audiences. Press coverage of the Harlem festivities was regular and wide-ranging, largely in papers published by and for the African American community.[23]

There is no evidence of such large-scale drag balls in Kansas City during this period, but there are numerous references to cabaret-based female impersonators during the Prohibition years. Musicians who performed in clubs during this time recounted such shows at different venues throughout downtown Kansas City. The Paradise Club on Fifteenth Street between Olive and Wabash, for example, had two floor shows each evening, both of which featured "a dozen gay transvestites: dancers, paraders, and female impersonators who worked for a producer who originated their routines and coached the dancers." Reported one club musician, we "got along fine; we used to visit their dressing rooms on our breaks, just to sit and watch them swish and carry on."[24] A local trumpet player, Booker T. Washington, described the impersonation scene at a second club, the Spinning Wheel, located on Twelfth and Troost Avenue, noting:

> the place consists more of female impersonators. . . . Each of them would do something different. They had a special to do, each one of them . . . they dressed like women. They stayed dressed like women. They went around throughout the crowd as women. You know and they didn't, wasn't nothing funny or faking with them, they were genuine. They were hired . . . they had between six and eight of them and they worked every night. . . . In fact, the most of them, that's where most of our money came from, the impersonators. They'd go out and do their numbers, and they would get tips and what tips they'd get, they'd throw in the kitty.[25]

When asked about local floor shows, saxophonist Herman Walder remembered, "They had female impersonators, mostly . . . they was sharp, too, man. . . . One of them was named Billy—that's the one I'd like to have a fight over . . . they would come from out of town . . . song and dance . . . they had all kinds . . . all kinds of artists."[26] Later Walder described the scene in greater detail. "In the black clubs they had female impersonators' night . . . on Monday—so and so's night—Tuesday—so and so's—next was Men's night—next is sissy night—they'd come on out then . . . female impersonators, they'd come on out . . . and everybody else, they'd come see 'em dance." The acceptance of the impersonators by these musicians was commonplace. "We judge people by what they want to be themselves, you dig what I mean," Walder explained. "And those people were good—they're always good to you. . . . They'd fill up the kitty, man—if they make some money man, they'd come and fill up the kitty."[27]

While club band members approved of the performing female impersonators, audience members who appeared in costume were not always as welcomed. A January 1927 account of the arrest of several men in drag at a local nightclub indicates the dismissive ire they sometimes encountered:

> *"Sissies" Brought in by Rude Police; Fined $500 Each by Judge*
> "It was just too terrible, my dear!"
>
> "The rude police have no sense of propriety," let the "sissies" of the city tell it. When the officers of the law raided a cabaret at 1520 East Twelfth Street, early yesterday morning, terror and consternation spread from manly breast to manly breast underneath the frilly garments of the feminine sex, worn for the evening's pleasure.
>
> When the last screams and squeals had coyly come forth from the throat originally designed for some he-occupation like calling hogs, the police had seven men—six were all clad in dainty chiffon things, cute little pumps, silk hose, and other frills.
>
> Yesterday morning the sight of six men in flimsy clothing evidently had a bad effect on Judge Carlin P. Smith because he fined each of the frequenters $500 each and also fined Ben Payne, the proprietor of the place, $500. They are the heaviest fines ever assessed against frequenters of a cabaret.[28]

The press coverage of this raid is significant not because it was standard practice but rather because it was so uncommon. In a city rife with violations of the law, Kansas City police rarely took action against social transgressions like impersonation.

Still, the implied flagrancy of the arrested individuals and the reporter's reaction to it reflected the national shifting of attitudes toward female impersonation and other forms of nonnormative behavior that emerged with the end of Prohibition. With the repeal of the Eighteenth Amendment to the US Constitution in 1933, the government increased oversight of liquor manufacturing and distribution. Local officials also gained greater control over the spaces in which liquor was consumed. The wild abandon and underground character of the speakeasies of the 1920s eventually disappeared as nightclubs assumed an aura of middlebrow respectability.[29] Accompanying this change in normative values was a disdain for the confusion of femininity and masculinity that female impersonators represented. These attitudes were already evident in the scandals surrounding actress Mae West. Her late-1920s plays, *The Drag* and *The Pleasure Man*, both of which featured female impersonators as major characters, were raided by police and shut down, with West arrested during the run of *The Drag*, for a third, similar production she authored and starred in. The result of the controversy was a widespread perception that female impersonation was offensive and obscene.[30]

By the mid-1930s, shifting audience tastes had driven drag from the cabaret scene, and several US cities passed laws banning female impersonation. Raids on drag clubs in Los Angeles resulted in the arrests of both performers and audience members.[31] In Chicago, clubs were harassed by law enforcement and, with the support of Mayor Edward J. Kelly, closed.[32] Female impersonators at the Garden of Allah club in Seattle were replaced by honky-tonk fare.[33] In New York, the nexus of the "pansy craze," a 1931 campaign by local newspapers against clubs that featured female impersonation led to police crackdowns on the clubs and drag balls in Times Square.[34] Smaller cities too became more restrictive, with female impersonators chased out of Rensselaer, New York; Milwaukee; and St. Paul in the first three months of 1935.[35]

Like these other cities, Kansas City revised its liquor control ordinance in 1934 to reflect the post-repeal regulatory environment.[36] Given that the city remained enmeshed in the Pendergast machine, however, these revisions were largely for show. Social life went on as before, with the relatively free flow of alcohol resulting in the expansion of Kansas City's already burgeoning nightclub businesses. Jazz pianist Mary Lou Williams recalled, "I found Kansas City to be a heavenly city—music everywhere in the Negro section of town, and fifty or more cabarets rocking on 12th and 18th Streets."[37] According to journalist Dave E. Dexter Jr., one section of Twelfth Street "boasted as many as 20 saloons and niteries in a single block."[38] And unlike other, more restrictive cities, numerous Kansas City clubs continued to offer female impersonation among their entertainment repertoires.

Many of these venues were on the east side of downtown, in and around the Eighteenth and Vine district. At the East Side Musicians Sunset Club, located at Twelfth and Woodland and billed as "a show place of the city," Tuesday night was female impersonator night.[39] The "Sepia Mae West," on tour from Chicago, had an indefinite engagement at the Harlem Nite Club in the summer of 1935.[40] During this period, a female impersonator was the featured performer at the grand opening of the Lone Star Garden at 1708 E. Twelfth Street, and in 1935, an impersonator was the highlight act of the July Fourth Dance at Paseo Hall, a performance that also featured the famous Bennie Moten band.[41] Friday nights were devoted to drag at Wolf's Buffet at 1522 E. Eighteenth Street, and even as late as 1938, small-scale drag balls were presented at the Lone Star.[42]

Despite the abundant drag shows on the East Side, in other parts of the Kansas City community the distaste for alternative expressions of gender paralleled similar attitudes in other cities where female impersonation had already disappeared. An unnamed reporter for *The Future*, a short-lived local conservative newspaper published in the mid-1930s, recounted an excursion into the "second-class Kansas City night club" scene. This rare account is worth quoting at some length:

> The majority of these spots are small, obscure and ephemeral, stemming directly from speakeasies. They are so much alike in décor, entertainment, choice of beverages and patrons that only the name distinguishes one from the other. Take an old store room, several bolts of black, red, or blue tarlatan, several cans of silver radiator paint, a second-hand bar and a ditto bartender and you have the makings of the average second class Kansas City night club. Your music will be supplied by a 3-piece orchestra who hammer out dance music for whatever coins fall into the yawning and ubiquitous kitty. The floor show, if any, can be made up of old burlesque acts, amateurs, or friends of the proprietor who are willing to oblige.
>
> We decided to make a calm, fairly sober analysis of this second rate phase of our city's night life; of those small, prolific places that bloom and fade rapidly despite the protection afforded them by the police and the powers that be. We started our investigations at 10:30 on a Friday night and closed them with the dawn. We did not go in a spirit of muckraking. We went to see and hear, hoping to find out why so many intelligent citizens spend their money and time sitting in these little unlovely places, breathing smoke and dust, drinking inferior beer and terrible whisky or plain strong alcohol, listening to generally wretched music and watching floor shows that are either embarrassingly stupid or stupidly indecent. We never found the answer, but we submit a detailed report for your consideration.
>
> We went first to Dante's Inferno, a small building with a smaller entrance. The interior is decorated with a lurid red substance, which must be as inflammable as the flames of hell it symbolizes. We were there for the first show, an extremely unpleasant ordeal, for the female impersonators who gave it were an inept and pitiful lot. One of them came to our table, sat down in all his finery, and ordered a sherry flip. Kansas City, he lisped, was the crudest place he had ever worked in. "The folks here sure are dumb. They don't get nothing subtle." He went on to explain that he worked on a circuit which extended from New York to New Orleans; he made pretty good money, but had to spend a lot of it on snappy costumes. He was wearing, at the time, a little tulle model, decorated grotesquely with a bunch of bananas. One look at the croupiers behind the gambling table decided us against trying our luck there. We left just as the soft-spoken Mr. Lusco was arguing with two young men patrons in an attempt to prevent them from dancing together.[43]

But like the 1927 police bust of a local nightclub mentioned earlier, this newspaper account is significant not for its critique of female impersonation but for

Interior shot of Dante's Inferno nightclub, showing its devil-themed decor, c. 1934.
Courtesy of the Kenneth Spencer Research Library, University of Kansas.

what it reveals about the entertainment culture of the city. This anonymous foray
into Pendergast-era nightlife provides an acerbic introduction to Dante's Inferno,
the Kansas City club that became known throughout the city for female impersonation. Located at the intersection of Independence and Troost Avenues, Dante's
opened in December 1933 and was billed as "never a nightclub setting like this!"[44]
Northside politico Joe Lusco, who had ties to organized crime, owned the club.
Eli Madlof was the popular master of ceremonies for the floor shows backed by
the Charles Perry Orchestra.[45] As the catty *Future* writer reported, the club was
decorated in a hellish theme, with red painted walls to represent Hades and satanic
knickknacks arranged throughout.

The richest source of information about Dante's Inferno is from performer
Edna Mae Whithouse.[46] Born in Indian Territory in the first decade of the twentieth century, Whithouse and her family relocated to Kansas City when she was a
child. They lived in midtown near Twenty-Ninth Street and Gillham Road. Her
father was a religious singer, but she took her vocal talents in a decidedly "infernal"
direction. She was both a waitress and a regular performer at Dante's almost as soon
as it opened. The waitresses' uniform echoed the club's décor. "We had a little devil

Edna Mae Whithouse and Billie Richards at Dante's Inferno, c. 1934. Courtesy of the Kenneth Spencer Research Library, University of Kansas.

suit, and horns . . . we had a tail, but that caused a little business," she recalled in an interview. "You'd go by with a tray of drinks and some sucker'd get a hold of your tail, so we eventually de-tailed the costumes." The uniform's designer also "made the monsters in there, and he made 'em move . . . they'd crawl out of the cave . . . spill somebody's drink, they'd jump and scream." As a singer, Whithouse supplemented her serving tips with additional gratuities earned during "table singing" stints. "I hustled those songs at tables. . . . I'd squat down at the table . . . they always wanted a little sad song, even the gangsters, even the tough guys," she recounted. "They'd sit there and blubber, just as tender as babies. . . . I'd get as high as a hundred dollars . . . you sing softly enough so if Mr. Jones at the other table wants to hear it he'd have to call you over."[47]

As part of the floor shows Edna Mae was billed as Eddie and paired in a duo with Seattle-based female impersonator Billie Richards. The act performed regularly, eventually becoming known as the Lynn Sisters, and was popular with local audiences and the entertainment press alike.[48] Whithouse described the Kansas City environment the female impersonators encountered: "When we first got them, they [audiences] were curious. People didn't know what to make of 'em. But the longer we had them, the more they liked them. They'd invite them to sit and they'd buy drinks for them." She recounts that the impersonators encountered difficulties with some African Americans at the club, not indicating whether the impersonators were staff or patrons. "The boys would make cracks to them," she remembered. "They slapped a couple of them, which is bad . . . theirs is just a business, it's nothing personal." Club management, though, stepped in to maintain order and decorum. "Brother Jim [Lusco] straightened 'em up. He said, 'Don't you bother these guys' . . . the other gays'd come down to see 'em . . . everybody'd come to see 'em."[49] The response of these black club patrons stands in direct opposition to the experiences of the African American musicians quoted earlier. While evidence of these differing responses is lacking, the fact that the female impersonators and the musicians were in professional collaboration may have contributed to the more positive perceptions of the performers.

Whithouse continued to perform at Dante's well into the 1930s, until she was recruited for a touring company of the *Follies of 1936*. Around that same time, Dante's relocated to 512 East Twelfth Street and discontinued female impersonation in its floor shows. Whithouse returned to Kansas City after touring for a few years and partnered professionally and personally with Joe Jacobs. In the mid-1940s they opened the Riverside Supper Club at the intersection of Highways 71 and 45. The restaurant and nightclub were housed in the building that formerly served as the clubhouse at the Riverside Jockey Club, established in 1928 by Tom Pendergast and Phil McCrory.[50]

At the onset of World War II, female impersonation largely disappeared from the record of civilian life, although there is a body of evidence demonstrating that it remained a regular feature of the military experience during the war.[51] By 1941, a reform government had been installed in Kansas City, which even the apolitical Edna Mae Whithouse described as a "big improvement" over wide-open Pendergast graft and corruption.[52] Kansas City, like the rest of the nation, got down to the serious and deadly business of war. The previous quarter century had presented Kansas City theater and cabaret audiences with local and national female impersonation for a longer period of time than in most other cities. At war's end, Kansas City, like the rest of the nation, busied itself with recovery and reclamation of something resembling "normal life."

Yet despite this embrace of the mainstream, in the late 1950s a second formidable cycle of Kansas City drag history reemerged at the Jewel Box, a nightclub at 3219

RAE BOURBON

A TRICK AIN'T ALWAYS A TREAT
Recorded Live From The
WORLD FAMOUS JEWEL BOX

To be Played
Very Late
at Night

For
Elderly
Delinquents

Very High in Fidelity
(Stereo Too)

Very High in Fidelity
(Stereo Too)

Rae Bourbon album cover, recorded at the Jewel Box in Kansas City, c. 1962. Courtesy of the LaBudde Special Collections, University of Missouri–Kansas City.

Troost. This new generation of impersonators embodied the shrill, hyper-artificial female characterization popularized by Bert Savoy, and was best personified by drag legend Rae Bourbon (1892?–1971). Bourbon was internationally known and previously had been featured at Dante's Inferno in several performances. According to Whithouse, Bourbon was "one of the world's greatest. . . . I guess second to Eltinge. He did an awful lot of swishing, but he didn't wear 'drag'—he dressed real classy. How ultra he was! He worked for us [Dante's] four times—he was a headliner."[53]

Throughout his career Bourbon toured the United States, and ultimately returned to Kansas City to cap his performing life in the early 1960s. He was regularly featured at the Jewel Box and released a live recording of a performance there. As an entertainer, Bourbon served as a bridge from the raucous vaudeville traditions that had kept female impersonation in the public eye to the emerging self-identified gay community of three decades later that found its first home in clubs like the Jewel Box. He helped perpetuate female impersonation in Kansas City long after it had disappeared in other cities across the United States, and he provided a direct linkage between these two distinct eras of a hidden Kansas City theater tradition.

Notes

1. "Into the New Orpheum," *Kansas City Times*, December 27, 1914, 5A.

2. "Plan Great Celebration for Opening of New and Beautiful Orpheum Theater Saturday Evening," *Kansas City Post*, December 20, 1914, 10A.

3. Edward Leroy Rice, *Monarchs of Minstrelsy: From "Daddy" Rice to Date* (New York: Kenny Publishing, 1911), 26.

4. Trav S. D., *No Applause–Just Throw Money: The Book That Made Vaudeville Famous* (New York: Faber and Faber, 2005), 65, 83.

5. Ibid., 54.

6. Sources investigated include Trav S. D., *No Applause*; Joe Laurie Jr., *Vaudeville: From the Honky Tonks to the Palace* (New York: Holt, 1953); Douglas Gilbert, *American Vaudeville: Its Life and Times* (New York: Whittlesey House, 1940); Anthony Slide, *The Vaudevillians: A Dictionary of Vaudeville Performers* (Westport, Conn.: Arlington House, 1981), and *The Encyclopedia of Vaudeville* (New York: Greenwood, 1994); F. Michael Moore, *Drag! Male and Female Impersonators on Stage, Screen, and Television* (Jefferson, N.C.: McFarland, 1994); C. J. Bulliet, *Venus Castina: Famous Female Impersonators Celestial and Human* (New York: Bonanza Books, 1928); and Robert C. Toll, *On with the Show: The First Century of Show Business in America* (New York: Oxford University Press, 1976).

7. *Kansas City Star* and *Kansas City Times*, 1880–1922.

8. *Main Street Studio: An Exhibition of Photographs of Famous Vaudeville Entertainers by Orval Hixon*, University of Kansas Museum of Art, May 2–June 27, 1971, plate 91. Exhibition organized and catalogue written and designed by James Enyeart.

9. Quoted in Toll, *On with the Show*, 248.

10. Toll, *On with the Show*, 247–248.

11. Laurence Senelick, "Lady and the Tramp: Drag Differentials in the Progressive Era," in *Gender in Performance: The Presentation of Difference in the Performing Arts*, ed. Laurence Senelick (Hanover, N.H.: University Press of New England, 1992), 26.

12. Ibid., 32.

13. "Most Gowns Lack Brains," *Kansas City Star*, August 9, 1913, 12.

14. See Senelick, "Lady and the Tramp"; Toll, *On with the Show*, 250–251; Slide, *The Vaudevillians*, 47; Thomas Bolze, "Female Impersonation in the United States, 1900–1970" (PhD diss., State University of New York–Buffalo, 1994), 74–77; and Daniel Hurewitz, *Bohemian Los Angeles and the Making of Modern Politics* (Berkeley: University of California Press, 2007), 34–38.

15. Senelick, "Lady and the Tramp," 33–37; Slide, *The Vaudevillians*, 134–135.

16. Advertisements, *Kansas City Star*, September 17, 1913, 9; April 22, 1917, 2; February 22, 1919, 3; and February 12, 1921, 3.

17. "Starbeams," *Kansas City Star*, May 2, 1917, 16.

18. Advertisements, *Kansas City Star*, September 30, 1917, 15; October 28, 1917, 13; December 12, 1917, 11; January 23, 1918, 8; February 19, 1918, 5; March 7, 1918, 8; April 14, 1918, 2; and May 15, 1918, 8.

19. Advertisement, *Kansas City Star*, February 11, 1917, 14C.

20. "With the First Nighters," *Goodwin's Weekly*, January 20, 1917, 10.

21. George Chauncey, *Gay New York: Gender, Urban Culture, and the Making of the Gay Male World, 1890–1940* (New York: Basic Books, 1994), 306.

22. Ibid., 294–295.

23. James F. Wilson, *Bulldaggers, Pansies, and Chocolate Babies: Performance, Race, and Sexuality in the Harlem Renaissance* (Ann Arbor: University of Michigan Press, 2010), 86; and Chauncey, *Gay New York*, 261–263.

24. Ted Dreher, *The Wicked Wicket: Prohibition's Effect on Kansas City's Early '30's Gin Mills*, self-published, 1992, 33.

25. Transcript Interview of Booker T. Washington, April 8 and July 8, 1977, Folder 36a, 81, Kansas City Jazz Oral History Collection (KC0012), State Historical Society of Missouri, Kansas City Research Center, Kansas City, Missouri (hereafter SHSM-KC). The "kitty" was a container, usually in the shape of a cat, placed at the foot of the stage where patrons could tip the house band.

26. Transcript Interview of Herman Walder, April 7, 1977, Folder 2, Kansas City Jazz Oral History Collection (KC0012), SHSM-KC, 81.

27. Transcript Interview of Herman Walder, June 8, 1977, Folder 3, Kansas City Jazz Oral History Collection (KC0012), SHSM-KC, 202–203.

28. "'Sissies' Brought in by Rude Police; Fined $500 Each by Judge," *The Call*, January 21, 1927, 1. The fines are equivalent to over $6,500 in current dollars.

29. Lewis A. Erenberg, "From New York to Middletown: Repeal and the Legitimization of Nightlife in the Great Depression," *American Quarterly* 38, no. 5 (Winter 1986): 766.

30. Bolze, "Female Impersonation," 201–214.

31. Daniel Hurewitz, *Bohemian Los Angeles and the Making of Modern Politics* (Berkeley: University of California Press, 2007), 121; Lilian Faderman and Stuart Timmons, *Gay L.A.: A History of Sexual Outlaws, Power Politics, and Lipstick Lesbians* (New York: Basic Books, 2006), 46.

32. St. Sukie de la Croix, *Chicago Whispers: A History of LGBT Chicago before Stonewall* (Madison: University of Wisconsin Press, 2012), 130–131.

33. Don Paulson, *An Evening at the Garden of Allah: A Gay Cabaret in Seattle* (New York: Columbia University Press, 1996), 9.

34. Chauncey, *Gay New York*, 331–333.

35. Bolze, "Female Impersonation," 226.

36. City of Kansas City, Missouri, Liquor Control Ordinance, No. 3437, Approved by

H. F. McElroy, City Manager, and Authenticated as Passed January 29, 1934 by Acting Mayor A. N. Gossett.

37. Quoted in Max Jones, *Talking Jazz* (New York: W. W. Norton, 1988), 187.

38. Dave E. Dexter Jr., "Moten and Lee Are Patrons Saints of Kansas City Jazz . . . Town Hits Its Peak in the 1930s as Spawning Ground for Musicians," *Down Beat*, January 1, 1941, 8.

39. Advertisements, *The Call*, March 22, 1933, 9; and November 9, 1934, 13.

40. "'Mae West' Well Known Female Impersonator Here," *The Call*, June 14, 1935, 11.

41. Advertisement, *The Call*, June 28, 1935, 9.

42. Advertisements, *The Call*, November 5, 1937, 15; and July 15, 1938, 9.

43. "Night Life of the Mortals," *The Future*, March 29, 1935, 1-2.

44. Advertisement, *Kansas City Journal Post*, December 2, 1933.

45. Edna Mae Whithouse Collection, Kansas Collection, RH MS P797, Kenneth Spencer Research Library, University of Kansas Libraries, Lawrence, Kansas (hereafter Spencer Library).

46. Edna Mae Whithouse was married three times and carried the names Riggs, Jacobs, and Mears. The oral history in the Kansas City Jazz Oral History Collection incorrectly lists her surname as Mintern, which was that of her daughter, who also took part in the interview. Other scholars refer to her as Jacobs (Amber Clifford, "Queering the Inferno: Space, Identity, and Kansas City's Jazz Scene," PhD diss., University of Kansas, 2007). Her papers are housed at the University of Kansas Spencer Research Library under the Whithouse name, which will be used in this chapter for clarity.

47. Interview 32, Edna and Ida Mintern, Kansas City, Missouri, January 24, 1980, Tapes 122-123, Kansas City Jazz Oral History Collection (K0012), SHSM-KC.

48. Edna Mae Whithouse Collection, Kansas Collection, RH MS P797, Spencer Library.

49. Interview 32, Edna and Ida Mintern, Kansas City, Missouri, January 24, 1980, Tapes 122-123, Kansas City Jazz Oral History Collection (K0012), SHSM-KC.

50. Edna Mae Whithouse Collection, Kansas Collection, RH MS P797, Spencer Library.

51. See, for example, Allan Berubé, *Coming Out under Fire: The History of Gay Men and Women in World War Two* (New York: Free Press, 1990), especially chap. 2, "GI Drag: A Gay Refuge."

52. Interview 32, Edna and Ida Mintern, Kansas City, Missouri, January 24, 1980, Tapes 122-123, Kansas City Jazz Oral History Collection (K0012), SHSM-KC.

53. Ibid.

CHAPTER SIXTEEN

Kansas City's Liberty Memorial

Remembering Then and Now

Keith Eggener

In 1915, as the European war dragged into its second year, spreading, intensifying, now taking American lives with the sinking of the *Falaba* and the *Lusitania*, sociologist Emile Durkheim wrote: "Without symbols social sentiments could have only a precarious existence. If the movements by which these sentiments are expressed are connected with something that endures, the sentiments themselves become more durable."[1] Three years later, with the Armistice signed, people the world over debated how best to make something enduring of their sentiments around the Great War's questionable gains, its incomprehensible costs, and the millions of lives lost to it.

Of the nearly 9 million soldiers who died in World War I, 441 hailed from Kansas City, Missouri. As the war wound down, calls for a memorial to honor them came quickly and spread fast throughout the city. The Liberty Memorial—a 217-foot limestone shaft set within a courtyard framed by two stark pavilions and two great sphinxes—stood at its dedication in 1926 as one of the country's largest and most lavish monuments. During the 1920s and 1930s it was praised internationally as among its best.[2] But time passes, and even the most seemingly durable sentiments fade. The memorial's story over the next seven decades—told elsewhere—is one of inexorable decline punctuated by well-intentioned but insufficient efforts to revive the aging structure.[3] By the 1960s, the once-prominent memorial was an outmoded and all-but-forgotten relic. In 1994, after years of neglect, it was declared unsound and closed to the public. When it reopened in 2006 it had changed, but then so too had its audience.

The Liberty Memorial was conceived and constructed during a period of "particularly intense monument-building," one that ran from roughly 1880 to 1930.[4]

The site was restored and expanded amid a second such period, beginning in the 1980s and continuing to this day. Locally, these two eras correspond with (1) Kansas City's emergence as a major urban center of high cultural aspirations and (2) its most ambitious and successful program of urban redevelopment. In each case and in different ways, Kansas Citians framed the war and its remembrance as a means to future gains. These framings offer telling views of the city's modern history, its greatest monument, and the changing nature of memory.

The Monument Rises

Calls for a memorial in Kansas City came even before the war's end.[5] The idea gained traction: public meetings were held, names were floated, and by December 1918, the Liberty Memorial Association (LMA), led by real estate developer J. C. Nichols and lumber baron Robert A. Long, had been formed. Their meetings included much discussion of type. Was the memorial to be a commemorative, functional building or perhaps a nonutilitarian monument? By April 1919, the LMA decided to erect "a monument plus a building, not for utilitarian purposes, but to house trophies of war."[6] A fund-raising drive begun that October netted more than $2 million in just ten days, with over 83,000 people (in a city of 325,000) contributing. In March 1920, American Institute of Architects national president Thomas R. Kimball signed on as "professional advisor" to the project. A site was acquired: thirty-three acres on a highly visible hilltop across from Jarvis Hunt's imposing beaux-arts Union Station, gateway to the city since 1914.

In December 1920, a competition was opened to all "bona-fide practicing architect[s]" in Kansas City and to five prominent firms invited from outside. The program called for "a memorial that shall symbolize the dawn of a warless age, and do honor to those who died that such an age might be a human heritage." The LMA stressed that the memorial—while it "shall set the keynote for an art, literary and musical center"—should have essentially no function but memorialization: "utilitarian features, if any, [should] be subordinate and incidental."[7]

The jury—consisting of architects Henry Bacon, James Gamble Rogers, and Louis Ayers of New York, John M. Donaldson of Detroit, and W. R. B. Willcox of Seattle—received eleven completed entries.[8] The most unusual was New Yorker Bertram Grosvenor Goodhue's proposal for a walled and ruined-looking acropolis with an immense blocky tower and a round-arched bridge over Main Street, linking the site to the neighboring hill to the east. His highly scenographic design received a politely dismissive fourth place. Third place went to Greenbaum, Hardy, and Schumacher for a giant fluted column rising from terraced gardens; theirs was the only local entry to place in the top four and the one most like the winning submission. Philadelphia's Paul Cret, whose design consisted of a high wall topped by a statue of Lady Liberty, earned second place. First place, by a unanimous vote, went to Harold Van Buren Magonigle of New York.

The earliest calls for a memorial in Kansas City had focused on the enduring significance of soldiers' sacrifices and the eternal debt of the living. It would be above all a place to remember and give thanks. Mayor James Cowgill's statement, published in the *Kansas City Journal* on November 18, one week after the Armistice, is exemplary:

> Chisel it from the whitest Parian marble, you cannot make it whiter than their sacrifice; or rear it of the firmest granite hewn from the everlasting hills, you cannot erect a monument that will be more enduring than their memory should be in the annals of the Nation. That such a monument should be erected there can be no question, though but an imperfect expression of the Nation's gratitude, for when bronze and marble and even granite shall have crumbled into dust their memory shall still live so long as the human heart shall pant for liberty.[9]

More than any of the others, Magonigle's entry captured this sense of timelessness. In one spectacular competition drawing he showed the memorial at night, seen obliquely and from below. In the dark foreground sits a stone sphinx, veiling its face enigmatically. Behind this a hidden light source illuminates a high wall covered with inscriptions and reliefs; this wall is crowned by a soaring column from whose top white smoke twists against a cobalt sky. Many of the competing images included human figures. One of Cret's showed a mustachioed man before a wall, pitching woo to his coy sweetheart. Others showed people standing about doing little more than pointing or lending human scale. Magonigle's drawing is unique in that it shows something happening, something that is more profound than pointing or wooing. The scene is a solemn pageant of some sort. The diminutive scale of the figures conveys the immensity of the structure and the distance between those living and those elevated and expanded by sacrifice. One tiny but powerful figure stands with legs apart, hands on hips, boldly silhouetted beside the sphinx. Others ascend the steps to the sphinx's right. Most are not seen at all but merely suggested by the flags they carry. Without the English-language inscriptions on the wall, the location and era would be completely indeterminate. Either Ramses or Reagan could assume his place atop the wall. Magonigle presented his concept not as the other entrants did theirs—as more or less attractive and commodious urban furniture—but as an object assuming a sacred and central role in the community, its forms capable of bearing their messages and authority for generations to come. A few years later, with construction under way, Magonigle told a reporter he saw no reason why the monument should not stand for 5,000 years.[10]

One of architect Harold Van Buren Magonigle's proposal drawings, depicting Liberty Memorial at night and capturing a sense of timelessness, c. 1920. Courtesy of the Avery Architectural and Fine Arts Library, Columbia University, New York.

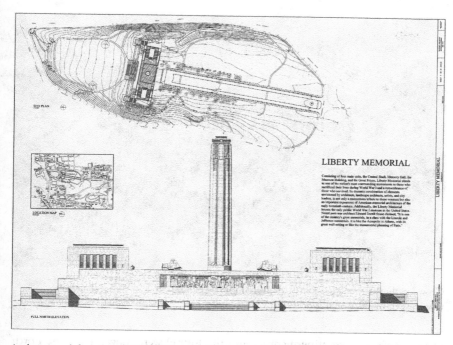

Architectural drawing of Liberty Memorial from the 2000 Historic American Buildings Survey. Courtesy of the Library of Congress Prints and Photographs Division, Washington, DC.

The recently cleared and graded building site was dedicated on November 1, 1921. In attendance were Vice President Calvin Coolidge, the five commanders of the Allied forces (including Missouri-born general John Pershing), and a crowd of 100,000. Construction, however, did not begin until 1923. As architects often do, Magonigle significantly underestimated costs, so substantial modifications were required. The entire design was scaled back and pared down. The memorial's central element, a great tapered shaft topped by four guardian spirits, was reduced in height. The matching classical pavilions on either side (a "memory hall" to be filled with murals and a museum for war-related "trophies") became severe, unembellished boxes. Originally set back from the shaft on a lower level, they now aligned with it on a single, long, east-west axis, forming a "memory court" with the shaft at the center. The once-elaborate north wall facing Union Station was made lower, longer, and almost featureless. It was to have accommodated a 400-foot-long frieze representing the "Procession of Civilization," to be carved by Magonigle's wife, Edith. Instead, the wall stayed blank until 1934, when Edmond Amateis's more modest 144-foot relief of the "March from War to Peace" was begun. The

Crowd gathering outside Liberty Memorial for the November 11, 1926, dedication.
Courtesy of the National World War I Museum and Memorial, Kansas City, Missouri.

two sphinxes (representing memory and the future) were moved from the north to the south side of the shaft and thus made invisible from Union Station. The north side's grand staircase and circular fountain were scrapped. Even with the sculptures and landscaping (by George Kessler and Frederick Law Olmsted Jr.), the final product appeared far more spare—and consequently, more modern—than originally intended.

On November 11, 1926, the not-yet-completed monument was dedicated in another ceremony marked by its size and modernity. Coolidge, now president, returned to address an audience of 150,000. Newspapers called this the greatest gathering in the history of the city and the largest crowd ever addressed by a president of the United States. People motoring toward the site caused one of the city's first traffic jams. Airplanes circled overhead before the speeches, dropping flowers on the masses below. Several distinguished guests were in attendance, including Queen Marie of Romania, whose travel expenses were underwritten by the Ford Motor Company. Loudspeakers carried the ceremony to the farthest reaches of the throng, while radio broadcasts carried it farther still. The ceremony was filmed and the reels carried by plane to New York so that theaters there could show it the following day. Klieg lights lit the memorial that night, making it visible from a great distance; twenty-five miles away in Olathe, Kansas, people reportedly thought a new star had appeared in the night sky. Critical response to the memorial was immediate, widespread, and generally rapturous.[11]

Boosting Kansas City

Scores of monuments were built across the United States during the first decades of the twentieth century. Many of these were connected to the concurrent phenomenon of boosterism—a nationwide movement by which local elites promoted their towns and cities, emphasizing economic development, real estate opportunities, tourist attractions, and civic pride grounded in the recognition of local history, culture, and community spirit.[12] Public monuments were among the leading material manifestations of this movement—both a symptom and an agent of the booster spirit—and at no time was their production greater than in the decade after the Great War. Across the nation, hundreds of memorials arose, commemorating heroes, events, and ideals related to the war. Many were of grand scale, but size had little to do with the numbers of local soldiers lost. Civic pride, ambition, and economic competition were far more significant drivers. The 1924 Indiana World War Memorial Plaza in Indianapolis, for instance, was among the largest in the country, even though that city's losses were not unusually high (nor were Kansas City's); it was built in large part to lure the American Legion to establish its headquarters there, with all the commerce and cachet this was expected to bring.[13]

Kansas City's booster machine had been gathering steam in the years before the war. Writing in 1908, local historian Carrie Westlake Whitney called it "simply the logic of destiny that Kansas City is to be the greatest metropolis on the American continent"—an overstatement, no doubt, but it illustrated an ambition that many then shared.[14] In the years between the two world wars, Kansas City did indeed take on the signifiers of a major modern metropolis. During the 1920s a new downtown skyline emerged, with twenty- and thirty-story office towers. A municipal airport began operations in 1927, the same year the Kansas City Art Institute moved to its new quarters near the site of the planned William Rockhill Nelson Gallery of Art and the Mary Atkins Museum of Fine Arts, later combined as the Nelson-Atkins Museum of Art. The University of Kansas City and the Kansas City Philharmonic were founded around the same time. Road construction, traffic signals, service stations, and parking lots and garages marked the city's growing automobility. Apartment construction surged, a sign of the city's mounting density. A key indicator of the city's new national prominence was its hosting of the 1928 Republican National Convention, described by Dustin Gann in Chapter 5 in this volume. Even during the Depression, construction continued unabated, funded partly by federal money and partly by local taxpayers. In 1931 voters approved a $50-million bond issue, the so-called Ten-Year Plan, for the city's continuing development. Among the projects were a new $6.5 million Municipal Auditorium capable of accommodating 10,000 people and a new Civic Center featuring skyscraper city hall and county courthouse buildings. Sports and convention facilities, parks, playgrounds, schools, hospitals, water treatment facilities, flood control projects, and zoo and airport improvements were all completed during this time. The city's Chamber of Commerce aimed, with only slightly less ambition than Whitney voiced in 1908, "to make Kansas City the greatest inland city in America."[15] Chamber of Commerce president Conrad Mann—"a pioneer in municipal advertising" and a leading proponent of the Ten-Year Plan and the Liberty Memorial—spent huge sums promoting the city nationally as "the Heart of America."[16]

Like many of their fellow citizens, the Liberty Memorial's planners anticipated and encouraged such achievements. They may have cast their work as a tribute to those killed in a war already receding, but what was sacrifice if not for the living and those yet to come? American war memorials, writes art historian Kirk Savage, helped further the "progressive narrative of national history," instilling a sense of closure that condensed moral lessons and allowed society to proceed toward new goals and achievements.[17] Moreover, in honoring their dead, Kansas City's living gained something that they sorely lacked, something that might enhance their civic image and sense of common purpose. "There are few cities in America that are so devoid of emblematic and memorial statuary as this," wrote LMA Secretary J. E. McPherson in 1921. "There is no conspicuous monument typifying the city's spirit and civic sentiment."[18] The Liberty Memorial would fill that void.

From the beginning the memorial was seen as an adjunct to future urban growth and glory. When Hunt's Union Station opened in 1914 its entrance faced not north toward downtown, but south toward the new suburbs just then being developed by future LMA vice chairman J. C. Nichols. Concerned with providing buffer areas along the lines of race and class and stabilizing land values at his elite subdivisions, Nichols, like other local boosters, was troubled by the view from Union Station's front doors. Across Twenty-Fourth Street stood Signboard Hill, formerly the site of Keck's Tivoli Garden (a popular picnic ground and dance hall of the 1870s), now a cluster of billboards, shacks, and scrubby vegetation.[19] Fearing the development of a larger and more entrenched slum, Nichols, along with Hunt, landscape architect George Kessler, and future LMA chairman Robert A. Long, urged improving the site to benefit the new station and visitors' first impressions of the city.[20] In 1919 the hill directly south of Union Station was chosen as the site for the new memorial and the land acquired by Nichols. He and Long hoped that a major cultural center—with museums and galleries, a concert hall and opera house, a library, and a university—would cluster around it. "Artistic achievements are absolutely necessary to our city's proper development and we must begin to plan for them," Long wrote. "The Liberty Memorial gives the opportunity to awaken all of our people to a realization of the need of this broader, more beautiful development."[21] Architect Magonigle would express similar sentiments, calling the site "a New Acropolis in a New Athens . . . the well-spring of a glorious future . . . your FLAME OF INSPIRATION."[22] Long picked up on this heightened rhetoric, evoking empire and linking Kansas City to other great urban centers. He cast the

View looking west at Union Station and "Signboard Hill," just south of the future site of Liberty Memorial, date unknown. Courtesy of the Missouri Valley Special Collections, Kansas City Public Library.

rising memorial as "the beginning of a great movement which we hope will establish Kansas City as the Mecca for all those ambitious and aspiring spirits who desire to develop artistic talents and which will place her as the cultural capital of her vast and favored tributary territory."[23]

Kansas Citians had for some time called their town the heart and hub of the United States. Now, in advertising it as such, they put the Liberty Memorial front and center. For example, a magazine advertisement of 1932 for the Missouri Pacific Railroad was headlined, "KANSAS CITY 'HEART OF AMERICA.'" This featured written testimony of the city's advantages (location, modern facilities) and amenities (art and music centers) and an illustration of its downtown skyline. In the foreground, smoke rising from its summit, stood the Liberty Memorial shaft.[24] The heart this imagery implied was geographical, for sure, but cultural and spiritual too.

Voicing Service, Quelling Dissent

Memorials, writes art historian Erika Doss, "are made because they correspond to immediate social and political needs."[25] Honoring soldiers, providing a place for mourning and remembrance, promoting cultural and economic opportunities: These were the evident social needs the Liberty Memorial addressed. Less overt were its political functions. World War I historian George Mosse identified "the Myth of the War Experience" and "the Cult of the Fallen Soldier" as elements of a widespread "urge to find a higher meaning in the war experience, and to obtain some justification of the sacrifice and loss."[26] In its aftermath and in more than one nation, the bloody war became a "sacred experience," a cornerstone of nationalist ideologies and of programs designed to discourage unrest and promote unity. Memorials and the speeches given beside them were among the principal tools of this conversion process.

The effort was not a seamless one. We see gaps, for instance, in the experiential fabric of those who fought and those who stayed home, between official rhetoric and private remembrance. With the signing of the Armistice, reported the *Star*, Kansas Citians were overcome with "the spirit of jubilation."[27] Talk of jubilation was commonplace and undoubtedly sincere for many, yet for those who fought in the trenches, a different mood prevailed. As novelist and former soldier R. H. Mottram recalled: "The news came. The enemy had signed our terms. I cannot speak for places in the rear, but, on what had been the battle-line, there was no glory, no jubilation. There was very little material for any festivity, and that little was hard to get, so bare and worn was everything and everybody."[28] More aggressive forms of dissent emerged and were met by still greater aggression. To question the war or the US government's motivation in waging it was to invite charges of sedition, and more than one Kansas Citian faced this charge. In 1917, Congress passed the Espionage Act, aimed at preventing interference with the war effort, insubordination in the military, or the support of enemies. The Sedition Act of 1918 extended this, prohibiting "disloyal, profane, scurrilous, or abusive language" about the US government or its armed forces. In Kansas City in 1918, high-profile sedition cases ended with the jailing of three journalists.[29]

In one very real and painful sense, memorials, like the wars they mark, represent failure, the breakdown of diplomacy and of a government's charge of maintaining the peace. War memorials—at least those built prior to the 1982 Vietnam Veterans Memorial in Washington, DC—have typically recast conflicts in triumphant terms that obscure this failure.[30] Much honest grief and gratitude undoubtedly fueled the building of the Liberty Memorial, just as virtuous feeling caused men and women to enlist. Yet by its end, this cataclysmic contest—resulting in more than 17 million soldier and civilian deaths and the wounding of 20 million more worldwide—was widely recognized as a disaster, a series of colossal and largely pointless mistakes. Anti-government and anti-militaristic sentiments were thus rampant in the United States and elsewhere in the years following the war. Framing the war as indisputably heroic and glorious, celebrating it publicly in polished bronze and stone, was not without its practical propagandistic value.

The competition program for the Liberty Memorial's design spoke portentously of "conditions of instability and change unprecedented in building history."[31] What exactly this referred to is unclear. What is clear is that conditions in the United States and elsewhere remained volatile well after the Armistice. The year 1919, for instance, saw political assassinations and revolt in Germany and the violent expansion of the Soviet Union. There was armed conflict between British, Indian, and Afghan forces; the USSR and Finland; France and Syria; and Hungary and Czechoslovakia. Between 1920 and 1926, American forces were sent to Russia, Panama (twice), Costa Rica, Turkey, China (four times), Honduras (twice), and Nicaragua; an invasion of Mexico loomed. At home during these years Americans faced political scandals, rampant organized crime, and a resurgent Ku Klux Klan. They clashed over Prohibition, women's rights and roles, race, immigration, and evolution. Labor activism and government crackdowns escalated nationwide, resulting in frequent violence. Race riots hit Chicago, Omaha, Tulsa, and other cities. Huge numbers of veterans were out of work, without benefits, angry, marching, and making demands.[32] In 1920, radicals bombed Wall Street, killing thirty-eight and injuring hundreds. Nationwide, raids on meetings of socialists, anarchists, unionists, immigrants, and others resulted in more than 10,000 arrests and numerous deportations. In Kansas City, a series of strikes from 1917 to 1920—including the bloody general strike of 1918, involving more than 25,000 workers—rocked the city and captured national headlines. Dozens of union members were arrested the following year on espionage charges, tried, convicted, and sent to the nearby federal penitentiary at Leavenworth, Kansas. Adding to this toxic state of affairs, between 1920 and 1926, when the *Missouri Crime Survey* was published, Kansas City laid claim to one of the nation's highest crime rates, its highest per capita murder rate, and one of its most corrupt and ineffective police forces.[33]

None of this was made visible at the Liberty Memorial, although it might help to explain the site's size and grandiosity and the peculiarly wary tone of President Coolidge's 1926 dedication address. Coolidge was invited to give the address by Irwin Kirkwood, husband of William Rockhill Nelson's daughter Laura and, with her, owner of the *Kansas City Star* after Nelson's death in 1915. A presidential address would draw favorable attention to the strike-prone, crime-ridden city and lend gravitas to the new memorial. The president initially declined but was won over by Kirkwood's offer of his luxurious and secluded compound in the Adirondacks, White Pine Camp, where the president and much of the White House staff spent most of the summer of 1926.[34] Paying his debt that November, Coolidge addressed the vast Kansas City audience. With "talking points" provided by *Kansas City Star* editor Henry J. Haskell, Coolidge spoke of the fairness of the federal government's new conscription policies (which now applied to rich and poor alike), its "boundless" admiration for veterans and the generous support it provided them (despite much evidence to the contrary), the nation's laudable ethnic diversity and peerless unity (race riots aside), and its lack of "imperialistic designs" (the long list of foreign invasions notwithstanding).[35] He denied that Americans profited from the war, though he admitted that "some individuals made gains." Repeatedly, he used the words "suspicion" and "distrust," and he insisted that these must be combatted.

The Armistice, he claimed, "did not mark the end of the war, for the end is not yet, it marked a general subsidence of the armed conflict." The world remained a dangerous place.

Yet the Liberty Memorial, he said, "raised to commemorate . . . the results of war and victory, which are embodied in peace and liberty," gave proof of "the whole martial spirit of this neighborhood . . . [whose] divisions were serving with so much distinction on the battle fields of France [while] their fellow citizens were supporting them with scarcely less distinction in patriotic efforts at home." Without providing specifics, Coolidge concluded that given "the present state of the world," American responsibility "is more grave than it ever was at any other time." But the Liberty Memorial stood as "holy testament that our country will continue to do its duty under the guidance of Divine Providence."[36]

Thus, exactly eight years after the Armistice, the war and its newest memorial offered indelible images of common purpose, noble sacrifice, and divine sanction. The memorial was a beacon, embodying the city's and the country's best instincts, modeling to all the virtues of unquestioning service and submission to authority. So much the better if it countered current social unrest or drowned out dissent.[37] His unwanted chore concluded, Coolidge and his wife got back on the train to Washington, just seven hours after their arrival in Kansas City.

Decline, Renewal, and Change

Memorials, historian Jay Winter writes, have a "half life, a trajectory of decomposition. . . . Other meanings derived from other needs or events may be attached to them, or no meaning at all."[38] Time passes, wounds close, memories fade, survivors die, new crises take precedence. By the early 1940s, with the country involved in a new world war, the Liberty Memorial faced the first of several budget cuts and closures.[39] Maintenance was deferred. A cycle of neglect, deterioration, and half measures set in. This was accompanied by a fundamental shift in public attitudes toward memorials after World War II. With the rush to commemorate the previous war still fresh in the minds of many, a kind of "memorial exhaustion" set in. The preference now was for modest plaques or, better still, for functional "living" memorials such as stadiums and community centers. Traditional memorials like Kansas City's were now seen by many as "useless and vulgar," demanding that people remember things they would rather forget.[40]

The Liberty Memorial's decline also mirrored that of the city surrounding it. The memorial's success had always been tied to that of the nearby Union Station, and indeed, as rail travel plummeted after World War II—with local passenger numbers falling from over 678,000 in 1945 to under 33,000 in 1973—so too did memorial visitor numbers decline. Meanwhile, through annexations, road building, and a dramatic rise in private automobile ownership, the city sprawled. Now isolated by freeways, Kansas City's downtown became increasingly shabby and depopulated. Urban revitalization efforts were conducted, but most had little real effect on the city's livability or image. Major natural and structural disasters hit hard, the local economy sagged, newspapers closed, airlines and professional sports teams left town, and racial divisions erupted. The civic pride and sense of unity the Liberty Memorial once represented ebbed. Between 1970 and 1990 the city lost population, especially in the downtown area and close-in suburbs. By the 1980s, the Liberty Memorial and its surroundings were a dangerous place, hosting a string of robberies, assaults, and murders. In 1994, following a suicide jump from its top and an engineer's report finding the structure in jeopardy of collapse, the memorial was closed.

Calls from veterans' groups to rebuild the memorial immediately followed its closure, but it was not until 2000, with money from a voter-approved city sales tax initiative and other public and private sources, that work began on a comprehensive restoration and expansion.[41] The National World War I Museum at Liberty Memorial opened in 2006, two years after its designation by Congress as the nation's official World War I museum. In 2014 President Barack Obama signed legislation re-designating the site as the National World War I Museum and Memorial. Today the museum is one of Kansas City's top tourist attractions, a source of local pride, and a major economic engine. The travel website TripAdvisor has twice named it one of the country's top twenty-five museums (out of more than 35,000 nationwide).[42] But as the site's new name suggests, the memorial now plays a secondary role.

The $102 million renovation project, overseen by Kansas City–based architects Abend Singleton Associates, involved a comprehensive restoration of existing structures and, on the memorial's south side, the construction of a terraced garden and reflecting pool. This provided the forecourt and entrance for a new, subterranean, 80,000-square-foot study center and museum with exhibits designed by Ralph Applebaum and Associates of New York (who also designed the exhibits at the US Holocaust Memorial Museum in Washington, DC). With more than 75,000 artifacts, the museum aimed to present a comprehensive experience of the war, shown from a variety of perspectives, not just American or even military ones. High-tech interactive tables, 3D, 360-degree images, soundproof listening rooms, wall-mounted videos, a 100-foot-wide movie screen, a walk-through bomb crater, and life-size trench re-creations immersed the visitor in the war experience. "We want to introduce people to this great cataclysm," said one of the exhibition designers. "Flashes, red fire, shells, battle sounds at night. We want to create a terrifying look."[43] Included were a café and a gift shop where one might purchase T-shirts embellished with screen-printed gas masks, hand-grenade mouse pads, and other like fare.

That any of this is now seen as desirable marks the fundamental distance between the early postwar era and ours. For soldiers and civilians who had lived through the

Modern photograph of Liberty Memorial and the Kansas City skyline, c. 2017. Courtesy of Visit KC.

war, it likely would have been unimaginable, appalling even, that anyone should want to experience such horrors anew or clothe themselves in images of death and destruction. But that generation is now gone. By 2006, when the museum opened, only thirteen American veterans of World War I were known to be alive.[44] The last, Missouri-born corporal Frank Buckles, died in 2011 at 110.[45] The memorial and museum are not for them. Who then are they for and what purpose do they serve?

The Liberty Memorial's revival is connected to several linked trends going on worldwide since the 1980s, trends identified by a variety of sobriquets, including the "Memory Boom," "Memorial Mania," and "heritage tourism." In nearly all fields of academic discourse, the study of memory, both personal and collective, has assumed a central position. Significant historical transformations—the aging and dying of the World War II and Holocaust generations, the end of the Cold War, ethnic and racial conflicts and the waves of violence and displacement that often accompany them, the civil rights movement and other social justice movements, the "cultural turn" in historical studies, and the rise of identity politics—have fueled our interest in collective memory and a nearly universal awareness of the stakes involved in controlling historical narratives. Who tells the story of a community or a nation, how do they tell it (what is included or excluded, emphasized or downplayed), and to what ends? In the arena of individual memory, billions of dollars are spent annually researching and treating the memory disorders that come with longer lifespans, in overcoming traumatic memories, and in trying to enhance memory's capacity and agility. Changing technologies for data capture, storage, and recall promise— or threaten—to alter the very nature of human memory. Within popular culture, memory-themed entertainments like the History Channel and Hollywood movies such as *Memento*, *Total Recall*, and *Eternal Sunshine of the Spotless Mind* vie for audiences with online memory games and a tidal wave of memoirs—memoirs being one of the strongest sectors of the publishing industry over the past two decades. Meanwhile, a worldwide surge in museum and memorial construction and of efforts to preserve and capitalize upon historic buildings, districts, and sites has occurred. These sites are often conceived as tourist destinations, feeding our culturally pervasive nostalgia and our hunger for authenticity, while promising jobs and cultural cachet for the communities that build and maintain them.[46]

Locally, the Liberty Memorial's restoration and expansion were early salvos in what has become one of the country's most ambitious and successful urban renewal programs of recent years. In 1996, work began on a $250-million restoration of Union Station, closed since 1985. The Liberty Memorial's rehabilitation followed soon after, and since 2000 upward of $8 billion has been spent on restorations of historic properties, new building projects, and other improvements, most of those within or near the city center. Projects include the new Kansas City Public Library, the new Federal Courthouse, the 19,000-seat Sprint Center, the Power and Light and Crossroads Art Districts, the Midland Theater restoration, the restoration and expansion of the Nelson-Atkins Museum of Art, the Kauffman Center for the Performing Arts, the *Kansas City Star*'s new printing plant, the Eighteenth and Vine Historic District, the MAX Bus Rapid Transit and short streetcar lines, hotels, office and residential developments, and much more. Since 2000 the number of people living downtown has grown by 50 percent to around 20,000, with plans to double that number once again.[47] Among the drivers of this recent growth are a robust regional economy and the political leadership and voter will necessary to approve bond measures and tax abatements. Attractively low real estate prices and numerous quality of life indicators, including a range of high-quality cultural amenities, draw still more people to the area and expand the tax base.

The Liberty Memorial, without abandoning its original goals, has positioned itself to aid and benefit from this new growth. According to a 2015 report from the LMA, "Every great American city has a strong arts and cultural life. But only one has the National World War I Museum. This is a gift to Kansas City and Kansas City's gift to the nation." Among other things, the museum's stated aims include being "the foremost interpreter and resource for insight into the Great War and its enduring impact"; providing "first-class visitor and virtual experiences . . . to diverse audiences"; being "a 'must-see' destination, and source of civic pride." The report calls the memorial court atop the museum "Kansas City's Front Porch," whose "iconic views" of the city make it perfect "for large group gatherings and special events," a prime "income-generating rental venue for private and corporate occasions." The site's total economic impact on Kansas City for 2013 "included spending outside the Museum that generated $10.7 million in economic output, $2.9 million in household earnings, and supported 110 jobs in the metro area." In contrast to the founders' conception of a towering memorial with a modest "museum for trophies," the site now showcases a major, world-class social history museum. And in this capacity, it aims "to positively effect social change" and encourage "informed decision making."[48]

The Meaning of Memory

Art historian Jules Prown has written of artifacts as "events" that live on into the present: concrete evidence of otherwise intangible, temporally situated human actions, beliefs, emotions, and aspirations.[49] The Liberty Memorial is such an artifact, but unlike many others—locked inside museum cases, frozen in time—it has evolved along with its urban setting. Its historical and functional trajectories are worth considering, not least for what these indicate about our changing notions of memory and commemoration.

In introducing his 1922 "guide-book to some of memory's most interesting facts," British popular psychologist T. H. Pear defined memory as "the recall of past experience . . . retained experience . . . actually being recalled."[50] Pear used the analogy of a gramophone record: experience fixes itself within the brain like the grooves on a phonographic recording; while playback (i.e., recall) might be affected over time by warping or erosion, the memories themselves are inherently unchanged. Seen in this light, a memorial is like a gramophone eternally replaying the same record; however faint or degraded the record becomes, it sounds essentially the same notes to all who listen. This conception accords with Emile Durkheim's notion, stated at the outset, of sentiments made to endure.

A few years after Pear, Durkheim's student Maurice Halbwachs opened the door to a much more dynamic view of memory, presenting it as something always malleable, always mediated by the experiences, perspectives, biases, and evolving interactions and agendas (conscious or otherwise) of those who remember. Though his work did not have much impact outside France until the 1980s, scholars since then have widely adopted and expanded upon his theories.[51] Memory is now broadly understood as not a passive thing we hold but a force that we possess and use to our own ends. It "is the very apparatus that enables change," writes memory scholar Astrid Erll. "Memory studies is therefore not an exercise in nostalgia, but . . . a method to discover and reflect the mechanisms and potentialities of culture change and renewal."[52]

The Liberty Memorial, built to serve a static view of the war and its meaning, one determined by elites and presumably accepted and shared by the larger public, today faces a more diverse and fragmented audience than ever before, one that expects and even demands an active, self-determined role vis-à-vis memory both individual and collective. People increasingly want to tell their own stories and develop their own interpretations of events based on access to available evidence. Today's audiences, further, are generally less interested in collective duties than in individual and group rights, and memory has become an important tool for pursuing these.[53] In other words, memorials today are less about the officially sanctioned pasts they mark than the individual and collective futures they might inform, enable, and activate; they are tools less for playback than for the exploration and expansion of self and culture. And unlike visitors of the 1920s or even the 1960s, no one going to the memorial today "remembers" the war. What we find and experience there now is history, not memory as scholars defined it, not the direct recall of lived experience, but stories handed down, told and retold.[54] Not everyone is happy about all of this, of course. In 2000, local preservation groups objected to the Liberty Memorial's expansion, in part because it emphasized the museum and thus "denigrate[d] the memory of those who gave their lives."[55] But trying to hold on to those memories without their changing is like trying to capture water in a net.

Certainly, some future-oriented thinking was present at the Liberty Memorial's conception, in the boosterism that brought the memorial to Kansas City and in the eyes of those who regarded it as an amenity to build upon. But the recent shift in emphasis from memorial to museum reflects the new stress on individual affect and experience, on those living now and in the years ahead. "War today is everybody's business," Jay Winter writes, not just that of cultural or social elites, veterans or survivors, architects or historians: "We need to acknowledge the messiness of remembrance, the absence of uniformity."[56] If memorials are to survive beyond a generation or two as anything other than curiously obsolete urban furniture, their sense of purpose must be regularly renewed and recast. We may say otherwise, but ultimately we build memorials not for the dead but for ourselves—for the living called upon to remember. If they do not speak to us, we are unlikely to listen to them.

Notes

This chapter draws on material previously published in Keith Eggener, "Up to Date in Kansas City: The Liberty Memorial as Modern Architecture," *Places: Forum of Design for the Public Realm* (November 2009), https://placesjournal.org/article/up-to-date-in-kansas-city/, accessed September 22, 2015. Used with permission.

1. Emile Durkheim, *The Elementary Forms of the Religious Life* (London: George Allen and Unwin, 1915, 1982), 231.

2. For more on the memorial's reception, see Eggener, "Up to Date in Kansas City."

3. Derek Donovan, *Lest the Ages Forget: Kansas City's Liberty Memorial* (Kansas City, Mo.: Kansas City Star Books, 2001). See also Cydney E. Millstein, "Liberty Memorial, Kansas City, Missouri, Historic American Buildings Survey Report," 2000, http://www.ahr-kc.com /reports/liberty_memorial/ (accessed September 22, 2015).

4. Dell Upton, "Why Do Contemporary Monuments Talk So Much?" in *Commemoration in America*, ed. David Gobel and Daves Rossell (Charlottesville: University of Virginia Press, 2013), 19.

5. An editorial in the *Kansas City Journal* called for a memorial on November 9, 1918, two days before the Armistice was signed. Donovan, *Lest the Ages Forget*, 18.

6. J. E. McPherson, *The Liberty Memorial in Kansas City, Missouri* (Kansas City, Mo.: Liberty Memorial Association, 1929), 6.

7. *Program: Competition for the Selection of an Architect to Design and Supervise the Construction of a Memorial at Kansas City* (Kansas City, Mo.: Liberty Memorial Association, 1920), 6, 8, 15, 21; and McPherson, *The Liberty Memorial in Kansas City*, 6.

8. All are illustrated in Donovan, *Lest the Ages Forget*, 32–49.

9. "Mayor Cowgill Indorses Victory Monument Plan," *Kansas City Journal*, November 18, 1918, n.p.

10. Magonigle, quoted in "Shaft Designer Inspects Sphinx," *Kansas City Post*, January 6, 1926, n.p.

11. This paragraph draws on contemporary Kansas City newspaper accounts of the dedication, all found in the Press Clipping Books, Liberty Memorial Library and Archives, Kansas City, Missouri. For more on this see Eggener, "Up to Date in Kansas City."

12. On boosterism see Paul J. P. Sandul, *California Dreaming: Boosterism, Memory, and Rural Suburbs in the Golden State* (Morgantown: West Virginia University Press, 2014); and Lee M. A. Simpson, "Boosters and the Selling of the American West," *Journal of the West*, 42, no. 4 (Fall 2003).

13. Relative to its urban population (324,410 in 1920), Kansas City's 441 losses were proportionately on par with most other sizable American cities. By comparison: Washington, DC (1920 pop. 437,571), lost 499 soldiers in the war; St. Louis (pop. 772,897) lost 1,075.

14. Carrie Westlake Whitney, *Kansas City Missouri: Its History and Its People, 1808–1908*, vol. 1 (Chicago: S. J. Clarke Publishing, 1908), 671.

15. James R. Shortridge, *Kansas City and How It Grew, 1822–2011* (Lawrence: University Press of Kansas, 2012), 73.

16. Harry Haskell, *Boss-Busters and Sin Hounds: Kansas City and Its Star* (Columbia: University of Missouri Press, 2007), 236. Haskell writes, "The flood stage of the booster campaign reached its high-water mark . . . with the long-anticipated dedication [in November 1926] of the Liberty Memorial."

17. Kirk Savage, "The Past in the Present: The Life of Memorials," *Harvard Design Magazine* 9 (Fall 1999): 2.

18. J. E. McPherson, "Kansas City's Liberty Memorial," Part I, *Arts and Decoration* 15 (June 1921): 98.

19. What had once been a single hill became two when Main Street was cut through it in the nineteenth century. The eastern half became the site of Crown Center during the 1960s; the western half is the site of the Liberty Memorial. Both were at various times called Signboard Hill.

20. A. Theodore Brown and Lyle W. Dorsett, K.C.: A History of Kansas City, Missouri (Boulder, Colo.: Pruett Publishing 1978), 169–179; Shortridge, Kansas City and How It Grew, 70–71.

21. "R. A. Long's Vision," Kansas City Star, October 26, 1919, n.p.

22. Harold Van Buren Magonigle, "Address at the Dinner of the Knife and Fork Club, Kansas City, Missouri, Armistice Day, 1924," 4, Liberty Memorial Library and Archives, Kansas City, Missouri.

23. Robert A. Long, "Our Liberty Memorial Is a Noble Civic Asset," Citizens' League Bulletin (January 23, 1926), 2. The Liberty Memorial's founders rarely mentioned its economic potential, though this was clearly a factor in Indianapolis's move to build the equally ambitious Indiana World War Memorial. See John Bodnar, Remaking America: Public Memory, Commemoration, and Patriotism in the Twentieth Century (Princeton: Princeton University Press, 1992), 86.

24. Literary Digest (April 6, 1932), n.p.

25. Erika Doss, Memorial Mania: Public Feeling in America (Chicago: University of Chicago Press, 2010), 212.

26. George L. Mosse, Fallen Soldiers: Reshaping the Memory of the World Wars (New York: Oxford University Press, 1990), 6–7.

27. Quoted in Donovan, Lest the Ages Forget, 6.

28. R. H. Mottram, Ten Years Ago: Armistice and Other Memories (London: Chatto and Windus, 1928), 17.

29. These were Carl Gleeser and Jacob Frohwerk (editor and publisher of the Missouri Staats Zeitung) and Rose Pastor Stokes (editor of the Jewish Daily News and author of a letter to the Kansas City Star calling out war profiteers). Patricia DeWitt, "The Espionage and Sedition Acts," http://missourioverthere.org/explore/articles/the-espionage-and-sedition-acts/ (accessed September 19, 2015). See also "Ten Years for Criticism," Literary Digest 57 (June 15, 1918): 13.

30. Andrew Shanken, "Keeping Time with the Good War," American Studies Journal 59 (2015): 2.

31. McPherson, The Liberty Memorial in Kansas City, 21.

32. Paul Duggan, "Back from Battle, a Generation Kept Fighting," Washington Post, November 12, 2006, http://www.washingtonpost.com/wp-dyn/content/article/2006/11/11/AR2006111101102.html (accessed September 21, 2015).

33. Haskell, Boss-Busters and Sin Hounds, 183–195, 216, 235.

34. Ibid., 236; Claude M. Fuess, Calvin Coolidge: The Man from Vermont (Boston: Little, Brown, 1940).

35. On most occasions, Coolidge wrote his own speeches, so Haskell's help here was unusual. Robert H. Ferrell, "Calvin Coolidge, the Man and the President," in Calvin Coolidge

and the Coolidge Era, ed. John Earl Haynes (Washington, DC: Library of Congress, 1998), 138; and Haskell, *Boss-Busters and Sin Hounds*, 236–237.

36. Calvin Coolidge, "Address at the Dedication of the Liberty Memorial at Kansas City, Missouri," November 11, 1926, http://www.presidency.ucsb.edu/ws/?pid=413 (accessed September 19, 2015). Themes from this address are echoed in other Coolidge speeches. See his comments on veterans in his annual messages to Congress for 1923, 1925, and 1926.

37. Along these lines, Steven Trout writes: "While the nation spent millions on war memorials, men disabled during the Great War received little if anything from the newly created Veterans' Bureau. . . . The United States' frenetic effort to memorialize the Great War perhaps derived less from confidence and conviction than from bewilderment and doubt . . . [from] the nation's urgent desire to impose order on a particularly complex and contradictory national experience." Steven Trout, *Memorial Fictions: Willa Cather and the First World War* (Lincoln: University of Nebraska Press), 18–19.

38. Jay Winter, *Sites of Memory, Sites of Mourning: The Great War in European Cultural History* (Cambridge: Cambridge University Press, 1995), 98.

39. This and the following paragraph are informed by Donovan, *Lest the Ages Forget*, 118–147. See also Shortridge, *Kansas City and How It Grew*.

40. Andrew M. Shanken, "Planning Memory: Living Memorials in the United States during World War II," *Art Bulletin* 84, no. 1 (March 2002): 130, 136, 140.

41. Donovan, *Lest the Ages Forget*, 156, 162.

42. "Top 25 Museums—United States," http://www.tripadvisor.com/TravelersChoice -Museums-cTop-g191 (accessed September 19, 2015). The list is admittedly idiosyncratic and inconclusive, formed by popular vote among the website's users; in 2015 the Kansas City museum was ranked number 21, just ahead of Nashville's Country Music Hall of Fame. But with 60 million registered members and 170 million online reviews, the site does represent an undeniably broad swath of public opinion.

43. Jim Jeffries, quoted in Donovan, *Lest the Ages Forget*, 155.

44. Duggan, "Back from Battle."

45. Buckles visited the museum and memorial in November 2008 but left no record of his impressions.

46. Astrid Erll's *Memory in Culture* (New York: Palgrave MacMillan, 2011) offers one of the best and most concise overviews of these phenomena, but the literature is vast. Along with Erll, Jay Winter, Erika Doss, Pierre Nora, Jan and Aleida Assmann, David Lowenthal, John Bodner, James E. Young, Terry Smith, and Paul Connerton have all produced valuable book-length studies along these lines. Much debate has also occurred about the relationship between memory and history, some of which Erll outlines. For Maurice Halbwachs, writing in the 1920s, memory was subjective and particular, while history was objective and universal. For Pierre Nora, "Memory is a perpetually actual phenomenon, a bond tying us to the eternal present; history is a representation of the past." Memory, he says, is absolute, while history is relative. See Nora's "Between Memory and History: Les Lieux de Mémoire," *Representations* 26 (Spring 1989): 8–9. Winter describes memory as a "counterhistory" that challenges the generalizations and exclusions of "official" history. For Erll, memory is an

umbrella term covering all our various ways of relating past to present, and history (i.e., evidence-based narrative reconstructions of past events) is but one means of pursuing this relationship.

47. Marie-Alice L'Heureux, "The Creative Class, Urban Boosters, and Race: Shaping Urban Revitalization in Kansas City, Missouri," *Journal of Urban History* 41, no. 2 (2015): 245–260. See also Shortridge, *Kansas City and How It Grew*, 163–176; Joe Gose, "Millennials Going to Kansas City, to Live and Work," *New York Times*, August 19, 2014, http://www .nytimes.com/2014/08/20/realestate/commercial/millennials-going-to-kansas-city-to-live -and-work.html?_r=1 (accessed September 21, 2015); and Jeffrey Spivak, "Turnaround Artist: Kansas City Mayor Kay Barnes Took Downtown from Dying to Thriving," *Planning* 73, no. 4 (April 2007): 24.

48. "Greater Kansas City Community Foundation, Nonprofit Search Profile: Liberty Memorial Association," 2015, https://gkccf.guidestar.org/profile/1096/liberty-memorial-asso ciation.aspx (accessed September 21, 2015). See also Anna Foote, "Value-Filled Events at the Liberty Memorial," Missouri Meetings and Events, http://mme.meetmags.com/2007/03 /value-filled-events-at-the-liberty-memorial/ (accessed September 21, 2015). This includes quotes from Mark Cox, development director for the association.

49. Jules D. Prown, "The Truth of Material Culture," in *History from Things: Essays on Material Culture*, ed. Steven Lubar and David Kingery (Washington, DC: Smithsonian Institution Press, 1993), 2–3.

50. T. H. Pear, *Remembering and Forgetting* (London: Methuen, 1922), x, 1–2. This definition, predicated on individual experience and the essentially static nature of individual memories, would have satisfied most of Pear's contemporaries. See also the more scholarly book by his contemporary, Beatrice Edgell, *Theories of Memory* (London: Oxford University Press, 1924).

51. Halbwachs, discussed in Erll, *Memory in Culture*, 6–8, 13–15.

52. Ibid., 174.

53. Comparing the Liberty Memorial with Maya Lin's Vietnam Veterans Memorial (VVM), Trout brings light to our changed relationship to memorials, what we expect and what we will tolerate. Unlike the VVM, the Liberty Memorial "emphasizes not the connection between the living and the dead but the distance between them—between the ordinary human beings who visit the memorial, who cannot help but be awed by it and the superhuman heroes whom it commemorates." Trout, *Memorial Fictions*, 19–20.

54. Compare to note 46.

55. This according to Jane Fifield Flynn, vice president of advocacy for the Historic Kansas City Foundation, quoted in Donovan, *Lest the Ages Forget*, 162–164.

56. Jay Winter, review of Steven Trout, *On the Battlefield of Memory: The First World War and American Remembrance, 1919–1941* (Tuscaloosa: University of Alabama Press, 2012); and John Bodnar, *The "Good War" in American Memory* (Baltimore: Johns Hopkins University Press, 2011), in *The American Historical Review* 116, no. 3 (2011): 755–758.

Contributors

Henry Adams is the Ruth Coulter Heede Professor of Art History at Case Western Reserve University. He graduated from Harvard University and received his MA and PhD from Yale University. He is the author of over 300 scholarly and popular articles, ranging over the American field from the seventeenth century to the present, as well as about fourteen books or book-length exhibition catalogues. He has won multiple awards. In 1989, in partnership with filmmaker Ken Burns, Adams produced a documentary on Thomas Hart Benton that was broadcast nationally on PBS to an audience of 20 million.

Kyle Anthony is an assistant professor of history and honors program director at the University of Saint Mary in Leavenworth, Kansas. He obtained his PhD in history from the University of Kansas and specializes in United States, military, and labor history.

Keith Eggener is the Marion Dean Ross Professor of Architectural History at the University of Oregon. Previously, he taught at the University of Missouri–Columbia, the University of Nevada–Las Vegas, and Carleton College. He has published books and essays on art, architecture, landscape, urban design, cinema, photography, and material culture, primarily of twentieth-century Mexico and the United States. He is a columnist for *Places* and editor of the *Journal of the Society of Architectural Historians*.

Dustin Gann is a native Kansan whose research examines the relationship between national culture and regional identity. He is especially interested in the processes and individuals that have shaped midwestern communities during the early to mid-twentieth century. He earned a PhD in twentieth-century US history from the University of Kansas and currently serves as an assistant professor of history at Midland University in Fremont, Nebraska.

Chuck Haddix is the curator of the Marr Sound Archives, a collection of 380,000 historic sound recordings housed in the Miller Nichols Library at the University of Missouri–Kansas City. Haddix hosts the *Fish Fry*, a popular radio program featuring the finest in Americana, blues, soul, rhythm and blues, jumpin' jive, and zydeco on KCUR (kcur.org, FM 89.3), Kansas City's public radio station. In 2005, he co-authored, with Frank Driggs, *Kansas City Jazz: From Ragtime to Bebop–A History* for Oxford University Press. His biography of Charlie Parker, *Bird: The Life and Music of Charlie Parker*, was published in 2013 by the University of Illinois Press.

K. David Hanzlick serves as an adjunct faculty member in the Nonprofit Leadership Program at the Helzberg School of Management at Rockhurst University and the Hauptmann School of Public Affairs at Park University. He has more than thirty years of experience in nonprofit leadership and fund-raising and is the director of program and development at Sheffield Place, a treatment and supportive housing agency for homeless mothers and their children in northeast Kansas City, Missouri. He is the author of the 2018 book *Benevolence, Moral Reform, Equality: Women's Activism in Kansas City, 1870 to 1940*, published by the University of Missouri Press.

John Herron is a professor of history and associate dean at the University of Missouri–Kansas City. A specialist in late nineteenth-century America, he explores the connections between the natural environment and American social and cultural history.

Stuart Hinds currently serves as assistant dean for special collections and archives at the Miller Nichols Library of the University of Missouri–Kansas City. He has an additional role as curator of the Gay and Lesbian Archive of Mid-America, a collecting initiative he co-founded in 2010 to collect, preserve, and make accessible documents and artifacts that reflect the heritage of Kansas City's LGBT communities. He is currently under contract with the University Press of Kansas to publish *Cowtown Queers: A History of Gay and Lesbian Kansas City*.

John W. McKerley teaches history at the University of Iowa. His publications include "'We Promise to Use the Ballot as We Did the Bayonet': Black Suffrage Activism and the Limits of Loyalty in Reconstruction Missouri," in *Bleeding Kansas, Bleeding Missouri* (University Press of Kansas, 2013).

Valerie M. Mendoza received her PhD in history from the University of California–Berkeley. She coedited a special issue of the *American Studies Journal* with Norma E. Cantu on Latinx social justice issues, which was published in November 2017. She currently serves as the director of programs for Humanities Kansas in Topeka, Kansas.

Jaclyn Miller earned her PhD in US history from the University of Kansas in May 2016 and serves as a permanent instructor of history at South Texas College in McAllen, Texas. Her research concerns banking history and the intersections of economics, politics, and the culture of capitalism within historical communities of the nineteenth and early-twentieth centuries.

Diane Mutti Burke is a professor and chair of the History Department at the University of Missouri–Kansas City. A graduate of Dartmouth College and Emory University, she has published books and essays that focus on the Civil War–era history of Missouri and the Missouri-Kansas border region, with a particular emphasis on the history of slavery and the experiences of civilians during the war. In her role as director of the UMKC Center for Midwestern Studies, she works to generate new research on the region and to bring this history to public audiences.

Jeffrey L. Pasley is a professor of history and journalism as well as the associate director of the Kinder Institute on Constitutional Democracy at the University of Missouri. A graduate of Carleton College and Harvard University, he is the author of the award-winning books *"The Tyranny of Printers": Newspaper Politics in the Early American Republic* and *The First Presidential Contest: 1796 and the Founding of American Democracy*, a finalist for the 2014 George Washington Book Prize. Before entering academia, he learned about journalism and politics directly as a reporter-researcher for the *New Republic* and as a speechwriter for Al Gore's 1988 presidential campaign.

Marc Rice is a professor of musicology at Truman State University. His research career has focused on the history of jazz in the Midwest, with a particular emphasis on the music of Kansas City. He also teaches courses on jazz history and ethnomusicology.

Jason Roe is a digital history specialist at the Kansas City Public Library and content manager and editor for the library's historical websites, The Pendergast Years: Kansas City in the Jazz Age and Great Depression and the Civil War on the Western Border: The Missouri-Kansas Conflict, 1854–1865, winner of the 2014 Roy Rosenzweig Prize for Innovation in Digital History from the American Historical Association. He earned his PhD in US history from the University of Kansas in May 2012 and received the History Department's George L. Anderson Award for Outstanding Doctoral Dissertation.

Sara Stevens is an architectural historian and an assistant professor of architectural and urban design history at the University of British Columbia–Vancouver. Her book, *Developing Expertise: Architecture and Real Estate in Metropolitan America* (Yale

University Press, 2016), studies real estate development in twentieth-century American cities.

Henrietta Rix Wood is an associate teaching professor in the Honors College at the University of Missouri–Kansas City. She is the author of *Praising Girls: The Rhetoric of Young Women, 1895–1930* (Southern Illinois University Press, 2016) and coeditor of *In the Archives of Composition: Writing and Rhetoric in High Schools and Normal Schools* (University of Pittsburgh Press, 2015).

Index